THE WRITING PUBLIC

THE WRITING PUBLIC

Participatory Knowledge Production in Enlightenment and Revolutionary France

ELIZABETH ANDREWS BOND

CORNELL UNIVERSITY PRESS

Ithaca and London

First published 2021 by Cornell University Press

Library of Congress Cataloging-in-Publication Data

Names: Bond, Elizabeth Andrews, author.
Title: The writing public: participatory knowledge production in enlightenment and revolutionary France / Elizabeth Andrews Bond.
Description: Ithaca, [New York]: Cornell University Press, 2021. | Includes bibliographical references and index.
Identifiers: LCCN 2020031941 (print) | LCCN 2020031942 (ebook) | ISBN 9781501753565 (paperback) | ISBN 9781501753572 (epub) | ISBN 9781501753589 (pdf)
Subjects: LCSH: Letters to the editor —France —History —18th century. | Mass media and public opinion —France —History —18th century. | France —Intellectual life —18th century. | France —Social conditions —18th century.
Classification: LCC DC33.4 .B65 2021 (print) | LCC DC33.4 (ebook) | DDC 070.4/42 —dc23
LC record available at https://lccn.loc.gov/2020031941
LC ebook record available at https://lccn.loc.gov/2020031942

To my parents

Contents

Acknowledgments   *ix*

Introduction   1

1. The Production and Distribution of the
   Information Press   17

2. The Writers, Self-Presentation,
   and Subjectivity   39

3. Reading Together, Book References,
   and Interacting with Print   60

4. Popular Science and Public Participation   87

5. Agricultural Reform and Local
   Innovation   112

6. Bienfaisance, Fellow Feeling, and the
   Public Good   133

7. Communicating the Revolution   155

   Conclusion   179

Appendix A   *185*
Appendix B   *189*
Notes   *203*
Bibliography   *239*
Index   *267*

ACKNOWLEDGMENTS

It is my pleasure to be able to thank everyone who has helped me research and write this book. Support from the Council for European Studies and the Andrew W. Mellon Foundation, the Princeton University Council of the Humanities, and the Fulbright Foundation made multiple research trips possible. The American Association of University Women, PEO (Philanthropic Education Organization), and the Council for European Studies Andrew W. Mellon Foundation Dissertation Fellowship afforded me two years to write. A National Endowment for the Humanities Summer Stipend supported the final stages of preparing this book.

My gratitude goes especially to Timothy Tackett for his mentorship. Tim has generously read countless drafts of this work over the years. At each stage, I have benefited from his critical eye and deep knowledge of the eighteenth century. It has been a privilege to work with such a gifted historian and engaged mentor. I am also thankful to Ulrike Strasser and Sarah Farmer for reading proposals, writing letters, and sharing their feedback. For her scholarly engagement with my research and for her friendship, I thank Helen Chenut. In Irvine and in Paris, Helen and Tim opened their home to graduate students and faculty from around the world. I have learned a great deal about scholarly friendship from them. Rachel Fuchs first fostered my interest in French history at Arizona State, encouraged me to pursue graduate school, and met me for lunch whenever I was back in Tempe. She was a wonderful historian and energetic advocate of junior scholars, and I am grateful to have known her.

My research in France was shaped by the generosity of historians there. I would like to thank Pierre Serna, Philippe Minard, and Antoine Lilti for inviting me to participate in their seminars while I conducted my research. Jean-Clement Martin drove to Poitiers on a very snowy day to show me around the *bibliothèque municipale* and the Société des antiquaires de l'ouest, and to share his advice on my project. While in Aix-en-Provence, Michel Vovelle invited me to his home to discuss my work. I am grateful for the kindness and intellectual generosity of all the historians who met with me during my time in France. My work was aided a great deal by the expertise and assistance of librarians and archivists in Paris and in the provincial collections where I worked. I would also like to thank the French families who extended their hospitality to me, especially Mary and Hervé Kergall. While I conducted research in the provinces, Fulbright alumni welcomed me to their homes, especially François Pitavy and Danièle Pitavy-Souques, Anne Raynaud-Reversat, and Elisabeth and Eric Limongi. Life in Paris researching this book was made all the more rewarding and fun by the friendship of the graduate students and early career researchers I met there.

I have shared facets of my work in progress at meetings of the American Historical Association, Western Society for French History, Society for French Historical Studies, Society for the Study of French History, the George Rudé Seminar, the Council for European Studies, the Consortium on the Revolutionary Era, and the International Society for Eighteenth-Century Studies. I am thankful to the many fellow panelists, audience members, and colleagues who have shared their insight and feedback on my work in progress. Special thanks go to Jack Censer who shared his expertise on the history of the press with me in the early stages of this project. Meghan Roberts read the manuscript with care and provided invaluable feedback. The participants in the Center for Eighteenth-Century Studies Workshop at Indiana University helped me work through an early draft of chapter 3. At Ohio State, the Premodernist Group and the History of the Book Group kindly invited me to share chapters in progress at key stages.

My colleagues in the Department of History have made Ohio State University a welcoming and intellectually rich place to finish this book. I am grateful to Alice Conklin and Kristina Sessa for reading the manuscript and sharing their advice. Randolph Roth and John Brooke met with me to discuss early drafts of the manuscript. Clayton Howard and Jennifer Eaglin provided helpful feedback on early drafts of chapters. I would also like to thank Theodora Dragostinova, Kristina Sessa, Mytheli Sreenivas, and Ying Zhang for the invitation to join their writing group, their comments on the introduction, and their moral support.

It has been a pleasure to work with the book team at Cornell University Press. I wish to thank Emily Andrew for her support of this project and for guiding the book through press. I am grateful to Lori Rider for her copyediting, Sandy Aitken for her indexing, and Jennifer Savran Kelly for overseeing the production of the book. I would also like to thank the anonymous readers for their thoughtful engagement with my work. They encouraged me to think deeply about my project.

Finally, I wish to thank my family. My love goes to my husband, Rob, who has supported and encouraged me since the beginning of this project. My sister, Madeline, has shared many phone calls and visits over the years as we have each pursued our own research. I am grateful for her insight and friendship. Some of my earliest memories are of my parents, Gail and Keith, reading to me. They shared with me their love of learning and supported my education at every stage. I dedicate this book to them.

THE WRITING PUBLIC

Introduction

On February 12, 1786, a letter to the editor appeared in the *Affiches du Beauvaisis* that described how readers interacted with the newspaper. The anonymous writer explained to the editor, "Your weekly papers are a sort of literary arena, where every athlete should have the right to present oneself, to choose an adversary and to combat them, without however, straying from the bounds of decency and one's public and private honesty." He expressed his disagreement with a letter to the editor in the previous week's newspaper, but he assured the editor that he intended only to combat his interlocutor in the press and to adhere to sociable norms of civility and honest conduct.[1] Newspapers like the *Affiches du Beauvaisis* formed a collective space that invited participation. In conceptualizing the newspaper as an arena, this writer reflected a sense of the affiches as a site for the horizontal exchange of ideas where writers could grapple with new information and with one another.

While this writer addressed the *Affiches du Beauvaisis* in particular, his comments described an entire genre of general information newspapers commonly referred to by historians as "the information press," which burgeoned in the 1770s and 1780s and persisted throughout the early years of the Revolution.[2] Such newspapers shared two key characteristics—a capacious coverage of various subject matter and the publication of letters from their readers. The editors of both Parisian and provincial newspapers expressed the same goal that this writer identified: to invite their readers into the conversation. Between 1770 and 1791, thousands of letters to the editor appeared in such newspapers, where writers participated in an iterative process of debate and exchange.

The newspapers that made up the information press proliferated after mid-century in Paris and in the provinces, where they appeared under such titles as *Affiches, annonces, et avis divers*, and were known generically as affiches. Such one-sheet in-folio newspapers soon appeared in dozens of French towns and cities, almost always on a weekly basis. Immediately following the front matter of the title and date, one could find a vast array of advertisements concerning services, property, and commodities, and then short articles covering all sorts of additional information. Featuring thousands of letters from their readers, the affiches were filled with fascinating and previously unstudied voices who had much to say about the society in which they lived.

Drawing on the letters to the affiches, my book traces the way that everyday readers participated in social and intellectual life from 1770 to 1789; an epilogue carries the story through the Revolution to the summer of 1791. Through the letters to the editor, the newspapers became a site for conversations about a range of pressing issues that readers confronted on science and medicine, economic and agricultural innovation, and social reform. Their conversations inform the historian not only about the proposed solutions, such as which particular crop to plant, how to navigate a hot-air balloon, or which medicinal remedy was deemed best. They also provide unique insight into the manner in which people read, communicated, and applied the new knowledge that was unquestionably being generated in the "century of Enlightenment." Such sources reveal the extent to which the shifting rational and emotional epistemologies associated with eighteenth-century life reached a diverse group of individuals who adapted such repertoires for their own purposes. They show how the exchanges between readers shaped changes in social habits and facilitated the formation of a public opinion in an era of dramatically accelerating change.

The affiches' letters to the editor form the heart of my study, because they capture the public's response to the new ideas they consumed. With the exception of historians of eighteenth-century French consumer culture who have drawn from the affiches' advertisements, these papers have tended to be overlooked in the cultural history of the eighteenth century.[3] For a long time, scholars of Old Regime and revolutionary France were most interested in answering the question of how politicized public opinion was by 1789. Because the affiches eschewed explicitly political criticism or commentary concerning church or state, they received far less attention in the cultural histories of the period than the clandestine and uncensored periodicals that were more philosophical and radical in nature.[4] But recently cultural historians have questioned the extent to which the coming of the Revolution was obvious to the general reading public, or even to the deputies who would lead the Revolution.[5] Researchers working on the eighteenth century are increasingly seeking to understand instead the importance of lived experience and the role played by contingency in the years leading up to the calling of the Estates General.[6] With this shift, the role of communication, rumor, conspiracy, and truth have become primary concerns for historians of both the Old Regime and the Revolution.[7] Letters from readers published in the affiches speak to this new scholarly concern with communication in late eighteenth-century life in original and significant ways. In sum, the affiches and the letters they contain merit fresh investigation.

Letters to the editor offer unique insight on pressing questions for historians, because their writers revealed who participated in them, what print matter they discussed, and what claims to authority were convincing to their readers. First, the signatures enclosed in the letters reveal a writing public with complex—and at times competing—interests who participated in the press. Identifying and counting who composed letters to the editor has an enormous advantage to the historian: it foregrounds the presence of otherwise marginalized voices in the history of ideas. Second, the mention in the letters of books and periodicals sheds new light on the print matter that readers consumed, critiqued, and valued. By attending to the works that informed their writing, the correspondence can reveal how Parisian and provincial readers accessed both clandestine and licensed works in France before the Revolution, and how the newspaper acted as a bridge through which readers shared the print matter they encountered. Finally, the letters are significant for the arguments that the writers made in them.

Based on an investigation of nearly seven thousand letters to the editor published in twenty-two Parisian and provincial affiches, I argue that newspapers fostered an interactive sphere where people could express opinions and invite responses on questions that mattered to them. They took each other seriously, responded to one another, and proposed and implemented reform. For many, the adoption of new ideas in the late eighteenth century came out of an iterative process of debate and exchange worked out in newspapers throughout the kingdom. Letters to the editor constituted a space for social learning, where writers engaged with one another's ideas as much as they did with other books. Their correspondence underscores that writers learned from one another, rather than from a top-down intellectual movement. Through their debates, writers and editors positioned the affiches as a site for reform-minded conversations.

The exchange of ideas about practical matters refashioned subjectivities and the public sphere itself. My book examines how writers negotiated a new sphere of virtual sociability in which they did not know their interlocutors. Writers had to make their case to the editors and to the newspaper's readers, and to evaluate competing claims made by other writers. In many instances, the editors were reluctant to step forward as arbiters, and the readers were left to evaluate what they read for themselves. It was around unsettled questions that the letters to the editor flourished. In this flourishing there lay a tension between the rich participation of diverse voices and the desire in the letters for information that was tested, true, and useful. Multiple possibilities emerged as more voices entered the forum the newspapers had opened. The negotiation evident in the press was foundational to the formation of civil society at the end of the Old Regime and in the early years of the Revolution.

Whatever the subject matter, writers began their correspondence by explaining why the editor ought to publish their letters. The most recurring explanation was that the affiches were the site where all practical knowledge that might inform and entertain readers ought to be gathered. Above all, they argued, their letter should be published because the information it contained was useful. For historians, their arguments are significant because they show how readers thought about the role of the press in Old Regime and revolutionary public life, and how they fashioned their own correspondence in response to such aims.

Addressing a public letter to a newspaper brought men and women well acquainted with domestic epistolary practices into a new, shared, and public venue—a forum that juxtaposed the thoughts of trained practitioners, amateurs, and enthusiasts concerning the arts, sciences, and social welfare. For many, a letter to the editor was the first and only way that their opinions would appear in print. The act allowed individuals from a range of backgrounds to articulate and share their views across the geographic and social space that otherwise separated them from other readers. It also necessitated new strategies for making a case before readers whose professions and positions in society differed from one's own. The practice of reflection took on new dimension as writers saw their own ideas in print before them. Letters to the editor allowed people to see their opinions juxtaposed against the ideas of others—to witness their thoughts contested, critiqued, and commended—by strangers they might not otherwise meet. Taken together, the letters expose just how widely shared new empirical and emotional epistemologies actually were, and how, through an innovative media form, readers debated, instructed, and learned from one another.

The Public Letter and Self-Fashioning

By studying the opinions of the letter writers living in the two decades before the French Revolution, my book provides fresh understanding of the ways that eighteenth-century readers responded to new ideas, and the role of the press in spreading such information. In addition to enabling a wide cross-section of literate society to participate in public debate, writing a letter to the editor also entailed a very personal dimension: a veritable assertion of the self. In sending letters to the editor, writers defined who they were and why their letters merited publication. In doing so they had to articulate their own subjectivity. Because writing a letter to the editor hinged the personal and the public, the letters in the affiches speak to the process of self-fashioning in a way that few other sources from this period can.

Historians have already extensively mined individual diaries, private correspondence, wills, and book catalogs for their perspectives on the experiences of individual figures and families living in the eighteenth century. However, analyzing a corpus of public correspondence in which readers from various backgrounds living in the 1770s and 1780s—figures whose thoughts and ideas might otherwise never have appeared in print—has a different advantage. It offers a way to assess on a much larger scale the popular reception of the new media of the late eighteenth century—the letter to the editor—and the role these media played in the formation of public opinion. In the press, thousands of writers pushed against the boundaries of authorship. At its heart, my book demonstrates how the spread of both new ideas and new communication technology intersected to shape French society at a critical moment in history.

The eighteenth century was, in a sense, a golden age of correspondence. Private correspondence among family, friends, and colleagues has been shown to offer an exceptional touchstone for the thoughts and ideas articulated by literate members of society. Epistolary practice shaped daily life, secured social ties, and oriented the writer's place within the wider world.[8] For the transitional period from the Old Regime to the French Revolution, private correspondence has underscored the contingency of individual responses to political and social change, change that was largely unanticipated even among future revolutionaries.[9]

By contrast, I consider how public letters fit within this genre, asking whether there was something fundamentally different about writing a letter to the editor. The Encyclopedists certainly made such a distinction. They defined the *lettre missive* as a personal, intimate letter meant to be kept private; sharing *lettres missives* with a third party was considered a breach of trust. But they also recognized the *lettre circulaire,* addressed to many people who had a shared interest in the letter's contents.[10] The philosophes wrote open letters with the intention that they would be shared and read aloud, and in some cases published. As Dena Goodman has argued, philosophes used such letters to bridge the divide between the salon and the public beyond, and to communicate new ideas. Moreover, the "epistolary commerce" of reading a letter—even a public one—required reciprocity.[11] Readers were obliged to respond, prompting a social habit.

The motives of those who wrote open letters for the affiches were more varied than were the open letters of the philosophes. Writers to the affiches sought to share information; to galvanize support for their cause; to advertise a product to inquisitive readers of means; to ask a question of a public that might have more information; or to counter the position of a previous letter to the editor. In all cases, however, the first goal was to convince the editor that their letter was worth sharing. The grounds on which prospective contributors justified the merits of their letters and their authority to speak are among the most revealing findings of my book.

In considering writing a public letter as an act of self-fashioning, my work is informed by histories of authorship and gender. In her study of women authors in the eighteenth century, Carla Hesse has emphasized that it was precisely self-reflexivity, mediated through writing—and for which literacy was essential—that made one modern.[12] Dena Goodman has demonstrated that it was through the very process of composing letters that eighteenth-century women came to understand themselves both as private persons and as women—and these self-definitions were made (and are always made) vis-à-vis a public sphere.[13] So too for contributors to the affiches, letter writing was an important means of articulating who they were and defining their relationship to the public. Writing a letter to the editor was simultaneously a personal and a public act.

By examining for the first time the affiches' public letters, I seek to break new ground in three of the longest-running debates among historians of the eighteenth century: first, that of the composition, timing, and extent of what has come to be routinely referred to as "the public"; second, the creation of a new sense of community thanks to the spread of newspapers;

and third, the ways in which what are conventionally called Enlightenment ideas permeated society.

Reconsidering the Public Sphere

The first contribution of my book is to offer a fresh analysis of the relevance of the "public sphere" that has generated much debate in eighteenth-century scholarship. As writers situated their letters before a public audience, they drew on repertoires that were rational, experiential, emotional, and social. Many writers made evidence-based arguments that emphasized and celebrated empiricism. They compared the results of their investigations with the contentions of others, and they took each other to task over errors they found in other letters. For them, the affiches were a collection of useful knowledge. But the space of the affiches was also affective.[14] The most frequently reprinted letters picked up by multiple newspapers encouraged emotional responses to faithful dogs or daring rescues. The space generated by the newspapers also possessed a commercial side. It was, after all, consumer culture and the publication of advertisements that initially made the affiches possible.[15] Some writers called on readers to buy French goods, or to examine botanical samples from the colonies; in so doing they situated Parisian and provincial readers within the nation and the empire. But for the majority of letter writers who sold nothing, the affiches were a way of shoring up one's authority and presenting one's civic engagement. In sum, a combination of rational, affective, commercial, and social interests of letter writers and editors shaped the formation of "public opinion" in the late Old Regime and the first years of the Revolution. While readers seldom spoke of themselves as a public per se, they did discuss what was best for the public good, and what a good citizen ought to do. The social conscience of the letters was always in evidence.

In studying the influence of the eighteenth-century press, Jürgen Habermas's 1962 classic formulation of *Öffentlichkeit*, commonly translated as "the public sphere," remains an influential model. Habermas envisioned a public sphere in which individual, private members of elite society with the education and resources to read and the time to reflect on what they read came together to participate in rational conversation. Through such interactions they developed critical reason, which they tried out first in print and later in politics.[16] Print culture and the public sphere grew concomitantly after mid-century. Access to books and other print media rose dramatically, and literacy rates increased, especially among those living in urban centers.[17] Habermas's model of the public sphere has remained salient in part because what we know about literacy and book publishing seems to reinforce its general contours.

In the decades since the English translation of Habermas's landmark work, historians have challenged the location, timing, and actors who shaped the formation of such a public sphere. While Habermas located his *Öffentlichkeit* primarily in eighteenth-century Britain, France, and Germany, historians have applied his model to the study of public life and participation throughout the world. Without a doubt, the rise of the public sphere was not just a European phenomenon.[18] In France, historians have also identified antecedents as early as the thirteenth century.[19] Even in eighteenth-century France, the public sphere was not the bourgeois world of a small, elite circle of private men that Habermas envisioned. The very category of the "bourgeoisie," how it was formed, what the name signified, and whether it existed at all, have been substantially reconsidered.[20]

Some historians have suggested it is best to set aside the social composition of the reading public. For them, "the public" is best understood as a normative concept that could be used by men of letters for political purposes, not as a group whose sociology mattered.[21] Others have argued for conceiving "the public" not only as a rhetorical concept but also as a communication network that reacted to theatrical works, literary fiction, and news reports.[22] Nor was such communication as separate from the state as Habermas had proposed; many of the people who shaped public opinion and participated in politics in the eighteenth century held public offices from which they implemented reform.[23] And the popular classes had repertoires for the expression of public opinion that were original and significant on their own terms.[24] Moreover, historians of the eighteenth century have convincingly demonstrated that the boundaries between public and private life that Habermas envisioned were not opposed to one another, but rather were permeable and overlapping arenas.[25] Habermas's public sphere is a model, a kind of Weberian ideal type, that has proven useful to think with, even as historians have shown that the unified, rational, elite public opinion that Habermas envisioned never indeed existed.

Despite the limits of Habermas's model, the question that he originally raised about the impact of print culture on the formation of public opinion, including its radicalization in the 1780s, has remained central to the cultural history of the eighteenth century. Robert Darnton's foundational study of Grub Street writers emphasized the difficulties of making a living as a writer in the eighteenth century. Shut out of Old Regime patronage networks, would-be philosophes survived by writing *nouvelles à la main* and other works of questionable quality. Darnton suggested that the Grub Street denizens became radical revolutionaries because of their years of professional marginalization.[26] Roger Chartier likewise argued for the primacy of print culture in shaping the course of the Revolution, but he emphasized the new patterns of thought that the practice of reading encouraged. For him it was not the particular ideas of Grub Street writers that made the Revolution but rather the creative, dynamic process of reading that prepared the revolutionaries to participate in politics.[27]

In recent years, historians have emphasized that looking to sources that engaged a wider audience shifts the social composition of the public sphere in meaningful ways. The writers who participated in essay prize competitions held by the French academies experienced a particularly democratic space for intellectual exchange in Old Regime France. Because each essay was anonymized prior to judging, Jeremy Caradonna has argued, it was above all the merits of one's ideas that shone through. Even farmers participated in such competitions, although they did not win.[28] In a similar manner, Lauren Clay has shown that theaters in Paris, the provinces, and the colonies reflected the wide-ranging character and consumer orientation of the public sphere.[29] The work of such scholars largely confirms what Harvey Chisick has underscored: "Ideas do not exist independently from people or groups of people who bear and articulate them. Any consideration of the social or political bases of public opinion shows this opinion to be divided, particular, interested and contestatory."[30]

As my book makes clear, to look carefully at public opinion is to glimpse particular interests. Appeals to the general public in the press may be read as the attempts by individual persons to claim authority. In looking to the affiches for the formation of public opinion, the public who read such newspapers emerges not as a homogeneous and singular entity but a range of dynamic and differentiated figures who found in the newspaper a new space for debate. I contend that the social composition of the writers is crucial to an understanding of the interests and aspirations they espoused. The letters to the editor that appeared in the affiches constituted a space in which individual writers from different social backgrounds debated shared concerns, situating the letters to the editor as a uniquely open and richly peopled sphere for discussion.

The Newspaper and Community

My book further contributes to our understanding of how modern newspapers helped create community. Through the very act of reading, the readers of public letters became part of an imagined group who shared their habits of newspaper consumption. Such ties were especially vivid and strong for the affiches' readers because their fellow readers wrote back. In corresponding via the newspaper, writers to the affiches enacted new habits of mind and new formulations of community. The letters published in the information press illustrate how practices of sociability were formulated by a much larger circle of figures. Their letters did not elide social difference, but they invited into the conversation writers who could not otherwise access elite salons, coffeehouses, or learned societies. In doing so, they adopted shared practices for sharing new and practical knowledge.

As Benedict Anderson famously argued, the experience of reading the newspaper transformed the way eighteenth-century readers thought about one another, prompting them to consider entirely new relationships in their lives. The juxtaposition of news from one's town, the capital, and other parts of the world made local, regional, and global ties visible and personal. Even when one read the newspaper alone in one's home, the act of newspaper reading brought people engaged in the same practice into an "imagined community."[31] Such an experience may also have created empathy for the people they read about. Lynn Hunt has argued that the social and legal reforms of the late Old Regime and especially the Revolution were only possible because of the empathy that individuals felt as they read epistolary novels.[32] Reading and contributing to newspapers have been equally as important in forging affective ties between readers who were otherwise strangers.

In the cultural history of the eighteenth century, the study of social relations is understood through the lens of sociability, as both a way of studying social relationships and a particular idea in the moral and political philosophy of the eighteenth century.[33] In a general sense, sociability is a shared set of practices that enable a group of individuals to relate to one another, when participation in that group is voluntary. For French historians, Maurice Agulhon's study of eighteenth-century Provence was foundational. Agulhon described sociability as a dynamic process: participants adhered to certain norms for interaction, but they also learned from one another, and in doing so they revised and adapted social practices.[34] While early scholarship on sociability primarily concerned politics, historians have since emphasized the significance of sociability for the republic of letters. Their work underscored that even as hierarchies and inequalities persisted until 1789, practices of sociability enabled French authors and playwrights to create a new and creative space for themselves "that was neither democratic nor absolutist."[35] Social relationships, correspondence, discussion, and friendship grew increasingly crucial to knowledge production in the eighteenth century.[36]

While the affiches did not discuss the philosophy of sociability in their letters to the editor, they did enact sociable practices that mirrored the general sense in which their contemporaries characterized it. In his article to the *Encyclopédie*, Louis de Jaucourt defined *sociabilité* as an attitude of generosity and kindness toward one's interlocutors, a reciprocal obligation to others, and a commitment to that which was useful.[37] It was especially in terms of their desire to be useful that writers made their cases in the information press.

Practicing the Enlightenment

My book also contributes to the history of the Enlightenment as it was experienced by a diverse community of writers. From the vantage point of the affiches, the Enlightenment was an approach to knowledge production that was, above all, practical and useful. Most of the writers to the information press did not oppose the philosophes, though in most cases they also did not directly mention them. Nevertheless, their writing shared with many eighteenth-century savants a sense of self-confidence and optimism about the age.[38] Their letters reflected the feeling that they lived in a unique moment where progress in the sciences and the conditions of everyday life were attainable. Through their correspondence, they took it upon themselves to participate in that amelioration.

My book engages with the historiography of the Enlightenment in two key ways. First, I take up Clifford Siskin and William Warner's call to consider the Enlightenment as a history of mediation.[39] In doing so, I highlight how writing, reading, and print informed one another. I also seek to convey a history of how ideas were shared and proliferated, and how such transmission shaped new forms of social interaction and practice. While many letter writers contextualized what they were doing as collaborative or useful to the public good, the forum of letters to the editor, like the Enlightenment itself, was a terrain of contestation. The forms of social interaction forged in the press equipped writers to participate in such debates.

Second, the book engages with Jeremy Caradonna's description of the Enlightenment being understood "as something that people *did* or *practiced*, rather than some specific set of beliefs or philosophical assumptions (even though these practices have obvious links to philosophical attitudes)."[40] By focusing on cultural practices, and considering the sites in which such knowledge was produced, my book underlines the ways in which the information press fostered a critical sphere of public exchange. Inspired by the work of Margaret C. Jacob, Jeremy Caradonna, Charles Withers, and others, it explores how a wide array of figures "lived" the Enlightenment.[41] My analysis of the letters to the editor of a broad group of eighteenth-century men and women calls attention to an important phenomenon that remains relatively understudied in the cultural history of the Enlightenment: how the emergence of the letter to the editor, a particularly novel form of communication, facilitated and shaped public participation in French intellectual life.

There is no question that the men and women who wrote letters to the affiches made references to living in a "siècle éclairé," and of spreading "les lumières" through their writing. But while they spoke with some frequency of practicing or sharing "lumières," they almost never explicitly defined what they meant by an "enlightened" age. In fact, the Enlightenment has been a complex and contested classification since the eighteenth century itself, and its study remains inextricably tied to the generations of literary critics, philosophers, and historians who have written about it from the nineteenth through the twenty-first centuries. Scholarly conversations over the nature of the Enlightenment and the scope of its participants have shaped much of the historiography in this field.[42] Especially since the 1970s, research on the Enlightenment has burgeoned, as historians have considered the ideas that European intellectuals debated in the long eighteenth century. J. G. A. Pocock has developed an interpretation based on the concept of plural "enlightenments" to capture the range and variety of such intellectual currents.[43] And various scholars since have proposed and explored the existence of the Religious Enlightenment, the Secular Enlightenment, the Radical Enlightenment, the Counter-Enlightenment, the Pragmatic Enlightenment, the Artisanal Enlightenment, and the Scientific Enlightenment, in all of its European, Atlantic, and global contexts.[44] Jeffrey Burson, by contrast, has argued against the proliferation of enlightenments and suggested instead that historians consider the Enlightenment "as plurality within an unfolding continuum, as process rather than atomistic, reified, hypostatic Enlightenments."[45] Other historians would go further still, arguing that the Enlightenment is largely a heuristic device, framed by historiography, informed by an evolving body of sources and historical perspectives.[46] In their varied interpretations of what it meant to live in an age of lights, the writers to the affiches mirrored the divergent perspectives within this scholarly field.

Methodology

The predominant methodological approach throughout my book is the close reading of 6,909 letters to the editor published in provincial and Parisian newspapers. This rich body of sources enables analysis that attends to the limits of sources for which few manuscript or archival records remain. Such limitations inform the approach I have taken to interpret the sources.

In doing so, my work is informed by the digital turn in the humanities, which has prompted questions about how computational research methods and large bodies of sources can increase our sensitivity to those social or gender groups too often excluded. In some cases when digitized corpora were available, digital humanists have been able to track down anonymous authors, rendering women's role in authoring eighteenth-century works more visible. While some of the tools they use differ from my own, their work has centered historical questions about the construction of archives and how historians study those people for whom few records remain. Digital history scholarship involves attending to the limits and inequities of archival records.[47] By studying the contributions of anonymous writers alongside the work of known authors, it is another ambition of my book to write a social history of ideas that engages with marginalized voices. Combining close reading with a quantitative analysis of the writers shows how the writers' social context informed their modes of self-expression.

Within digital humanities, network analysis is a particularly apt method for studying the relationships between periodicals. Network analysis is the study of the structure of social relationships. Such networks take many forms, but every network consists of individuals known as nodes and the ties that connect them with one another. In adopting this method to study the information-sharing relationships between newspapers, I am joining a number of historians who in recent years have used network analysis to illuminate the structures through which relationships were formed, ideas were spread, and values were shared in the early modern period.[48] Thus, network analysis has served as an apt approach to examine the impact of marriage and social mobility in Renaissance Florence.[49] It has likewise served as a useful way of conceptualizing those who fit within and fell outside a self-referential "Republic of Letters."[50] Emma Rothschild employed a similar technique to explore the relationships between global commerce and the interior economy of eighteenth-century Angoulême, while at the same time considering the impact of such trends on individual lives.[51] The quantitative approach in my book participates in the kind of work that Rothschild has done in her economic history of Angoulême: to write a history of information that begins with individuals in the provinces and their local circumstances, and then to trace the larger system in which even isolated figures who left scant written records participated.

The Structure of the Book

The book begins with the advent of the affiches in the 1770s, traces the participation of letter writers in their rise and evolution under the late Old

Regime and the Revolution, and then ends in late summer 1791 as the letters began to fade from the newspapers. For the writers of the affiches, the habits of mind formed in the late Old Regime would shape their revolutionary experience.

The first chapter examines the production, regulation, and distribution of the affiches, likely the most widely read domestically produced newspapers in Old Regime France. This chapter traces how the content of the newspapers was shaped by the editors in each town, a complex web of state licensing and censorship, and by the postal system that delivered the periodicals. In doing so, chapter 1 considers how the production of such sources informs the questions that guide this book.

Chapter 2 turns to the letters to the editor published in the affiches, and in particular to their authors. Using both quantitative and qualitative approaches, this chapter identifies the startling diversity of those who wrote to the information press. And while nearly half of the writers indicated who they were, many writers obscured their identities. This chapter limns what the historian can know about who the authors were and what the forms of self-presentation in the letters communicated. Writers exercised a range of approaches to self-fashioning that were shaped by the simultaneously public and personal act of writing a public letter.

Chapter 3 situates the affiches within a larger information context by examining how the letter writers interacted with print. A quantitative investigation of the books and newspapers that readers cited underscores the capacious interests of the newspaper-reading public. Writers engaged with some of the most celebrated savants of the eighteenth century, but their letters also highlighted the persistent influence of writers from the seventeenth century and antiquity. A close reading of the sources reveals that letter writers used the newspaper to reflect on many modes of reading, but above all, they used the affiches to practice reading together.

Chapter 4 investigates two scientific spectacles of the 1780s—hot-air balloons and electricity—that were covered regularly in the information press. Savants and amateurs alike wrote letters to share the experiments they had carried out. For savants, letters on ballooning and electricity afforded an opportunity to garner widespread support for scientific work. And yet once their letters appeared in the press, they found that the uses that other writers made of their findings were difficult to control. As they shared their conclusions, posed questions, and contested results in the press, writers devised strategies for situating their authority around unsettled scientific questions.

Chapter 5 concentrates on the avid participation in the affiches around agricultural reform. Agronomists and farmers alike used the newspaper to communicate new techniques and to convince other readers. Like the debates in chapter 4, letters concerning agriculture generated widespread interest in experimentation; what set them apart was their ability to encourage the implementation of new practices. By privileging material results worked out on one's own land, such letters emphasized know-how based on experience. They also cultivated a style of journalism in which anecdotes and facts described as self-evident became particularly powerful rhetorical strategies. Writers made cases to the paper based on a desire to be useful to society and to position the affiches as the repository for useful knowledge. In doing so, they opened up possibilities of who could speak with authority in the press.

While writers advocated reform in one another's fields and pastures, collective action was most evident in the letters to the editor that concerned the practice of philanthropy known as *bienfaisance*: the single most popular topic that letters to the editor addressed. Chapter 6 shows that when it came to social welfare, letter writers negotiated reform via the press at a wide scale. Communicating about bienfaisance afforded more writers—including some figures who did not write on other subject matter—a means to participate in the press. It was in the letters to the editor on bienfaisance that marginal figures became agents in their own stories.

The habits of mind that letter writers had practiced over the previous two decades would soon be put to new and unanticipated uses during the Revolution. Chapter 7 traces the information press during the first three years of the French Revolution. The end of Old Regime censorship and licensing presented newfound opportunities for writers to communicate directly about revolutionary politics. The affiches were integral to that collective political education, as writers used their letters to interpret the political events in which they participated, and deputies to the National Assembly used letters to the editor to communicate with their constituents. At the same time, the affiches continued to publish letters about the wide range of issues that had characterized the information press of the 1770s and 1780s. Such continuities underscore the ways in which the habits of mind fostered by writing a letter to the editor persisted and adapted into the early years of the Revolution.

While people participated in the Enlightenment in all manner of collective and active endeavors, the conclusion argues that writing a letter to the editor differed meaningfully from other kinds of participation. It required time and consideration. Writing a letter to the editor relied on the writer's assumption that other people would want to read what she or he had to say. Moreover, a letter to the editor reflected a desire to be a part of a public conversation. Writers' claims were affective and material, as well as instructive and civic-minded. People took their contributions to the newspaper so seriously because the issues they addressed impinged on their own lives. Such participation was only possible in the media landscape that emerged in the last decades of the eighteenth century.

CHAPTER 1

The Production and Distribution of the Information Press

In the spring of 1782 the English writer Sarah Goudar spent her mornings in her apartment overlooking the Palais-Royal. Each day her maid set a table alongside the balcony for her, where a teakettle, teapot, teacup, sugar bowl, bread, butter, and the Parisian daily *Journal de Paris* were all arranged before her. For Goudar, reading the newspaper was part of a daily routine by which she learned of the "lettered world." One morning she spilled her tea on the paper and destroyed it, so she wrote to the editors to request a new copy. In her published missive to the editor requesting a new edition of the paper, she chronicled her reading habits, emphasizing the daily practice of reading in her home.[1] Goudar painted an image of print consumption as a time of daily enjoyment, yet the place of the newspaper in the quotidian habits of Parisian and provincial consumers was a rather recent phenomenon.

The *Journal de Paris*, the Parisian *Journal général de France*, and the provincial newspapers published under the title *Affiches, annonces, et avis divers* were launched, for the most part, in the 1770s, when they began to flourish throughout France. While similar newspapers had appeared as early as the 1750s, many of those papers had struggled to survive. Drawing on the historiography of the press and original archival research, this chapter traces the production, distribution, and consumption of the information press. To understand the newspapers that emerged in the 1770s and 1780s requires an examination of the relationship of newspapers to three Old Regime mediators: the network of censors who regulated the printing industry; the postal system through which editors delivered newspapers to subscribers; and the editors themselves. Such structures guided editorial decision-making and are thus essential to understanding the way that the information press presented content to and invited contributions from readers.

Establishing the Affiches

Before mid-century, newspapers circulated in urban centers, but readers outside Paris had little access to periodicals. The scant number of newspapers in the kingdom reflected the elaborate state system of assigning printing monopolies known as *privilèges* to select publishers. In the seventeenth century the French government had given the exclusive rights to print newspapers to the *Gazette de France*, which consisted of short reports written by the ministry of foreign affairs, and provided readers with a sense of geopolitical news that favored king and church. The most prevalent publications in the countryside were reprints of the *Gazette*. The printer's privilège granted a title of possession and permission to publish on a renewable basis, in exchange for the submission of all published content to government censorship. In principle, the royal privilège allowed the printers of a periodical a monopoly to publish on specified subjects and protected editors from infringement by other publications.

By the eighteenth century, the monopolies on content were split between three newspapers: the *Gazette de France*, the *Journal des sçavans*, and the *Mercure*.[2] The *Gazette* maintained a monopoly on all geopolitical news. All remaining subjects were the domain of the two other privileged publications: the *Mercure*, which published on literature, theater, and society and court gossip, and the *Journal des sçavans*, which concerned learned subjects in the sciences and medicine. While other newspapers and magazines did appear in the seventeenth and early eighteenth centuries, the system of privilèges stifled the domestic market, and many periodicals failed.

The history of the emergence of the affiches is more complex. In 1749, after four generations in the Renaudot family, the privilège to publish the *Gazette* was sold. Two years later, its new owners, the chevalier Denis Rabiot de Meslé and the financier Louis Dominique Le Bas de Courmont, launched a second paper titled *Affiches de Province*, which shared the advertising format of the *Feuille du Bureau d'Adresse* that Renaudot had published in the seventeenth century. The *Affiches* targeted provincial readers and printed on various domestic topics. By 1753 Rabiot de Meslé and Le Bas de Courmont devised a plan to expand their enterprise by printing similar papers in all the major cities of the kingdom. They envisioned a network of offices for editing and publishing each paper, called *bureaux d'adresse*, which they intended to set up in each city.[3] Their goal was to sell the offices to provincial notables and to oversee the communication of news between the various *bureaux*. Ultimately, the plan was too ambitious, and Rabiot de Meslé and Le Bas de Courmont were unable to sell their vision to investors.[4] Plagued by personal and familial debts, Rabiot de Meslé lost influence over the *Gazette* and the affiches he had launched; he died in 1763. In contrast, his business partner's fortunes increased; Le Bas de Courmont became a *fermier général* and continued to oversee ownership of the *Gazette* and the *Affiches de Province*.[5]

After 1756 Le Bas de Courmont adopted a new strategy—to grant the right to publish a newspaper in the style of his *Affiches de Province* to one person in each town in exchange for the payment of an annual fee. Aimé Delaroche, a bookseller-printer in Lyon, had already negotiated this kind of arrangement for his *Affiches de Lyon* in 1750.[6] Soon papers titled *Affiches, annonces, et avis divers*, commonly known as affiches, began appearing in port cities such as Marseille, Nantes, and Bordeaux, and along the borderlands of the kingdom in Lille, Besançon, Metz, and Strasbourg.[7] Over time, more affiches were launched throughout the interior. The affiches published on a wide range of general information subjects, including weather, legal proceedings, commercial news, literature, and fashion, which editors adjusted to suit local and regional interests. The price Le Bas de Courmont charged publishers for the exclusive rights to publish in a given town varied, but most paid between 100 and 200 livres for the privilège. By 1778 Courmont's total annual revenue from such license fees throughout the kingdom had reached 5,000 livres.[8]

Once Le Bas de Courmont began selling the rights to publish in provincial towns, the number of affiches published in France grew, but many of the early papers were unable to stay in business for more than a year. Historians of the press have described the decades between 1750 and 1770 as an initial phase, when printers experienced difficulty in finding a market and sustaining their publications.[9] After 1770 their fortunes changed. The royal edict of June 1771 mandated that royal printers circulate published contracts of sale, and many printers seized on the opportunity to supplement their newspaper content with such listings. While affiches had certainly existed before, Gilles Feyel has argued that the edict of June 1771 gave them a newfound staying power.[10] Newspapers founded after 1770 were much more likely to remain in business.

While the edict provided stability to affiches throughout the kingdom, the content of the papers diversified to reflect the interests of individual editors and the markets where the papers appeared. By 1775 approximately twenty more cities were publishing affiches, including Dijon, Grenoble, Avignon, Aix-en-Provence, Montpellier, Perpignan, Montauban, Limoges, Poitiers, La

Rochelle, Tours, Amiens, Reims, Meaux, Sens, Auxerre, Le Mans, Angers, and Bayonne.[11] Among the fifty largest towns in the kingdom, two-thirds now had their own newspapers. Most such towns were capitals of their *généralités* or seats of a *cour souveraine*. Another strong indicator of whether a paper would appear in a town was the presence of a *chambre de commerce* or a *consulat marchand*—70 percent of affiches had such a commercial institution.[12] More than demography, literacy, or the presence of specific administrative institutions, an active market and the development of strong readership were the necessary factors for the success of the affiches.[13]

Meanwhile, the media landscape in Paris underwent its own transformation. In 1751 Le Bas de Courmont and Rabiot de Meslé had secured the rights to publish the *Affiches de Paris*. After Le Bas de Courmont died in 1777, the privilège for the Parisian paper was sold, and the paper reappeared under the title *Annonces, Affiches et Avis Divers, ou Journal général de France*.[14] The Parisian affiches also faced a new competitor when the *Journal de Paris* began publication in 1777. Whereas the affiches were usually published on a weekly basis, the *Journal de Paris* was the first daily newspaper to appear in France. In page format and in content, it resembled the provincial and Parisian affiches.

By the 1780s most major towns had a newspaper of their own, and the number of newspapers publishing in the interior had grown substantially. The *généralités* of Paris, Orléans, and Tours had three affiches each, while the *généralités* of Lille, Châlons, Dijon, Rennes, La Rochelle, Bordeaux, Montpellier, and Aix-en-Provence each had two papers.[15] The density of newspapers was especially high in the north, the northeast, and the Parisian region. By the eve of the French Revolution, forty-four towns had their own newspapers, and the affiches became the main source for local and regional news.

The Editors

The editors of the provincial and Parisian affiches were usually prominent businessmen from regional centers who remained in the town to edit and oversee the publication of their newspapers. Most of them already held the position of *imprimeur-libraire*. As printer-booksellers, they were responsible for printing government decrees for local distribution. They also published books and pamphlets, and some owned bookshops where they sold the works they had printed. The affiches thus provided a useful vehicle for maximizing their profits in an enterprise for which they already possessed the technology and an experienced labor force.[16]

The editors who were not printer-booksellers came from a wide variety of backgrounds. Five were lawyers (*avocats*), one was a notary, one a *procureur*, and two others were professors. An apothecary and a master clockmaker were among the founders of the *Journal de Paris*. For a few years, a dentist ran the *Affiches de Montpellier*. At least two of the editors had some religious training. The editor of the *Journal général de France*, Louis Abel Bonafous, Abbé de Fontenay, was a Jesuit until the suppression of the Society of Jesus; Albert Brondex, the editor of the affiches in Metz, had received a Benedictine education, though he never entered the order. Nevertheless, more editors (twelve) described themselves as printers and booksellers than any other profession.

For at least five of the editors, running the newspaper took on a social and professional significance, which they indicated by taking on the title of *journaliste*. By the 1780s the people publishing newspapers had begun to think of themselves not merely as *gazetiers*, that is, as compositors and distributors of information, but rather as *journalistes* who exercised judgment over their content. While the self-description of *journaliste* originated in Holland, it grew in popularity in French literary papers in the 1720s and 1730s. Denis Diderot's entry in the *Encyclopédie* for "journaliste" transformed the meaning and accelerated the adoption of the term.[17] In his estimation, a *journaliste* was responsible for publishing excerpts on literature, the sciences, and the arts, but also for helping the reader understand them—a journalist ought to instruct readers and exercise fairness in evaluating the information presented in the paper. Diderot's *journaliste* was also guided by two aims: the progress of humanity and the love of truth.[18] The self-description of *journaliste* thus emphasized the creative, authorial role that working on the affiches entailed. This reformulation was further underscored by newspaper editors in the 1780s who began changing their titles from *affiches, annonces, et avis divers* to instead include the word *journal*. These shifts in the self-presentation of editors and the names of their papers were emblematic of the changing ways that editors thought of their work.

Some of the editors were themselves affiliated with the same social circles as men of letters. Jean Milcent, the director of the affiches in Rouen, was a member of the *société littéraire* in Bayeux and the Académie des Palinods in Rouen. He was introduced in Marie Thérèse Rodet Geoffrin's salon by Jean le Rond d'Alembert and Diderot, and he wrote poetry.[19] Louis Couret de Villeneuve, the editor of the *Affiches de l'Orléanois*, was the father-in-law of the prominent printer Charles-Joseph Panckoucke, who was known especially for publishing the *Mercure de France*.[20] Panckoucke's sister, Amélie Suard, was a salonnière and writer; her husband was a journalist. René Jouyneau-Desloges in Poitiers and Jean-François Blouet in Metz were members of learned societies and academies.[21] Some editors also revealed a particular interest in bienfaisance; the editors of the *Journal de Lyon* and *Journal de Paris* were especially active in founding and supporting philanthropic societies.[22]

Many editors expressed their interest in belles lettres, beneficence, and a desire to print useful content; such values were widely shared throughout the kingdom.

Among the editors and printers of the newspapers under study, women produced at least five. All identified themselves as widows, a status that by law and custom entitled them to run the family business as printer and bookseller.[23] When the *imprimeur-libraire* André Giroud died in Grenoble, his wife, Justine Souverant, took over the family printing shop and bookstores. She founded and edited the affiches as a means of augmenting her business, and she successfully ran the paper until 1792.[24] The publisher of the *Affiches de Rennes*, Jeanne Le Saulnier du Vauhello, took over her husband's print shop when he died in 1771; she ran it until 1823.[25] Élisabeth Charlot, the widow of Louis Godart, printed the affiches in Amiens until 1777.[26] For some of the women who produced affiches, very little is known except for the requisite references on the newspaper page. Identified only by her husband's surname; the widow Nicolas printed the *Affiches d'Artois* in Arras.[27] The widow Barbe-Thérèse Lefebvre Marchand would take over the paper in 1789. Marguerite Pagès-Marinier, the editor of the *Affiches de Montpellier*, was a dentist who also ran a reading room (*cabinet de lecture*). Much of her story survives because of Pagès-Marinier's protracted legal battles with another printer in Montpellier and with Le Bas de Courmont over the right to publish the *Affiches de Montpellier*. Rather than paying for the privilège to print in Montpellier, she had instead secured local permissions from provincial authorities. It took ten years and the intervention of royal authorities for Courmont to wrest publishing rights from Pagès-Marinier.[28]

In general, the editors were men and women from middling backgrounds living in urban centers who were well educated and well established in their communities. In many cases they had inherited a print shop from their fathers and would eventually pass on the business to their children. Far from the Grub Street writers who penned *nouvelles à la main* in Paris, the editors of the affiches were local notables interested in preserving the revenues the affiches provided.[29] The evolution of their newspapers after 1789 would reveal a range of ideologies from conservative monarchist to Jacobin, but such political outlooks were obscured before the Revolution. In their content analysis of the revolutionary press, Pierre Rétat and Claude Labrosse have argued that it was possible to determine the general political inclination of a newspaper's editors based on the content they chose to publish.[30] Yet before the outbreak of the Revolution most editors eschewed overtly political content, and the political positions of the men and women who published affiches would be shaped by the very experience of the Revolution. As a result, this book does not trace a political genealogy of the editors.

Finding an Audience

Before beginning to print their newspapers, editors published a prospectus to explain the content they intended to cover. In it, editors identified their prospective audience, outlined general content areas, and invited their subscribers to participate in the affiches by sending letters to the paper. Editors played a key role in framing the content and circulation of the affiches, both by inviting contributions from readers on particular topics and in choosing which responses to print. The prospectuses of the affiches have received extensive treatment in histories of the press, beginning with Eugène Hatin's foundational study.[31] Jack Censer has argued that the prospectuses of the affiches demonstrated the "overwhelming inclination" of the editors to recognize their publications' audiences. The prospectus served to communicate the editor's aims to two audiences: the officials who had to approve the paper and the readers who would eventually purchase a subscription.[32]

The newspapers the editors designed were short, four-page publications consisting of one piece of paper folded in half on the left-hand side. At the top of the first page, the title "Annonces, Affiches et Avis Divers" of the town or généralité appeared.[33] Titles evolved as their prospective markets expanded or shrank; some papers even printed under different titles depending on the newspaper's destination.[34] While some affiches, such as the papers published in Nantes and Chartres, featured an engraving depicting the town, most newspapers were very simple and displayed minimal ornamentation, as illustrations were costly. Each edition included the issue number, the title, and the date; the pages were typically numbered consecutively for the entire year. Most affiches appeared on a weekly basis, though the *Journal de Paris* appeared daily, and the *Journal général de France* published three times a week. The *Journal de Paris* also included meteorological and astronomical observations on the first page.

Below the front matter, the paper was printed in two columns. The first page featured the *annonces*: the lists of properties sold, as required by the 1771 edict, along with a series of advertisements featuring goods, land, and houses for sale. Families looking for a cook, domestic servant, or tutor often took out ads in the paper.[35] Dentists, oculists, and itinerant craftsmen advertised their services to potential employers. Few manufactured goods were advertised, with the exception of books.[36] The occasional notice of a lost dog appeared. Many editors inserted announcements from their subscribers free of charge as a way to generate more subscriptions. The affiches typically charged 12 sous to print an advertisement from nonsubscribers, though the cost varied by the length of copy and the newspaper in which it appeared.[37] A newspaper's last page had a series of rubrics; announcements of theatrical spectacles, the price of goods, lottery results, and word puzzles were among the topics featured.

The remaining space on the front page and the two pages in the middle of the affiches were composed of an array of content that included news and all other information relevant to the "utilité générale," which varied from week to week: belles lettres, the sciences, the arts, geography and travel, history and the classics, agriculture, medicine, bienfaisance, jurisprudence, administration, obituaries for prominent figures, current events, and human-interest pieces. To date, Jack Censer and Gilles Feyel have done the most comprehensive content analysis of the affiches.[38] They estimate that after publishing the advertisements from subscribers and the announcements required by state and local officials, editors had control of approximately two-thirds of the content of the paper, which they filled with an assortment of topics that touched on daily life, including administrative announcements, current events, anecdotal stories, book and theater reviews, agricultural and scientific observations, and medical remedies. Among this content, there was also "a rich body of letters from readers, who intervened often on the major issues of the moment."[39] Historians of the Old Regime press have noted the robust presence of letters to the editor in the affiches, but no one has systematically analyzed who wrote the letters and what the letters had to say. Published letters to the editor speak to an entirely new realm of eighteenth-century lives and social activity. They are especially important because historians have shown that private correspondence serves as a powerful touchstone of social, cultural, and political life in the eighteenth century.

In general, letters from readers under the heading "A l'Auteur du Journal" or "Au Rédacteur du Journal" followed a similar structure. They opened with an address to the editor and often included the date and location of their composition.[40] The body of the letters varied in content, depending on the subject matter and aims of the writer. The writers of the letters ended with a closing such as "yours, etc.," and they then commonly specified their name.[41] As chapter 2 explores in depth, in some cases writers indicated their social position or profession. Other writers did not want their name published in the paper, although they might well offer a pseudonym, or their initials, or sign simply as "a subscriber."

In the 1770s the letters to the editor became a regular feature of the information press. Letters varied in length from a paragraph to several pages. The amount of space dedicated to letters varied from newspaper to newspaper.

The affiches in Lyon, Marseille, and Angers, for example, published letters only on an occasional basis. In Paris, Poitiers, Dijon, and Metz, by contrast, published letters became a regular component of the newspapers' content. The total number of letters published in a given newspaper reflected editorial choices. Some editors seemed to design their publications from the outset with correspondence in mind, even printing regular appeals for letters from their readers. In their prospectus, some editors included a call for letters from readers that explained the newspaper's aims and contents to potential readers, and they even indicated the topics of correspondence they would like to receive. The strategies for publishing letters from readers also varied. Some editors collected a set of letters on a particular theme or question, which they published together in one issue. Others published letters as they were received in a more serialized fashion. But inevitably the space devoted to letters had to be balanced with other content that was also considered essential, such as advertisements and administrative reports.

The rate of publication of letters to the editor grew over time. While they first appeared in a few affiches as early as the 1760s, their sustained publication took off in the provinces only after 1770, as the number published rose from an occasional letter to more than a hundred per year. After 1782 the number of letters published in the provincial press more than doubled, a volume of correspondence that was sustained through 1789. In Paris the aggregate number of letters published increased even more dramatically, from fewer than ten a year before the *Journal de Paris* to more than three hundred letters a year after it began publication in 1777. In contrast to the weekly publication cycle of most provincial affiches, the *Journal de Paris* had four pages to fill every day, and letters quickly became a key component of the periodical. As more newspapers were launched in the 1780s, the letters became a fixture through the beginning of the Revolution. Nearly seven thousand letters appeared in the affiches between 1770 and the end of 1788. The growth in the publication of letters over the last two decades of the Old Regime corresponded to the process by which editors honed their abilities to foster discussion and curate correspondence with their readers.

The editorial style of journalism in such newspapers did not yet resemble that of the nineteenth and twentieth centuries. Rather, theirs was a journalism "de type épistolaire," through which the editor made a call for contributions from his or her readers.[42] Such epistolary journalism relied heavily on the contributions of readers and subscribers. After all, editors depended on the intellectual and social circles in their town and in provincial society more broadly to buy the newspaper. Affiches flourished where they were able to engage their readers in ongoing conversations and debates.

Editors structured their papers in ways that made room for dialogue by posing questions to readers, inviting responses from subscribers, and printing various observations and debates that juxtaposed competing points of view. In doing so, they conveyed the notion that the newspaper was in conversation with its readership.[43] In some cases, the editor left a brief *note du rédacteur* at the end of a letter to the editor to offer more context or assure readers that a response was forthcoming. The editors of the *Journal général de France, Affiches des Trois-Évêchés et Lorraine,* and the *Affiches de Toulouse* all indicated in such notes that they would provide comments on a subscriber's letter in the next number of their newspapers.[44] In Poitiers, Michel-Vincent Chevrier offered to print the excerpts from the *Mercure* that a letter writer referenced.[45] The editor of the *Affiches de Rennes* included her own lively responses to the letters she printed; on one occasion she checked the math in a letter she published.[46] Editors also used notes to make their decision-making process more transparent to their readers, by explaining why the paper had chosen to print or not print a particular piece they had received. For example, the editor of the *Affiches de la Basse-Normandie* invited a letter writer to contribute more letters and explained that the correspondence would be printed serially because of its length.[47] Such editorial interaction no doubt shaped the kinds of letters that the papers received from their subscribers. They also helped encourage the flourishing of letters to the editor in the affiches, which continued to grow over the two decades preceding the Revolution.

Moreover, editors shared and reprinted content from similar publications. Editors routinely cut information from other periodicals and used that content to fill the pages of their own newspapers. The practice of the "scissors editor," where editors cut content from other newspapers and reprinted it in their own, often without attribution at all, persisted in this period throughout the Atlantic world.[48] The men and women who published affiches likely also reprinted content without acknowledging the content's origin, but in at least 440 of the letters published between 1770 and 1788 (approximately 6.4 percent of the total corpus), the editors indicated that they had reprinted the letter from another newspaper. For example, Justine Giroud indicated some of the letters in her *Affiches du Dauphiné* were "au Rédacteur des *Affiches de Metz*" or "Aux Auteurs du *Journal de Paris.*"[49] The periodicals on which the editors drew were mixed. They republished content from other affiches in Paris and the provinces, from specialized journals, and from other periodicals from the surrounding region.

Figure 1.1 presents a network visualization that traces the information flows from their source to the newspaper that reprinted them. A network plot is a way of visualizing a set of relationships through a depiction of nodes and ties. Each node represents an individual, in this case one newspaper. Each tie (or edge) indicates one connection between two individuals. In this figure, each tie represents one case of republication, where an editor cut a letter to the editor from another newspaper and pasted it into the paper she or he produced. To distinguish the original source of publication from the affiches where the letter was republished, the arrow points away from the newspaper where the letter originally appeared and toward the paper that republished it. A density of ties between two particular newspapers indicates that such papers republished content with greater frequency. The more central a particular newspaper within the figure, the more often it was cited by several of the surrounding newspapers. In contrast, the nodes on the periphery of the visualization with a single tie were republished in only one case, by only one newspaper. This network figure is particularly useful for identifying the relationships between papers, gauging the significance of a particular newspaper for other affiches, and identifying the other types of periodicals to which editors turned for content. Significantly, letters to the editor appeared not only in the information press but also in learned journals and other censored and uncensored periodicals.

The Parisian newspapers were a popular and frequent source from which provincial editors took information. The centrality of the Parisian publications (nodes 11 and 12) shows that most of the provincial affiches drew content from their Parisian counterparts. The ties between the affiches show that editors republished the most letters from Parisian newspapers, but the Parisian papers were not the exclusive sources of information. The clustering of provincial affiches near the center of the network (nodes 2, 7, 8, 9, 10, and 13) shows that provincial affiches also shared content among themselves. Some of the republished content was regionally oriented. For example, the *Affiches d'Aix* (node 1) reprinted content from the *Journal de Provence* in Marseille (8). In the southwest where newspapers were scarcer, the *Affiches de Bordeaux* (18) reprinted letters from the *Affiches de Montpellier* (19). Literacy rates, density of newspapers, and regional connections and interests mattered.

Moving toward the periphery of the network, the ties become less dense, and specialized journals (indicated as triangles) and regional newspapers (represented as circles) become more prominent. In many cases, such publications were linked to provincial affiches by just one letter (that is, one tie). The surrounding circular and triangular nodes suggest that the markets for each newspaper had particularities to which the editor was attentive, and editors published content according to the interests of their particular readership. For example, the *Affiches de l'Orléanois* (node 10) published content from nearby

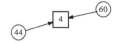

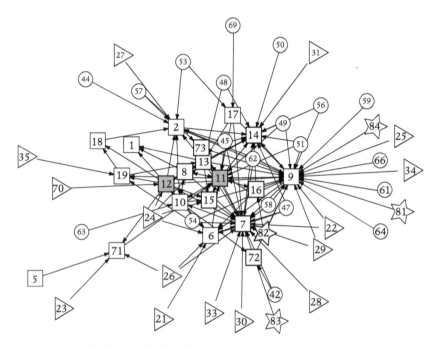

Figure 1.1   Reprinted content in the affiches, 1770–1788.

Each node represents a newspaper, and each tie indicates one letter an editor republished after its initial appearance. The shapes indicate types of newspapers as follows:

Squares: all the provincial newspapers under study in this book, including the affiches published in Angers (2), Grenoble (7), Marseille (8), Metz (9), Orléans (10), Poitiers (13), and Troyes (15).

Squares shaded gray: the Parisian newspapers, the *Journal de Paris* (node 12), and the *Journal général de France* (node 11).

The remaining shapes indicate other periodicals from which the Parisian and provincial affiches drew content:

Stars: newspapers published abroad.

Triangles: specialized journals on the arts, sciences, health, or literature.

Circles: general information newspapers not consulted in this study.

The unique identifier number in each node indicates a particular newspaper. All newspapers are listed in full by their unique identifier in appendix A.

Angers (2) and from Paris (11 and 12), but also from provincial newspapers further afield such as the affiches in Marseille (8) and Verdun (63), as well as the *Morning Herald* from London (82). The *Affiches de Toulouse* (14) republished content from the Parisian *Journal général de France* (11), but also from the specialized periodical the *Journal militaire* (31), from newspapers in the southwest, such as the *Affiches de La Rochelle* (50), and from northern and central France, such as the *Feuille de Flandres* in Lille (49), the *Affiches de Normandie* in Rouen (16), and the *Affiches de Moulins* (56). The network visualization of reprinted letters shows that the affiches shared content with one another and with other periodicals in France and abroad. Together they formed a circuit to share practical information from one newspaper to another.

Censorship

The content of the affiches was influenced not only by the editor but also by a complex system of censorship at the local and national levels. In principle, the system of royal privilèges set the limits for what could appear in print in France. Privilèges delineated the subject matter of each publication, but they also enforced material quality control by indicating, for example, the kind of paper that the printer had to use and the aesthetic quality of the type setting.[50] They also required that the editor designate who was authorized to print the publication; the specified publisher then had to register with the guild of booksellers and printers. This requirement protected the interests of master craftsmen and distinguished authorized publications from counterfeit and clandestine copies. Alongside this system of licensed publication, a burgeoning clandestine book trade and the circulation of newspapers published abroad for a French audience also existed.[51] Finally, publications required an approbation, a formal sanction delivered by royal censors that stated they had reviewed and approved content.

For the affiches in particular, the process began with securing the necessary license to print from the *propriétaire du privilège*, Louis Dominique Le Bas de Courmont (and later his successor, Pierre Benezech). Since the privilège for all affiches technically originated in the privilège granted to the *Gazette*, the royal ministry officially in charge of censoring the affiches was the secretary of foreign affairs. In the case of the *Gazette*, the secretary of foreign affairs had the oversight to censor information concerning geopolitical affairs that impinged on the way the monarchy was perceived. Once the necessary provincial and royal authorities approved the prospectus, the editor printed their paper on a weekly basis and sent copies to both their fellow editors who published affiches in other French towns and the royal censor in the Department of Foreign Affairs who gave "directives, compliments, and reprimands," based on the content.[52]

Traces of the changes that censors required of the editors of affiches are rare, though a few records exist. Colin Jones has emphasized the petty nature of the changes that censors required in his evaluation of the editor's proofs of the *Affiches de Province* before and after censorship. Beyond the *Affiches de Province*, there is little evidence that the censor in Foreign Affairs exercised any role in suppressing other affiches' content. The affiches generally covered topics that were more local and practical in nature, and in doing so they steered their content away from topics that might run afoul of the censors. The affiches rarely experienced suspensions or printed formal retractions, though there were exceptions. The intendant suspended the *Affiches des Trois-Évêchés et Lorraine* in April 1782; the paper resumed publication in July. The editors of the *Affiches de la Haute Normandie* in Rouen and the *Affiches de Nantes* received reprimands for their content and adjusted their future editions accordingly.[53] In Toulouse the publisher Jean-Florent Baour faced two lawsuits in which powerful local legal officials argued that he had exposed private matters in his *Affiches*. Despite winning both cases, the cost of defending himself was too much; he gave up his privilège to the paper in 1776.[54]

The *Journal de Paris* experienced greater scrutiny. Vergennes, the minister of foreign affairs, together with the support of Jean-Charles Lenoir, the lieutenant general of the Paris Prefecture of Police, surveilled the daily.[55] Between June 4 and 27, 1785, they suspended the *Journal de Paris* for printing a poem that ridiculed Princess Maria Christina of Saxony, a relative of Marie-Antoinette. For their part, the owners of the *Journal* insisted they had printed the verses by pure ignorance; they had no intention to offend the royal family, whom they said they counted among their subscribers.[56] In December 1786 the censor assigned to the *Journal* was reprimanded for allowing an *éloge* to the comte de Guibert to appear in the paper.[57] There is little archival evidence to suggest that provincial newspapers received the same level of scrutiny as the *Journal de Paris*, and some editors tested the political and philosophical waters. The criticism of royal policies and institutions published in the *Affiches de Bordeaux*, for example, further illustrates the laxity of censorship for some of the affiches.[58]

The records of the editors publishing affiches from the 1750s through the 1780s reveal that maintaining the rights to publish and determining which parties must approve newspaper content was complex and often confusing for the printers. Most newspapers, after all, were censored not by the Department of Foreign Affairs but rather by the *chancellerie*, which also oversaw the French book trade.[59] Where archival records of the affiches survive, they concern three key questions: disputes between rival printers in the same town over who had the right to publish the newspaper; confusion over which local and royal institutions had the right to designate the editor; or inquiries regarding who had the right to censor a particular paper.[60]

In practice, the system of censorship was made more complex because of the potential impact of the powerful head of the royal *chancellerie*, provincial networks of patronage, and local politics more generally. By the 1760s Guillaume-Chrétien de Lamoignon de Malesherbes, the director of the royal publishing office, had successfully challenged the sole authority of the secretaries of state to censor the affiches, so editors needed not only a license from Le Bas de Courmont but also the approval of the *chancellerie*, who assigned censors to read the paper. Once the central administration had reviewed a request for the rights to publish, they would contact local authorities to request their approval before they permitted the printer to move forward with publication. The decision went to the intendant of the province, then to a local magistrate in the town, and in some cases to the lieutenant general of police. In urban centers under the jurisdiction of a *parlement*, the court also had to authorize the publication. If all of the provincial authorities granted approval, the editor would then produce a prospectus that described the paper he or she intended to publish, which was posted around the town for consultation. Editors who met the expectations at each step were then awarded the exclusive right to publish the affiches in the town.[61]

In addition to this lengthy approval process, according to their licensing agreement, each edition of the paper was supposed to be read by a local censor. In practice, the authority that held this responsibility varied from town to town, as evidenced in the particular approbations at the end of each issue of the newspaper that testified that the content of the paper had been seen by the appropriate authority. These notices usually took the form "with approval," "read and approved," or "seen and approved," and they were followed by the visa of the lieutenant general of police or the general notice "permission to print and distribute."[62] Since the *chancellerie* did not name censors systematically, some affiches were submitted only to the local lieutenant general of police; his approval sufficed to indicate that the content of the paper was not offensive to the royal person. However, in other locations the *parlements* also assumed an active role in regulating the content of the paper; *magistrats* and *procureurs du roi* could and sometimes did denounce the contents of the paper.[63]

Other affiches had specifically designated royal censors. In Orléans the Abbé de Reyrac, the rector and curé of Saint-Maclou and a friend of Condillac, censored the affiches. In Caen the royal censor assigned to the affiches was Le Paulmier, the rector of the Univérsité de Caen, a member of the local academy, and a subdelegate to the intendant.[64] The regulation of censorship and assignment of censors to the affiches generally aligns with the processes Malesherbes described in his correspondence as chief censor from 1750 to

1763: censorship was a negotiated process that encompassed a great deal of collaboration between authors and censors. Censors saw themselves as men of letters who were enhancing literary quality. Their correspondence centered on discussions of tone and style—that is, on the quality of books—as much as content. Publications that received an approbation had to express the right ideas about the king and the church, but they also had to be written in good prose.[65]

In short, the manner in which an individual royal censor carried out his work varied. In some instances, censors did not read the copy they were assigned to police, and the printer moved forward with publication, thus implicitly allowing indiscreet content to slip into print. Alternatively, Malesherbes sometimes tacitly responded to publishers' requests for leniency by directing the censor in charge of the particular publication to show greater forbearance in their evaluation of the content. Thus, while the system of censorship for newspaper editors in the 1770s and 1780s was extensive, the ostensibly stringent guidelines on the content of the domestic press were rather unevenly enforced, generating a climate of tolerance between editors and censors.[66]

For writers from the 1750s until the end of the Old Regime, censorship was a process of collaboration between state censors, publishers, and authors. While the royal administration maintained a commitment to censorship, correspondence between censors shows a complex process of negotiation, which was intended to serve not only the interests of the state but also those of guilds and of well-established men of letters. After all, authors and censors often came from the same social circles, and many censors were themselves authors. What is more, censorship was often a secondary occupation: most censors were members of the clergy, lawyers, doctors, and professors; some were state administrators. Working as a censor was not particularly profitable in and of itself, but it did impart a sense of prestige and the possibility of acquiring a wealthy patron or a more lucrative appointment.[67] As such, most censors took their work seriously, even assuming the role of copyeditor, correcting spelling and arithmetic, and revising poor grammar. They worked closely with authors, so much so that the director of the book trade often asked editors of a particular book which censor they would prefer to work with. Censors routinely negotiated content with the authors whose work they reviewed.[68] The extent of collaboration is further underscored by the low percentage—only about 10 percent—of books refused publication.[69]

The structure of royal censorship is particularly salient for the study of the affiches because it underscores how much one's social networks and financial resources shaped one's ability to publish a book. For most literate men and women, the path to publishing a book was beyond their means and social connections, and it necessarily relied on patronage, financial resources, and knowledge of the intricacies of the royal bureaucracy. But publishing a letter to the editor of a newspaper was significantly more attainable.

The Distribution of the Affiches

Once the editors had navigated the necessary licensing and censorship barriers, they mailed the newspaper to their subscribers via the royal post. Ensuring that the affiches had an audience required editors to get the publication to their readers quickly and consistently. The royal post, which was authorized to deliver all letters and newspapers, made such circulation possible. The press and the post had long been intertwined, for the earliest "news papers" in Europe were published by the postmasters themselves.[70] In the late eighteenth century, subscribers to newspapers, including the affiches, still received their newspapers in the mail.

Paris was firmly situated at the center of the postal distribution network. Parisians could post correspondence to the provinces from seventy-eight mailboxes found in shops and bakeries around the capital, or they could mail the letter from the general post office on the rue Platrière.[71] The postal roads that connected major cities and towns throughout the kingdom emanated from Paris like spokes on a wheel, dotted with relay stations. The state-sponsored postal system had since the fifteenth century required relay riders to travel via these "post roads." Over the eighteenth century this exchange network had grown ever more connected, nearly doubling the number of relay stations where travelers and mail couriers could find a place to rest, a fresh horse, and news. By 1788 a total of 1,426 relay stations stood along the king's roads. By 1792 twelve of the fifteen postal roads from Paris had daily mail departures.[72]

In the late eighteenth century, the fifteen main postal routes were served by coaches that carried mail and newspapers along set routes, with a network of secondary roads reaching the more remote interior of the kingdom. This system of roads enabled timely communication in the north and in the towns surrounding Paris. Correspondence from Paris arrived in Rouen within one or two days, whereas postal delivery to Bordeaux took five to six days, and delivery to Lyon required six days. In general, mail from Paris arrived within eight days to sixty-four major towns and cities in France.[73]

Sending a letter from one provincial town to another typically took longer and incurred an additional fee, as letters were routed along the major highways through the hub of Paris. For example, a letter sent from Paris to provincial centers such as Lyon or Bordeaux would reach such distant destinations more rapidly than a centrally located town such as Clermont-Ferrand that was not on a main postal road. Even given these constraints, figures from the early 1790s suggest that one could receive information by post from anywhere in the kingdom within a twenty-day time frame, depending on the sender's and the recipient's proximities to major postal routes.[74] The time frame between the printing of a newspaper and its arrival to the subscriber in part explains the tendency for the affiches to print useful information, rather than particularly timely stories. Moreover, while such conveyance may appear slow by twenty-first-century standards, Jay Caplan has argued that the prevalence of idioms from this period such as "post-haste" in English, *en poste* in French ("with haste, at full speed"), or *con la celerità de la stapheta* in Italian ("as fast as a mounted courier") underscore that for preindustrial Europeans the post moved at a pace that was quite swift indeed.[75]

Securing enough subscribers was critical to the financial viability of the affiches, and postage costs were a considerable concern for editors and subscribers. After mid-century, two innovations reduced the financial risk of producing a newspaper and encouraged more subscribers: lower postage costs and a new subscription model. First, lower postage costs strengthened the economic viability of starting and sustaining a newspaper. The cost of mailing newspapers via the royal post decreased in 1763.[76] While the royal post continued to convey newspapers and letters from town to town, by the 1760s intra-urban exchanges known as *petites postes* emerged, first in Paris and then in provincial centers, including Bordeaux, Rouen, Lyon, Nancy, and Marseille. The *petites postes* had two key advantages: they were much quicker than the royal post, with pickups as often as nine times a day in Paris, for example; and they were much less expensive than the royal post. Moreover, they allowed the sender to prepay for a letter, thus relieving the financial burden on the recipient. Up until this point, the recipient of a letter typically paid the postage on its arrival, and the rate paid varied depending on the type of letter or package sent and the distance it traveled.[77] The custom persisted until the 1840s, when postage stamps were first issued. The system of city-wide postal delivery made possible by *petites postes* was faster and less costly, though mail still occasionally reached the wrong recipient or was lost altogether. House numbering was just beginning in the late eighteenth century.[78]

Second, newspaper producers began to include the fee for transport (known as "franco" or "franche de port") in the cost of the subscription, which they collected in advance of delivery. Editors advertised the cost of a subscription, along with instructions about how and where to subscribe in their prospectus and in notices in the newspaper throughout the year.

The price of an annual subscription to the weekly affiches published in Angers, Bordeaux, Caen, Dijon, Grenoble, Lyon, Montpellier, Orléans, Reims, Toulouse, and Troyes was six livres for those who lived in town. In Aix-en-Provence, Amiens, Compiègne, Metz, Poitiers, and Rennes, annual subscriptions to residents in town were between seven and eight livres.[79] The affiches published in Rouen and Arras were the most expensive, with annual subscriptions of twelve livres in town. All affiches also advertised subscription prices for delivery throughout the kingdom, which included the cost of postage. The price for such subscriptions was typically 7 livres, 10 sous for those papers that charged 6 livres in town, and 9 livres for those that charged 7 livres in town, but the papers in Rouen and Arras charged 15 and 13 livres, respectively.

The cost of a subscription to the affiches was relatively inexpensive in comparison to other periodicals. Annual subscriptions for the affiches cost approximately half of what subscribers paid for a year of the *Journal des dames*, and a fifth the price of a subscription to the *Mercure de France*. In 1777, when the *Journal de Paris* began publishing on a daily schedule, the cost for an annual subscription was 24 livres in Paris itself, and 31 livres, 4 sous for the provinces. Most editors advertised their office address along with a series of addresses of notaries and lawyers in nearby towns so that potential readers in the region could pay for subscriptions locally. The affiches in Arras, for example, allowed subscriptions with nine notables in the region, including a bookseller in Douai and one in Lille, a notary in Béthune and another in Lillers, the directors of the post in Hesdin and Dunkerque, a customs officer in Péronne, a goldsmith in Aire, and a cloth manufacturer in Saint-Omer.[80] The editor of the *Affiches de Reims* even circulated preaddressed envelopes so that his subscribers in nearby Troyes could more easily subscribe to his paper with the local notary, Jean-François Delion.[81] The publishers of the *Affiches d'Aix* used similar prefilled forms as receipts for subscriptions.[82] Taken together, the subscription model and lower postage costs reduced the risk to newspaper owners and increased access for subscribers. Whereas the early affiches in the 1750s had often failed, most of the newspapers launched in the 1770s stayed in print well into the Revolution.

Estimating the Readership

Precisely how many copies of the affiches circulated through the post remains unknown, since complete subscription logs or print runs no longer exist that would indicate the total number of newspapers printed and sold. Lacking complete records, historians of the press have combined the claims made by printers and partial subscriber lists to estimate total circulation for most affiches between 200 and 750 subscribers, although some affiches had more than 1,000. From such estimates, historians of the press have extrapolated a total number of subscriptions to the approximately forty affiches as somewhere between 8,000 and 30,000.[83]

Yet total readership was invariably higher than the total number of subscribers. In Reims the editor of the affiches estimated the readership for the paper was at least four times the total number of subscribers, while the editor of the *Affiches de Provence* claimed each copy of his newspaper reached twenty or thirty people.[84] Moreover, by mid-century, individuals did not have to subscribe to a paper in order to read it because they had access to a range of reading rooms and local lending libraries. Urban French readers could pay to read the international gazettes and various other newspapers in *cabinets de lecture*, privately owned reading rooms that allowed members to read a variety of publications on the premises—and sometimes to rent items to take home. Often run by booksellers, such reading rooms provided access to new literary works and major periodicals at an economical price.[85] In the case of the *Journal de Provence* in Marseille, the publisher himself ran a reading room where the entire run of the paper was offered free of charge. The greater flexibility in the fees charged and the pay schedules in *cabinets* meant that a more diverse public could read the publications offered there.[86]

Still other readers joined *sociétés de lecture*, which were associations of literary enthusiasts who pooled their resources to buy copies of one or more publications; the members of such literary cooperatives established time frames during which members could take a book or periodical home before passing it on to the next cosubscriber. *Chambres de lecture* also existed, as book clubs, where individuals gathered in one space to read and debate the papers they purchased collectively. Since the 1750s the number of such venues had increased rapidly. Nantes, for example, had six, with a readership of about a hundred people in each collective. By the end of the Old Regime, most provincial towns in France had at least one, and these reading rooms remained active long after the Revolution.[87] Their members tended to be minor members of the nobility and doctors, lawyers, and businessmen. Occasional newspaper advertisements written by the editors publicized local reading rooms and listed the publications available and the cost of dues for access to the collections.[88] One particularly evocative description of a reading room was written by a member of a *chambre* in Niort in 1775, where "minds are enlightened by communication, hearts are united by approaching one another, taste for society is purified, confidence and concord maintained." In the reading room, readers met to pose questions, propose problems, and

develop hypotheses; in short, those in attendance could "find enlightenment and advice" in a space that was "suitable to sociability, to the common
interest."[89]

For those living in urban locations, reading rooms provided an economical alternative to a private subscription. Furthermore, a range of other spaces
including cafés and clubs made newspapers available to their customers for
free.[90] Such spaces provided access to print, were well lit and heated, and
offered an opportunity for readers to discuss publications with one another.
Café reading was social, and it fostered public opinion through discussion
and criticism of periodicals.[91] Moreover, the prevalence of newspapers in
such spaces suggests not only that the total readership of a given newspaper
was higher than the total circulation but also that reading and discussing collectively were common practices.

The practice of sharing print and reading collectively persisted not only
among the middling classes and members of the liberal professions but also
among the popular classes. According to notarial records, most domestic
workers in Paris knew how to read by the latter half of the eighteenth century, and they had access to reading material in the households where they
worked. They attended public readings that took place in cafés and gambling
rooms, which were often elaborations on information contained in newspapers. There were also public readings on the streets of Paris. Daniel Roche has
argued that the only portion of the press inaccessible to the popular classes
was likely the literary periodicals, which assumed a formal education.[92]

In the provinces, literate villagers read newspapers aloud to their neighbors. The oral transmission of news was shared in places of work, especially
the blacksmith's shop, the market and fountains, and the benches that typically lined the *place publique*, as well as inns and drinking establishments.[93]
Provincial chateaus had libraries, the very existence of which created the
possibility for people to borrow or take print matter. Inns also offered readers
in the countryside access to periodicals. Some fifty postmasters subscribed
to the *Mercure*. And many itinerant individuals that traversed the countryside
brought print with them: stewards, agents, butlers, servants, and occasionally coachmen brought books and new ideas to the countryside.[94] In the winter months, peasants gathered in a barn or private house for a *veillée d'hiver* to
share folklore and news; while predominantly a space for the transmission of
local oral tradition, there were occasions when a literate intermediary read
aloud to the group.[95] Letters published by country noblemen in *La Feuille
Villageoise* early in the Revolution recounted the way they gathered together
with "their" peasants in the evening to read the paper together. After the
Revolution had begun, one writer referred to the experience of reading the

newspaper aloud as a "civic catechism" through which the minds and the souls of the farmers who gathered were enlightened.[96] Much less is known about what the peasants themselves thought of the messages conveyed in such publications. Nevertheless, news circulated widely, even in rural settings.

Taking into account all of the spaces where people congregated to read and discuss news, and the spaces where newspapers were available—from libraries and reading rooms to cafés and workshops—the total audience of the affiches went well beyond the number of newspapers published. Jeremy Popkin has argued that the *Gazette de Leyde* with a subscriber list of four thousand likely found its way into the hands of 50,000 to 100,000 readers. A similar extrapolation suggests that the provincial and Parisian affiches may have had 130,000 to 200,000 readers, and perhaps more.[97] Indeed, the readers of the affiches made up a significant portion—and likely the majority—of the French newspaper-reading public.

Since the 1770s the affiches had only grown in popularity. By the eve of the Revolution, they were key sources of local and national information for the French reading public. Invariably, the content of the newspapers was mediated by the editors who produced them, the censors who policed them, and the postal system that distributed them. Nevertheless, the editors designed their papers to give their readers the sense that they were participating in a dialogue. Editors crafted prospectuses that advertised the paper to invite such participation. As chapter 2 will show, editors printed letters from their readers, and they responded to their subscribers' contributions with editorial notes. Such letters to the editor became a critical component of the information press.

Writing a letter to the editor afforded the opportunity for men and women to see their ideas in print. Publishing a book or a pamphlet required economic means, a professional network, and a certain know-how. Such thresholds restricted the group of people who would become authors. By comparison, the costs of writing a letter to the editor were low. In the format of a public letter, those eager to share their ideas found in the affiches a comparatively smooth path to publication.

CHAPTER 2

The Writers, Self-Presentation, and Subjectivity

On March 3, 1780, Siméon-Prosper Hardy wrote in his diary that he had published a letter to the editor in the Parisian daily newspaper the *Journal de Paris*. Hardy's letter discussed the establishment of a hospice for the poor in the parish of Saint Jacques du Haut Pas, near the Jardin du Luxembourg, and he had asked the Parisian daily to publish his comments. In his diary Hardy transcribed a copy of the letter along with an explanation of just how the letter had come to appear in the paper. Hardy's neighbor, the engraver Charles-Étienne Gaucher, knew the editors of the *Journal*.[1] Gaucher ensured that Hardy's correspondence received attention from the editors; the letter appeared in print, signed with Hardy's initials, on March 10. In some ways Hardy's story was unique. As a bookseller he was well acquainted with the printing industry and those who worked within it. Moreover, Hardy and his milieu are well known today because of his unusual practice of keeping a diary over four decades from 1753 to 1789, which grew to eight manuscript volumes. And yet, in writing a letter to his local newspaper Hardy was not so exceptional. In the 1770s and 1780s thousands of letters written by readers and subscribers appeared in the Parisian and provincial press.

Writing letters was a popular—even ubiquitous—activity among the literate in eighteenth-century France. The epistolary form was the basis for popular novels, especially best sellers such as Samuel Richardson's *Clarissa*, *or the History of a Young Lady* and *Pamela, or Virtue Rewarded* and Jean-Jacques Rousseau's *Julie, ou La Nouvelle Héloïse*. Letter-writing manuals were sources of both instruction and entertainment; volumes directed toward young people and women of various social stations reflected this dual purpose.[2] Letters moved the plot forward in several works performed at the Opéra-Comique.[3] Paintings and engravings depicted the act of reading or writing a letter. And a consumer industry accompanied epistolary practices: the desk, papers, ink, and pens all situated the letter writer in relation not only to the recipient of the letter but to the market and to *le monde*.[4] Correspondence across vast distances secured emotional bonds between family and close friends and undergirded the commercial and political success of family networks.[5] The degree of sentiment, the frequency of correspondence, and the adaptation of one's style from formal language to local dialect all served as modes of conveying one's intimacy with the recipient of the letter.[6]

Letter writing played a profound role in cultural and daily life and in structuring social networks. In addition to writing private letters intended for family, friends, and colleagues, some men and women wrote public letters intended for a wider audience. In the 1770s the information press began publishing letters from readers in their weekly papers. By the eve of the French Revolution, letters to the editor routinely appeared in provincial and Parisian affiches. The analysis in this chapter includes all letters to the editor published from 1770 through 1788 in the Parisian information press, the *Journal de Paris* and the *Journal général de France*, and in provincial affiches in Aix-en-Provence, Amiens, Angers, Arras, Bordeaux, Caen, Compiègne, Dijon, Grenoble, Lyon, Marseille, Metz, Montpellier, Orléans, Poitiers, Reims, Rennes, Rouen, Toulouse, and Troyes.

Writing a public letter to the newspaper certainly differed from writing a private missive to a friend or family member; writers to the paper could not assume privacy, nor could they rely on a rapport formed through interpersonal interactions. And yet, as discussed in the introduction, those who wrote public letters did rely on a certain reciprocity from their audience. Writers to the affiches used their opening and concluding remarks to invite the newspaper's editor and readers to consider their opinion and to respond, by writing back or trying out the suggestions they had made. Letters to the editor also afforded writers a means of conveying themselves in transparent and in masked forms.[7] Their correspondence prompted affective and social expectations for the writer and for the readers of such letters.

Signatures made by the writers themselves allow the historian to reconstruct a partial prosopography of the periodical reading public during the last decades of the Old Regime. Within the 6,909 letters examined in this book, half (50.2 percent) of all published letters were signed, and 37.5 percent of the letters indicated the author's profession or social position.[8] The variation in signature styles did not emerge all at once. In the affiches' early years of publication, most letters were published without a signature, or at most with initials. The trend changed by 1775, when signed letters became the most prevalent signature type. Figure 2.1 shows the signature styles that letter writers adopted over time.

The most common style was to sign one's letter with a name. The next most popular approach was to offer no name at all. Writers also identified themselves by their initials, a pseudonym, or simply as "un/e abonné/e" (a subscriber). By describing oneself as a subscriber, the writer indicated that he or she played a role in the commercial success of the newspaper and that the editor ought to pay attention to their comments. Figure 2.1 treats all letters published across the kingdom, but the proportions of signature styles were similar in Parisian and provincial newspapers. Signed letters constituted 51.5 percent of the letters published in the Parisian newspapers and 47.8 percent of the letters published in provincial newspapers.[9]

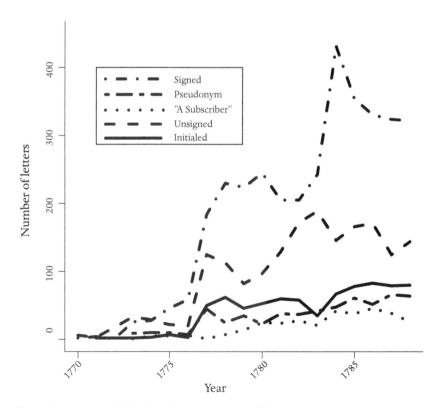

FIGURE 2.1   Letters published in Parisian and provincial affiches, 1770–1788, by signature type.

Table 2.1 traces the proportion of writers who signed one, two, three to five, six to ten, or more than ten letters to the editor. Some of the signatures that writers adopted consisted of abbreviated names such as the "Abbé de St. L***" or only of one's initials, such as "A . . ." To account for the possibility that multiple authors may have used the same initials, all abbreviated or initialed names were tagged as ambiguous signatures. The second column in the table includes such names in the calculation. The third column excludes all of the initialed and abbreviated names from the analysis. In both cases, the proportion of writers within each category is strikingly similar, which suggests that the pattern of the number of letters written by a given author is not sensitive to the inclusion of ambiguous authors in the analysis.

Among the signed letters, the vast majority of writers had only one letter to the editor published. Approximately 22 percent published two to five letters in the affiches, and 3 percent wrote between six and ten letters. Although there were some serial contributors who wrote numerous letters to the editor, they constituted a small proportion of the letter writers. Less than 2 percent of all the writers published more than ten letters. Rather than representing the work of a small group, the forum of letters to the editor favored many unique contributors.

Identifying as many of the writers as possible involved a process of recording and interpreting the signatures. The first step was to record three distinct elements from each signature: the name, the social position, and the profession exactly as they were printed in each letter. Some letters included only a name, or only a description of the author's profession. Once all three elements of the signature were recorded, each letter was classified by the signature, social position, and profession according to a standardized schema.[10] Next, the names given in the signature were categorized into five groups: signed, unsigned, initialed, signed with a pseudonym, and signed "un/e abonné/e" (a subscriber). The names were also disambiguated from similar names in the paper. All letters signed with a name, pen name, or initials were

Table 2.1   The number of signed letters published in the *affiches* by each writer.

NUMBER OF LETTERS SIGNED BY AN AUTHOR	PERCENTAGE OF ALL WRITERS (INCLUDING AMBIGUOUS SIGNATURES)	PERCENTAGE OF ALL WRITERS (NOT INCLUDING AMBIGUOUS SIGNATURES)
1	73.2	73.3
2	13.0	12.9
3–5	9.3	9.6
6–10	3.1	3.0
11+	1.5	1.2

assigned a disambiguation name to account for variations in publishing practices, such as typos, or the editorial decisions to include or exclude titles such as M., Mme., Fr., and Abbé, or the credentials for a given writer. For example, even in the same year in the same newspaper, letters by Henri-Alexandre Tessier appeared under both the signature "l'Abbé Tessier, Docteur-Régent de la Faculté & de la Société de Médecine" and simply as "l'Abbé Tessier."[11] The signature was first recorded as it appeared in each particular letter; all such letters were also assigned the disambiguation name "Tessier" to ensure that all of his letters were examined together.

Each signature style afforded the writer certain benefits of revealing or obscuring who they were. The approach taken in this book acknowledges the limits of identifying all of the men and women who participated in writing letters to the editor based on their signatures. Some writers likely exaggerated their status in hopes it would increase their chances of publication. Others wished to portray themselves as an everyman when they were in fact a well-known savant. Condorcet, for example, adopted an anonymous and humble persona in his letters to the *Journal de Paris*. And as the example of Hardy at the beginning of the chapter makes clear, even known figures sometimes concealed their identities. Moreover, some writers wrote anonymously more than others; it is likely that this was especially the case for women navigating the gendered social contexts within which they wrote. Despite the limitations of the sources for identifying the exact proportions of letter writers from a given social position, the letters do reveal the interests of writers from a wide array of social and professional contexts who consumed and responded to the information press.

A Prosopography of the Writing Public

Among the signed letters, a prosopography of the writing public begins to emerge. Approximately 50.2 percent of the letters published between 1770 and 1788 were signed by their authors, the majority of whom also included their social position or profession. The data from all published signatures formed the basis for the prosopography of letter writers. Identifying the writers according to their self-descriptions inevitably means that social and professional categories at times overlapped or were impossible to pinpoint more precisely. For example, the only writers classified as nobles in this prosopography are those who explicitly identified themselves as such. The social positions of the letter writers who did not share one remain unknown, and their positions in society may have differed in meaningful ways. The number of letters signed by profession are displayed in Figure 2.2.

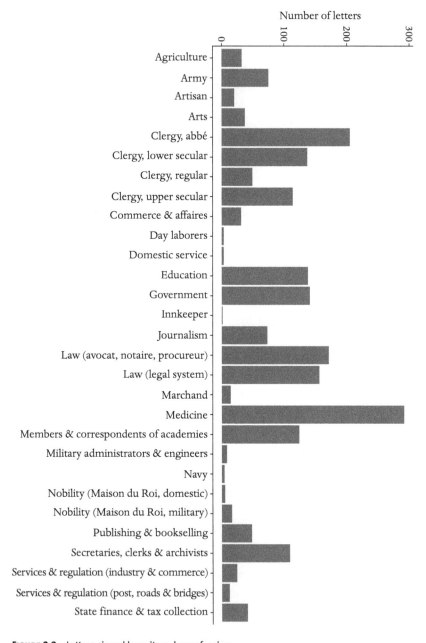

Figure 2.2 Letters signed by writers, by profession.

Members of the clergy were regular contributors to the information press. Men affiliated with the church known as abbés wrote 205 letters, more than any other group within the clergy. In the eighteenth century the title abbé was used to identify oneself as a tonsured clergyman whether or not one was ordained to the priesthood. Their correspondence covered literary, scientific, and practical subject matter. The lower secular clergy, composed of parish priests (curés) from middling backgrounds, wrote 137 letters, most of which concerned the material and moral care of their local parish. The subject matter of their letters included descriptions of potato farming, setting up scholarships for poor boys to enter the priesthood, offering alms for the poor in the parish, and caring for the sick. Among the secular clergy, parish priests wrote more letters than any other group. The upper secular clergy consisted of bishops, archbishops, and canons, most of whom came from the nobility; they wrote 114 letters to the editor. The regular clergy, that is, members of religious orders, authored far fewer letters than the secular clergy with 49 letters.

By comparison, nobles wrote far fewer letters to the editor. The composition of the nobility had had changed significantly over the eighteenth century. While precise figures do not exist for the entire century, approximately ten thousand men and their families were ennobled in the eighteenth century through the purchase of venal offices.[12] Attaining nobility remained a meaningful signal of social advancement, as evidenced by the continual rise over the century in the cost of venal offices for those seeking noble status. In the information press a small proportion of writers identified themselves as members of the nobility in their signatures. The majority of the nobles who signed their letters indicated that they were retired members of the army, and this group consisted for the most part of military officers and military surgeons. As Christy Pichichero has shown, reform-minded public letters by members of the armed forces dated back to at least the 1760s during the campaigns to reform capital and corporal punishments for desertion. Drawing on the language of humanity and sensibility, they tried to convince the crown and the public to listen.[13] Other members of the military who did not divulge their particular position in society also wrote letters to the editor. Men employed in the military administration, engineers, the constabulary, and the navy wrote fewer than ten letters each. Members of the king's royal household wrote twenty-one letters.

Only nine of the men who signed their letters described themselves as a bourgeois, and their correspondence appeared in the affiches published in Paris, Toulouse, Troyes, and Grenoble. "Bourgeois" was a juridical category that brought with it certain privileges in prerevolutionary France. In prerevolutionary Paris, bourgeois privilege was hereditary. As a self-descriptor, "bourgeois" indicated that one was an inhabitant of a particular town, or that one was associated with small business.[14] In short, "bourgeois" was an ambiguous signifier, and few letter writers spoke of themselves as such.

Educated men in the liberal professions and the government were active and vocal participants in the social and cultural life of their local communities, a role that extended into the information press. Among those without noble or clerical positions, men from the liberal professions, especially doctors, lawyers, notaries, and others employed in the legal system and in the royal bureaucracy, wrote the most letters to the editor. Their letters often reflected their professional and social investment. Members and corresponding members from French academies wrote 124 letters; their social position as noblemen or commoners remains unknown. Their contributions met the public interest in the arts and sciences in a short, manageable way. The range of topics covered in the letters to the editor written by corresponding secretaries covered a similar spectrum as the essay-writing competitions held by regional academies.[15] Whereas the academic concours invited all to submit their essays to a jury of judges, the affiches afforded writers the space to try out their ideas and debate one another in a public arena.

Doctors, surgeons, dentists, and apothecaries contributed 292 letters. Nearly every letter written by a doctor concerned medicine: a report on a new technique witnessed at a hospital, a statement advocating inoculation, or a recipe for an effective remedy. They shared information for public adoption, especially medical remedies for everyday ailments such as the common cold. In their letters concerning childbirth in particular, surgeons emphasized how important their know-how could be. Medicine would remain one of the hallmarks of the information press. For doctors and surgeons alike, letters to the editor afforded them a channel to improve public health by circulating useful information. At the same time, and much to the consternation of the doctors, the information press also made it possible for the occasional charlatan to market his cure-all, or for untested treatments to gain recognition. The efforts of doctors and surgeons to police the boundaries of medical knowledge in the press were emblematic of the ways that the affiches enabled the spread of new information and conversations, just as they exposed the contestation of knowledge production.

Lawyers contributed approximately 171 letters that covered topics from the law to current events to belles lettres. Lawyers are represented in Figure 2.2 under the category of law. The legal system category includes all those who identified that they worked in *parlements*, presidial, *baillage, sénéchaussée, prévôté*, or seigneurial courts, and those who worked in special jurisdictions. The 156 contributions from government officials came from various state offices, including intendants and subdelegates, but also municipal mayors, court clerks (greffiers), and bookkeepers employed by the state or by local governments. Mayors wrote in to provide information about local current events and projects to improve the town, and intendants suggested ways to enhance agricultural practices or road conditions in the areas they administered. Tax collectors and censors also contributed occasional letters. Reform-minded provincial administrators used the affiches to facilitate their campaigns for public works, agricultural innovation, and commercial growth.[16]

Although such men figured prominently in the pages of the affiches, they were by no means the only contributors. In fact, letters to the editor were authored by an expansive group of educated men and women, including architects and engineers who contributed to the preoccupation with public works in the newspapers. Booksellers, writers, and printers wrote forty-eight letters to the affiches. Writers and publishers often wrote to the newspaper when their personal reputation was at stake. They used the venue of the newspaper to advertise new books, to air their grievances with another writer for stealing their work, or to disavow a publication they had not authored appearing under their name. Secretaries, archivists, and librarians also wrote to share their interests in history and law in the affiches. Students and teachers wrote 138 letters on subjects relevant to their own areas of learning. The letters written by performers and artists publicized the spectacles in which they would soon appear.

Newspapers also published correspondence from abroad, but the authors of such letters tended to be wealthy individuals or well-known published authors. Some wrote in the form of travel narratives, which were growing in popularity at the time. In general, they sought to contribute to a growing body of knowledge about the wider world. Doctors worked collectively, comparing notes in the hope of treating their patients more effectively. International travelers sought to understand France's relationship to its empire and to the wider world. In general, such writers shared a comparative approach, and their careful notation of difference reflected the early anthropological literature available in popular novels, philosophical texts, and current news periodicals.[17]

What made the forum of letters to the editor unique among eighteenth-century venues for debate and discussion, though, were the contributions by men and women lower in the social strata in towns and in the countryside, including farmers, artisans, and merchants. In rare instances, those employed in domestic service and even someone calling himself a day laborer (*manœuvre*) contributed letters. In the case of the *manœuvre*, his correspondence referenced his own expertise with canal and bridge projects in the town.[18] Historians of the *Journal de Paris* have emphasized that the Parisian daily was popular reading material for domestic workers.[19] Their correspondence generally concerned their work. An innkeeper and a postmaster wrote letters to the editor.[20] Luxury cloth merchant manufacturers, a milliner, and a second-hand clothing dealer each wrote letters.[21] The artisans who wrote to the Parisian press included locksmiths, a master bookbinder, and a master joiner.[22] Letters from clockmakers and a tanner appeared in provincial papers.[23] Some of the artisans who wrote letters were quite wealthy master craftsmen; for example, the queen's stringed-instrument maker wrote two letters to the *Journal de Paris*.[24] In short, men and women from the working and artisanal classes not only read newspapers but also participated in them by writing letters to publications in Paris and in provincial urban centers.

Writers from the countryside also included agricultural workers from an array of social statuses. Most farmers specified that they were of a higher economic status—such farmers were landowners, plow owners (*laboureurs*), or leasers of seigneurial land. *Laboureur* was the name for "middling landowners and tenants."[25] But *laboureur* could also connote rather different positions: a commercial status, which included landownership and grain production; a reference to a merchant's family background from the peasantry; or a designation as a *fermier* who shared a business orientation toward grain production.[26] One writer to the *Affiches de Troyes* signed his letter as a "receveur de terre," a wealthy farmer who leased seigneurial land and buildings.[27] Three letters by winegrowers appeared in the affiches in Poitiers and in Paris.[28] The other farmers who indicated their profession described themselves as *cultivateurs* or *agriculteurs*.[29] On one occasion, a *cultivateur* also indicated he was a landowner.[30] For the most part, the correspondence from farmers focused on agriculture. As was the case for the writers who were merchants and artisans, their letters appeared in a mix of Parisian and provincial newspapers. As chapter 5 will show, agronomy and those who carried out agricultural work were salient topics of interest in the capital and in towns throughout the kingdom.

The juxtaposition of voices made the newspapers a unique locus of information exchange, if at times a cacophonous one. The general informational nature of the affiches afforded interested parties a venue to speak to different audiences. At times, writers' interests pushed against one another. Writing a public letter to the newspaper also prompted writers to consider why a vast and varied public ought to listen to them. The published correspondence thus revealed both the engagement of newspapers with the ideas of their day and the rhetorical strategies that writers employed to reach a more expansive audience. To be sure, writers from agricultural, artisanal, and merchant backgrounds wrote a smaller proportion of the total correspondence that appeared in print. Nevertheless, their presence in the pages of the affiches was significant. Their voices were situated on the newspaper page along with the contributions of writers from more elite circumstances. Few other eighteenth-century spaces made room for people from such a spectrum of social backgrounds to participate in the same conversations.

As a public venue that one accessed remotely, writing a letter to the newspaper enabled women to take part in public conversations from the privacy of their own homes. Letter writing was widely regarded as a respectable practice, and women from various social positions wrote to the papers. Among the corpus of 6,909 letters, women who identified their gender explicitly signed seventy letters. Precisely who many of these women were remains difficult to determine in the majority of cases, because they concealed their identity. In the Parisian press, and occasionally in provincial affiches, writers identified themselves only as "une Abonnée," a subscriber.[31] In at least ten cases, the writer indicated she was a countess, a marquise, or a baroness, but she omitted her name.[32] Letters written by women who signed "Madame ***" were just as frequent.[33] Four letters were written by young women, who referred to themselves as "une jeune demoiselle".[34] It is likely that many elite women wrote anonymously out of adherence to social norms of modesty and privacy, though there were other reasons to choose anonymity. Contemporaneous norms in Britain have shown that anonymity was widespread in the eighteenth century, owing to a range of motivations, including the genre in which one wrote.[35] Moreover, just as Mary Louise Roberts has shown for Marguerite Durand and the women who wrote for her fin de siècle newspaper a century later, women who participated in journalism navigated a space for themselves by presenting a public image that was culturally acceptable. Such a "strategic repetition of old roles in new contexts" enabled women to maintain an image that was at once respectable and transgressive.[36] So too the women who wrote to the affiches navigated a space for themselves that was public and innovative, even as they abided by certain gendered norms of respectability.

Some women identified themselves by name. Dressmakers such as Madame Guedon indicated their name and their profession, as did Galet the dentist and De Rousset the schoolmistress.[37] Widows of well-known men also signed their names to letters in which they publicized their late spouse's work and memory. The widow of the chemist and apothecary Guillaume-François Rouelle wrote to the *Journal de Paris* to correct errors in a false advertisement concerning her late husband and nephew.[38] The widow Weisse also wrote, out of "duty to the public and to the memory of M. Weisse," to rebuff criticism of his medicinal remedy for postpartum complications. She also submitted her husband's remedy to the Société Royale de Médecine and received a pension.[39] Some women used the self-descriptor of "widow" to publicize their own work. The widow of Nicolas-Bonaventure Duchesne published her letter to the *Journal de Paris* and her books under the name "Widow Duchesne."[40] In a letter advertising her book of proverbs, the writer and moralist Madame de Laisse described herself as a widow.[41]

In at least one case, a widow was assisted in the composition of her letters to the editor. Jean-Jacques Rousseau's partner, Thérèse Levasseur, sent two letters to the *Journal de Paris*, discussing the posthumous publication of Rousseau's work. Her letters were republished in the *Affiches de Dijon*.[42] Levasseur's May 1779 letter was written by the publisher of Rousseau's complete works, François d'Ivernois, according to a sketch provided by Rousseau's friends, Paul-Claude Moultou and Pierre-Alexandre Du Peyrou. Rousseau's last student, René-Louis de Girardin, marquis of Vauvray, then edited the letter before Levasseur signed it, and the letter was sent to the editors of the *Journal de Paris*.[43] Levasseur's private correspondence differed in orthography and clarity of expression from the published letters that appeared under her name in the press. The differences between her private correspondence and her published letters are significant. But even in the case of Levasseur, where scholars know more about the many hands that labored in her letters, the extent of editorial intervention in her letters remains unknown, precisely because of the collective efforts to write them.

Celebrities also wrote to the newspapers. The actress of the Comédie Française, Françoise Marie Antoinette Joseph Saucerotte, wrote to the Parisian papers in 1778 using her stage name, Mademoiselle Raucourt.[44] A letter from Mademoiselle Beaumesnil, the composer and singer at the Paris Opéra, was published a month later.[45] The actress Andrée Coche also wrote a letter as Madame Vanhove; her husband, Charles-Joseph Vanhove, was a *comédien du roi*.[46] Although such letters were less common in the provincial press, Marguerite Brunet wrote to the *Affiches de Normandie* under her stage name, Madame Montansier. La Montansier was a powerful figure who maintained exclusive rights to balls and performances at Versailles, as well as the privileges for playhouses in Brittany, Normandy, Picardy, and Anjou.[47]

Women discussed an array of subject matter in their correspondence. In the case of the *Journal de Paris*, women wrote on topics ranging from literature to philanthropy, and from music to scientific discoveries. Some touched on issues of marriage or divorce; others addressed the experiences of women as authors and advocated for the equality of women. One reader noted that the variety of the newspaper content was suitable for the women who read it at their toilette, where the paper would "adorn her mind" while she prepared her head.[48] Writing letters that were intended to be shared also became a critical avenue for the political formation of women such as Rosalie Jullien, who remarked on the newspapers she read in her family correspondence, and who later wrote a public letter to the *Journal patriote de Romans* in 1790. Through writing a public letter, Jullien articulated her own public identity and, during the Revolution, her own political opinions.[49]

The process of writing a letter to the newspaper gave women's individual experiences new meaning and significance. While women wrote on themes such as the moral education of one's children and charitable efforts for the poor, their correspondence in the *affiches* made clear that all subject matter concerned them. One pointedly critiqued the editor for printing content concerning Rétif de la Bretonne's views on women.[50] For many women, their letters to the editor were their first and only published works. The practice of writing allowed women from an array of backgrounds to, as Carla Hesse describes, "separate [themselves] from their ideas, to take possession of them, and to exchange them with others across space and time."[51] A letter to the editor was a means of making oneself visible, both to the writer who penned the letter and to others.

Over the eighteenth century, France had grown more wealthy, populous, and urban than ever before, and the people who wrote to the *affiches* in part reflected such social changes. Most letter writers in the information press were from educated but middling backgrounds. Men from the liberal professions, parish clergy, and correspondents with the academies were all prevalent interlocutors. Very few writers were merchants or manufacturers. Moreover, many contributors worked for the state, in the legal system, as administrators, or as tax collectors. Parish priests wrote letters regularly. Thus, rather than indicating a bourgeois domain driven by equity among consumers, the letters to the editor suggest the interests of individuals from differing social positions, corporate statuses, and professions. The wide array of social backgrounds of the writers influenced the scope of perspectives in their letters. As each writer made their case for the editor to print their letter, the *affiches* displayed the social jostling that was transpiring on the newspaper page and beyond it.

For the prerevolutionary press, some writers' self-descriptions eluded straightforward classification according to a social rank or corporative status. The discursive space of the newspaper afforded writers the opportunity to assert their authority in new ways, even as Old Regime structures of power persisted. With their signatures, letter writers identified themselves in ways that reflected the shifts in social value placed on economic, social, and professional status in the late eighteenth century. Some who benefited from corporate statuses indicated their affiliation in the *affiches*. However, it is significant that many writers did not use the vocabulary of rank or profession to describe who they were. Instead, they sought an equity in social recognition, what John Shovlin has called in other contexts a "parity of esteem."[52] For many who did not have a social position, the newspaper presented writers with room to make other claims about why readers ought to listen. Reputation and experience were repertoires from which writers from disparate social, commercial, and professional contexts could draw in the press.

Pseudonymous Writing

Some writers did not divulge their identity and social position and instead adopted strategies to conceal or suggest a public persona. The limitations on newspaper content specified in each paper's privilège and regulated by the royal censors shaped not only the topics discussed in the letters to the editor but also the willingness of some contributors to reveal their identities. While approximately half of writers chose to identify themselves by name, 8.3 percent of letters published between 1770 and 1788 appeared under pseudonyms, both false names and self-descriptions of various kinds.[53] The pseudonyms included classical allusions, literary references, archetypal figures, and professional descriptors. Pseudonyms offered writers a means of sharing potentially unpopular or controversial opinions without requiring the author to bear the social, professional, or legal consequences.[54] For much of the seventeenth and eighteenth centuries, pseudonyms had protected writers working under censorship. In the affiches, letters signed with a pen name remained a small but consistent trend.

Pseudonyms situated a writer's authority to speak on a given subject. This was especially the case for names that emphasized the writer's profession, for example, "an artist from the old Academy of Saint-Luc"; "the publisher of the *Journal des Théâtres*"; "a parish priest from the vicinity of Civrai"; "a country farmer (*cultivateur*)"; or simply "a doctor." By identifying themselves by their profession, the writers presented an archetype, which the reader could then fill in with their own assumptions about the writer's experience. Such names expressed a level of familiarity with the subject of the letter, as a priest would know the needs of his parish, and a farmer would understand the health of grain in his region. Such descriptors encouraged the reader to imagine the person who possessed an opinion on a given topic. Moreover, by including letters from men and women in various professions, the newspapers provided a collective portrait of the audience the editors intended to reach.

Some pseudonyms omitted any mention of profession and instead focused more directly on the writers' relationship to the topic they discussed. Their names identified the writers as experts, like the contribution written collectively by the group "the lettered persons from Senlis," or amateurs, such as the writer who chose the English pen name "Tom Reader." Pseudonyms served a rhetorical purpose by identifying writers as social elites or as everymen, and they set an expectation in the mind of the reader for the kind of argument that would appear in the letter. Likewise, the authors of missives by "a hermit from the Sennar forest," "a solitary patriot and farmer from Dauphiné," "the spectator," "the unknown hermit," or "the English traveler" painted themselves as outsiders whose isolation granted them objectivity, or at least a fresh perspective.[55] Alternatively, some signatures included place names, like "un Lexovien," to convince the reader of the author's identity as a resident and interested party from Lisieux, a town in Lower-Normandy.[56] In the *Journal de Paris*, partisans who signed their letters as "Les Gluckistes" and "Les Piccinistes" debated opera.[57] By their pen names, writers established their authority and proximity to the subject matter of their letter.

The use of a pen name could also function as a mask—both obscuring the true identity of the writer and allowing for the creation of a public persona. In the case of the *Journal de Paris*, pseudonymous writers became for the newspaper's readers a vivid cast of characters, such as "le Marin Kergolé" or "Nigood d'Outremer." Readers could track the letters printed in the newspaper, much as they would follow characters in a serial novel, citing their favorites, following their contributions, and critiquing and defending them.[58] Even if the reader knew the true identity of the writer behind the pen name, the pseudonymous identity took on a life of its own, much like a fictional character might. At this time in the early American republic, pseudonyms functioned in a similar manner. The American affinity for Latin pen names was tied to the author's effort to relate a larger political situation to a classical figure or ideal, in order to make abstract concepts in political philosophy more legible to the reader.[59] While those who wrote letters to the press in France were not as fond of Latin pen names—"Pro Patria" and "Symbulus" were rare exceptions in the French newspapers—pseudonyms in the affiches did valuable rhetorical work to explain the position of the writer.

Pseudonyms served not only as masks for their authors but also as rhetorical tools deployed by writers to support their arguments. One writer used both literal and figurative masks to distance himself from the claims in his letter. Taking on the identity of "Scaramouche" as his pseudonym and as his costume at a masked public ball in Toulouse, he related an encounter at the Carnival festival with an elegant woman. She described the experience of Lent in the present age as one of pleasure and amusement, which had diminished the fervor and piety that had characterized the season in ages past. She confided that she found "morality in the Heart of honest men," and she boasted, "I laugh as much as I can, because gaiety is the balm of life."[60] The entire letter used a series of masks—the mysterious woman, the masked man, and the pseudonymous author—to distance the writer from the unorthodox opinions on morality and religion that he espoused in the paper. Selection of an appropriate pen name served to make the author more distant or more proximate, more objective or more invested in the letter he or she wrote. Pen names also served as shorthand for a set of social expectations that the writer could then uphold or subvert in the letter.

Initialed and Unsigned Letters

Anonymous letters to the editor made up approximately 30.4 percent of all the letters published in Paris and in the provinces between 1770 and 1788. Such letters were either unsigned or, in 4.7 percent of cases, signed simply as a subscriber, "un/e de vos abonnés/e."[61] The nearly 5 percent of writers who signed their letters as "one of your subscribers" situated themselves as stakeholders to whom the editors should listen. Their claims of subscribership placed demands on the editors to print their work or face the possibility of losing a customer.

In the early 1770s anonymous contributions to the provincial affiches were rare, but the number of anonymous letters increased sharply in 1777 when the *Journal de Paris* began publication. Approximately a hundred unsigned letters appeared each year throughout the late 1770s and 1780s. Indeed, eighteenth-century editors were much more willing than editors in the twenty-first century to accommodate writers who wished to remain anonymous. Today, most newspapers reject anonymous letters automatically. Among eighteenth-century newspapers that relied heavily on letters from subscribers to fill their pages, editors printed letters without signatures, although in many cases the editor knew the author. Anonymity was a ubiquitous approach to publishing in the eighteenth century because it served many purposes for the writer and the editor.

Some researchers have tried to identify the early modern writers of such anonymous letters by comparing internal evidence within the letters themselves with other documents of known authorship. In one such study to verify that a series of anonymous letters published in the *Journal de Paris* were indeed the work of the economist and Encyclopedist André Morellet, Dorothy Medlin compared Morellet's private correspondence with Benjamin Franklin, five manuscript letters housed in a Genevan archive and the municipal library in Lyon, and the anonymously published letters to the editor. While it is possible in rare cases like this one to find anonymous letters that can be matched to well-known writers, the lack of extant manuscript letters and the sheer number of letters published anonymously makes a large-scale investigation of this sort impossible. Nevertheless, the example of Morellet's anonymous letters underscores that both known intellectuals and marginalized individuals adopted anonymity.

Most anonymous letters appeared in the paper simply without any signature. The lack of explanations for anonymity by the writers or by the editors who published them indicates that neither party felt an obligation to explain why writers did not sign their names. In a sample of ten years of publication in the *Affiches de Dijon*, where anonymous letters appeared throughout the decade, only three anonymous letters were printed with an editorial explanation for the unsigned letters. In the vast majority of cases, no explanation appeared at all. When authors did mention why they wished their letters to remain private, the rationale was that the writers preferred not to risk their reputations by attaching their names to a letter. In the text of the letters, writers insinuated that the editor of the *Affiches de Dijon* knew their identity, but they asked for editorial discretion in omitting their name. One such writer asked the editors for anonymity out of fear that his letter's frankness would upset his mother. Another concluded his letter by assuring the editor that while he was sure that his medicinal remedy would work, he would rather that the paper leave out his name and in effect shield his professional reputation.[62] Such requests emphasized the potential costs writers could experience if their letters' contents were not well received. By concealing their identities, they sought to protect their public names. Letters concerned with charitable and philanthropic action asked for anonymity instead out of a sense of public virtue. In such cases, it was the very anonymity of such acts of goodwill that made them charitable, as benefactors were not supposed to be interested in receiving public recognition for their contributions.

When anonymous letters included a postscript from the editors, the editors provided information about the professional background or the public stature of the anonymous contributor. In an editorial note, the editors of the affiches published in Metz included the writer's profession as a way of distancing the newspaper from the content of the letter: "This letter is signed by a well-known amateur in this town who has asked us to publish it without naming him. We think we should give warning that, on this occasion, in reporting the various letters addressed to us, we do not pretend to adopt any system, nor to take any side."[63] The editor of the *Affiches du Dauphiné* noted that one letter was written by a professor of law "known for his *lumières* and for his patriotic love," but she did not name him. In a particularly specific editorial note in the *Affiches du Dauphiné*, Souverant specified not only the author's profession but also the courier who had delivered the letter to her: "This article is by a *physicien* from Grenoble. It was handed to the director of this paper by a magistrate of the city, who is very zealous for the progress of the sciences, to whom the author has paid homage." Over time, her claims about the writers she published grew much more general in form, attesting only to their status within the community, as she did in the following two letters: "This article was addressed to us by a person of consideration of this city," or "This article is from a very enlightened and highly regarded person."[64] What these references tend to suggest is that even if the letters did appear anonymously in the paper, the contributor's identity was usually known to the editors. They tended to be members of the community whose reputation and ideas the editor respected and, in some cases, felt compelled to publish.

Finally, writers chose to identify themselves by their initials, sometimes including their town of residence and their profession. Initialed letters were not adopted until 1773, when they first appeared very occasionally in the *Affiches de Trois-Évêchés et Lorraine*. Such letters composed approximately 11.1 percent of all letters published from 1770 to 1788.[65] Initialed letters obscured the writer's identity to the newspaper's readership as a whole, but they provided those in the same town, profession, or social circle with information to identify the writer. In this way, one could remain anonymous to the general reading public of the newspaper while at the same time revealing oneself to a smaller subgroup of fellow readers. This tactic lent writers a coded means of communicating to friends, colleagues, and correspondents in the know about their identities. As the example of Hardy at the opening of this chapter illustrates, an initialed letter could be claimed by the writer and shown to one's friends once it was published. Furthermore, printing a public letter was an efficient means of getting the word out; for individuals looking to garner support for a local project or publicize a current event, submitting one's thoughts to the paper saved the time and resources of writing many letters to various friends and acquaintances.

Most letters signed with initials were accompanied by a description of the writer's social position or profession. For example, perhaps in an effort to avoid outright conflict with health practitioners whom he vehemently denounced as charlatans in his letter, a doctor writing to the *Affiches de l'Orléanois* signed only with his initials.[66] The editors of the affiches in Metz included a small note distancing themselves from an unknown author: "We do not permit ourselves any reflection about the letter that you are about to read; it suffices to observe we do not have the honor of being known to the artist who wrote it, and that we have never had the least relation with him, even an indirect one."[67] In cases such as this one, signing with one's initials and one's profession gave the reading public an indication of who the writer might be without conveying certainty about the individual's identity. Moreover, individuals who did not sign their letters may have adopted this approach when their letters consisted of plagiarized or fictional content drawn directly from or in emulation of epistolary novels, operas, or letter-writing manuals. Initials allowed both the letter writer and the editorial staff to distance themselves from the content of a letter that could become controversial.

Letter Writing and Authorship

In order to assess whether writing a letter was indeed the first foray into print for the readers of the affiches, an author search of the Bibliothèque nationale de France's online catalogue was conducted for all signed letters in a sample set of newspapers. The sample test included all of the 449 letters published in four newspapers from Poitiers, Metz, Dijon, and Paris in 1774, 1779, and 1785.[68] Three years were selected in order to assess change over time. The letters signed by writers who were already published constituted nearly a third of all signed letters within the sample set. The prestige of such writers varied; some had published only one pamphlet related to their profession. For example, doctors occasionally published a pamphlet related to best practices in their field, such as how to prevent postpartum blood loss or how to treat rabies. Others were rather prolific authors: playwrights such as Honoré-Antoine Richaud-Martelly, Carlo Goldoni, and Joseph Marie Piccini; scientists such as astronomer Joseph Jérôme Lefrançois de Lalande, engineer Jean-Claude Pingeron, chemist (and later deputy to the Legislative Assembly) Louis-Bernard Guyton de Morveau, and *physicien* Joseph-Aignan Sigaud de la Fond; moralists such as l'Abbé Méry de la Canorgue; and a libertine writer, Simon-Pierre Mérard de Saint-Just, were among those who wrote pamphlets and books in addition to their letters "aux auteurs du journal." The investigation into a sample of four newspapers confirms that the majority of letter writers were previously unpublished when they wrote to the newspaper. Among the published authors, both prolific specialists and occasional pamphleteers wrote to the affiches to discuss a range of questions.

While published letters were a commonplace in the Old Regime press, little manuscript source material exists to corroborate the identity of the writers who identified themselves, and historians will probably never know with certainty who wrote the unsigned letters. Eighteenth-century publishing practice was for the editor to send original manuscript letters directly to the printing shop. Once the type was set and the pages printed, the printer would typically recycle the paper on which the letters were written or sell it for scrap.[69] As a result, manuscript letters to the editors are exceedingly rare. Indeed, the only newspapers with extant archival records are those that were seized by the police in cases of bankruptcy or political offense.

The manuscript records that do exist from subscribers to the editors have received thorough investigation.[70] Such extant newspaper records were preserved because the papers were shut down for their conservative political leanings during the French Revolution, and their records were seized. The confiscation of prerevolutionary publication records is even more rare, with the exception of the women's newspaper that published without a royal privilège until it was shut down in 1778, the *Journal des dames*.[71] For moderate newspapers such as the affiches that for the most part avoided shutdown, little manuscript records remain about the editors or their contributors. With the exception of François Moysant in Caen and Jean Florent Baour in Toulouse, the editors to the affiches left few manuscript records concerning their work; even in their cases, the extant records do not encompass their decisions about what they chose to publish in their newspapers.[72]

The individual letters received by the editors, and the editors' decision-making processes of what to print, what to reject, and what to modify, remain obscured. My own extensive investigation of the personal papers and scant records of the editors of affiches published in Toulouse, Troyes, Poitiers, Dijon, and Caen, held in provincial libraries and archives, unearthed only a few manuscript letters in the municipal libraries in Poitiers and Troyes that were written to the editors of prerevolutionary affiches.[73] Such editorial practices in France are consistent with contemporaneous practices in Britain. A comparison of extant manuscript letters written to the editors of the English *Tatler* and *Spectator*, Joseph Addison and Richard Steele, with the newspapers themselves indicated that the letters preserved were precisely those the editors never published.[74] Furthermore, as was the case for letters to the *Tatler* and *Spectator*, even when it is possible to locate manuscript letters, the historian learns very little about why particular letters were or were not published. The editors never left any explanation.

Since no external evidence of editorial practices remains in the extant manuscript letters, nor in editors' diaries or personal correspondence, the historian must develop other means for reading these valuable sources. The approach in this book is a detailed analysis of the internal evidence of the letters themselves and an attention to the questions that the writers' self-fashioning allow the historian to consider. In the French case, the very array of topics covered in the letters, the stylistic variation in prose, and the number of letters published by known authors all suggest that the editors sought to represent a wide cross-section of the French reading public. Although it is also possible that some of the letters might have been written by the editors themselves or by paid correspondents, the differences in orthography, rhetorical approaches, and content strongly suggest that this was not often the case. Indeed, published correspondence in Anglophone North America followed a similar trend: the vast majority of letters were written by readers, but some were produced by the editors or were composites of several letters on a given topic compiled into a single piece.[75] The writing styles of the letters published in the French information press likewise varied, indicating a multiplicity of contributors.

The men and women who voiced their opinions in the affiches came from disparate backgrounds and adopted varied strategies for presenting their identities. More than half of all contributors gave some indication of their name or profession. Although previously published authors penned letters, writers who were otherwise unable to get their ideas into print also participated in the forum of letters to the editor. As one writer to the *Journal de Paris* explained in his letter to the editor, "I have neither the courage nor the talent to make a book, but it is pleasant and easy for me to put on paper the ideas and observations that my travels and studies have put me within reach to collect."[76] For amateur writers with ideas to share, the information press afforded a path to publication. The range of social positions and professional interests—which included not only men of letters but also women, farmers, and craftsmen—set apart the forum of letters to the editor as an especially open sphere of eighteenth-century sociability.

Writing a letter to the editor was the bridge by which a wide array of literate men and women entered into public debate. They articulated who they were with a public audience in mind. But writing a letter was also personal, as writers asserted who they were. In writing letters to the editor, the authors defined themselves as private individuals, and in doing so they articulated their relationship to and space within the public. Self-fashioning was mediated through the act of writing. For the writers, the simultaneously public and private act of writing a letter to the newspaper provided a space for known authors and marginal figures alike to try out public personae. In writing to a wide audience, most of whom were unknown to the author, letter writers had to convince the editors that their comments were worth sharing. In making the case that the editor ought to print the letter, writers made claims about what the information press was for and what their fellow subscribers ought to read. Their answers were capacious and contestatory ones.

CHAPTER 3

Reading Together, Book References, and Interacting with Print

In 1779 a merchant named Chevalier wrote to the *Journal de Paris* about how much he loved to read. "I am not a man of letters," he confided; "the details of a fairly large trade occupy the best part of my time; but I like literature, and above all poetry, so every moment that I can spare without prejudice to my profession as a merchant, I willingly share between the reading of our poets and the conversation of my friends."[1] Like most of the consumers of the information press, Chevalier was not a writer who traveled in literary circles. He found his livelihood in another profession, but he nevertheless wanted to participate in the cultural life of the city. Rather than writing to a literary magazine, he and many subscribers shared their affinity for reading in the information press. They introduced the works they had read, and they began a conversation in the newspaper about them.

This chapter examines the ways that writers signaled to their fellow readers what they were reading and, on occasion, how they explained the experience of reading itself. To study the texts that the French newspaper-reading public accessed and how they read them, this chapter begins by discussing the books and other print matter that letter writers referenced in their correspondence. The case study consists of the citation strategies in all of the letters published in 1778, 1782, and 1788 in newspapers from Aix-en-Provence, Amiens, Angers, Arras, Caen, Compiègne, Dijon, Grenoble, Lyon, Marseille, Metz, Montpellier, Orléans, Paris, Poitiers, Reims, Rennes, Rouen, Toulouse, and Troyes. Not all letters mentioned a book. Among the 1,567 letters published in the three-year sample, 24.1 percent of the letters to the editor referenced book titles. By comparison, 24.7 percent cited another letter to the editor or an article that they had read, either in the same newspaper or in another periodical.[2] The remaining letters referenced no print works at all. Over the three years sampled, readers identified 441 unique titles in their letters. In addition, they referenced 204 authors in general, that is, without reference to a specific title. (For a complete list of the titles cited, see appendix B.) Writers cited books and authors to support their own arguments or work through their own ideas.

This chapter also investigates the writers' experiences of reading. The analysis is drawn from the corpus of 6,909 letters published between 1770 and 1788. In their critiques and close readings, the writers to the press expressed their emotional and analytical processes of participating in a world of print. Together, the body of letters offers a window into the reading practices of a large and diverse community. By situating their responses in the information press, they invited the newspaper's consumers to read alongside them.

Writing to the Affiches

The style of referencing previous content from the newspaper reinforced the editors' claims that the affiches were in dialogue with their readers. Writers indicated in general, and in some cases with reference to a particular issue number or date of the paper, that their correspondence was a response to a previous article or letter. In some cases where writers cited a particular letter to the editor, debates ensued between two or more interlocutors over the ensuing weeks. The debates in the press also underscored the limits of what was known and accepted by all. Writers responded to share new evidence on an issue of debate or to offer a different interpretation of the evidence already in the paper.

References to previous newspaper content were also a means of correcting the record, as editors did not typically print retractions. Instead, they published letters from readers that referenced another article or letter in the paper, and then they offered factual revisions, such as updating the proper address for a business or place of residence. More complex amendments included cases where the letter writer claimed or denied authorship of a published work that had appeared in the press under another name. Even quite well-known authors faced challenges of distinguishing authoritative and counterfeit work. As discussed in chapter 2, Thérèse Levasseur wrote a letter to the editor to specify the only authentic copies of a volume of

Rousseau's *Ouvrages*.[3] Counterfeit books proliferated as soon as the first run of a book was successful, and printers tended to order fewer copies of a given book for each edition they produced.[4] As such, the possibility for error, even in authorized titles, was rather high. By sending updates and corrections on other print matter to the affiches, writers situated the newspapers as public record keepers. The serialized fashion of the calls for revision encouraged newspaper consumers to stay up to date in their reading.

By using their letters to reference other periodicals, writers opened up the information press to political and philosophical conversations. Approximately 1 percent of the letters to the editor published between 1770 and 1788 were responses not to previous content the writer had seen in the affiches but rather to literary periodicals such as the *Mercure de France* and *L'Année littéraire* and specialized journals on the law, the military, and medicine. All such periodicals were published with the requisite licenses and according to the Old Regime censorship strictures. Notably, letter writers also wrote to the affiches in response to newspapers published abroad, citing the *Journal encyclopédique ou universel* published in Liège and the *Annales politiques, civiles et littéraires*, which was published in London and, from 1780 to 1784, in Brussels.[5] They cited the London-based *Courier de l'Europe*, a French-language gazette for circulation in Great Britain that openly took positions on political questions. A second edition was published for the continent; in France the *Courier* was personally censored by the minister of foreign affairs, Charles Gravier, comte de Vergennes.[6] The *Journal encyclopédique*, the *Courier de l'Europe*, and the *Annales politiques* were periodicals that had the support of French polymaths and men of letters, including Jean-Louis Castilhon, Jean-Baptiste-René Robinet, Pierre-Augustin Caron de Beaumarchais, Jean le Rond d'Alembert, and Voltaire. While they made up a small proportion of the total correspondence, letters to the editor that engaged with such publications cited content beyond the limits of censorship. The references to these publications reveal that the affiches' readers accessed a range of periodicals, censored and uncensored. Information was shared between periodicals such that the affiches were not isolated from the political and philosophical ideas that circulated in the late eighteenth century. Selective citation was one strategy that made it possible for subversive content to appear, even in censored general information newspapers.

Book Title References in the Information Press

Nearly one in four letters included a reference to a book title or author.[7] To investigate the range of book titles cited in the affiches, this section draws on a three-year sample of letters to the editor where letter writers referenced 441 unique titles. The books cited in the affiches are organized in figure 3.1 according to the schema used in the eighteenth-century Parisian bookseller's catalogs, which divided all books into five major categories: literary works (belles lettres), arts and sciences, history, jurisprudence, and theology.

As figure 3.1 shows, works of literature were cited in the information press most of all, composing 37.0 percent (163 titles) of the titles cited. Books and pamphlets on the sciences and arts constituted 29.5 percent of the works cited (130 titles), and history was the next most referenced category, with 22.4 percent of all book titles referenced (99 titles). The number of titles on jurisprudence (2.3 percent, with 10 titles) and theology (3.6 percent, with 16 titles) constituted a much smaller proportion of the books referenced in the information press. Approximately 5.2 percent of the titles referenced

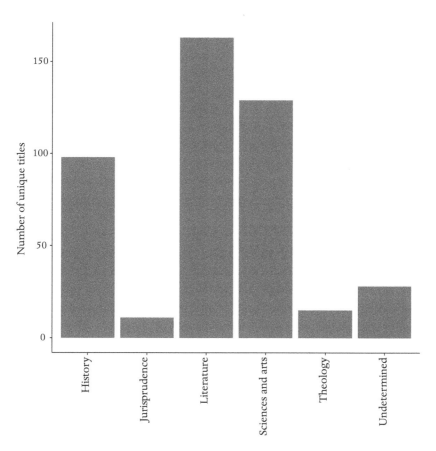

FIGURE 3.1   The number of unique book titles cited in the affiches, sorted by catalog subject matter schema.

by letter writers fall into the "undetermined" category. Works classified as "undetermined" included two kinds of books: titles that included too little information to identify them with certainty as a particular publication, and works that were not listed in the general catalog of the Bibliothèque nationale de France.

The titles referenced in the affiches encompassed an assortment of well-known and obscure books. In the eighteenth century, books were categorized according to catalogs kept by Parisian booksellers. This system emerged in the seventeenth century as an attempt to order all print knowledge in one system; the schema was shared by the Parisian booksellers and then adopted by booksellers and cataloguers.[8] From such book catalogs, historians have traced the scale of book production and exchange in France.[9] In addition to accounting for the books that were produced, bought, and sold, the catalogs divided books according to their subject matter. Each subject contained a series of subcategories with smaller subcategories of their own. For example, the category of sciences and arts included pyrotechnic art, the arts, natural history, mathematics, medicine and surgery, metaphysics, philosophy, and physics. The arts, for example, contained an additional outline of subcategories: architecture, art of painting, gymnastic and other athletic arts, military art, mechanical arts (*métiers*), dictionaries of the arts, and games. The catalogs reflected the efforts of booksellers and producers to conceptualize and order an increasingly vast print environment.[10] Over the eighteenth century, the catalogs show the evolution in reading tastes toward an ever-wider range of print matter. Figure 3.2 presents a more detailed visualization of the books cited in the press according to the more descriptive subcategories within the catalog.[11]

More than any other category, letter writers cited literature. Among the 163 titles within the larger category of belles lettres, polygraphs, dictionaries, novels, and poetry were the most referenced works. Compilations of selected writings known as polygraphs accounted for thirty-two of the titles, which included volumes of the works of writers who had recently died, such as Jean-Jacques Rousseau, Charles-Pierre Colardeau, Germain-François Poullain de Saint-Foix, and Voltaire. Letter writers mentioned eighteen dictionaries or grammar books, including Pierre de la Ramée's *Grammaire latine* and *Grammaire française*. Other reference books included dictionaries dedicated to music, Italian poetry, ariettas, diplomacy, the French language, and synonyms. Writers referenced twenty-two novels in their letters, including Voltaire's *Candide* and Montesquieu's *Lettres persanes*. Treatises on education that adopted the form of a novel, such as Caroline-Stéphanie-Félicité du Crest, Madame de Genlis's *Adèle et Théodore* and Jean-Jacques Rousseau's *Émile, ou*

FIGURE 3.2   The number of unique book titles cited in the affiches, sorted by catalog subcategory.

de l'éducation, also appeared in letters to the affiches. Epistolary novels referenced in the information press included Samuel Richardson's *Clarissa, or, the History of a Young Lady*, Jacques-Henri Bernardin de Saint Pierre's *Paul et Virginie*, and the *Orpheline angloise, ou Histoire de Charlotte Summers*. Even a relatively unknown picaresque work, Jean-François Dougados's *Voyage*, was written in the style of an epistolary novel.[12] Eighty-seven of the titles cited were works of poetry, including thirty-one plays or operas written in verse.

After literature, the sciences and arts garnered the most attention. The titles under sciences and arts encompassed practical guides on agricultural or geological subjects; observations on animal behavior and disease; explanations of chemistry experiments; medical and surgical treatments; philosophical works; and books on the arts of painting, hunting, and swimming. Among the 130 titles within the category of *sciences et arts* that appeared in the information press, twenty-five of the titles were works on the arts. Among them, five works each concerned architecture and the art of painting. One book covered the mechanical arts. Two titles—Jacques-Antoine-Hippolyte, comte de Guibert's *Essai général de tactique* and General Gordon's memoirs—were cited on military arts. Three books entailed the physical arts of hunting and swimming. Nine were encyclopedias, including Denis Diderot and Jean le Rond d'Alembert's *Encyclopédie, ou dictionnaire raisonné des sciences, des arts et des métiers*. The other dictionaries were dedicated to new inventions, or dictionaries of "Grands Hommes" or "hommes illustres."[13] Posthumous tributes to esteemed figures were prevalent both in the books that writers cited and in the affiches themselves as "nécrologie," where the editors printed letters dedicated to renowned men in the style of an obituary.

The books that fell under the category of the sciences covered philosophical and practical studies on all aspects of the natural world. Sciences and arts encompassed mathematics (10 titles), medicine and surgery (26), metaphysics (3), natural history (23), philosophy (30), and physics (10). The books on mathematics encompassed studies of astronomy, geometry, and optics, including two works by Jean-Paul Marat, the future revolutionary. Books in the category of medicine and surgery included pharmacological texts, studies of health and illness, and fifteen titles on chemistry, such as essays by Joseph Priestley, John Pringle, and Pierre-Joseph Macquer. The three works on metaphysics concerned the occult; one of the titles in question was a treatise on werewolves by Paul Grillandus, a sixteenth-century exorcist. Natural philosophy books included practical works on botany and agriculture and observational studies of animals by Georges-Louis Leclerc, comte de Buffon, the Abbé Alexandre Henri Tessier, and Jacques-Henri Bernardin de Saint-Pierre. The category of philosophy also encompassed pieces on commerce and state finance by Adam Smith and Victor de Riquetti, marquis de Mirabeau, the economy of the home, and works of morality by Jacques Necker. Finally, philosophy also included political treatises and philosophical essays from antiquity, such as the work of Aristotle, and from celebrated eighteenth-century men of letters such as Rousseau and Voltaire. Among the ten works in the category of *physique* were Jean-Antoine Nollet's work on electrical experimentation and instruments, *Leçons de physique expérimentale*, and Francesco Lana de Terzi's seventeenth-century aeronautical study, *Magisterium naturae et artis*. The books on the sciences discussed in the information press suggest that readers were aware of and interested in recent breakthroughs in fields such as chemistry, and in new ways of thinking about natural philosophy, economics, and political philosophy.

Writers referenced ninety-nine works of history in the information press. The publications on historical subjects reflected the interest of readers in France in particular. Seven books were local in scope, including histories of the city of La Rochelle and the provinces of Dauphiné and Anjou. Twelve titles concerned the French monarchy. History subject matter also encompassed travel narratives, geographies, and atlases, which together accounted for twenty-two of the books referenced. Some periodical literature also fell within the category of history; fourteen almanacs and literary magazines were referenced in the information press. Letter writers also commented on histories of Italy, Germany, Russia, Turkey, China, and the Americas. The history books that appeared in the letters to the editor indicated the global and local, ancient and contemporary interests that writers brought to the information press. In citing histories, letter writers signaled to one another a curiosity about the world, an orientation that was shared by Parisian and provincial readers alike.

Histories of Ancient Greece and Rome also appeared in the affiches. Most of the books on antiquity cited in the newspapers were written in the eighteenth century, including works by Gian Rinaldo, comte de Carli-Rubbi, Gabriel Brotier, and Cornelius de Pauw. But letter writers also referenced titles from the classical past. One writer cited Plutarch's *Lives*, a first-century work that had circulated in French translation since 1559.[14] Another letter writer cited Titus Livius's *History of Rome*, which had been available in French translation since the fifteenth century. Other books covered Greek music and philosophy, or the history of Rome's public figures. Letter writers discussed antiquity avidly, even when they did not reference a particular book title. They commented on the Roman ruins in their vicinity, local history, and the Roman objects they collected.[15] The eighteenth-century interest in antiquity was in part fostered by the Grand Tour. Yet even at the local level, collecting antiquities and corresponding about them was a popular hobby.[16] The newspapers formed another layer in the social networks through which objects and information from antiquity were shared.

Works of theology constituted sixteen of the 441 titles referenced in the affiches. Two of the books were dedicated to the lives of saints: Godfrey Henschen's *Acta Sanctorum*, a seventeenth-century encyclopedic hagiography of the saints, and a book on Jeanne-Françoise Frémiot, baronne de Chantal, a French saint canonized in 1767. Writers who referenced theological books mentioned the sixteenth-century Jesuit Émond Auger most of all, including his sermons, catechism, and treatises on the duties of a Christian prince. Auger's *Metanœologie* was referenced in seven letters to the editor; only Diderot and d'Alembert's *Encyclopédie* appeared in the press more. Most theology titles were devotional works, catechist texts, or collections of sermons, all of which were read by the laity in the eighteenth century.[17] While the Bible did not appear in any references, an annotated edition of the Books of Lamentations and Psalms was cited in one letter. Notably, there were also religious works from outside Catholicism referenced in the affiches. One letter writer discussed the Koran. Another discussed Pierre François le Courayer, whose reform-minded beliefs included support of Jansenism and the Anglican Church.[18] Taken together, the titles on theology suggest that religion was not a topic of regular discussion in the information press, even while the Bible and other devotional works remained best sellers. For those that did reference theological works in the affiches, books that supported religious practices were the most popular.

Books concerning jurisprudence spoke to a more specialized audience who consumed the provincial affiches. The works in this category included the *Gazette des tribunaux*, a compendium dedicated to legal proceedings and published essays written by lawyers on recent edicts. Two seventeenth-century books on French inheritance law, Jean-Marie Ricard's *Traité des donations entre-vifs et testamentaires* and Denis Le Brun's *Traité des successions*, were also referenced. While most of the titles concerned French law, works on the English legal system and on natural law also appeared in letters to the editor. The most prominent theme across such titles was criminal justice reform. William Blackstone's *Commentaries on the Laws of England* appeared in translation and was referenced in two letters. André-Jean-Baptiste Boucher-d'Argis was referenced in one letter for his *Observations sur les loix criminelles*. Nicolas de La Mare's administrative works on policing, the *Traité de la police*, which were published in a series of volumes between 1707 and 1738, appeared in one letter. Composing only ten of the 441 book titles referenced, the works on jurisprudence do not fully reflect the dynamic level of engagement with criminal justice reform that was taking place in these decades. The limits of censorship and licensing of content likely restricted such discussions in the information press in ways that are evident today only by their absence.

Frequently Cited Titles

The vast majority of the titles cited in the information press appeared only once, with approximately 81.0 percent of the books (357 titles) referenced in one letter to the editor. Fifty-four works (12.2 percent) were mentioned twice.

Within the sample set of letters written in 1778, 1782, and 1788, writers cited thirty book titles three or more times. Repeated references to the same books suggest that those titles garnered greater discussion in the information press than did most books. Among such titles, works of literary fiction were particularly popular; they accounted for two-thirds of the works cited at least three times. James Macpherson's epic poem *Ossian*, which appeared in French translation in 1777, was mentioned in three letters. A new French translation of Homer's *Iliad* garnered attention in 1782, when four writers referenced it in their letters. The most often cited poem was Voltaire's 1723 epic in homage to Henry IV, *La Henriade*, which five writers mentioned in their letters. *Clarissa*, the epistolary novel by Samuel Richardson, was cited in three letters, as was Montesquieu's *Lettres persanes*. Caroline-Stéphanie-Félicité du Crest, Madame de Genlis's *Adèle et Théodore* appeared four times. Theatrical works such as Molière's *Tartuffe*, as well as lesser-known plays such as Léonor-Jean-Christin Soulas d'Allainval's *L'Embarras des richesses* and Louis Abel Beffroy de Reigny's *Aîles de l'amour*, were each referenced in three letters. As the total number of references to each work suggests, the most popular books in the press were either written in the eighteenth century or recent translations. The ten most cited works are displayed below in table 3.1. Half of the titles were literary works, four were on the sciences and arts, and one was a theological text.

Writing a letter to the newspaper was a way of participating in a collective endeavor not unlike an encyclopedia. The most popular book referenced in the information press was the most widely known reference work of its time, Diderot and d'Alembert's *Encyclopédie*, which was referenced in eight letters to the editor. Similar works, such as the *Dictionnaire de l'Académie*, d'Origny's *Dictionnaire des origines*, and Macquer's *Dictionnaire de chymie* were also among the top ten most cited books. Such compendia brought together many contributors on one shared project. The juxtaposition of information in these volumes was echoed in the organization of the newspaper page itself, which was also a multiauthored work where short articles on diverse topics were juxtaposed with one another.

However, for the most part book references in the information press did not cluster around a small corpus. Most books were mentioned only once in the newspapers. Rather than returning to a shared set of titles, letter writers instead signaled outward to an array of books and interests. Because the writers cited so many unique titles instead of repeatedly citing the same ones, letters to the editor reveal little about the best sellers of the eighteenth century.[19] Instead, the references show the ways that writers used books to consider their own subjectivity and construct their own arguments.

Table 3.1   The ten most cited books in the *affiches'* letters to the editor.

BOOK TITLE	BOOK AUTHOR	NUMBER OF REFERENCES	CATALOG CATEGORY
L'Encyclopédie, ou dictionnaire raisonné des sciences, des arts et des métiers	Diderot, Denis, and Jean le Rond d'Alembert	8	Sciences and arts
Dictionnaire de l'Académie	N/A	7	Literature
Metanœologie: sur le suget de l'archicongrégation des pénitens de l'annonciation de Nostre Dame et de toutes telles autres dévotieuses assemblées, en l'Église sainte	Auger, Émond	7	Theology
Lunes	Beffroy de Reigny, Louis Abel	6	Literature
Courrier des planètes	Beffroy de Reigny, Louis Abel	5	Literature
Étrennes de cousin	Beffroy de Reigny, Louis Abel	5	Literature
La Henriade	Voltaire	5	Literature
Dictionnaire des origines	Origny, Pierre-Adam d'	5	Sciences and arts
Dictionnaire de chymie	Macquer, Pierre Joseph	5	Sciences and arts
Études de la nature	Bernardin de Saint-Pierre, Henri	5	Sciences and arts

In certain cases, citing a book served commercial purposes. Some references were likely surreptitious attempts to promote books one had written, or those one was selling. The references to Louis Abel Beffroy de Reigny's work in the affiches were just that.[20] While some letters were no doubt thinly veiled advertisements, the majority of letters mentioning specific titles gave no indication that they were trying to sell the book they discussed. Even in cases where the newspaper's editor was a bookseller-printer, the works discussed in the paper were rarely available in his shop. A comparison of the books referenced in the affiches in Dijon, Orléans, and Poitiers with the lists of books the printer-booksellers had ordered from the Swiss publishing house the Société Typographique de Neuchâtel revealed only two titles: a volume of the collected works of Voltaire and a guide to vineyard cultivation by the agronomist Maupin.[21] Thus, while it is possible that some writers did write letters to enhance their literary reputation, or printers published certain letters to drum up sales of their books, such cases were rare. There is not enough evidence in most cases to know with certainty what the motivations of the writers were. As a result, this study does not distinguish between the titles in the rare letters that may have been advertisements and the rest of the corpus.

In publishing general information newspapers, the editors likely privileged certain kinds of works over others. For example, the low proportion of theological books referenced in the letters to the editor does not indicate that the readers of the affiches did not own or read the Bible, devotionals, or other theological works, which remained best sellers throughout the eighteenth century. Rather, the absence of such references may indicate that the discussion of theological topics was either redacted by the censors overseeing the press or self-censored by editors who chose not to print on such subject matter. The absence of citations could also allow for writers to slip more controversial discussions past the eyes of the censors. As studies of the citation practices in the *Encyclopédie* have shown, the most often cited books were works that both identified the author openly and had the official permissions and protections to publish. Nonattribution, and even misattribution, were effective strategies that writers used to evade the censors and place more subversive content in print.[22] The absence of certain works in the affiches reflected the strategic choices of editors and letter writers.

Frequently Cited Authors

Some writers referenced an author without indicating a particular book or pamphlet at all. Table 3.2 presents a list of the twenty authors who were most referenced in the affiches, ranked by the number of total references. Voltaire and Rousseau were by far the most often referenced authors; both died in 1778, and several of the references to them were eulogies published that year. Racine and Corneille ranked just below Rousseau and Voltaire. And many of the references to Racine, Corneille, and Voltaire cited all three authors together. Voltaire may, in part, have inspired such a connection by his own commentary on Corneille and Racine.[23]

As the references to authors illustrate, the affiches were not entirely separated from the world of the philosophes. The letter writers directly referenced some of the leading political philosophers, historians, and natural philosophers of the eighteenth century. Among the twenty most cited authors were five Encyclopedists: d'Alembert, Jean-François Marmontel, Montesquieu, Rousseau, and Voltaire. Yet the authors who were mentioned in multiple letters were not all contemporary figures; letters referenced poets, playwrights, philosophers, and theologians from the Grand Siècle with as much frequency as those of the eighteenth century. The most cited authors

Table 3.2   The twenty most referenced authors, without citation of a particular title.

AUTHOR	NUMBER OF REFERENCES
Voltaire	35
Jean-Jacques Rousseau	21
Jean Racine	15
Pierre Corneille	10
Molière	7
Jean le Rond d'Alembert	6
Bernard le Bovier de Fontenelle	6
Jean de La Fontaine	6
Montesquieu	6
Virgil	6
Nicolas Boileau-Despréaux	5
Cicero	5
Jacques-Bénigne Lignel Bossuet	4
Aesop	4
François Fénelon	4
Horace	4
Jean-François Marmontel	4
Pliny the Elder	4
Francis Bacon	3
Jean-André Deluc	3

also included five poets, philosophers, or historians from Greek and Roman antiquity. Antiquity was a subject of fascination in the eighteenth century, as a tool of legitimization of the present and a way to participate in the celebration of the past, but above all as a creative field that afforded writers more expansive opportunities to revise and reimagine familiar stories than did theological texts.[24] The references to authors suggest that the readers of the affiches shared interests in philosophy, literature, and natural philosophy, and they drew on a cadre of classical, seventeenth-century, and contemporary authors to explore their interests. The writers to the affiches participated in an Enlightenment culture that was informed by such authors whose ideas permeated the lives and worldviews of late eighteenth-century figures from various social backgrounds.

The citations made by readers to periodicals, books, and authors revealed part of the information context in which the newspapers were consumed. Writers used references to books and periodicals as signposts to point the affiches' readers toward a wider world of print. The books and authors mentioned in the press did not constitute a complete inventory of the books that newspaper readers accessed in late Old Regime France. Thus, the absence in the affiches of particular titles that historians have identified as eighteenth-century best sellers does not indicate that such books were not consumed by the readers of the information press. Referencing a particular book title or author was a way of substantiating one's argument in the short format of a public letter; book references caught the attention of the reader and linked the opinions of the letter writer to the works they mentioned. Citation was a means by which letter writers made sense of print and formulated their own ideas.

Interacting with Print

In addition to revealing books they read alongside the affiches, letter writers spoke self-reflexively about the experience of reading itself. Situated at the crux of the personal and the public, letters to the editor prompted readers to articulate their own subjectivities and the communities to which they wrote. While the principle purpose of a letter to the editor was to make an argument or present one's case on a particular subject, writers also explained their experiences of reading in a range of interpretive and emotional forms. By studying the published correspondence that men and women shared about their reading habits, this chapter underscores what Leah Price has described as the "impossibility of separating individual reading practices from literary communities."[25] The placement of individual reactions in the information press linked personal and collective reading experiences.

In their letters, subscribers described when and how they read the newspaper. In Marseille "La Comtesse de ***" sketched her daily habit of reading the *Journal de Provence* at the start of each morning. She spent the rest of the morning perusing the *Journal de Paris*, then the *Mercure*, before dining with the *Gazette de Santé* right in front of her, and falling asleep with the English papers.[26] A *laboureur* named Emme Gourdaut described his practice of keeping copies of the *Affiches de Troyes* at home and reading each issue seven or eight different times.[27] For some, reading the newspaper was a shared process. A writer who described himself as the "Suisse du Cirque" explained a copy of the newspaper only came to him once everyone with whom he worked had read it.[28] On one occasion, a writer to the *Journal de Paris* admitted that he did not read the *Journal* regularly because he did not know how to read properly; the paper was read to him.[29] As these cases illustrate, writers approached the newspaper page with distinctive habits, skills, and aims.

Letters to the editor also offered glimpses into the physical circumstances under which people read, as even letters that were not primarily concerned with books or periodicals nevertheless touched on the material contexts of reading. For example, a young woman wrote to the *Affiches d'Angers* to report on her recovery from cataract surgery; she named being able to read again, with the aid of glasses, as a sign of her progress.[30] A writer to the *Journal de Paris* concerned primarily with ventilation in the home identified being able to read in one's bed without fear of smoke or fire among the merits of properly constructed chimneys.[31] For some, reading the newspaper was a way of spanning the distances that separated subscribers. An anonymous writer explained to the editors of the *Journal de Paris* that while he was some sixty leagues from Paris, he continued to read the paper for both education and amusement.[32]

In short, the contributors to the affiches read the paper in varying ways—extensively each day with other newspapers or intensively at home; borrowed from one's coworkers or alone and far from the site of publication. They read the paper for information and entertainment. And they wrote back to the paper to continue the conversation. For the readers of the information press, reading had become a necessary and ubiquitous pastime; writing back to the paper was, as one writer put it, a means of recognizing the newspaper's usefulness and supporting its success.[33]

References to newspapers and books also featured readers' responses to particular content by justifying their own letters in response to the feelings or questions that previous newspaper content inspired. A letter signed by "three of your subscribers" exclaimed that they "had been unable to read without emotion" a description of filial piety that appeared in the previous day's paper.[34] In response to an article published in the same paper, one writer noted that he read the piece in the *Journal de Paris* "with as much interest as sensibility."[35] Trassart, the vicar-general at Saint-Papoul, described how he read "with tenderness" a touching letter that appeared in the paper.[36] While descriptions of emotional responses were the most prevalent, letter writers also demonstrated their willingness to share differing perspectives. The flurry of correspondence over Émond Auger's theological treatises and sermons illustrated this phenomenon, when writers shared their own interpretations of Auger's work via the press. By referencing one another as well as books, those who wrote letters to the editor practiced reading collectively.

In the published correspondence in the information press, three trends emerged. First, the writers responded to books in emotional terms. Those who documented the experience of reading often emphasized the depth of feeling that gripped them, especially when they spoke of reading novels. Second, writers took seriously their role of critiquing the books and periodicals they had read, and they wrote to the affiches to offer corrections and suggest revisions. Readers of encyclopedias and other multiauthored works were especially active participants. Finally, they asked the editors to print excerpts of what they were reading so that they could comment on the text in greater depth. Such close readings were especially common in discussions of poetry. Together, the letters conveyed the multifaceted ways in which people of varying backgrounds interacted with print.

Reading with Emotion

The capacity of literature to draw out an emotional response in the reader was most evident in the letters to the editor that concerned popular sentimental novels. Epistolary novels in particular burgeoned in the period between the 1760s and the 1780s, with thirty new novels appearing each year in France in the 1770s and forty new novels published annually in the 1780s.[37]

A letter by the future revolutionary Antoine-François Delandine that was published in the affiches in Grenoble and in Paris aptly demonstrated the personal impact of this trend. He responded to his recent experience of reading Bernardin de Saint Pierre's epistolary novel *Paul et Virginie*, which chronicled the moral and social education of two children raised in an idealized state of nature on colonial Mauritius (Isle de France). Moved by the descriptions of an island paradise and the sentimental renderings of the characters, Delandine wrote a glowing review to the newspaper: "I found the heart I had at eighteen and it took me until the sublime and consoling passage that ends the work to compose myself. Maybe there were some digressions that were a bit too long, nevertheless one wouldn't want to remove a sentence, not a single word." He saw the novel not only as a source of entertainment but rather as an emotional and moral journey: "With Paul and Virginie, I found myself satisfied with my existence." Reading the novel was not only an aesthetic experience for Delandine, but one that gave him satisfaction in his own life and made him want to be useful in the lives of others. As he put it: "For a long time, I had not read something where the imagination was more varied, more brilliant, or where the moral at the end was better fulfilled. It is impossible to read it without desiring to be useful and without feeling better. There you have it—an occasion worthy of being seized upon by an enlightened Company, a protector of true talents and of their proper use."[38] Delandine suggested that *Paul et Virginie* should receive an annual prize for "écrits utiles." As his letter illustrated, reading was a way of relating to the experiences of fictional figures. But the language of feeling also motivated his care for society, which he intended to demonstrate by finding ways to be useful.

Delandine's reading of *Paul et Virginie* was emblematic of a style of sentimental reading that was especially pronounced in response to novels. Rousseau's *Julie, ou La Nouvelle Héloïse* inspired similar responses. In their letters to Rousseau, readers described being consumed by the novel in ways they experienced both emotionally and physically. They related to the characters, they shed tears as they read, and they felt a trepidation of Julie's death that drove them to illness. They spoke of the depth of their feeling for the characters, and for Rousseau by extension.[39] Through such correspondence with Rousseau, readers shared their earnest, heartfelt experiences of reading—the pleasure and affinity that *Julie* had inspired. What the sentimental reading in the information press makes clear is that readers' responses to Rousseau were not exceptional in their depth of feeling. And while many readers confided only in a novel's author or in their personal diaries, some shared their responses in their local newspaper.

The influence of sentimental epistolary novels was so moving for some writers that they wrote to the papers to clarify what happened in fictional worlds, just as they clarified reports of current events. One anonymous writer to the *Journal de Paris* reacted to a recent description in the paper of the tableau designed by Mademoiselle la Ville, which depicted a scene from Richardson's *Clarissa*. The letter identified what the writer called a "double error," for the newspaper had misrepresented the plot by describing the tableau as Clarissa's brother leaving to fight the villain Lovelace. As the writer put it, "everyone knows" that Clarissa's brother had dueled Lovelace at the outset of the novel, and it was in fact her cousin, Colonel Morden, who killed Lovelace. The second error was the newspaper's description of the tableau itself, which depicted a scene between Morden and Clarissa.[40] While the record in question was a fictional story, the writer had decided that the epistolary novel was important enough that the newspaper ought to make sure the story was presented faithfully.

Invited into the interior lives of fictional figures via the familiar letters that made up the novel, readers formed emotional ties with characters whose most intimate thoughts and experiences were known to them. Moreover, the protagonists in such novels were ordinary people—people like the readers themselves. Lynn Hunt has compellingly suggested that the immediacy and intensity of readers' engagement with the novels they read made them more sympathetic to the lives of others, more moral, and, indeed, more capable of inventing human rights.[41] As the letters to the editor illustrate, some readers felt so strongly about what they had read that they wrote to the newspaper to share their personal investment in novels. Writers felt a responsibility to get the story right, even when that story was a novel.

Especially in the case of Rousseau, the affinity for a protagonist extended to the novel's author. Jean-Jacques Rousseau prompted heartfelt responses from the newspaper-reading public, especially in the months after his death. The playwright and novelist Claude Joseph Dorat wrote to the *Journal de Paris* to reflect on the personal impact of Rousseau's memoirs on his own life. In his letter to the editor, he said that he had conveyed the same letter privately to a woman of his acquaintance.[42] Sharing a familiar letter as a public one, Dorat blurred the lines between life and epistolary fiction in much the same way that Rousseau had in his novels. One particularly vivid account of Rousseau's impact was written by a woman who recalled being in her carriage with her husband, son, and two friends, when the conversation turned to the memory of Rousseau. For her, the shift in conversation "was enough to awaken in my soul a tender admiration" for a man she had never met. She acknowledged his profound influence on her: "I spoke of J. J. Rousseau, to whose works I owe the little that I am worth, and the principles, dare I say virtues, in which my heart loves to feed." Then she described the moment in the carriage when "everything moved me": her husband's conversation, her child's touch, which she called "the secret and pleasure of all mothers." She described the moment of thinking of Rousseau in the carriage and taking comfort in her family as an "emotion that had deliciously occupied me" but one that she did not have the strength to pursue more deeply.[43]

Historians of emotion remain divided on what to make of the responses of readers to the epistolary novels of the eighteenth century. William Reddy has argued that the heightened sentiment in eighteenth-century literature, such as readers who were brought to tears by a novel, was an exploitation of the power of emotional expression that readers at the time questioned as sincere.[44] The responses to Bernardin de Saint-Pierre, Rousseau, and Richardson in the information press sometimes quibbled about the facts presented in the paper, but they did not question the earnestness of readers' emotions. Instead, the emotional responses that appeared in the newspapers of the 1770s and 1780s align more closely with what Barbara Rosenwein has called "emotional communities," where groups understood the norms for expressing such emotions and shared a consensus about which emotions had value.[45] For eighteenth-century readers, the capacity for fellow feeling became a central virtue.[46] In the affiches, letter writers drew on one another's emotional repertoires as they shared their responses in the press.

Critical Responses

The letters to the editor also welcomed criticism, and writers often corresponded to the paper to show how actively they had read a particular work. Especially when they discussed reference works, letter writers approached books in much the same way that they did the newspaper—as an iterative, collectively authored work where their perspective mattered. For example, a letter written in response to Jean Dubreuil's *Dictionnaire lyrique portatif* recommended revisions for the next edition of the volume. The letter writer in Le Puy-en-Velay suggested an updated version include new opera pieces, but also more varied musical forms: ariettas, vaudeville, and romances ought to all appear in the *Dictionnaire*, each with a short preceding analysis. He generally approved of the organizational structure of the volume, but he asked the author for more guidance. The writer also recommended clear titles of the *pièces de théâtre* at the top of the corresponding pages, uniform page layouts, and alphabetical tables of contents at the end of each volume listing all pieces by title and by the first few lines of verse.[47]

The calls for more labels, tables, and illustrations in the letters to the editor reflected the interests of readers who desired information that was ordered, standardized, and clear—tools that would lend a volume to easy consultation. Writers such as the critic of Dubreuil's *Dictionnaire* also expressed the notion that a book was a provisional work that could and should change. Even Diderot and d'Alembert's *Encyclopédie* relied on the assumption that its readers would interpret and improve on it.[48] In a similar manner, a certain "D. R." wrote to the *Journal de Paris* to note the limits in a definition he had read in the recently published book *Mélanges tirés d'une grande bibliothèque*. In general, he found it to be a useful and well-made volume, one that "replaced a crowd of absolutely useless books." By identifying errors in a book that he esteemed, he sought to enhance future editions so that the editor could place in the book "all the perfection he can give it."[49] In their responses in the press, such writers approached books as objects that would change, and they took it on themselves to participate in formulating such changes.

In their critiques of books, most writers underscored that they read carefully, and they focused their letters on flagging the errors they found. One of the *Journal général de France*'s subscribers was hopeful that in a new edition, he would find "one pure source that one can draw from with confidence," in an encyclopedia that contained "neither the lies, exaggerations, nor the big errors that disfigure the old."[50] The search for comprehensive and trustworthy sources preoccupied many. Writers contacted the affiches routinely to rectify errors that they found, especially when those errors concerned the reputation of an author. For example, after the *Affiches de Rennes* had printed a fable, which the paper attributed to a M. Fron., readers wrote letters to the editor explaining that the fable was in fact the work of the Abbé Aubert, who had published it at least thirty years earlier.[51] Other letters warned about subscribing to volumes that would never be published, counterfeit volumes of the posthumously collected works of known authors, or unauthorized changes to an author's book.[52] The concern with the authority and validity of information presented in books and newspapers surfaced in the letters to the editor.

While most writers chose to share portrayals of themselves as confident readers and curators of the information they consumed, some revealed instead the uncertainty that troubled their reading. As one writer to the Parisian *Journal général de France* put it, "I read exactly, yet sometimes I do not understand what the author is trying to say."[53] He complained to the editor of the problems of learning the specialized vocabulary as he made his way through the *Nouvelles éphémérides économiques*, and of discerning whether an individual author was sincere or joking. The challenge of parsing truth from wit was shared by a writer who warned in his letter about reading the English-language *General Advertiser*, "One must be careful to not mistake a joke for a fact."[54] For some eighteenth-century writers such as Anthony Collins, the concept of ordering knowledge was itself a joke.[55]

The sense of overwhelm generated by print was not new in the eighteenth century. As Ann Blair's work has shown, the feeling there was too much to know had grown so pressing by the sixteenth century that European scholars devised all manner of management techniques in an effort to organize the information explosion that print technology had intensified.[56] In the information press of the eighteenth century, letter writers voiced similar feelings. One anonymous subscriber wrote to the paper to express the challenge of keeping track of all of the new books published, especially those produced beyond French borders.[57] The sense of confusion or information overload that readers expressed reflected larger processes. In France alone, the number of books published after 1750 increased by 113 percent over the total number of books produced in the first half of the century.[58] By the eve of the French Revolution, the number of books in a given household had risen substantially, and the range of subject matter had diversified. Print was more affordable than ever before. Confronted with the proliferation of books, eighteenth-century readers believed that they lived in an age when the number of books was not only too many to read but indeed had surpassed human capacity to know their names or count them.[59]

Moreover, the audiences who accessed the inundation of print had expanded. Literacy had risen slowly over the century. Among men, literacy throughout the kingdom had reached 50 percent by 1789; historians estimate the percentage of women who could read was much lower.[60] Literacy rates for urban and rural notables were much higher than the averages for France as a whole. Especially in Paris, some members of the working classes, and domestic servants in particular, bought and shared books with one another.[61] The social composition of the French readership had expanded by the end of the eighteenth century.

How readers acted on their feelings of information overload were significant too. In the sixteenth and seventeenth centuries, early modern readers interacted with books in a variety of ways, and such differing styles of reading were in part a response to the overabundance of books.[62] The readers of the eighteenth-century press adopted individual and collective strategies for, to borrow Blair's term, "processing" new knowledge.[63] Writers to the affiches made choices about what was worth knowing and what made knowledge trustworthy. The following chapters will show that book knowledge was but one source of authority among many in the information press.

Interpreting Verse

When writers to the affiches discussed reading closely, they often turned to poetry. Poems and theatrical works written in verse composed 19.5 percent of all the works cited in the information press in the sampled years.[64] The prevalence of verse in such discussions was in part owing to the four-page format of the newspaper itself, which no doubt privileged reprinting and discussing short excerpts. One writer noted that composing a letter to the editor required one keep their critique concise, since "your *journal* does not lend itself to long dissertations."[65] But the public interest in poetry was not simply a product of verse suiting the length of the paper.

Writers included excerpts from poems that meant something to them, and they asked the editors to print the lines they found particularly interesting or charming. They commented on poems that made them feel deeply, even when such feelings were painful.[66] Others described local provincial programs and prizes dedicated to the recitation and analysis of poetry.[67] Events and festivities prompted creative responses in the newspapers. A letter writer named De Varennes was so inspired by a poem he had read in the affiches that he had written some verses of his own, which he asked the editors to print. François-Jean Willemain d'Abancourt even wrote his letter to the editor in the form of a poem.[68] In citing particular titles, writing out full verses, and commenting on poetry, such letters illustrated how readers participated in literary conversations. By situating those conversations in general information newspapers, they invited a wide readership to respond with them.

Some of the poems cited in the information press were well-known classics, such as the translations of Homer's *Iliad* that multiple readers discussed in the Parisian newspapers. An anonymous writer praised Charles-Joseph

Loeillard d'Avrigny's and Pierre-Nicolas André-Murville's adaptations of the *Iliad*. The writer admired Murville's verse, noting its beauty, noble style, and pleasing form. The writer selected and shared excerpts that communicated both the depth of feeling between the characters and the detailed description captured by the author. In his or her estimation, what distinguished great poets was a talent for description.[69] Some letter writers acknowledged they lacked the reading knowledge of Greek or Latin to evaluate the accuracy of such translations. For example, in his letter to the editors, the "Marquis de V**" responded that the latest translation of the *Iliad* was written in a lively style which had inspired his enthusiasm for the epic. And yet the marquis found much to criticize in Homer's work. He did not care for the morals of the gods or heroes, whom he found cruel and deceitful. Rather than offering a close reading of a particular passage, he expressed instead his lack of interest in the characters: "Don't we have the right to be a bit tired of Agamemnon's family?"[70] The marquis's letter highlighted that readers approached even widely read works with disparate aims and preferences in mind.

Later that year, a certain Salaun wrote to the *Journal général de France* to convey his satisfaction with the newspaper's rigorous reviews of literary works, especially in light of what he saw as the "mediocrity of modern productions." And yet, in the critiques that the newspaper had published of the *Iliad*, Salaun believed the paper had gone too far.[71] Salaun's assessment was no doubt an effort on his part to appear knowledgeable to other readers. He did not describe his own process of reading. Nevertheless, his letter suggested the differing levels of background knowledge that subscribers brought to the paper. His comments also showed that he understood not all readers would interpret literary merit in the same way.

As the letters to the editor on Homer's *Iliad* revealed, discussions of poetry at times assumed a certain level of education, both a know-how for reading verse and a familiarity with Latin (and in the case of Homer, Greek). Even discussions of current events could turn on such skills. For example, in celebration of the demonstration of a steam engine at Jacques-Constantin and Auguste Charles Périer's workshop in Chaillot, an anonymous writer to the newspaper in Marseille reacted with a Latin couplet. His letter was a close reading of two lines, which included a discussion of the syntactical errors in the couplet. He lamented how difficult it was to write verse that was both pleasing to hear and precise in its meaning. This was a common complaint in the affiches. In a letter to the affiches in Compiègne, the poet and writer François-Félix Nogaret noted the difficulties that students and Racine alike had faced in setting their sentiments to verse without "the help of several superfluous words."[72]

Nevertheless, the writer in Marseille noted that the steam engine in Chaillot and the Latin couplet it had inspired "had reawakened the Latin muses of the kingdom," as more people had tried their hand at writing verses on the same subject. The letter ended with five exemplary Latin couplets gathered for the occasion, which he presented "without criticism or praise" for the readers of the paper to evaluate.[73] As the affinity for Latin verses in letters to the affiches indicated, many newspaper readers had the requisite education to participate in such conversations and, from time to time, write a few lines of poetry of their own. Moreover, the invitation of the letter concerning steam engines and Latin verse made clear that letter writers discussed poetry in the paper, at least in part, so that their fellow newspaper readers could participate.

Most of the poems cited in the information press appeared in only one letter, but Voltaire's epic poem *La Henriade* was an exception to this trend. Originally published in 1723, it was distributed throughout the century in new critical editions, including a bilingual version of the poem in Latin and French in 1772 that made the work suitable for teaching in school; it was included in a collection for the dauphin's education in 1790, which further solidified its status as a classic of French literature.[74] Some writers to the affiches were so confident that the poem's prestige spoke for itself that they referred to Voltaire not by name but rather as *La Henriade*'s author.[75] Citing *La Henriade* and *Mérope* in particular, one writer described Voltaire's "ardent love of justice and humanity that burst forth in all of his good works."[76] Like the writers who responded to novels in the press, this contributor noted Voltaire's ability to convey emotion and inspire virtue in the reader.

Other references in the information press to Voltaire's epic poem focused on the poem's style, structure, and originality. Pierre Laureau de Saint-André quoted two verses from *La Henriade* in his letter to the *Affiches de Dijon*, which was later printed in abridged form in the *Journal général de France*. Laureau noted that Voltaire's description of Rome, which was recognized by some critics as a particular beauty of the work and by others as a bombastic phrase, was not Voltaire's work at all but rather Godeau's *Epistle to My Library*, which he had "read with the greatest surprise" and recognition. He suggested that Voltaire had "drawn" Godeau's work "from the dust."[77] Whatever the origin of the particular verse, his letter shows how readers consulted new works in ways that were informed by what they had read before.

An anonymous writer to the affiches in Metz likewise used comparison, in this case to read *La Henriade* and Jean-François de Saint-Lambert's *Les Saisons* side by side. The writer began by noting the importance of learning to read well and acknowledged that verse and prose demanded different attentions and skills of the reader. Moreover, reading well required attending to the sounds and cadence of a verse. Citing full verses of Saint-Lambert and Voltaire, the writer compared each author's modes of expression in describing a gathering storm, a feat that Saint-Lambert accomplished in thirty verses while Voltaire dedicated only six to the subject. By presenting two poems side by side, the writer to the *Affiches des Trois-Evêchés et Lorraine* invited the newspaper's consumers to read along with her.[78] Voltaire's ability to communicate his ideas efficiently in verse caught the attention of multiple writers. In his letter to the editor, the writer and future revolutionary Jean-Louis Castilhon held up Voltaire's *Henriade* as an example of economy of expression, even as he noted it contained some four thousand verses.[79] The letters to the editor concerning poetry fit within the information press because of their short format and because they invited responses from other readers. By publishing letters from their readers that invited the public to read and interpret a particular passage, the affiches became an important space for reading together.

Social Reading

How the men and women who wrote letters to the editor understood their contribution to a newspaper was shaped by reading practices that often took place in shared spaces, where the written word was transmitted orally, and where the audience discussed information they heard. There was a range of such spaces dedicated to collective reading during the late eighteenth century, which varied according to one's geographic location and social status. As chapter 1 has shown, venues for collective reading increased the overall circulation of the information press. The content of the letters shows how the habits of reading and writing to the press forged new social practices.

In both Parisian and provincial centers, reading was both a means of conveying information and a way of participating in society. In a letter to the *Affiches de Normandie*, a woman advocated against a reading room in her town, which she feared would exclude women and provide a venue for only men to socialize. She asserted that access to information and the discussion of such information among both men and women of the town was essential to the social life of her community. Citing the popularity of summer gatherings, she explained, "The men and women assemble. We converse, play games, dance sometimes, but above all we talk about the news; not only news of the state, but of our city and neighborhoods and other nearby places. There is nothing more delicious than this sort of news. . . . It is in the little towns where one finds the fine flower of critique."[80] While opening a reading room in town would foster the fascination with news, her letter to the editor underscored the social and gendered disparities that such a space would intensify. For her part, she sought to preserve a space where men and women could cultivate the habits of criticism and conversation together.

Criticism was perhaps as much an indication of the social status and refinement with which the writer identified as it was a reflection of her interest in the intellectual life of the town. Nevertheless, her letter underscored the centrality of print in the social lives of the urban elite. As literacy rates rose in the eighteenth century, one's ability to read no longer served as a clear marker of social status. Instead, how and what people in one's social circle were reading grew in significance among notables.[81] The attention to the circulation of local news within elite society also reflected the practices cultivated in salons, where reading aloud functioned not only as a form of entertainment but also as a way to invite novelty. Such was the case when *salonnières* invited writers to share their new work, such as the marquise de la Vaupalière, who invited sixty guests to her home to hear Beaumarchais read selections from his *Mariage de Figaro*, or Madame du Deffand, who welcomed her friends to la Harpe's reading of *Barmécides*.[82] While *salonnières* were particularly well-known figures who invited their guests to read aloud, such practices were shared by many. One anonymous writer to the *Journal de Paris* described the commonplace practice in his social circle, where men were called on to recite verses before company. To prepare for such an occasion, he thought it best to reflect on the verses one would recite, as continually exercising one's ear could inure the speaker to the feeling verse communicated.[83] Reading new works together fostered conversation and fused social ties. Discussing such practices in the information press underscored their significance.

Men and women read aloud in all manner of public spaces, such as coffeehouses, halls, reading rooms, gardens, and concerts. Eighteenth-century books on elocution in religious and secular settings alike emphasized the importance of tone, gesture, and other nonverbal cues, because the aim of reading aloud was to communicate feelings.[84] Some readers of the information press suggested that newspaper editors provide even more spaces for such readings to take place. One letter writer named Colleville explained that his eyesight was beginning to fail him, so he asked the editors to facilitate public readings by printing his letter. He hoped that others interested in public readings on various genres could find one another via the newspaper, and perhaps together they would establish such a service. "I love reading," he wrote. "It has always been my principal occupation."[85] For Colleville, reading together was a practical solution to the loss of his vision and a remedy against social isolation.

But especially among elite men and women, the home was an important locus for social reading. In the eighteenth century, those who could afford to do so dedicated one of the rooms in their home to a library, where the family and their guests gathered to read collectively in the evenings. The father of a student named Lili Rosset made it his habit to read the paper in the young letter writer's presence.[86] Rosset's was not the only letter that featured families reading together. One subscriber to the *Journal de Paris* described his practice of reading with his wife, mother-in-law, and children each morning. As he explained, his eldest daughter would read aloud to everyone, and then each member of the family shared their own reflection about the reading. After recalling the previous day's passage, the children compared and pondered the two texts and asked their father questions. He noted how their faces lit up as they enjoyed the daily activity, leading him to conclude they learned without effort.[87] The writer echoed the ideas of François Fénelon, John Locke, and Charles Rollin, who believed that a child's reading should amuse while offering instruction—that children should be enticed to love learning.[88] Didactic literature read as a family at home cultivated self-control in children, instructed behavioral norms, and prepared children to participate in society.[89] The letter writer who described reading together each day understood reading and discussion as a foundation for his children's intellectual and social growth.

Readers also took their books and newspapers outside with them to read together. In their gardens and on their walks, picnics, and longer voyages, readers brought along a book to share.[90] The letter to the editor critiquing Dubreuil's *Dictionnaire* focused on the need for the book to be published in a "convenient and portable format" and at a reasonable price.[91] In short, the material form of a book affected who would be able to read it and where. In a similar manner, the accessibility and portability of the short-format newspaper made it ideal for transport. Social reading was widespread in eighteenth-century cultural life, and the affiches were an important virtual space to carry out the practices of reading together. What set the forum of letters to the editor apart from other reading spaces was its capacity to reach so many participants.

The letters to the editor were a venue for social reading that flourished in the 1770s and 1780s, where writers could reach a wider audience. Their references to books and to one another speak both to the relevance of specific kinds of works in their debates and to larger questions about the range of subject matter that was up for debate. Referencing books was a way for members of the newspaper-reading public to participate in the literary life of the age. Through their citations of books, pamphlets, and verse, they signaled to their fellow readers the larger network of print that they read alongside the affiches.

Writers cited works of literature, especially reference works, novels, and poetry. Books on the sciences and the arts also appeared in their letters, composing nearly a third of all references. History publications covered the history of France, antiquity, and the wider world. Books concerning jurisprudence and theology appeared much less frequently; together such books constituted less than 6 percent of all the titles referenced in the press. Rather than returning to the same titles again and again, most letter writers introduced books that no other writer mentioned. The array of titles cited in letters suggested the capacious interests that readers brought to the periodicals. Moreover, the fact that literary discussion took place in general information newspapers at all is noteworthy.

More significant than what they read, the letters show how newspaper readers responded to books and other print matter. The forum of the newspaper enabled letter writers to begin conversations about books with other readers. Such conversations were no doubt amplified and extended into other reading circles throughout the kingdom, where collective reading practices and habits of discussing books were widespread. The debates about print matter in the information press equipped readers with new habits of mind, which they would bring to their discussions of popular science, rural reform, and social welfare. As the following chapters demonstrate, citing a book was but one method letter writers would adopt to present evidence and make their case.

The letters revealed the avid engagement of newspaper readers with print media. And yet we know the mind is not merely soft wax onto which ideas are stamped; reading was a complex and creative process.[92] The responses that men and women offered in the affiches about reading are thus particularly rich. Writers characterized the newspapers both as a space where readers could discuss and debate what they had read and as a public record that offered instruction to the community. As a writer to the *Affiches de Toulouse* publicizing his Literary and Patriotic Society in the town of Gimont explained, the purpose of the literary society he had founded in particular, was to share their work and to inspire "the love of the useful."[93] The letters to the editor serve as a remarkable record of the responses to a growing body of print media by a wide readership. At the same time, the letter writers made claims about what such knowledge was for. The impulse to create and share useful knowledge, as the writer from Gimont emphasized, would become the guiding ethos of the information press.

CHAPTER 4

Popular Science and Public Participation

In November 1783 a letter to the editor appeared in the *Affiches de Toulouse* that likened the significance of the introduction of hot-air balloons to Archimedes's famous lever. "All of Paris, Monsieur, all of France, all of Europe is occupied in this moment by the *Ballon aérostatique*," the letter read, "*physiciens* and non-*physiciens*, everyone celebrates the glory so justly earned by the gentlemen Montgolfier." He described the unique nature of the age in which he lived, when, after two thousand years, "the fruit of [Archimides's] principle had ripened."[1] As the anonymous writer saw it, the Montgolfiers had discovered the natural laws that governed the physical world, and their Montgolfière balloon demonstrated to *physiciens* and laypersons alike the tangible, spectacular outcome of a centuries-long process. The brief letter expressed a fascination with the visual, spectacular outcomes of discovery. By applauding the significance of the innovation, the writer reflected the ways that men and women in the late eighteenth century conceptualized the potential for future breakthroughs.

This chapter investigates letters to the editor concerned with scientific innovation through two case studies: the advent of hot-air balloons and electrical experimentation. Hot-air balloons and electricity were scientific phenomena that built on eighteenth-century innovation in natural philosophy and chemistry. In 1783 and 1784 the first balloons were launched in France, and electricity became the subject of two causes célèbres. In these years, savants turned to the affiches to generate public interest in scientific inquiry by publishing their results. In part, the spectacular and public nature of such experiments invited popular participation, which readers voiced in their letters to the editor. The efforts of experts to engage newspaper readers were successful; over the two-year period of 1783 and 1784, 462 of all of the 1,287 letters published in the affiches concerned the sciences.[2] As the range of participants trying out experiments or offering innovations on their own grew, it became more difficult for savants to control the messages conveyed in the press. After all, the affiches' editors printed side by side the learned and amateur letters regarding balloons or electricity. The writing public wanted not only to learn but also to contribute.

The discussions of popular scientific experimentation in the affiches reflected a widespread optimism that human understanding of natural philosophy would continue to grow in ways that were just becoming clear. The letters concerning ballooning and electricity demonstrated how readers translated this general optimism into specific scientific contexts. The process of empiricism and the purposes of new knowledge guided their correspondence. In tracing their conversations, this chapter is not a study of the mechanics of hot-air balloons or electricity, because the writers themselves did not adhere to shared understandings of the mechanics. Rather, this chapter is an examination of the ways that spectators and practitioners participated in scientific spectacle and inquiry. Ballooning and electricity were vivid illustrations of the ways in which popular scientific conversations situated empiricism as the basis of authority and by doing so destabilized assumptions about who could participate in making new knowledge.

Ballooning Culture

The first hot-air balloon took flight in France on June 4, 1783, in the town of Annonay. The affiches avidly followed the events, dedicating consistent attention to the early experiments and public responses. The Montgolfier brothers, Joseph-Michel and Jacques-Etienne, were the inventors behind the first public balloon launch. Before becoming balloonists, the brothers ran a paper manufactory and maintained keen interests in chemistry and the physical sciences. News of Henry Cavendish's identification and isolation of hydrogen, which he called "inflammable air," and Joseph Priestley's discovery of "dephlogisticated air," or oxygen, in 1774 had traveled to France and sparked the imagination of the early aeronauts. In June 1783 Antoine Lavoisier replicated Cavendish's findings. Inspired by the research into the relative weight of oxygen and hydrogen as compared to common air, Joseph and Etienne devised a hot-air balloon, which they unveiled in June 1783 in a public demonstration.[3] Over a brazier they kindled wool and dry straw doused with alcohol, which filled the balloon above it with hot air. When released from its tethers, the balloon ascended rapidly to 3,000 feet and was carried more than a mile and a half into a vineyard where it landed and caught fire.

By July the Montgolfiers had decamped to Paris, where they continued their demonstrations. Before the summer's end they were faced with competitors, especially Jacques-Alexandre-César Charles, a public lecturer in physics who devised a balloon filled with hydrogen. He was aided by the brothers Anne-Jean and Marie-Noël Robert, who were both royal engineers, and Barthélemy Faujas de Saint-Fond, an enthusiast for natural history who launched the subscription to raise funds for the hydrogen balloon. Each team developed their own approach for the appropriate gas to use and how best to treat the balloon itself so that it would hold the air that filled it. Charles's team, for example, made their balloon of patterned silk, which they soaked in rubber. The Montgolfiers used untreated fabric. While *nouvelles à la main* testified to the fierce competition between the balloonists, the general information press instead adopted what Mi Gyung Kim has called "a hegemonic transcript of the balloon's scientific and public utility."[4] Conflicts between ballooning teams for the most part stayed out of the affiches.

The balloons, which were often called *globes aérostatiques* or *machines aérostatiques* in the press, dominated the letters to the editor in 1783–84. Enthusiasm for the balloons spread quickly. Women adopted the "chapeau au ballon," a new style of hat made of silk gathered into a puffed crown and paired with a wide brim.[5] Other hat styles featured ribbons taken from the balloons and used as trim. Novelty merchants sold miniature balloons for three to eight livres, which enthusiasts could take home and launch in their own homes and gardens.[6] Parades, portraits, and poetry all reflected the excitement and consumer culture that quickly emerged around the new invention.

The affiches were no different. Updates on ballooning appeared in the newspapers frequently. Especially in the early accounts from 1783, such letters consisted of eyewitness testimony of ascents conducted in Paris and its environs. Over time, the impulse in the letters shifted to more regionally oriented efforts to raise funds for a particular city's own project to launch a balloon. As the desire to participate in this phenomenon overtook the country, notables in provincial towns, along with academicians, sponsored projects and solicited donations. Amateurs also took part in the conversation by proffering advice on ways to apply or improve the nascent technology.

The enthusiasm for the balloons was widespread, even as the purposes that writers proposed for the new technology jostled against one another in the press.

Whereas most of the content of the censored affiches was rather restrained, it was not so with ballooning. Writers expressed claims of genius and discovery. They voiced the feeling that they lived at the pinnacle of human achievement. The awe they expressed for ballooning verged on the spiritual.[7] As observers and participants, writers depicting balloon launches could get a bit carried away. The lofty language in their correspondence communicated a confidence in innovation that many perceived as boundless. But in that hope, there was also a tension, for *physiciens* and enthusiasts saw in the balloon differing possibilities.

Aeronauts Engage the Public

Balloons captured the public imagination and influenced letters to the editor throughout the kingdom. The first letters in the provincial press on ballooning appeared anonymously in the *Affiches du Dauphiné* on September 19, 1783. The letter opened confidently, declaring that "all *physiciens* ought to—I think—believe now in the possibility of aerial navigation."[8] The hard work of getting the balloon into the air accomplished, the writer thought it would be rather simple to sort out the steering, takeoff, and landing. The best way to make this happen was to encourage collaboration on such problems through a "society of Savants and Amateurs" who would fund the construction of a globe which the writer agreed to pilot. The letter ended by specifying precisely who the writer was addressing: "Protectors of the sciences, illustrious savants, renowned artists, it is up to you to facilitate and perfect this sublime discovery, which should prove, more than any that has ever done, the power and genius of man."[9] By directly identifying the people whom the writer invited into the proposed society, he or she attempted to delineate a boundary of who should participate in such projects.

During the fall of 1783 and the winter of 1784, the letters on ballooning attempted to reproduce in the mind's eye of the reader the early ballooning demonstrations and to convey how the scientific process worked. The contributions generally conformed to an outline where the writer walked his reader through an experiment. The writer related a series of tests that were modified slightly each time a launch was conducted in order to measure the effect of small changes on the result. The correspondence also emphasized precision: the size of the balloon, the weight of the structure, the exact height the balloon reached, and how long it remained aloft.

Precise measurements, repeated tests, and the sharing of results all invited enthusiasts to follow along.

There were limits to the participation that experts wanted from the public. Barthélemy Faujas Saint-Fond, previously a lawyer and prominent geologist, was fascinated by ballooning and published descriptions of experiments conducted with aerostatic machines in 1783 and 1784. In a letter to the affiches in Grenoble, he outlined a series of experiments conducted on October 15, 1783, which had attracted a large audience with divergent interests: "We had been careful to warn that the experiments that we planned to do with this beautiful machine concerned savants and that the more interesting they were for physics, the less they would interest people attracted by simple curiosity." The balloon, which was piloted by Jean-François Pilâtre de Rozier, ascended into the air to 80 feet, which was the length of the tether, and remained there for four minutes and twenty-five seconds.[10] Two days later, on October 17, the balloonists performed the same trial, but this time the wind did not cooperate, and the balloon would not ascend. The failed launch did not disappoint the other specialists gathered, who generally understood how hot-air balloons worked. Faujas Saint-Fond suggested that "persons practiced in the art of experiments who know how many circumstances they depend upon" were generally satisfied with the results. But the writer derided those who attended simply for the show, whom he characterized as all those who had solicited an invitation with the intention of attending a party. Faujas Saint-Fond indicated in his letter the factors that explained the balloon's rise and fall, but he also articulated his concern that the interests of specialists and of the general public of spectators were rather different. The reading public was swept up in the moment of discovery. Practitioners fashioned themselves in contrast as serious empiricists. By providing detailed measurements, experts communicated how the experiment was conducted so that their results could be replicated and compared. For amateurs, the same letter conveyed an outline for how *physiciens* worked and built on principles of empiricism. While Faujas Saint-Fond took care to explain that some experiments were intended for experts alone, enthusiasts paid little attention to the *physiciens'* efforts to police the boundaries of scientific knowledge.

The third experiment took place on the nineteenth of October with more than two thousand people in attendance. The balloon filled with hot air within five minutes, and Pilâtre de Rozier piloted it 200 feet aloft, where he stayed for six minutes without having to refill the balloon. Next, the aeronauts repeated the same experiment, this time refilling the balloon and ascending to 250 feet, where Pilâtre de Rozier stayed for eight and a half minutes. The wind swept him toward some trees, so he renewed the gas to regain equilibrium, "rising pompously in the air at the sound of public cheering." Then the same experiment was repeated a third time, this time with André Giroud de Villette accompanying Pîlatre de Rozier. The two pilots ascended to the end of the balloon's tether, which measured 324 feet, where they stayed for nine minutes. The writer offered his own calculations; he counted only nine minutes on his watch, while several others affirmed the balloon's position for nearly a quarter of an hour. Finally, a fourth experiment repeated the third experiment, though this time Pîlatre de Rozier was instead accompanied by the marquis d'Arlandes for an eight-and-a-half-minute flight. The letter closed with a statement that "progressive successes of these various experiments are the best answer that can be made to the detractors of this astonishing machine."[11] To see a balloon launch was to be won over by it.

While *physiciens* may have belittled the carnival spirit that animated the balloon launches, the public participation in ballooning had a profound impact on those gathered. Balloon launches invited an audience made up of all orders. The potential for celebration and upheaval that accompanied the success or failure of a launch has been read by historians as a reflection of social tensions simmering in urban centers in the 1780s, as violence erupted at some failed balloon launches.[12] While the evidence in the affiches does not suggest that ballooning served as a rejection of social stratification or as a precursor of revolutionary crowd action, the letters to the editor do make clear that ballooning garnered the enthusiasm of many who responded personally to the successes and failures of the launches. The public launches and the letters to the information press by *physiciens* captured the interest of many spectators who began to envision experiments of their own.

Provincial Ballooning and Local Knowledge Production

Over time, letters on balloons departed from the early pattern of big demonstrations made by famous aeronauts and instead focused on new goals: launching similar demonstrations in one's own town; improving the technology behind the *globes aérostatiques*; or using the public interest in balloons to advertise one's own scientific endeavors. Letters about bringing balloons to provincial centers aimed to share the breakthroughs that *physiciens* and spectators had witnessed around the capital with a provincial audience. The campaigns for provincial balloons relied on collaboration with regional academies and other learned societies interested in the sciences. In one such case, a writer to the *Affiches d'Angers* expressed disappointment at the lack of support for bringing a balloon to Angers, where despite "the universal enthusiasm inspired by Monsieurs Montgolfier and their imitators, I was distressed to see the kind of immobility of my compatriots, citizens like me of a city where all the sciences have been taught for more than three centuries." The writer also underscored that Angers was a town where scientific inquiry was well established, even if his campaign for a balloon launch had thus far proven unsuccessful among people like him.[13] Large-scale balloon experiments were captivating but expensive endeavors that required substantial resources. In provincial centers, funding a hot-air balloon of their own communicated both a town's prestige and its commitment to the sciences.

Raising funds to support the building of balloons throughout France grew in the press and relied on learned local partners. In Dijon, one writer solicited subscriptions for an aerostat in Burgundy, which the local academy was cosponsoring. The writer took the public response to his call for contributions as a sign of "the general interest this project has caused among our fellow citizens." The first sixty subscription tickets had sold so quickly that the writer expressed confidence in the public understanding and support for "the importance of this Experiment."[14] The letter specified that the total cost of such a balloon was 7,000 livres, and concluded with a brief note that the subscription would remain open until all the costs were covered. A similar style of letter concerning subscriptions for a balloon in the town of Angers appeared in February, despite the challenges fundraisers there had faced the previous year.[15] Follow-up reports on fundraising efforts were published in the subsequent months.

The correspondence in the affiches situated provincial centers as sites of innovation. In the case of Dijon, a letter appeared just three weeks after the initial call for donations to update readers on the balloon under construction by the academy. The writer expected the balloon, which would measure 27 feet in diameter and carry two passengers, to be ready within two weeks' time. The work of early aeronauts such as the Montgolfiers, Charles, and Pilatre de Rozier had "stirred all minds, even in the provinces," spurring the construction of balloons and the continued experimentation that such an apparatus made possible.[16] In Nancy balloon experiments conducted by a Professor Nicolas led one writer to declare that "each province has its own Montgolfier, and Lorraine like any other wants to launch its own Balloon."[17] Those who wrote to their local affiches with ballooning updates emphasized the innovators everywhere in the kingdom.

The desire to have one's local city launch a balloon reflected the more widespread sentiment among provincial notables that scientific achievement and local esteem were linked. Natural philosophers enjoyed a rising prestige in the eighteenth century, as noblemen set up private laboratories in their homes, and natural philosophy became a topic of worldly conversation in salons.[18] Perhaps the most influential institutions in increasing the stature of scientific inquiry were the provincial academies. While the academies dated to the seventeenth century, their role in provincial intellectual and cultural life intensified after 1750, when they became a central site for reviving local pride and strengthening efforts to spread knowledge as widely as possible. As the academies dedicated newfound attention to the sciences, the reputation of such fields rose. Provincial academicians were increasingly seen as reform-minded men who were eager to promote change and share knowledge.[19]

As the participants in provincial intellectual life expanded, they devised new social practices to communicate with one another. A high proportion of provincial notables, ranging from the clergy to the nobility, participated in academic activity. United by manners and uniform practices that were shared by learned societies throughout the kingdom, the academies formed social ties with one another, even as they defended their particular organization's autonomy. This new intellectual culture of *académisme* in the provinces was aided by the influence of intendants, governors, and church officials such as bishops, who were able to organize local resources and stimulate the political support of Paris.[20] Since most provincial centers had just one, the provincial academy was unique for its organization, which brought together all intellectuals in the region into one circle.

The influence of new social ties on scientific knowledge was evident in the letters in the affiches. For example, in a letter to the *Journal de Lyon* describing the Montgolfiers' first demonstration of a balloon launch in their city, the writer gave particular attention to the sponsors who had brought the event to Lyon: the provincial academy and Jacques de Flesselles, the intendant of Lyon.[21] He described Flesselles as a man who was "always zealous for what he can contribute to the good of the province or the progress of the sciences and arts."[22] While the case of Flesselles's involvement is one particularly vivid example, the academies depended on the sponsorship and at times the intervention of state and church officials to sustain their activities.[23]

The academies also influenced the discussions of natural philosophy for inhabitants of the provinces who were not members, especially through the affiches and essay competitions. Between 1670 and 1793, provincial academies held at least two thousand essay competitions known as *concours*, which were open to all. The essay prize competitions are well known for launching the careers of aspiring men of letters such as Jean-Jacques Rousseau, the Abbé Grégoire, Pierre Bertholon de Saint-Lazare, Antoine

Lavoisier, and Jean-Paul Marat. Yet the *concours* invited submissions that were anonymized and reviewed on the merits of their argument, so the contestants included savants but also more marginalized figures who were looking for a way to participate in the world of letters. The questions posed in the *concours* of the 1770s and 1780s were concerned with improvement that relied on expertise in engineering, medicine, or natural philosophy.[24] The affiches shared the preoccupation with improvement and useful knowledge that could be shared as widely as possible. On occasion, they published the very questions posed by the *concours*.[25] By publishing letters to the editor that bridged the academy and the provincial readers outside of it, the information press fostered social practices of information sharing. Between the affiches, the *concours*, the culture of *académisme*, and the support of projects such as hot-air balloons, scientific culture in the provinces was vibrant and participatory.

The Balloon as Laboratory

In their efforts to participate in the burgeoning scientific culture in the provinces, inventors billed their balloons as floating laboratories. Letters to the editor charted the spread of ballooning culture throughout the kingdom, but they also educated readers through technical descriptions of the balloons and detailed records of their flights. Writers characterized the *Machine aérostatique* as a space for observation and experimentation ideal for investigations into the buildup of electricity and condensation that produced rain, as well as various other experiments on clouds. They sent animals aloft and took barometric readings.[26] Writers expressed their preoccupation with the possibilities in nascent innovation in a manner that underscored their intellectual and emotional responses.

The records of the aeronauts' flights conveyed that each balloon flight was an experiment in itself. Letters by participants in such voyages brought firsthand accounts of the thrill of flight and of the scientific potential that balloons held. Writers profiled the aeronauts, giving fellow readers a glimpse of the innovators in action. Giroud de Villette accompanied Pîlatre de Rozier on his October 19 experiment and sent his observations to the *Journal de Paris*; the *Affiches du Dauphiné* soon reprinted the letter. Once they were airborne, Giroud de Villette surveyed the city below them: "As I turned around, I made out the boulevards from the gate of Porte Saint-Antoine to that of Saint-Martin, all covered with people, which seemed to me to form an elongated bed of various flowers." The Butte de Montmartre appeared to be less than half the height of the balloon; Giroud de Villette then looked into the distance toward the outlying suburbs, where he easily identified Neuilly, Saint-Cloud, Issy, Ivry, Charenton, Choisy, and perhaps Corbeil in a light fog. This bird's-eye view of Paris not only instilled wonder in the writer but also focused his attention on the balloon's utility that he believed in time they would perfect. He suggested that from the vantage point of the balloon, war could be revolutionized, for the balloon was relatively affordable, and it would enable the army to identify the enemy's position, maneuvers, and marches and to convey signals to one's allied troops.[27] He recommended that balloons could be effective over sea too.

While in some letters the balloon's flight was the extent of the experiment, letters such as this one describing a flight over Paris suggested the potential utility the balloons could serve. An anonymous writer to the paper in Metz suggested powering a balloon with electricity.[28] Some with more interest in recent discoveries in chemistry used their letters to compare the weights of various gases and offer their suggestions on how lighter gases might affect the balloon's flight. For example, M. Proust wrote to the editor of the *Affiches d'Angers* to invite readers to his experiments on various forms of gas and their effect on balloons launched from the local chateau's courtyard.[29] Whether as an arm of military surveillance or, as other writers suggested, as a laboratory for meteorological observation and chemical experimentation, balloons were understood as both a symbol and a site of future innovation.

For their part, writers noted "a prodigious quantity" of letters on the subject of balloons asking for more information on how they worked and what adjustments would improve them. In one such letter, the writer recommended a brochure that covered ballooning topics while they waited for more ballooning reports to appear in the newspaper.[30] The confluence of newspaper content with literature on ballooning was further evident in cross-references made by the editors and by letter writers to one another. Editorial notes, references, and reproductions underscored the expanding body of research that *physiciens* and amateurs alike generated in the early years of the balloon.

Balloonomania

The correspondence from the early balloonists and other savants was so successful in building public engagement that enthusiasts began to write back via the affiches. The suggestions writers submitted regarding further improvements to balloons conveyed both the enthusiasm they felt for innovation and the limits of their own scientific understanding. As writers suggested adjustments, they made clear that they did not understand precisely how the balloons worked. Some letters recommended different materials be used to construct the balloon, or that the balloon's power source be modified. One such submission in the *Affiches de Toulouse* described a balloon made of paper he had witnessed in Auch.[31] Inspired by the *physiciens'* letters, writers offered ideas of their own about how to improve on the balloon.

Letters concerning navigation highlighted one of the most predominant problems that the early aeronauts faced: they had little ability to steer the balloons once they were in the air, leaving them at the mercy of the wind. The challenge of steering continued to plague balloonists throughout the nineteenth century. During the Franco-Prussian War, French military forces in Paris would use balloons for reconnaissance and communication with forces outside the besieged capital. Unable to control the steering of the balloons, they were swept off course by the wind, hampering French strategic efforts.[32] A reprinted letter that appeared in the *Affiches du Dauphiné* identified this common problem: "All the attention of savants and artists seems to turn to the art of directing the Aerostatic Machine." The writer suggested, why not harness birds, as one would harness horses or oxen on land? He had even worked out the finer points that one would need to address in order to bring this idea to fruition: First, find the species of bird that would be the best for such a task. Second, train the birds to pull the balloon. Third, devise how to best harness the birds for the takeoff and landing. Fourth and finally, pinpoint the place on the balloon or the basket to affix the harness so that it would not tip the whole apparatus over.[33] Having read about a challenge faced by balloonists, the writer sought to participate in working out a solution. The editors may have printed the eccentric letter for amusement, but the letter's presence in the affiches also showed that spectators without specialized knowledge actively processed the hot-air balloon launches they observed.

In a similar manner, a frequent writer to the *Affiches du Poitou* was motivated by the puzzle of aerial navigation and the dramatic aerostatic experiments he had seen in the environs of Poitiers. He proposed modeling the shape of the balloon after a fish, since fish could easily move up and down in elevation, as well as manage horizontal motion and steering with ease. He suggested that flaps attached to the balloon with little pivots or hinges would help with steering. After all, he remarked, there were aquatic birds, and the difference between flying and swimming was not so great.[34] The writer of this particular letter was a lawyer and minor official who eagerly weighed in with his opinions in letters to the editor on agriculture, natural philosophy, and reform over more than a decade. By explaining how they had come to their suggestions, amateurs showed the space between their approaches and those of savants. Even spectators who had not mastered the chemistry and physics that made flight possible were nevertheless fascinated by ballooning. They wanted to participate, and the editors of the affiches printed their reflections. The solutions that writers such as these suggested were esoteric additions that the editors may have published purely for entertainment, but their presence also signaled to readers the range of perspectives the affiches would publish.

In their efforts to puzzle out how the balloons worked and how to guide their flight, writers adopted the metaphor of a machine. Some of the writers who shared their ideas for flying machines acknowledged the whimsical nature of their letters, as did a certain J. R. D. who confided that if the affiches in Montpellier published his letter, he would take it as a signal that his work was not an "entirely chimerical idea." Wishing to contribute something to the discovery of hot-air balloons, the writer proposed a balloon with an internal mechanism like a clock, which would power wings in unison. The letter included a multistep explanation where the author described the role of spokes and gears in moving the wings he would affix to his flying machine.[35] In this case, the writer had attempted to translate his technical know-how of clocks to the popular interest in ballooning. In their enthusiasm for new balloon models and applications, writers tried out hypotheses that pushed against what was possible.

Finally, letters on balloons used the public interest in spectacle to lead readers to advertisements for other inventions. One man opened his letter with a declaration of how wonderful it was to live in an age of flying machines, but the body of his letter was concerned with his own contraption—shoes that enabled him to walk across water. He wrote to publicize his upcoming demonstration on the Seine from Pont Neuf to Pont Royal. Through the publication of his letter to the editor, he solicited donations that would help him defray the cost of his travel to Paris, which the newspaper agreed to collect and document on the writer's behalf. The letter was republished in the *Affiches des Trois-Évêchés et Lorraine*. The public responded enthusiastically, and the *Journal* collected 3,243 louis in all. Even the marquis de Lafayette donated to the experiment.[36] When it was revealed that such a shoe did not exist, the paper donated the funds to charity instead; the demonstration never took place. As this thinly veiled ad for a bogus invention illustrated, the affiches were used by some contributors as a marketplace where both goods and ideas circulated before reader-consumers.[37] However, most letter writers sold nothing at all. For most participants in the press, ballooning functioned as a way to participate in an ongoing debate about questions that remained unsettled.

Not all of the letters on flight were lofty portrayals. One of the first letters to the editor concerning balloons made the argument that ballooning led to madness. By far the most widely reprinted letter on the subject of ballooning was originally written to the *Journal de Paris* and reappeared in the affiches of Angers, Toulouse, Poitiers, Grenoble, and Metz in October 1783.[38] Following the style of a Voltairian satire, the anonymous letter chronicled the writer's efforts to save his uncle who had grown obsessed with ballooning. His uncle had become "occupied, like all people with the métier of this accursed invention of the Aerostatic Balloon, whose authors God wishes to confound." He recounted how he constantly told his uncle to leave balloons alone, for innovators and novelties were always dangerous. The letter related an argument between the uncle and a fellow *physicien* about the uncle's plans for his own balloon. After the spat, the uncle fell ill and then fled, as the writer put it, "like a bird." The nephew's letter ended with a physical description of his uncle who had escaped in a state of undress, wearing his dressing gown and only one shoe.

Letters on ballooning topics dominated the newspaper page at this time, and the popular letter about a disturbed uncle's plans for an aerostat of his own fit within that larger trend. The letters about him were like stories in an epistolary novel of sorts that appeared in serial installments in the papers. The story may well have been for sheer entertainment; its adaptation of the epistolary form and the tone of satire likely resonated with contemporary readers. Satirical prints, plays, and verses from this period poked fun at a set of amateurs who used balloons to fly away from life's troubles.[39] The story of the balloonist uncle was especially dramatic in comparison even to letters on the spectacle of ballooning. Whatever the aims of the particular writer, the story served as a counterbalance to the optimistic narrative that ballooning often generated. This negative critique of innovation stressed the destabilizing force that technological change could render and underscored the ambivalence members of the public could harbor about such changes.

Over the *longue durée* of the affiches, letter writers privileged incremental and practical improvements, but even for them, the advent of balloons represented a paradigm shift. The kinds of comments that writers made on witnessing these balloons in flight focused on the spectacular, sublime experience. Such letters articulated a veritable balloonomania—the *globes aérostatiques* were all that anyone could talk about, dream about, think about. The letter with which this chapter opened sums up the ways eighteenth-century readers contextualized this innovation, as the fruition of work some two millennia in the making. The accomplishment of flight was a breakthrough, and the letters to the editor about this feat communicated a momentousness that was rather unusual for letters published in the information press.

Through the advice for further improvements, the suggestions for practical applications, and the advertisements of related goods, published correspondence on balloons aligned with the goals of letters to the editor more generally. The desire to put balloons to use appeared within the first few months of their existence, and the emphasis on utility persisted. As with many of the debates in the press, the correspondence on ballooning provided a space that made room for experts and amateurs alike. Writers with expertise in ballooning commented repeatedly in the press that they wrote to other *physiciens* and savants, and they tried to set clear boundaries around who their work was for. And yet, the affiches published letters from enthusiasts who contested the savants' ideas. No longer content to witness the launches and follow along in the press, writers participated in the debates and challenged the *physiciens'* exclusive hold on the topic. As writers' perspectives pushed against one another on the newspaper page, the letters to the editor became a field of contestation.

Electricity and Empiricism

The interest in scientific spectacle, especially where uncertainty persisted, expanded in the affiches beyond ballooning to electricity. Popular interest in electricity dated back at least to the invention of the Leyden jar in 1745, which allowed the experimenter to accumulate an electric charge that they could then release at will and all at once. The visible and dramatic nature of electrical experiments allowed observers to see and feel the forces at work. Yet *physiciens* struggled to explain precisely what was going on. Even among experts such as Benjamin Franklin or Jean-Antoine Nollet, causal explanations for electricity were troubled by gaps, uncertainty, and lack of consensus.

Electrical debates turned around not merely the nature of electricity but especially around its usefulness. It was in disputes over the uses of electricity that, as Larry Stewart has suggested, "philosophical controversies explicitly invited a public adjudication."[40] Because electricity was so confounding to explanation, and because its utility held such promise, it continued to be a subject of scientific and popular fascination in a range of learned and popular print matter well into the nineteenth century.[41] The particular resonance of electrical processes in letters to the editor in 1783 and 1784 reflected these long-standing trends, but they were also especially timely, as they coincided with two notorious incidents: a legal trial over a lightning rod in 1783 and the investigations of Franz Mesmer in 1784.

Electricity became the subject of protracted and widespread discussion in the 1780s, in part because of the legal battle over a lightning rod in the small town of Saint-Omer. In 1780 the amateur *physicien* Charles Dominique de Vissery de Bois-Valé installed a lightning rod on his chimney, but the grounding tube extended over the roof and down the wall of his neighbor's home. What began as a local dispute over private property and the placement of the lightning rod became a veritable cause célèbre that culminated in the summer of 1783 with the decision of the Conseil provincial et supérieur d'Artois, the court of last appeal in the province.[42] Vissery's case was argued by the lawyer and *physicien* Antoine-Joseph Buissart and his young assistant, Maximilien Robespierre.[43] In the appeal before the Conseil d'Artois, Robespierre set aside theoretical explanations of electricity and dismissed the need to consult experts. Instead, he argued that the judges could use their own experience to observe the self-evident facts before them; the court decided in favor of his client.[44]

The particulars of Vissery's case and discussions of lightning rods appeared in newspapers throughout his legal battle from 1780 through 1783, including the *Mercure de France*, the *Journal de Luxembourg*, the *Journal de Paris*, and the *Affiches de Flandres*. Antoine-Joseph Buissart, a fellow *physicien* and lawyer for Vissery, published two letters in the *Affiches de Flandres* under the pseudonym Nostradamus.[45] And Robespierre's plea was published and sold in Arras and Paris; advertisements and reviews for the publication appeared in the *Mercure de France*, the *Journal encyclopédique*, and *L'Année littéraire*.[46] Vissery's case raised interest in lightning rods and all manner of discussions about how electricity worked. The coverage of the affair in the provincial and Parisian press sustained those conversations.

In 1784 the two royal investigations into mesmerism likewise inspired coverage in the press. Two commissions organized to investigate Mesmer's work were composed of prominent savants and public figures, including Benjamin Franklin, Antoine Lavoisier, Jean-Sylvain Bailly, Antoine Laurent de Jussieu, and Pierre-Isaac Poissonnier. Up until that point, Mesmer's conceptualization of animal magnetic fluids was understood as plausible because it relied on an idea that had guided early electrical experimentation: that electricity was communicated through an imponderable fluid. Once again, the possibility and uncertainty surrounding electrical communication fostered discussions in the press.

Campaigns for the Lightning Rod

Letters concerning electricity differed from the published correspondence on ballooning in key ways. Electricity did not foster the frequent attention in the affiches that ballooning did in 1783 and 1784. But the correspondence on electricity shared the preoccupation with usefulness that conversations regarding balloons possessed. Letters on lightning were occupied first with the observation of natural phenomena, and then with the possibility of directing electrical power. Their language focused on comprehending natural laws, the knowledge of which could ameliorate conditions in the countryside. Such letters touched profoundly on the theme of harnessing nature to suit the needs of humanity.

To begin with, electricity in the form of lightning held a lethal power over communities. An anonymous writer shared one particularly vivid account from Beaumont-de-Lomagne with the *Affiches de Toulouse* on the lightning storm that had passed through the town that week. Without warning, the calm night vanished as "the sky soon disappeared under thick clouds: the thunder scattered all over our horizon, announcing itself with a dreadful noise, its bursts multiplied and, coming from different places at the same time, produced a dissonance and a crash so frightful that they could only give us an idea of the dissolution of the whole world." As the storm shrouded the town with fear, lightning struck in two places. First, the parish bell tower was hit, and the church and those inside it were enveloped in smoke. A second later, lightning reached the other end of town, striking an artisan's home. Although the artisan was hit, he somehow survived. Aside from the holes bored in his hat and the singed hair on his leg, he emerged relatively unscathed from what the writer assumed would have been a fatal incident. The man's remarkable survival was the reason the writer sent a letter to the paper, since "journalists eagerly collect these macabre epochs, the public discusses them with tenderness," and he wished to honor humanity by sharing it.[47] While this particular writer emphasized the danger, chaos, and lack of control to which lightning reduced the countryside, other writers emphasized that such vulnerability need not be the case.

Calls to study and redirect lightning were sometimes made at the expense of those they claimed to help. In his contribution to the *Affiches de Troyes*, a certain M. Joly explained that he wrote his letter so that a phenomenon that was so terrible for the common person, whom he described as *le vul-gaire*, might be explained and given order. As chapter 5 will show, peasants were often described in letters to the editor as sympathetic figures who were essential to France, but in the correspondence on natural philosophy, writers used the peasantry as a foil against which savants could demonstrate their own authority.

Joly's letter to the editor conceptualized lightning as only one of electricity's many manifestations. He explained, "Today *lumières* and sound philosophy prevail almost everywhere; today the famous experiments of Leyden and Marly-la-Ville leave no doubt that thunder is in the hands of nature, that electricity is in ours, and that both proceed from the same principle." Joly asserted that electricity now rested in the hands of men, who, having unpacked the principles of electricity through experiments, could manipulate it to serve their own purposes. Summarizing the findings of famous experiments and demonstrations, he explained simply that when iron was isolated and exposed in the open air it would attract lightning, as all elevated bodies would. And thunder "consists only of a wave in the air." Joly argued that the thorough investigations of *physiciens*, especially in "a century as enlightened [*éclairé*] as ours, where men are natural observers," enabled examination of electrical phenomena more and more closely. His own study of lightning had convinced him that it was only an effect of general laws. His argument relied on the general premise that while the effect of lightning could be destructive, the universe as a whole tended toward its own preservation even if the particular physical processes for that maintenance were unclear to the natural philosopher. What was important was the observation of phenomena by the senses. His style of thinking was emblematic of treatises on electricity by even its most well-received proponents such as Benjamin Franklin and Buissart.

Rather than fearing the forces that generated it, Joly argued the storm needed to be understood, and lightning was the manifestation by which one witnessed "the presence of a cloud in action." He juxtaposed his causal explanation of general principles with a description of the powerful force of the storm: "The imposing and majestic sound that resounds in the air, these sparkling furrows piercing the breast of a dark cloud, this confused mixture of light and darkness, fire and water." He argued that observation ought to elevate the observer's thoughts and feelings to the wonders of nature, for fear of lighting need not bring down one's soul. Furthermore, he claimed that it was not for himself that he felt compelled to explain such events, but rather for the peasantry who feared lightning and attributed it to supernatural causes. He recommend the use of lightning rods, especially on churches.[48] The social juxtaposition between his own understanding and his description of the perspective of the peasantry highlighted that Joly's claims to knowledge rested on exclusion. At the same time, he identified a shared concern, because fires started by lighting and requests for donations for those who were injured or reduced to homelessness by them were the basis of letters to the editor throughout France. The local responses to fire are discussed at greater length in chapter 6. Letters to the editor that proposed lightning rods underscored the practical impulse that guided the information press.

Writers worked out the problem of property damage caused by lightning in the affiches, because lightning was understood as a public problem. Eighteenth-century debates on the safety and effectiveness of lightning rods became collective concerns in part because they were installed on structures that were both highly visible and also seen as belonging to the community, such as churches, powder magazines, and other public buildings.[49] In the affiches in Montpellier, a writer described a lightning strike on the parish church of Saint-Denis, documenting the injuries people had suffered and the damage to the structure. The writer recommended that the church invest in a lightning rod from the Abbé Bertholon, a *"physicien* of the first merit." He also cautioned readers not to ring the church bells in an effort to dispel thunderclouds, as the risk of the bell falling and injuring someone was significant. A "multitude of observations" made the writer confident that ringing the bells to deter lightning did not work.[50] In their efforts to shift attitudes toward lightning, writers underscored the efficacy of prevention techniques. Situating their campaigns for the lightning rod in the affiches underscored the public utility that editors and letter writers articulated for the newspapers.

The effort to offer convincing explanations that would reform popular practice was evident in the press even before 1783. In a letter to the paper in Dijon, the chemist and future revolutionary Louis-Bernard Guyton de Morveau underscored that examples had the most profound influence on the general opinion, because they were perceptible and prompt. Knowing their influence, he argued the newspapers should publish examples, as they could serve to establish useful facts.[51] Guyton's preoccupation with usefulness in the press showed how *physiciens* sought to reformulate popular beliefs in their effort to win over opinion in favor of lightning rods. Having just overseen the construction of a lightning rod on the Notre-Dame church in Bourg-en-Bresse, he spoke with experience about the efforts under way to protect churches in the region. He also cited similar efforts documented by Professor Toaldo, who had directed lightning rod construction in Venice and Padua the previous year. Lightning rods in France, as elsewhere in Europe, were instrumental in shifting public opinion over to "the Enlightenment ideal of a law-obeying universe."[52] Advocates of the lightning rod in France spoke of electricity in terms of the laws that nature obeyed, and they emphasized that such laws were visible to the untrained observer.

In the letters advocating for lightning rods in the 1780s, writers combined their justifications for them as a means of preventing fire and injury, with discussions of the merits of spreading knowledge about lightning's causes. Buissart's letter to the affiches reflected these principles. He noted comparative studies in Germany on the effectiveness of lightning rods and Benjamin Franklin's experiments to bolster his claims. Citing Franklin's findings, he asserted that lightning generally fell on church steeples, which had iron crosses, or on the weathervanes of houses. Tall oak and fir trees were also frequently hit, but Buissart noted that the lightning tended to find metals. As he saw it, the best way to avoid lightning strikes was to plant a tall tree on the easternmost edge of each town and affix rods to draw the lightning to the tree rather than to other tall edifices in the vicinity.[53] Writers such as Buissart preoccupied themselves with explaining natural laws in order to inform the reader and improve daily life in the countryside. Their focus on usefulness was underscored by the detailed suggestions for practical implementation in their letters and their sense that education via the information press would make a difference.

Trials with Electricity

Letter writers also documented the uses to which they put electricity in their everyday lives. Practitioners argued for the health benefits of electric shocks, especially for those suffering from paralysis and epilepsy. Medical applications of electricity were proposed as early as the 1750s, though results from such treatments were considered inconclusive. Jean-Antoine Nollet thought electrical treatments would improve circulation and in so doing purge disease from the body.[54] He implemented a systematic trial of electrical treatment for paralyzed soldiers at the Hôpital des Invalides but ultimately found the results of his efforts to be "too uncertain to be worth mentioning."[55] Franklin hypothesized that electrical shocks could treat paralysis and possibly insanity.[56] While claims about the efficacy of electrical cures remained cautious in academic contexts, by the 1770s electrical machines were widely available. Traveling practitioners offered public demonstrations and treatments in consumers' homes. Even John Wesley, the founder of Methodism, used electricity as a tool for healing in his pursuit to combine medicine and moral instruction.[57] By the 1780s the variety of medical electrical instruments had grown affordable and specialized. In an effort to convey electrical fluid to the appropriate part of the body, new tools were produced for ailments including toothaches, eye problems, rheumatism, tumors, and deafness. In the marketplace, electrical experimentation grew in popularity, even as academics maintained skepticism in their reports.

In the information press, letter writers put electrical instruments to use in their own homes and experimental cabinets. Letters on the subject of electricity came from amateurs who tested properties of electricity that they had witnessed in demonstrations or read about in periodicals. In his letter to the editor of the *Affiches de Franche-Comté*, Louis Filiol de Raimond acknowledged he was neither a doctor nor a *physicien*. In fact, he managed the post office in Besançon. Nevertheless, he had read about electrical experimentation and saw himself as sufficiently informed to run his own experiments at home. His test subject was his much beloved cat Angora, who had recently begun to suffer from epilepsy. By rubbing the cat's fur against the grain, he produced electric sparks in such a great quantity that he said the poor animal looked as if she were on fire. He then recorded her responses to the treatment, which he found to be consistent with the findings of state *physiciens* and faculty doctors whose published work he had read. He noted she experienced no loss of consciousness or foaming, but her coat bristled, and she moved, with an "extreme vivacity," around the room for a half hour. Her owner feared she might injure herself in her agitated activity, but he reported that she calmed down and became more affectionate than ever. Three months later, she had presented no epileptic symptoms whatsoever. He concluded his letter with the request that other readers evaluate his results, which he left to *physiciens* in particular to examine. Not only did this amateur lay out each step of his experiment and his findings, but he also submitted it to the newspaper so that his findings could be judged by a community of experts. His letter was reprinted in the *Affiches du Dauphiné* and the *Affiches de Toulouse* in the following weeks.[58]

Contributions that documented electrical experiments were organized around empirical practice that yielded a result one could see or feel. Amateurs such as Angora's owner introduced electricity as a stimulus and recorded the results. His letter and other contributions by amateurs adopted a step-by-step, detailed approach, and they concluded with the request that the public conduct similar experiments and report back on their findings. Letters to the editor thus offer new and surprising evidence of how widespread empirical epistemologies were. Having read about documented experimental procedures by savants, the writing public adapted scientific methods for their own purposes.

Some writers took their experiments a step further and tried out their ideas on human subjects. Electrical demonstrations such as the "electric kiss" were popular parlor games in late eighteenth-century France. In the electric kiss, a woman stood on an insulated platform, where she was surreptitiously connected to a charge like a Leyden jar. One of the men in the audience was then invited to kiss the woman, eliciting a spark between their lips.[59] The newspapers published letters from electrical enthusiasts who tried out similar experiments on their friends in their homes or in electrical cabinets, like those around the Palais-Royal in Paris. One such enthusiast was Jean-Louis Carra, a future revolutionary inspired by aerostatic inventions and mesmeric fluids.[60]

Jean-Louis Carra submitted to the newspaper his findings from an electrical experiment that he had conducted. In his letter, he explained the basic logistics of the experiment as follows: he placed the subject on a stool that wouldn't conduct electricity, then connected him to a metal rod attached to an electrical machine, and when the person was electrified, Carra placed his hands over the person's clothing to feel the electricity. Noting what both he and his subject felt, he then modified the experiment to see what effect small changes would generate. For instance, he noted that when he placed sulfur rods in his jacket, the number and intensity of sparks between himself and his subject increased dramatically. Furthermore, by running his hands along the person's body, he produced "a rolling fire of electricity" that caused the subject to break out in a sweat. Rather than producing large sparks, he asserted that the electrical atmospheres divided into small concussions or vibrations that reacted inside the body of the person, and caused the perspiration he observed. Then Carra tried out the same experiment on a new subject and reported how she tolerated the same process. A third person then took his turn. Carra noted that all of his volunteers were in good health, and he had not tried out his experiment on anyone ill. He ended his letter by asking the public to help verify his results: "I leave it to the *amateurs* to repeat and vary these experiments."[61] The appeal to other practitioners to replicate their findings was a common refrain in the amateur experimenters' letters. Carra's effort to become a *physicien* relied on his experiments, but also on his correspondence with the press and his participation in academic *concours* on ballooning.

Other amateur writers ran electrical experiments of serious consequence. A M. Sans, who specified that he was not a doctor, explained his medical application of electricity in his "cabinet électrique," which he found to be particularly effective in eradicating epilepsy in children. He corroborated his assertions with the results of a recent demonstration at Versailles on nineteen young subjects, and he reported the procedure had stopped their seizures. His treatment, he assured the public, was safe and free of any sparks or shocks. He was confident that the amount of electricity was so gentle and the treatment so easy that the least educated mother could use it to cure her child. Harnessing the power of electricity, he pitched his treatment for a common childhood ailment "to the good of humanity."[62] Depicting his process as safe, effective, and fast-acting, he hoped to expand his remedy in neighborhoods throughout the city in a number of cabinets, which he estimated could save a tenth of the children who would otherwise perish from epilepsy. Sans's *cabinet électrique* attempted to adapt a new technological innovation to fit a social need.

The style and tone employed by these letter writers specified the limits of their knowledge, but they did not surrender the use of electricity to the experts. Instead, such writers took part in experimentation, outlining for their fellow readers the problems they faced, the treatment they applied, and the results they gathered. In the case of Carra, he even repeated the experiment with multiple subjects to track the effects. Writers also endeavored to replicate their findings by asking other readers to repeat the experiments on their own and report back to the affiches.

The emphasis on experimentation and tactile experience in their correspondence served to validate, and in other cases to discredit, the claims of fellow experimenters in the press. For example, a M. Jal de Muntel wrote a letter critiquing a book that the Abbé Pierre Bertholon de Saint-Lazare, a *physicien* and academician, had published on electricity. He questioned how Bertholon could make claims about electrifying spaces as large as the Sainte-Geneviève gardens, or that an electric current could kill all the aphids and caterpillars in a garden.[63] Finding Bertholon's book too outrageous to be believed, he tried to discredit the abbé in the press by suggesting the *physicien* thought his readers too naive to discern the falsehoods in his book. He found the proof that the experiments had worked unsatisfactory, and he doubted whether Bertholon had actually conducted the experiments. Jal de Muntel wanted evidence, not lofty assertions designed for a credulous public: "We are no longer in the time of Pythagoras," he wrote. "'Magister dixit' has no place in physics." He juxtaposed the ideas presented in Bertholon's work with a vision of how "true *physiciens*" would present evidence: "All those who are interested in the propagation of the sciences cannot protect too much the simple and prejudiced readers against an infinity of assertions devoid of proof, which can contribute only to giving false notions and maintaining them in error."[64] The writer indignantly argued that it was not enough to take the word of a well-known figure; instead, concrete evidence was needed for an author to be believed. Jal de Muntel's blustery letter reflected a prevalent role that *physiciens* articulated for themselves in the press as the arbiters of scientific knowledge. For them, true *physiciens* were considered responsible not only for presenting evidence for the sake of empiricism but also for guiding the way the public would interpret their findings. Letters on electricity—whether anchored in a lightning rod, as medical treatment, or as the stimulus in an experiment—addressed directly how the public would make sense of electric forces. Writers expressed a responsibility to explain natural phenomena in a clear way that adhered to a cause-and-effect relationship, and to protect credulous readers.

Discussions of electricity characterized the optimism of the age, by which electricity was transported from the hands of nature to the hands of men, as Joly put it. Such power could be channeled, mitigating the damage and uncertainty it had previously rendered on the countryside. Rather than leaving it at that, though, practitioners looked for ways to better understand electricity and to put it to use. In this way, electrical experiments became a way for amateurs and enthusiasts to understand natural laws for themselves. The writers were preoccupied with figuring out how things worked and ensuring that information was shared so that others could test their findings. To their credit, the principle of replicable findings remains essential to a good experiment today. Whereas letters to the editor on ballooning expressed that the flight was a triumph in and of itself, electricity was applied. Whether by grounding lightning through rods that protected churches, businesses, and homes, or by using electric currents as a medical treatment, the letters about electricity focused on improving the conditions of daily life.

The letters to the editor on ballooning and electricity revealed the widespread growth in scientific culture. The increased esteem that the sciences enjoyed in the 1780s was the result of a decades-long process that the provincial academies, supported by state officials and church leaders, had accelerated. Their success bolstered the reputations of scientific practitioners. The burgeoning correspondence in the affiches show that by the 1780s, associating oneself with endeavors in the sciences was a way to take part in such changes, increasing one's prestige in the process. In their letters to the editor, writers made claims that they were both enlightened and philanthropic. Their correspondence revealed that claims of participation in the Enlightenment were also a reflection of struggles over exclusion, expertise, and empiricism.

In their efforts to establish authority, writers focused in part on who was eligible to write on scientific subject matter. Letter writers who discussed topics related to ballooning and electricity differed from the general population of letter writers. In the full corpus of letters to the editor studied in this book, 50.2 percent of letters were signed, and 30.4 percent were published with no signature. Those who wrote on the sciences were less likely than the average letter writer to publish anonymously. Among the letters published in 1783–84 on scientific subject matter, authors identified themselves in 63.4 percent of those letters.[65] Furthermore, with the exception of just one *comtesse* who contributed a letter on a local ballooning demonstration, men wrote all of the signed letters. Educated practitioners also figured prominently within this group.

While the writers who discussed ballooning and electricity tended to represent a more elite population, the audience that they referenced as their readership varied considerably. In the case of the letters on hot-air balloons, one writer saw the new technology as universally relevant for the interest that ballooning experiments inspired "in all orders of citizens." In contrast to this rather ecumenical sense of the impact of ballooning, some amateurs acknowledged the limits of their abilities to win over readers. One pseudonymous writer lamented that to be sharp in one's assertions in the sciences, one needed an authoritative name and credentials.[66] As these two illustrations suggest, writers imagined rather different audiences would engage with their contributions than the wide-ranging prosopography of letter writers presented in chapter 2 revealed.

To be sure, letters on subjects related to natural philosophy and popular science tended to favor savants, but theirs were not the only voices. Amateurs, hobbyists, and salesmen wrote as well. Clearly, readers could learn to distinguish the letters written by well-known, trained practitioners from those of self-declared amateurs, since savants signed their contributions. The extent to which a reader would then equate the individual's social position with his or her expertise remains a more difficult question. As this chapter's case studies have demonstrated, enthusiasts did not accept the efforts by *physiciens* to police the participation on ballooning and electricity; amateurs took part in debates. Writers on the topic of electricity were rather straightforward about what their credentials were, but they also intimated that credentials were not most important. They couched their authority on a subject instead in their extensive experience. They argued that they had done the experiment themselves, and they had clear findings. Furthermore, they asked their fellow readers to repeat their experiments and to write back to compare results. For them, expertise did not matter as much as one's adherence to empiricism. While their knowledge of physics or chemistry certainly varied, such writers were only in rare instances charlatans out to dupe readers or make easy money. For the most part, the letters penned by amateurs to their local papers reflected the earnest desire of practitioners to figure things out: to share their observations and to debate their fellow readers. In doing so, they showed their willingness to question elite claims to knowledge.

In their accounts of balloons and electricity, the juxtaposition of voices in the affiches thrived on debate and uncertainty. Writers suggested improvements and reported their results, but it was the very lack of definitive answers that fostered correspondence. The notion of a collective working through ideas and experiments together drew the reader into a shared, virtual process of discovery. The lack of consensus about why one had found the results they did left readers to discern the truth for themselves. The claims to authority that amateurs articulated suggest that the terrain of expertise was shifting; legitimacy in the letters to the editor rested on the experience of having conducted one's own experiments with certainty. As chapter 5 will show, for most, the translation of empiricism to one's own experiences was found in more practical applications. In farms and gardens across the kingdom, men and women launched experiments of their own. The affiches became a primary locus for the circulation of their results.

CHAPTER 5

Agricultural Reform and Local Innovation

On May 25, 1786, the *Affiches du Poitou* pub-
lished a letter to the editor by the agronomist Maupin concerning the viticul-
tural experiments and demonstrations he had performed. He contended that
the results of his work should speak for themselves: "Facts, especially such as
those that I present, are the very light to the blind. With this light, it is impossible to not see. And there is no man, however ignorant, who is not in a position to have an opinion, to judge and pronounce in the very matters in which
he would have the least knowledge." As he saw it, "the allegation of ignorance
could only be a false pretense, and consequently a lie."[1] In his letter, Maupin
privileged empiricism based on concrete evidence, which he argued all should
be able to understand. He believed that when presented with clear evidence,
all would come to the same conclusion about what they saw before them.
He argued that those who differed in their interpretation were not merely
mistaken but lying. Maupin's letter was particularly bold, but he highlighted
the way that many agronomists used the information press to link empirical
evidence and *lumières*. They argued for an approach that many letter writers
employed in the affiches: presenting material evidence that they themselves
had observed and conveying confidence in their findings.

Maupin's letter was one of many on agricultural improvement that
filled the pages of late eighteenth-century newspapers. Recent innovation
in chemistry, botany, engineering, and other scientific fields had begun to

influence thinking on agriculture, which by the nineteenth century would revolutionize agricultural practice in Europe. Yet in the decades before that revolutionary shift was apparent, the diffusion of new agricultural knowledge remained a local phenomenon.[2] The affiches were an important site for sharing such information across geographic and social divides.

This chapter traces how new ideas about agricultural improvement were shared and debated in the press. Such conversations were informed by the political economy of the physiocrats, and by rather immediate, material concerns of food insecurity. The subject matter of their letters tended to converge around land reform, the implementation of new crops, and the prevention of disease in crops and livestock. In all cases, they were emblematic of a much larger trend among the letters: to explain in detail the experiments under way in the countryside. Letter writers recounted how long they had run their experiments, how much land each test occupied, the particular treatments applied to each field, and comparisons of the results at stages throughout the growing season. The letters in the information press thus reveal how widely agricultural reform efforts had spread. By showing the ways that diverse writers made their case to experts and practitioners, the letters to the editor offered a glimpse into the writers' claims to authority. The information press was a significant vector through which new techniques circulated, and where practitioners and experts could share in the same conversation.

Physiocracy, the State, and the Peasantry

The widespread interest in agronomy garnered the attention of men of letters and newspaper readers alike, and it was shaped by the influence of economic thought. The prevailing economic model in France since mid-century was physiocracy, which was guided by the idea that commercial growth came from agricultural growth. François Quesnay first posited the ideas underlying the economic theory in his 1758 work *Tableau économique*. He also wrote the articles for "farmers" and "grains" in the *Encyclopédie*, where he emphasized the role of agriculture in creating the renewable wealth for the kingdom that nature alone could produce. Through comparisons of prices, expenditures, arable land, and harvests, Quesnay argued that large farms produced the majority of the food supply. Given that assessment, he argued that the state ought to do more to support farmers. In general, his call for the state to implement reform emphasized economic liberalization, including rationalizing taxation, cutting duties and tolls, and scaling back market controls on grain.[3] Later, Pierre-Samuel Dupont de Nemours coined the term "physiocratie," meaning "rule of nature," to describe in his 1767 essay the economic outlook Quesnay had first posited.[4]

The physiocrats defined their philosophy not only in terms of agriculture and political economy. Physiocracy was also a theory of knowledge. And it was a moral philosophy that privileged evidentiary argumentation. The physiocrats envisioned education as a key element of their philosophy that would enable the public to "imbibe the true dictates of Nature."[5] They designed primers, pamphlets, and demonstrations geared toward specific audiences, including princes, adults, and children. Physiocratic thought was especially fashionable in the 1750s through 1770s, when its strongest advocates, the so-called *économistes*—Quesnay, Anne-Robert-Jacques Turgot, and Victor de Riqueti, marquis de Mirabeau—were influential in royal economic policy, where they promoted fiscal reform and free trade in grain.[6]

By the 1780s agronomists and political economists did not adhere strictly to all of the ideas formulated by the physiocrats, but elements of physiocratic attitudes echoed in their treatises. The continued influence of the physiocrats was also evident in the press, where writers argued that changes to agricultural practice could increase productivity. A piecemeal approach to economic principles was common at the time, as even the proponents of physiocracy did not necessarily adopt wholesale its economic and political implications.[7] Strands of thought inspired by the physiocrats continued to resonate in the prerevolutionary decades: the belief in growth coming from the land, the support for modifying the countryside, and the characterization of the peasant as a sympathetic and decent figure were all present in the letters to the affiches.

By the 1770s and 1780s French government authorities and landowners were turning resources and attention to reform. Official reports on public works drew on local grievances and observations as well as the expertise of engineers.[8] Royal administrators addressed all manner of environmental issues, including deforestation, swamps, water pollution caused by artisanal trades such as tanning, and the delivery of potable water. Academies also proposed essay contests concerned with explaining and safeguarding economic growth in agricultural and manufacturing sectors. The regional academy in Marseille posed the question, "Why has commerce grown in Marseille, and what are the means to ensure prosperity?" The Royal Society of Agriculture of Paris asked whether agricultural flourishing had a greater impact on the manufacturing sector or vice versa.[9] State officials also wrote repeatedly to the affiches to propose and implement reforms in land management, public works, and agriculture.[10] Through all of these channels, the importance of safeguarding and improving agricultural land received significant attention.

The information press participated in such discussions by inviting experts to share their opinions and by publishing local reports from practitioners. Some of the letters they published spoke rather directly to physiocratic principles. For example, one writer explained in the *Affiches du Poitou* the efforts to construct a new road in the Vendée from Cholet to Les Essarts. The engineers were drawing up the necessary plans; the local seigneur, Jacques d'Escoubleau, comte de Sourdis, had asked for the road; and the council had authorized construction. The writer described the count as a "good citizen and enlightened man" who understood the advantage of facilitating travel and transport for "the good of agriculture and commerce."[11] With similar aims in mind, Jacques Dumoustier de la Fond invited the affiches in Poitiers to publish the calculations concerning how to make the river Dive more navigable so that the public could evaluate them.[12] The framing used to justify the merits of new roads and improved waterways echoed broad physiocratic principles.

Arguments about the need for commerce and agriculture to work together were directly addressed in a letter from "un ancien Négociant" to the *Affiches de Troyes* in 1784. In it, the anonymous merchant argued that "agriculture and commerce have a natural and necessary relationship: one forms the basis of our riches, the other implements its benefits." Noting the significant attention commerce already received, he asked why there was not more state intervention in the realm of agriculture. He suggested at least two officials be assigned to oversee agricultural efforts for each province so that they could support new projects, including clearing land, developing mines, building canals, and other hydraulic interventions, all of which he characterized as means to "produire les lumières."[13] For this writer, the Enlightenment was something one made. His correspondence underscored the overlapping interests that writers identified in commerce, agriculture, and reform.

Ultimately, the anonymous merchant suggested that the farmer ought to receive some of the material benefits from such interventions. He suggested that administrative officials should support the efforts of seigneurial lords to implement such changes, to "exciter l'émulation" in the provinces. In doing so, the merchant emphasized that economic success relied on provincial notables, and he argued that landlords should lead land improvement projects. His outlook aligned with the physiocrats, who linked agricultural regeneration with renewal of the nobility. Quesnay had emphasized that agricultural improvement relied on the seigneur investing his revenue in the land. Mirabeau also celebrated noble landowners who lived on their estates and actively and personally managed the land, because in his estimation agriculture was the very foundation of the nation's economy. Depictions of landlords' direct involvement with the agricultural improvement of their estates were prevalent in literature, such as the fictional Wolmars, and in life, such as Antoine Lavoisier.[14]

Some landlords echoed such a seigneurial role in the information press. In his letter to the *Affiches de l'Orléanois* the comte d'Essars synthesized the results of his agricultural observations in several nearby provinces, and in doing so, he presented himself as a landlord with keen interest and direct knowledge of agricultural production on his estate.[15] Some writers underscored the position of landlords in the press by writing their appeals directly to them. For example, an anonymous letter to the *Affiches de Toulouse* invited the paper's readers, in particular the curés and seigneurs who read the affiches, to ask their plowmen to verify some observations he had made.[16] The letter concerned the impact of wind conditions on increasing the difficulty of plowing fields, but his letter was emblematic of the influence ascribed to provincial landlords and priests as instruments of reform.

Letters by landlords and parish priests also argued that concern for agriculture was a key component of good citizenship. One curé's letter to the affiches in Poitiers suggested that observing nature served agricultural and religious purposes by preserving one's well-being through food production, but also by encouraging one to think of nature's author. His methods for doing so were empirical; he encouraged parish priests to record the meteorological variations of the year and the results of the harvest, so that local observations could support agricultural improvement. By emphasizing the role of the clergy as record keepers on agricultural matters, he envisioned the priest as a contributor not solely to religion but also to the state. He argued that attending to agricultural matters would bring priests to better "exercise of charity, humanity, and the duties of a citizen." As chapter 6 will show, charity, a sense of shared humanity, and claims to citizenship were often linked in the information press. This priest's letter called on the paper's readers to remember that, "the needs which attach us to the plow still require such urgent work."[17] In the press, the material results of the harvest prompted a sense of urgency from writers, because it concerned their day-to-day well-being. They argued for participation in agricultural knowledge production out of necessity, and because it made one a good citizen.

Writers considered the impact such environmental and land management shifts would have on the peasantry. In their calls to modify the French countryside, writers relied on the physiocratic assumption that the land was inherently abundant. Their descriptions of the countryside were emblematic of visual and literary representations of the harvest in the eighteenth century, which emphasized the intrinsic potential of the land through depictions of gathering, binding, and gleaning that underscored nature's bounty. In lieu of the muscular peasants laboring in the fields in seventeenth-century imagery, the peasantry in eighteenth-century visual culture were recast as decent, unthreatening, and sympathetic.[18]

In the letters to the affiches, writers considered the condition of the farmer in sympathetic terms, formulating a vision of the peasantry as essential members of the kingdom. In one letter published in Troyes, a schoolmaster wrote to the paper asserting that people in the countryside should be assured "an honest subsistence."[19] In the Affiches de l'Orléanois a surgeon underscored that agricultural welfare was the basis for national welfare, and as agricultural producers, peasants were the most important group to the state, even though he noted they were not treated that way.[20] In a letter to the Affiches du Poitou, a curé described his attempts to educate plowmen on the treatment of soil in fallow fields, but his letter acknowledged their agency, for "the key to the granaries is in the hands of the laboureurs."[21] The priest asserted that the willingness of laboureurs to adopt new techniques would make all the difference. As such examples illustrate, writers expressed an optimism that it was now within human capacity to change the conditions of the peasantry, even as they suggested that such changes should be led by state officials and traditional social elites. Even in the arenas of reform advocated by the affiches, social hierarchies persisted. Their correspondence communicated the material limits that the peasantry faced as they argued for change.

In the press, reform relied on a sense of fellow feeling for the farmer. For example, a letter to the newspaper in Troyes appearing under the title "économie" described a rich area of at least five thousand acres of arable land along the banks of the Aube that had once been very fertile but was depleted at present. The poor soil conditions were compounded by the river's patterns of rising over the banks, which caused flooding that endangered the peasantry and their crops: "Far from contributing to the cultivateur's prosperity, the flooding tends, on the contrary, to substantially diminish his means. . . . One feels how such inconveniences are prejudicial to the general good and to his own."[22] In addition to describing the material effects of the overflow, empathy for the peasantry was central to the letter writer's argument. To prevent further flooding and ensure consistent harvests, the writer suggested a public works project to raise the banks of the river. Letters such as this one that considered the condition of the peasantry emphasized their ties to the agricultural and financial health of the state. The recasting of the peasantry as significant, sympathetic figures with agency of their own contributed to the social imaginary the press fostered. Letter writers established the importance of the material experiences of food producers and in doing so situated the affiches as a space that was interested in their perspectives.

Facing Real-World Problems

The desire for agricultural reform was driven in part by persistent food insecurity. The profound irregularity in securing the grain supply continued throughout the early modern period and was compounded by unpredictable weather and inequality in resources. Historians now know that the seventeenth century was indeed the Little Ice Age, a period of particularly cold winters and short growing seasons that were a product of lower solar activity, increased volcanic activity, and an especially high frequency of El Niño storm systems (ENSO).[23] The climate in Europe in the eighteenth century was generally warmer after the end of the Little Ice Age in about 1715. The conditions of the winter of 1788–89 are particularly well known by historians of France, but that winter was part of a longer period of erratic climate that spanned from the 1760s to approximately 1820. In these years, irregular weather patterns caused by ENSO, volcanic eruptions, and a period of decreased solar activity known as the Dalton minimum brought cold winters in Europe and North America, drought in India, and massive hurricanes in the Caribbean.[24] Especially after 1788, letters to the editor published in the affiches commented directly on the impacts of the climate on growing conditions throughout the kingdom.[25]

The preoccupation with food security remained prevalent in the eighteenth century. As Daniel Roche has emphasized, food supply in France relied "to a huge extent" on grain consumption. Most of France still depended on grain for making bread, which constituted the majority of a peasant's diet. Grain consumption accounted for between one-half and two-thirds of one's expenditure, and average daily bread consumption was approximately 1,200 grams.[26] The process of provisioning French cities was an arduous task, and while Paris was mostly supplied with wheat flour, provincial centers searched for a viable supplement for wheat flour out of necessity. The pursuit of suitable, nutritious substitutes preoccupied a wide group of experts who campaigned for new crops and studied the nutrition of bread.[27]

While eighteenth-century innovations in new crops, land management, and agricultural techniques had alleviated food insecurity somewhat, fluctuations in grain harvests triggered spikes in bread prices throughout the last decades of the eighteenth century. In an effort to resolve the subsistence problems that had troubled France for centuries, the French government undertook massive reforms by liberalizing the grain trade, first with domestic deregulation in 1763 and then with freedom of export in 1764. The implementation of the reforms coincided with a subsistence crisis, which began in 1765, when grain shortages were exacerbated by the disruption in the supply trade. Prices doubled and, in some places in the kingdom, tripled. As economic conditions worsened and public opposition grew, the government decided to end the plan in 1770. Ending the policy brought new problems, as the police system imposed after 1770 was resisted, and in the case of the Midi, violently so. Then Louis XV died in May 1774. In September 1774 Anne-Robert-Jacques Turgot liberalized the grain trade once more. Famine and a series of riots known as the Flour War followed in 1775. The failed reforms would influence Louis XVI and his finance ministers, especially Jacques Necker. The preoccupation with subsistence was such a powerful force for the people of France that it drove royal policy responses. Moreover, through the reform attempts of the 1760s and 1770s, provisioning had become a subject for public debate.[28] Correspondence published in the information press responded to long-standing concerns, which were especially heightened and timely owing to the recent debates over liberalization.

The Agricultural Enlightenment

At the same time, farmers began trying out new approaches in their own fields. How and why farmers who decided to adopt a new technique did so was, as Peter Jones describes it, a "highly complex and multifaceted" process where small adjustments to existing methods played the major role. And yet pinpointing and describing these incremental changes remains a puzzle for the historian—information circulated widely, but in what formats? Most eighteenth-century farmers resisted book knowledge and instead found local and material results much more convincing.[29] Plow trials, for example, garnered expansive public interest and participation.[30] The idea that applied knowledge was more useful than books was shared by Antoine Lavoisier who lamented the lack of empirical evidence in theoretical agricultural writing. Lavoisier's model farm at Fréchines was an attempt to offer concrete proof of the benefits of new agricultural approaches.[31] The notion that model farms such as Fréchines might influence farmers in the region to change their techniques was a popular one in the late eighteenth century. Agricultural societies founded experimental farms in Limoges, and there were similar efforts undertaken in Lyon and Riom. Learned societies launched competitions to reward farmers with increased productivity and organized the distribution of new seeds.[32]

The forum of letters to the editor was one of the rare places where book learning and practical knowledge came together. The widespread interest in field demonstrations in the affiches rested on the premise that improvements that yielded material results encouraged the wider adoption of new techniques. At the same time, agricultural writers produced theoretical tracts for the most part, rather than concerning themselves with the work done by the people laboring in the fields. Writers to the affiches were aware of the resistance between the two circles. As one parish priest writing on the condition of field workers near Civray put it, in his experience, "We often learn much better with a good *laboureur* than with *traités d'agriculture.*"[33] It was in the information press that the diffusion of new, applied knowledge and techniques happened.

Eighteenth-century discussions between savants and field workers were rare, but in the affiches they participated in an ongoing conversation. Writers used the vocabulary of *économie*, or reform efforts to better manage one's existing resources and maximize new ones, to discuss and debate agricultural improvement; a shared vocabulary afforded reformers from a range of backgrounds a basis for formulating improvements.[34] Public interest in economic reform expanded in the eighteenth century, as agronomists and lay readers consumed a growing literature concerning natural history, agronomy, and technology. The extensive correspondence on agronomy and animal husbandry reflected, at least in part, that writing on this topic was considered polite, a suitable topic for genteel conversation.[35] Moreover, the affiches offered an avenue for expanding agricultural discussions to a wider audience. By comparison, at the university, even in fields such as botany and agronomy, gardeners and amateurs were treated as participants but not full partners in the research they conducted.[36] In short, agriculture was a socially acceptable basis for writing a public letter to a provincial newspaper and a topic with which many had direct experience. Rather than focusing on one's position in society, the debates over agriculture in the information press turned around firsthand knowledge.

The Circulation of Practical Models

Writers to the affiches privileged practical suggestions that their fellow readers could implement, and their letters reflected the major areas of attainable innovation in eighteenth-century agriculture. Soil fertility garnered considerable attention across Europe at this time.[37] The French information press was no exception to the trend. As the discussion above of the press coverage of the peasantry indicated, writers throughout the kingdom wrote to the affiches to offer suggestions on how best to prepare fields. They debated the methods of clearing and preparing land for grain cultivation. Because they relied so heavily on wheat, French farmers had to leave some of their land fallow in order to allow for tired soil to regain the requisite nutrients. Whether cultivators ought to enrich the soil by burning their fields, letting them lie fallow, or using fertilizers were all up for debate in the affiches, and the letters from readers cited books, other accounts in the paper, and their own experience on the subject.[38] While the particular solution proposed varied, the published correspondence shared a how-to format that could serve as a resource for practitioners.

In the information press, a popular solution to soil conditions was to plant fodder crops that would feed livestock. The adoption of fodder crops was likely informed by British techniques, where farmers raised root vegetables such as beets and turnips and foraging legumes that supported larger herds of livestock; in turn, these crops supplied nutrient-rich manure for the soil. Writers to the affiches tried out similar approaches for themselves. One anonymous writer compared the merits of sainfoin, alfalfa, and clover, which he had cultivated alongside one another; he also weighed his own experience against what he had read about the crops. Ultimately, he found that sainfoin was not so abundant at the first harvest as his reading had led him to anticipate. Rather, he suggested that there was much land where sainfoin and alfalfa did not thrive; in his comparison, clover was less delicate to raise but less useful as livestock feed.[39] Alfalfa and sainfoin were used at first in the manner that this farmer employed them—to enrich soil for cultivation. Alfalfa, sainfoin, and clover all had the added benefit of serving as fodder crops, and most farmers could sell their clover crop at market or graze their livestock on it.[40] The strategy of raising fodder crops for livestock was a model that continental reformers supported. In the French information press, writers put fodder crops to the test.

Among the letters that discussed the adoption of British agronomy in France were those from one of the leading agronomists of his day, Abbé Henri-Alexandre Tessier, whose letters appeared in the papers in Paris, Grenoble, and Poitiers. His earliest letter to the *Journal de Paris* appeared in 1777, shortly after the agronomist and physician became a member of the Royal Society of Medicine. Most of his correspondence with the information press took place after 1783, when he entered the Academy of Sciences and the Society of Agriculture of Paris. In 1787 he would become the director of the royal experimental farm at Rambouillet. Tessier's letters included detailed accounts of total seeds planted and crops harvested at Rambouillet and comparisons throughout the kingdom.[41] His letters in the 1780s demonstrated how the experimental farm implemented British techniques; he designed Rambouillet and the letters he wrote about it as a model that other farmers could follow.

Tessier emphasized in his correspondence that the timing for planting fodder crops was key, and on this point, unknown farmers writing to the affiches agreed. "Le pauvre Laboureur" emphasized the importance of planting at the proper moment in his letter to the *Journal général de France*. The anonymous plowman sowed his fields, which he would otherwise have left fallow, with fodder crops as soon as he had harvested his rye. He described his process of irrigating the field in advance to prepare the seeds for germination in hopes that the fodder crop would begin to grow in October before the winter set in.[42] Writers also shared methods of fertilizing the soil with lime in the affiches. Lime neutralized the acid in the soil, which enabled farmers to use fields that they would otherwise have had to let rest, but it required substantial resources to quarry, burn, and transport it to fields.[43] Fodder crops, by contrast, were a rather affordable alternative.

In their discussions of agricultural innovation, the affiches also touted the merits of root vegetables such as the turnip, beet, and potato. Such vegetables were cultivated in kitchen gardens in the eighteenth century. Root vegetables allowed for a break in the monotony of grain-centered diets, and the diversification in diet through vegetables helped stave off scarcity.[44] Root vegetables were hardy and caloric, and they served as a supplement to a wheaten bread diet. Agronomists' advocacy for the turnip, the beet, and above all the potato appeared in specialist publications with a new urgency in the 1780s.[45]

The letters to the editor in the information press reveal that the campaigns for the root vegetable won over adherents throughout the kingdom. Writers to the affiches on this theme included the intendant of Paris and members of the Royal Society of Agriculture. According to a letter by the marquis de Lormoy, turnips were suitable for farmers who wanted to graze their animals on the same land where the root vegetable grew.[46] He organized his estates in Marquenterre according to the English farming model.[47] In his letters from Lorraine, the Abbé de Commerell presented specific instructions about how to sow root vegetables, prepare the soil, and determine when the crop was ready for harvest. He used his letter to advertise the beet to cultivators who might wish to grow root vegetables the following season, and he enclosed instructions about how to subscribe with him.[48] The information press touted the ease with which root vegetables could be cultivated and encouraged their adoption.

Letters lauding the potato's merits were especially prevalent in the newspapers. Potatoes were a subject of popular interest throughout the 1770s and 1780s because of their hardiness and high caloric content. For their part, the Academy of Besançon had dedicated their 1772 essay competition to the study of nutritious vegetables that could ward off famine. Antoine-Auguste Parmentier won with his essay on the potato, though all five of the essays submitted argued that the potato was the best solution to food insecurity.[49] Recipes that included potatoes appeared in the information press.[50] State and local officials interested in agricultural reform commented in the papers on the conditions of the growing season and their effect on the potato harvest.[51] Writers to the affiches celebrated the potato for its utility as food suitable for people and livestock alike.[52] Curés wrote letters about the fields they set aside for potato crops and the distribution of the harvest to those in the parish. A curé living near Alençon also referenced research that informed his potato farming, such as pamphlets published by François-George Mustel and by the botanist Henri Louis Duhamel du Monceau.[53] A notary and *receveur* cited Roger Schabol and Claude Durival's work on potato cultivation and suggested its benefits for feeding livestock in his letter to the affiches published in Metz.[54] The references to books and pamphlets in the letters to the editor situated the information press as a site for distributing and debating new and useful information. As writers shared their experiences from their own fields, gardens, and books, they commented on the methods they tested and applied.

The search in the information press for suitable supplements to wheat flour underscored the common concern and collective efforts of writers to improve access to bread. For example, one anonymous writer suggested acorns as a supplement, which when soaked and boiled were edible. The writer insisted that his recipe was at least better than black bread, which consisted mostly of rye flour.[55] The campaign for the potato grew with the advocacy of Antoine-Augustin Parmentier, whose 1777 manual, *Avis aux bonnes ménagères des villes et des campagnes sur la meilleure manière de faire leur pain*, included recipes for potato bread that required only hot water, salt, potato pulp, and starch. The finished loaf had the appearance of wheaten bread, and it did not require expert handling.[56] Antoine-Alexis Cadet de Vaux, one of the editors of the *Journal de Paris* and a friend of Parmentier, published content in his paper on the utility of the potato. But the descriptions of potatoes as a basis for bread appeared in newspapers throughout the kingdom.[57] The potato was by far the most popular alternative to wheat flour in the press, and the campaign for its adoption in the affiches showed the widespread interest in nutrition in provincial centers.

Writers also proposed new wheat alternatives in which they underscored how effective the newspapers were in prompting their decision to try a product for themselves. New crops advertised in the papers included a variety of buckwheat they called *blé noir* (which was also referred to as *blé de Siberie*, or *blé de Tartary*). In the affiches in Compiègne a merchant named Lange documented his success in growing the new buckwheat. He urged anyone interested in trying the crop to write to him, and he would sell them any amount at three livres a bushel.[58] In a similar letter published in Grenoble, the writer explained that the grain was suitable for planting between April and July, and each plant produced "50, 100, 1000 to 2000 grains, according to the bounty of the earth or to the fertilization and preparation one had done—the grain succeeds in all sorts of situations and terrains." While it needed more water, the grain was particularly hardy, made a nourishing bread, and held up well in storage since it was resistant to pests. The writer to the *Affiches du Dauphiné* trusted that the merits of the grain were so extensive that he concluded his letter with the declaration, "In a few years, we will not cultivate any other grain; it will be a great resource in case of scarcity."[59] The problem of scarcity was not merely a rhetorical flourish. Poor harvests and food insecurity were especially persistent in France outside of the Paris basin.[60]

The Limits of Agricultural Knowledge

Finally, the problem of pests and diseases that afflicted crops preoccupied many writers, especially when the remedy was unknown. In some cases, they offered home remedies to eradicate pests without knowing exactly why a particular solution worked. For example, a writer to the affiches in Metz shared how he had effectively kept dormice from destroying his espalier fruit trees by applying crushed fern leaves behind the fruit. He warned the editors, "Do not ask me why, sirs, the fern could produce such an admirable effect, because I confess I do not know." For him, it sufficed to know the technique yielded results: "I know an expedient to preserve my fruit, and that is enough for me."[61] Letters that shared remedies to eradicate rodents, caterpillars, aphids, and wasps adopted a similar approach, as they offered a solution the writers had devised even when they were unsure of exactly why their technique proved effective.

Animal husbandry in particular presented a host of questions that writers were ill equipped to answer. Veterinarians wrote letters to the editor describing diseases and known remedies for livestock. Letters documenting the spread of the *maladie rouge* that attacked sheep and other livestock, especially in the Sologne region, garnered repeated attention in the press. The disease afflicted livestock who were put out to pasture and then later would evacuate blood, even from the nose and eyes. Letters to the affiches in the provinces documented the disturbing symptoms and debated how the disease was communicated. Henri-Alexandre Tessier was among the experts who worked on the disease.[62] Most of the discussion of diseases in livestock read like local observational reports, which writers eagerly sent to the press. The primacy of letters in the information press that relied on direct experience at times exposed the limits of the contributor's knowledge and instead settled for increasing awareness.

The most common complaint of disease appeared in letters from farmers, priests, and agronomists throughout the kingdom, who wrote to the affiches to describe a wheat blight they called *blé carié, chamois,* or *charbonné*—a fungus that afflicted wheat, turning grain into a putrid dust that quickly infected healthy grain in the field and the storehouse. The Royal Society of Medicine commissioned research into the cause of the disease in 1777. Throughout the 1770s and 1780s, the interest in understanding the cause and curbing the contagion preoccupied lay practitioners too. Through published correspondence, they tried to "crowdsource" some way to stop its spread.

The lack of definitive answers about the causes of the wheat rot led many editors to publish letters from their readers that addressed the problem and proposed a remedy. By inviting their fellow readers to confirm their findings, writers working on wheat blight adopted a collaborative approach that connected state officials with practitioners. Such was the approach of a curé writing to the paper in Amiens who recommended storing harvested grain in baskets, which in his experience had kept the grain free of contamination.[63] Henri-Alexandre Tessier offered his expertise on the ongoing debate over wheat blight to the press in August 1785. While his findings were more detailed, he traced analogous questions and followed a similar format to the other letters to the editor on the disease. His solution was to treat the seeds with diluted lime. He explained the conditions for soaking the seeds, provided concrete numbers on how much lime was suitable to use per bushel of wheat, and explained why the fungus that attacked the wheat was so problematic. His letter relied on evidence-based reasoning in which he had tested the theories described in treatises through his own extensive experimentation.[64]

Investigations into wheat diseases foregrounded the role of collaboration with farmers in finding a remedy. The Abbé Genty, a secretary for the Royal Agricultural Society in Orléans, suggested a lime bath was not enough to protect seeds from disease: "Convinced by numerous experiments," he argued that the best way to get rid of the fungus was to beat and clean the grain set aside for seed, and to keep it sealed in the barn, away from the straw. Genty's recommendation relied on experiments that a plowman from

Saint-Florent had conducted, and on the results he had communicated to the agricultural society.[65] A few days later, the paper in Poitiers published an account that also relied on a method that a skilled *cultivateur* had applied.[66] The results that were published in the affiches were ones worked out in fields by agronomists and farmers together. As one anonymous letter published in the *Journal général de France* put it, "Agriculture is an art founded upon the experiment."[67] The knowledge privileged in the press consisted of methods that the writers had tested or observed. As the fine-grained descriptions of the wheat blight and how to stop it suggest, the explanations in the letters were at times contradictory, leaving the readers to discern for themselves which approach to employ.

Emulation in the Information Press

The affiches relied on material and observational results to convince readers of the efficacy of new agricultural approaches. The emphasis on experimentation within the letters enabled writers to link the arenas of learned expertise reliant on print with the practical results they had worked out in fields. The emphasis on applied knowledge in the affiches underscores that the agricultural Enlightenment was overwhelmingly practical.[68] A culture of emulation was central to agricultural reform in the eighteenth century, when plowing races, fairs, and model farms fostered imitation and competition. The letters in the information press communicated the importance of applied knowledge on a wide scale. Writers expressed the hope that their fellow readers would try out the methods published in the newspaper.

Once again, writers focused on a range of agricultural topics that collectively articulated the newspapers as a key site for the diffusion of useful knowledge. Situating the information press in this way also bolstered the calls for emulation in the letters. Especially in the correspondence on agriculture, the newspapers privileged precise and simple instructions. Lottinger, a correspondent of the Royal Society of Medicine, emphasized the importance of instruction when he wrote to the affiches in Metz to share his method of fermentation for wine production. He listed his observations and offered step-by-step direction about each stage of production, guided by the principles in the enologist Olivier de Serres's *Théâtre d'agriculture et mésnage des champs*. Lottinger thus intended for other readers of the affiches to be able to follow along and replicate his findings. In the editorial note after his letter, the editors suggested Lottinger consider the use of the hydraulic valve by D. Casbois, of which they assumed Lottinger was unaware when he made his observations.[69] The feedback between writer, editor, and the works they cited reinforced the sense that the steps a writer had followed could be picked up and applied by other readers of the newspaper. The dialogic, iterative nature of the affiches was foundational to the way that letters writers interacted with the paper.

The particular crop or cultivation technique varied from letter to letter, but writers participated in the information press by sending in how-to suggestions of their own. They offered technical advice on vineyard cultivation, plowing techniques, and wine making.[70] In a letter touting his method for promoting better growth of arbors and hedges, Huvier de Mes followed the organizational structure that other letters had modeled; he identified a common problem, then offered an explanation of just how he had devised a solution. He described the amount of shrubs he planted, the appropriate distances between plants, the size of the plants, and so on, so that others could replicate his work. Then he assured the reader that the approach was well tested on his own land for the past three years. He also eschewed credit; while he said he was the first to adopt this approach in his town, he noted he had not invented it, as the technique was in use in other provinces.[71] How-to accounts like this one spoke to the success of a method—in this case the cultivation of hedges—that the writer had tested. Their explanations also identified what they had read, how long they had worked on an approach, and just how they had accomplished their task. Moreover, they offered concrete evidence—material proof that the approach worked.

Some writers went further still, suggesting that the affiches were critical to the diffusion of useful and proven improvements. The academician and agronomist Jacques Joseph Ducarne de Blangy wrote to the *Journal général de France* to express what he felt "the interest of humanity" demanded. Blangy read multiple papers and pamphlets, and he wrote to the Parisian paper to corroborate findings in other sources.[72] In doing so, he connected the affiches throughout the kingdom together as a collective repository of practical information.

A particularly forceful letter on the role of the paper in collecting knowledge appeared in the *Journal général de France*, where a writer urged the paper to take a more systematic approach to the publication of agricultural information. Since "agriculture is one of the essential parts of the *journal*," the anonymous writer suggested the editors should insert more crop surveys from different parts of the kingdom, and all such accounts should appear in the same form. The letter included a template of just what the surveys ought to include: the distance from Paris and from the main highways, the amount of land, the number of houses and other structures per acre, the conditions of the soil, the crops cultivated by acre, and the harvest yielded.

While he expressed some uncertainty over what other possible questions correspondents ought to include in their reports, he thought collecting such details was important. As he put it, "I think [the reports] would be useful because of their accuracy."[73] In calling for the collection of accurate and useful knowledge, writers asserted that the affiches should play a critical role in data collection.

The newspapers were influential for readers that craved standardization and distribution of trustworthy evidence, and some writers reflected on the impact the information in the affiches had on their behavior. Subscribers noted the influence that previous accounts in the paper had on their decision to change their planting practices. A letter from Poitiers made such a case: based on previous articles in the paper about the merits of a new variety of buckwheat, the writer decided to test it on his own land. He bought a bushel of seeds, shared them with his neighbors, and planted them. Based on his initial results, he speculated that the harvest would provide enough bushels so that he would not need to rely on seeds from neighboring provinces in the future.[74] By situating himself and his target audience on the same plane, the writer suggested that people like him could benefit from his experience. Moreover, he emphasized that to appreciate its merits, the crop had to be tried out.

While the particular crops or techniques they advocated differed, letter writers throughout the kingdom identified common problems and offered solutions they had tried for themselves. Their letters adopted a how-to format that offered precise details so that readers could follow along and implement the techniques on their own. Moreover, they argued that the information press had a key role to play in cultivating emulation. They asked the editors of the affiches to publish more letters on agricultural topics, and they called for the standardization and proliferation of accounts from the provinces. Moreover, the contributors came from a range of social backgrounds, which included academicians, local notables, and cultivators. In this way, the newspapers bridged the arenas of learned expertise reliant on books and of technical knowledge practiced in fields.

Claiming Authority

Through their published correspondence, writers established their authority to speak on social and empirical grounds, and in doing so they situated the affiches as a channel that spanned geographic distance and social distinctions. The agronomist Maupin used the information press to advocate for greater public interest in agriculture: "The public, so curious and so eager for an infinity of things that often have little or no importance, is, in general, so cold on all matters of agriculture." Maupin took it on himself to educate and inspire the public, as he put it, to warm it to instruction and, above all, to put new and sound techniques into practice. For him, sharing useful knowledge was not enough. Maupin noted he had twenty-seven years' experience in vineyard cultivation, had published his first work of instruction twenty-three years earlier, and had spent the past fourteen years in the employ of the state. Moreover, he wrote that he had worked on comparative and what he called "authentic" experiments consecutively for the past nine years.[75] In describing the extent of his experience in the field, his published writing, and his employment, Maupin situated himself as an authority on the subject whose work the reader ought to trust. To do so, he emphasized his time in the field much more than his education or erudition.

The communication of agricultural knowledge in the affiches relied on empirical, firsthand evidence. Much of the correspondence on agriculture communicated examples the writers had worked out for themselves. A writer to the *Affiches de l'Orléanois* described his twenty years of experience and the sixty years of experience of a *cultivateur* with whom he worked as the basis of his solution to wheat blight in his fields. He explained that his recommendations were built on a series of experiments he had conducted, and he provided step-by-step instructions so that readers could adopt his technique.[76] By sharing not only their results but also their methodologies, writers offered material proof for the newspaper to distribute. In doing so, writers actively shaped a role for the press and justified their own contributions.

By privileging material results, letter writers also identified the people they wanted to convince. For example, in one account written under the pseudonym of "un pauvre laboureur," the writer offered the results of his experiments on fertilizers and seed preparation. He had divided his land into three sections of ten acres each, and each section received a different treatment to vary the acidity in the soil where the seeds grew. The writer ultimately discovered that all of his plants were susceptible to blight, so he asked his fellow readers to offer suggestions on how to combat the contagion. In soliciting their feedback, he said their responses would provide "the most essential service to several honest *laboureurs*, who, like myself, seek only their own education and to improve agriculture." He asked the editor to make his letter public "after having given it a more suitable form; for I know how to plow better than to write, but both have their utility." The editor included a short note at the end of his letter indicating that he printed the *laboureur's* letter as he received it, since he "wrote as well as he plowed."[77] Whether the letter was written by an actual plowman or not, it is nevertheless significant that the affiches printed letters from the vantage point of farmers. In publishing content from agronomists and farmers alike, the newspapers claimed that the affiches served both audiences.

For those who could not rely on their own experience, connections to well-known figures bolstered their claims. The naturalist and future revolutionary Pierre Marie Auguste Broussonet wrote to the *Journal général de France* to explain how to cultivate mulberry trees and remove silkworms from the bark of the trees.[78] Citing the work of Olivier de Serres, he asked the paper to publish his letter, because de Serres's work was not widely known, and because of its timely relation to the large-scale trials at the Royal Veterinary School of Alfort, where his friend and supporter Louis-Jean-Marie Daubenton was chair of rural economy.[79] Networks of tree nurseries existed not only in the environs of Paris but throughout the provinces. Languedoc had since 1723 supported the exchange and cultivation of mulberry trees, and a similar nursery network for olive trees was set up in 1785.[80] Similar projects were under way in Burgundy.[81] By allying himself with a prominent public figure and a widely known practice, Broussonet sought to bolster the significance of his own contribution.

Social ties based on one's status as a parent also served to strengthen the cases for land management made in the paper. For example, a woman wrote to the affiches in Poitiers to argue for the draining of the Saint-Hilaire marshland. She also admitted that she wrote to the paper to see what people would say about her ideas. For her part, she asserted that there were many acres of land lost to the marsh, which could instead be used for grain cultivation. She defended her right to share her opinion by referencing her motherhood: "The earth is the nurturer of all of us; as a mother and as a citizen, I have the right to be as interested as men in the needs and resources of society."[82] By fashioning herself as a mother, she drew on a popular notion of eighteenth-century maternal devotion, which relied on both sentiment and personal experience. The image of an idealized mother who devoted herself entirely to the emotional and physical care and education of her child circulated in the eighteenth century in print and visual media.[83] Emphasizing her particular stake in society as a mother and citizen, this writer drew on a familiar and compelling rhetorical framework to gain her readers' attention, articulate her commitment to society, and claim the authority to speak in the press.

While some writers identified their concern via their role within a family, others expressed the authority of their contribution in light of their concerns for humanity as a whole. In a letter to the *Affiches de Troyes* in 1784, Pierre Collot described in detail the experiments he had conducted with a new wheat variety, listing what he did on each day, what the weather conditions were at that time, and the state of the wheat at each stage. He also credited the newspaper with introducing him to the product in the first place. Once he had read about the wheat strain in the paper, he found a farmer "respected for his dignity and zeal for humanity" who had given him some seeds to plant. In his letter he shared his findings, and he was prepared to share the wheat with other "curious *agriculteurs*" interested in doing small trials of their own.[84] His approach reflected the values shared by many "sentimental savants" in the eighteenth century.[85] In framing the farmer's credibility in light of his zeal for humanity, Collot underscored his preoccupation with the public good and situated himself as a sociable writer who cared for others.

For many writers, the authority to speak in the affiches rested on one's ability to demonstrate that their findings could be observed, tested, and, above all, put to use. Such an affinity for usefulness was not an end in itself but instead an expression of one's public virtue. One anonymous writer to the newspaper in Orléans appealed to the editor to publish his letter on the basis of its usefulness, which he said was a credit to the newspaper: "If periodicals deserve the recognition of the region for which they were made, it is doubtless when their object is public usefulness. This one at whose head you are, is among their number: the merchant and the landowner find here instructions and *lumières* concerning their mutual interests."[86] In a similar manner, a letter published in the *Affiches d'Angers* and republished in the *Affiches de l'Orléanois* emphasized that usefulness was the heart of the affiches' role. The writer opened the letter by arguing that as far as he was concerned, "to make oneself useful to your fellow citizens is, according to me, first among our duties."[87] Writers argued that their investment in society was manifest in the usefulness of their letters.

The sense of responsibility to one's fellow citizens was direct in letters on agronomy, which emphasized the material impact of agricultural reform on people's lives. The justifications that writers gave for their ability to speak emphasized empirical facts, social ties, and usefulness. In making such claims, writers offered a vocabulary for the kind of knowledge that was valuable, and they situated the affiches as a key locus for information sharing. They also gestured toward the audiences they wanted to reach by invoking farmers and agronomists in their correspondence. Even more than the published correspondence on lightning rod implementation in chapter 4, letters about agricultural improvement revealed how writers tried to convince one another to adopt new techniques.

While practitioners were not treated as equal partners in university settings or scholarly discussions of agronomy, those with practical knowledge became part of the conversation in the affiches. The reliance on material results in the press opened up an opportunity for those with experience to make new claims about their social or professional authority. Editors cultivated conversations about empiricism and authority by printing letters from theorists and practitioners who presented evidence that their fellow readers could evaluate. By printing letters by engineers and agronomists, amateurs, state officials, seigneurial landowners, parish priests, and actual farmers, the affiches acted as a bridge for the diffusion of useful and practical knowledge.

As the debates in the press around agricultural subject matter, such as fodder crops, buckwheat, and wheat blight, illustrate, letter writers did not necessarily reach a shared conclusion about how to proceed. Nevertheless, their debates show the curiosity of the writing public, who wanted to compare their own findings with the work of other practitioners across the kingdom. Although some letter writers lamented that the public was not interested in agricultural questions, the information press makes clear that, on the contrary, people could not stop talking about them.

Agricultural innovation in the eighteenth century occurred in a small-scale manner, but the affiches reveal how new knowledge was communicated and applied by practitioners. Motivated by their desire to be useful, to support the public good, and to ensure the wealth and well-being of France, agronomists wrote to the newspapers to inspire emulation among their fellow readers. Such letters emphasized the applied, experimental nature of their work. The processes that writers and editors described in the press reflected a preoccupation with incremental innovation that would improve the material circumstances of everyday life.

The practical examples published in newspapers shed new light on the early and incremental processes of agricultural change that would become so evident in the nineteenth century. Beyond books and laboratories, practical agronomy took root through model farms, seed sharing, and letters to the editor. Contributors asked the paper to print more reports, they offered suggestions about what kinds of correspondence they would find most useful, and they explained how previous letters in the paper had inspired them to change their cultivation practices. Even in remote provincial regions, collaborative work thrived. As one writer with a new method put it, he believed his technique was "too interesting to not announce it publicly, so I am using the route of this paper which is spread throughout the province."[88] The information press had become an important vector for the communication of reform.

CHAPTER 6

Bienfaisance, Fellow Feeling, and the Public Good

In 1777 the *Affiches du Poitou* published a letter from a law student named Dupuy describing a wedding in the nearby town of Pouzioux, where the bride, the groom, and their families invited "all the poor in the region" to partake in the festivities. According to the writer, the "compassionate charity" of the two families, both of whom were *fermiers*, was well known, so it was little surprise to the writer that they had included the peasantry in their celebration. They invited peasants to the church for the wedding ceremony, and then the wedding party and all of their guests went together to the village, where the couple distributed a piece of bread weighing three pounds to each person in equal portion, so that "none was forgotten, and so that no one had more than the other." The writer praised the contributions made by the bride's and groom's families and the sensitivity they felt for their fellow man. This account of giving at a wedding underscored two themes prevalent in the discussions of social welfare at the time: first, that benefactors saw the poor as like themselves, in the words of their letters to the editor, as "leurs semblables," and second, that they acted out of a sensitivity and emotional connection (*sensibilité*) to the condition of the poor. That evening at the dinner and dancing that followed, friends and fellow villagers gathered to celebrate with the bridal couple. On observing the nuptial feast, the writer exclaimed, "O sainte humanité!" He had witnessed the couple enact love for and support for their fellow man, which he described as "the most beautiful light of virtue that brings humanity closer to its author." The letter concluded with a call to the readers to receive and admire this great example of bienfaisance, in the hope that the public might in turn emulate it.[1]

Letters from readers throughout the kingdom chronicled their own accounts of spontaneous and organized philanthropic and charitable work that invoked a similar vocabulary of fellow feeling, sensibility, and virtue. The affiches described these acts as bienfaisance. Between 1785 and 1789, writers authored more letters to the editor on bienfaisance than any other topic.[2] In the correspondence describing bienfaisance, writers expressed their concerns about the material conditions of people in their community, people they described as like themselves. Their letters reflected an earnest philanthropy, but they also were a way of presenting oneself and establishing one's credentials to the readers of the affiches. The scale of their work tended toward the local, but the steps that members of the public took and the way that writers described their philanthropic action revealed the importance of emotion in their decisions. They also suggested that the scope of social change the literate public imagined was possible. In their letters, they justified why they themselves were the ones to enact that change. Participation in the social welfare projects documented in the affiches was a way to express public virtue and demonstrate the sincerity of one's empathy through action. Through their letters, writers found new ways to situate themselves not only as beneficiaries but also as active contributors to society. Above all, letter writers wanted to be useful. Bienfaisance was a significant avenue to finding practical solutions to the difficulties of daily life. In their letters, writers expressed a sense of confidence that they could ameliorate their condition.

This chapter begins with a discussion of what bienfaisance meant in the eighteenth century in both theory and practice. The information press reinforced some long-standing practices of social welfare by supporting Old Regime charitable authorities, including parish clergy, foundling hospitals, and local relief after fires. While such practices were not new, the language of sentiment and the material emphasis that writers used to describe their efforts were novel. The affiches also printed proposals and progress reports about new philanthropic organizations, which illustrated the expansive visions for social change that circulated in the last years of the Old Regime. In all of the letters describing charity and bienfaisance, the letters to the editor situated the information press as the public record for philanthropic work that served the public good. Finally, while bienfaisance took many forms, the anecdotes describing beneficent action provided models of what virtue looked like for men and women according to their social station. While bien-faisance did not elide social difference, it made room for men and women from a range of backgrounds to exercise their agency in the press. By offering myriad portraits of bienfaisant action, letters to the editor encouraged fellow feeling and emulation. In doing so, editors and writers pushed the information press beyond the aims of entertainment and information as they sought to move readers to empathy and to action.

Situating Bienfaisance in the Affiches

The popularity of bienfaisance in the affiches reflected, at least in part, the interest of the newspaper editors themselves. The editorial team of the *Journal de Paris* was especially involved in philanthropic projects, and bienfaisance was part of their rationale for starting the paper in the first place. Moreover, the history of newspapers as employment centers and pawnshops facilitated this connection. Since their seventeenth-century inception, general informa-tion newspapers had functioned as a public and secure venue for getting the word out about philanthropic work and support for the poor.[3] By the late eighteenth century, calls for bienfaisance included notices that the public could make donations to the editor's office with the assurance that the funds would go toward the specified cause.

Published correspondence in the information press depicted how read-ers interpreted and applied the idea of bienfaisance in their own lives. Like Dupuy's letter describing the wedding feast, their correspondence interwove a new orientation toward emotion, fellow feeling, and virtue with religious explanations. In eighteenth-century France, charity and poor relief were still largely organized by the church and by urban and rural institutions such as hospitals.[4] Over the century, the explanations for why one ought to support such institutions began to shift away from traditional religious explanations of charity as an act of Christian love and duty that usually consisted of alms-giving or caring for the sick, poor, or orphaned. Charity was understood as an act of love of God. In its place, the discourse for bienfaisance emphasized the material conditions of the poor and compassion for the well-being of other people. When the Abbé de Saint-Pierre coined the term "bienfaisance," he described it as an inclination to do good toward others.[5] Bienfaisance was something one did. Only the king was beneficent in character, whether he enacted good works or not. And yet even he was described in the affiches as a "Roi bienfaisant," because he cared for the happiness of his subjects.[6] Voltaire would later popularize "bienfaisance" in more utilitarian and pater-nalistic terms through care for the poor, orphaned, and hungry.[7] Diderot and

Rousseau emphasized sympathy for others who shared a mutual condition; to be bienfaisant was in part to commiserate. Jean-Baptiste Greuze's engravings likewise introduced a visual repertory of bienfaisance, through which one could envision the proper recipients and enactors of philanthropy.[8] Popularized in visual and print media, bienfaisance, which emphasized compassion for the material conditions of the poor, was widespread by the end of the eighteenth century.

The rationales for social welfare in the press were likewise complex and often drew on both religious and secular repertories. Historians of religion and charity have tended to view the eighteenth century as a period of transition, during which an increasingly less devout French populace was no longer as motivated by the church's precepts, and they acted instead out of a more secular impulse to improve society. Such a shift in attitude toward virtue and compassion was evident, for example, in the language in wills in eighteenth-century Provence, which drifted away from traditional and religious charity.[9] Yet charity before and during the eighteenth century was not uniform or unchanging. Charitable practice had long ebbed and flowed with the material needs of the community, periods of spiritual renewal, and gender politics, and it would continue to do so well into the nineteenth century.[10] Moreover, emotional and religious rationales for charity and poor relief had long been intertwined.[11] For many writers to the affiches, charity and bienfaisance remained connected, even as the editors labeled their correspondence as bienfaisance.

Discussions of pragmatic and local social welfare efforts were a frequent occurrence in the information press. To motivate donors to support bienfaisant causes, philanthropists relied on a vocabulary that appealed to fellow feeling when they wrote to the affiches. They made the case that the poor or sick whom they wished to help were like themselves, save for unfortunate circumstance. While some writers used religious language to describe beneficent action, they combined the discussion of their faith with sentimental and material motivations. Indeed, the letters show a general shift toward bienfaisance, but one in which writers traversed the blurry boundaries between religious and secular philanthropy.

When it came to framing their accounts of bienfaisance, the readers of the Parisian and provincial papers underwent an education of sorts. Letter writers responded to previously printed content, adopting the topics or language that other writers had employed. In one such letter in the *Journal de Paris*'s first year, the writer proposed donations to a "society for the public good," and the writer invited a response from an anonymous locksmith who had proposed a similar project in the paper.[12] Early letters on bienfaisance drew on readers' personal experiences. Writers emphasized the way that their larger concerns about the public good were reinforced by personal testimony, especially in cases when the bienfaisance in question was a medicinal remedy. For example, one writer documented a remedy for fevers; when he sent the recipe to the paper, he expressed the hope to see it in print in terms of his duty to humanity and usefulness.[13] In sharing their remedies, writers such as this man situated the paper as a repository of helpful knowledge, in this case of medical information for a lay audience. In the information press, recipe sharing was an important way to provide useful knowledge and to express one's social-mindedness.

The letters concerning bienfaisance that proliferated in the 1770s emphasized that their particular experience had merit because it would benefit humanity. Their contributions to the press were, by the 1780s, a sustained conversation. In the winter of 1783–84 the Parisian daily the *Journal de Paris* was printing at least two discussions of philanthropy a week, though the paper had long exhibited an interest in such work.[14] Thereafter, the Parisian press dedicated sustained attention to bienfaisance. Much as the correspondence on agricultural improvement had relied on personal anecdote in order to convey results, letters on bienfaisance emphasized the writers' own experiences. The precise and personal nature of the accounts of bienfaisance bolstered the claims made in the letters. The immediate benefit the writer had witnessed was conveyed as a public good once published by the affiches.

In their letters to the editor writers often described medical treatment as acts of bienfaisance, which spread good deeds and conveyed humanity. An anonymous writer from Saint-Léger wrote in these very terms to describe the local seigneur's establishment of a surgeon to care for the poor in the vicinity free of charge.[15] Doctors wrote letters in which they offered not only their medical expertise but also their concern about improving the lives of others. And patients wrote letters to the editor in which doctors were described as bienfaisant figures.[16] Writers also asked the editors of the affiches to print medical recipes, and they couched their requests in the belief that sharing the remedy served the public good. When the letter writers were themselves the recipients of bienfaisance, the help they had received almost always manifested in the form of health care, as a medical cure or expert knowledge ensured their recovery. For example, an anonymous woman wrote in to report on her husband's successful treatment for chest pains and fever and to commend the doctor Helvetius who first devised the recipe that had delivered her husband "from the arms of death."[17] As historians of early modern England have shown, sharing recipes was a critical way of making and circulating knowledge about the natural world—a process that experts and practitioners shared.[18] In the information press, recipe sharing likewise encouraged the spread of knowledge among readers from disparate backgrounds. The anonymity of many of the writers to the affiches underscored the altruistic claims they made as they eschewed credit or personal notoriety in their letters to the editor.

Writers who contributed information on medical treatments and noted the efforts of local *bienfaiteurs* who helped the ill pressed readers to emulate their behavior. They blended religious and secular justifications for carrying out good works. The letters situated the paper as the storehouse where such good works were entrusted.[19] In addition to the importance that writers ascribed to the newspaper, they also made larger claims—they acted to inform, to reform behavior, out of love or duty, because of piety, or for *la patrie*. For the readers of the affiches, learning how most effectively to express philanthropic concerns, motivations, and activities was a dynamic process that required a changing set of approaches in their efforts to engage the public.

Organizations of Bienfaisance

One of the avenues that editors pursued to support bienfaisance was to print letters by individuals associated with establishments of charity and bienfaisance, such as local churches, schools, hospitals, or orphanages, and new private organizations. Their correspondence drew attention to local efforts to care for those in need by advertising, soliciting donations, or offering suggestions for an institution's improvement. They provided poor relief, assistance for disaster victims, and monetary aid for the release of debtors. In doing so, the press participated in ongoing activities.

The affiches also offered new explanations for traditional practices. The church continued to hold a predominant influence over social welfare projects. Parish priests often wrote letters to the editor to advertise charitable efforts or solicit public support for the social services they provided. Clergymen sometimes wrote in the same vein as the letters that referenced medicine as bienfaisance. For example, a Brother Bernard wrote in to discuss the prevalence of a medical treatment, addressing his letter to the paper as a way to "instruct the Public."[20] Priests also acted as trustworthy mediators, and in some cases they supported the charitable work of anonymous benefactors by acting as a go-between for interested parties. In one such letter, a village curé wrote to advertise a small ivory sculpture of Jesus on the cross; the anonymous owner, knowing its full value, had bequeathed it to a poor orphan so that its sale could pay for his education and establishment in the clergy. The curé informed his fellow readers that the work would be on display at his home every day in the afternoons until someone offered an appropriate price to fulfill the intentions of the anonymous benefactor.[21] Such an act was not particularly novel: the concept of a pious donor who would help a boy enter the clergy was common in the post-Tridentine period. What was new was that the newspaper had become an intermediary in such practices, by vouching for the truth of the priest's fundraising campaign, and by spreading the announcement to a wider audience.

The example of the priest facilitating the education of young orphans was emblematic of eighteenth-century writing about the figure of the *bon curé*, the good priest. The model of the good priest emphasized the role of parish clergy in the civic and social life of the community. Such depictions emphasized the priest's generosity and morality, both as a teacher and as a "servant of humanity."[22] This role was crafted not only by writers but also by the clergy themselves, who took on the role of a "citizen priest" by acting as tutors and servants to their local community—functions the communities largely welcomed.[23] The published correspondence by parish priests reflected these roles they had fashioned for themselves. In their letters to the editor, priests fused their concerns for the material and moral conditions of their parishioners. For example, M. Tallerye, the archpriest of Parthenay in the Aquitaine basin and curé of the Chapelle-Saint-Laurent, wrote that among the laudatory words guiding the occasion of his new appointment was that "bienfaisance will walk before you."[24] Another priest petitioned the newspaper's readers for help with the illnesses and poverty faced by his parishioners.[25] Other writers adopted a similar vocabulary to describe parish priests. One anonymous writer to the *Journal de Lyon* described priests as particularly aware of the needs of the people in the countryside.[26] In the information press, bienfaisance had become a characteristic of the clergy too.

Priests also took on roles as intermediaries and as caretakers in the press. A letter written to the editors of the *Affiches de l'Orléanois* retold the efforts of a M. Vervoort, a curé on the outskirts of Paris in Rosny-sur-Montreuil, who had recently died of the same fever that was plaguing his parishioners. The anonymous letter writer described the curé as a man who was "faithful to all his duties, who held all the poor in his heart." His treatment of the poor and infirm extended beyond the duty of his profession and conveyed the depth of his commitment. Without fear or precaution for himself, he was "as assiduous in his care for them as a father with his cherished children." The tribute to Vervoort emphasized both the fatherly duty and the personal dedication of this parish priest.

The idea of the philosophe as father was a popular conceptualization in the eighteenth century. Men of letters in the eighteenth century had come to understand their intellectual life and family life as concomitant strands of their identity, and their usefulness to society relied on their ability to embody both.[27] Letters to the editor show that some priests had adopted a similar framework. The author described the curé's care for his parishioners as an apt work that, "enlightened by religion, honored humanity." He described the curé like a father caring for his children; the priest located a doctor who could treat the sick and continued to attend to them until his death. Such behavior mirrored the traditional conceptualization of the priest's religious and social duty, and the imagery of Vervoort as a father certainly drew on a long tradition within Christian theology. But the writer also described Vervoort as a "Christian philosophe" who had sacrificed himself to support those in need. The letter concerning Vervoort fused traditional notions of the clergy with new ideas that animated his public service as a curé bienfaisant, a Christian philosophe.[28] The correspondence about priests enacting bienfaisance connected the language of feeling, social responsibility, and enlightenment.

The memorialization of bienfaiteurs who had died was also emblematic of a larger effort by the editors of the information press to take on a new journalistic role by crafting the genre of *nécrologie*, not merely as a listing of a figure's actions in life but rather as a narrative of a life that would connect with their readers. The *nécrologie* was a short-form article developed by the editors of the eighteenth-century press to celebrate remarkable figures who had died. Anne-Marie Mercier-Faivre has described such articles as a "Panthéon de papier."[29] Being worthy of such obituaries also relied on the assumption that the public already knew the person; they were tributes to public figures.[30] In the 1770s and 1780s, some writers adopted the style of the *nécrologie* in their letters to the editor in order to celebrate the social commitments of those who had recently died. Their accounts built affective ties by prompting their readers to consider the actions of the exemplary figure they eulogized.

Philanthropic institutions also used the press to propose new solutions to the problems they faced. Suggestions for small yet meaningful improvements animated much of the correspondence. In February 1781 a writer who wished to remain anonymous offered a detailed account of the administration of foundling hospitals and an innovation to improve their work. The letter described the manner in which infants were taken from Paris's foundling hospitals and distributed to wet nurses in the countryside; some fifteen or so babies at a time were transported by carriage from the foundling hospital, accompanied by only two or three women. The writer was pessimistic about the fate of the orphaned babies, as most did not survive their time in the countryside, and the children that did survive suffered other maladies owing to malnutrition. As the writer saw it, the major problem was that wet nurses were so poor that they took in more babies than they could care for.

Unable to address the systemic problems of poverty or infant mortality, the writer turned instead to a small but implementable remedy. To that end, he or she suggested a new kind of carriage that would transport sixteen babies at a time in little baskets so they would not touch each other or sleep on one another. The carriage also made room for five attendants, thus increasing the care they received on their journey to the country. According to the writer, the nuns who ran the foundling hospital liked the idea of the new carriage, and both the writer and the women religious overseeing the hospital hoped to see it implemented soon.[31] The proposal received support in the following days in the form of a subsequent response to the paper that emphasized the importance of work on behalf of foundlings. The writer was deeply moved to live "in an age where the love of humanity acts so powerfully upon sensitive souls."[32] By outlining the way a particular charitable institution ran, highlighting the problems inherent in it, and suggesting means of improvement, such letters articulated an interest in innovation and a confidence that material solutions could ameliorate the conditions of others.

Letters concerning the care of orphans and the funding of foundling hospitals continued throughout the 1780s. One letter that appeared in the *Journal de Paris* and then in Grenoble's affiches called for contributions that were "so useful and so necessary" for the foundlings' shelter at the Bicêtre Hospital. The letter elaborated on the history of such institutions by drawing the readers' attention to a plaster statue of Saint Vincent de Paul in the Cour du Salon at the Louvre, which featured two foundlings at the saint's feet. The two children symbolized the first foundling hospital in France and Vincent de Paul's role in its founding. The writer elaborated, in 1638, the police established a foundling shelter [*hospice*] at rue Saint Victor, "But is it enough to found one? Properly administering is truly the character of bienfaisance."[33] Bienfaisance by its definition involved an investment in the community that provided for those in need, foundlings in this case. But the formulation of bienfaisance articulated in this letter also fused public and administrative interests; the responsibility of continued management inherent in the concept of bienfaisance suggested that the public had an interest and duty to care for the ongoing needs of the poor, sick, and orphaned—a commitment that municipal administrators shared.

The role of local leaders in carrying out bienfaisance also surfaced in cases of emergency. Letters about fires were vivid examples of "faits divers," that

is, timely and local news stories that featured emotional accounts of danger
and neighborly aid. But the narratives also described the responses to fire as
acts of bienfaisance. In these accounts, administrators took responsibility for
fighting the fire and caring for those displaced by it. Members of the clergy,
nobility, state administration, and in some cases, the military also appeared
in letters reporting on fires. In one such letter, Montplanqua, a doctor from
Nogent-sur-Seine, reported on a fire in his town in detail. His account ended
with an assurance that the local seigneur, "who always spreads his benefits
on his vassals," took measures to give them aid, and a lady who had spent the
previous summer at the nearby château contributed a sum to support those
affected by the fire.[34] The letters by local doctors or priests that drew attention to the actions of local nobles emphasized that the landlord was fulfilling
his responsibility by supporting the victims of the fire. In other cases, a curé
acted, according to the letter writer, with courage and patriotism to contain
the fire in Aix-en-Othe. A priest also wrote the letter to the paper documenting the loss of homes, furniture, and livestock in the fire in Courtenot. He
beseeched the paper to print his letter soliciting support, which he specified
the secretary of the subdelegation would collect.[35]

Writers in the provinces who described bienfaisance in the wake of a
fire also emphasized the swift response from the military. For example, the
Affiches des Trois-Évêchés et Lorraine reported the 300 livres that a passing regiment had donated from their own salaries to help the villages of Juville and
Moncheux south of Metz rebuild after a fire. The letter's author, a lawyer by
the name of Bauquel, included the aside that "the Major added that he had
not had the time to know the intention of all the soldiers, but he was sure
they were also in a hurry to deprive themselves to relieve the unfortunates
for whom they had already worked so effectively."[36] Whether the regiment
felt the same way is unknown, for the paper did not print any comments
from the soldiers. The *Journal de Provence* printed a similar letter from Varange,
an eyewitness and retired captain of the Normandy regiment, which listed
the exact amount of donations made by Charles-Joseph, Prince de Ligne
immediately after a fire in the village of Velaines not far from Ligny-en-
Barrois in the northeast of France.[37] The letters covering poor relief in the
wake of a fire underscored the importance of local-level responses, which
they framed as acts of bienfaisance.

Most discussions of fire emphasized administrative institutions. Officials themselves wrote letters to the editor reporting on the aid mobilized
to help victims. A *surnuméraire* employed by the *Ferme générale* wrote the
letter concerning a fire in Crest. The letter by a notary documenting the

fire in Saint-Dizier noted how the town magistrates felt the suffering of the public.[38] The lieutenant general of police in Paris wrote a series of letters to report the donations made in response to a report of a fire that had left many homeless in the cul-de-sac Basfour, a pedestrian corridor in the Saint-Denis neighborhood. The letters submitted by the lieutenant general consisted of a register with the amount of donations made to the victims of the fire and the names of the people who contributed, although most of the donations were printed anonymously or with an attribution that read, "a servant on behalf of his master." In all, some 2,669 livres were raised to support the Parisians left homeless by the fire.[39] Letters printed in provincial newspapers throughout the kingdom reported on fires and recorded the amount of funds collected. In cases of fire, the affiches functioned as a record keeper where a mix of administrators and traditional figures responsible for charity, including the military, nobility, and clergy, appeared as agents responsible for the welfare of the community.

Finally, leaders of private charitable or philanthropic societies wrote to the affiches to publicize their work and solicit support. De Boissy, the treasurer and administrator for a private organization to support families of men in debtor's prison, which he called the Compagnie de MM. de Charité pour l'assistance des Prisonniers & la délivrance des Débiteurs, wrote at least a dozen letters published toward the end of each month in the Parisian daily. In each letter, he offered an account of those who had donated funds. The letters included the precise amount that each party contributed and specified the use to be made of the funds. Occasionally, de Boissy would include the name of the contributor—though most gave anonymously. The reasons for their contributions often invoked religious explanations. One anonymous woman contributed funds "with the intention of appealing to God's benediction for her marriage." Another anonymous donor gave "in thanksgiving of healing from a disease."[40] De Boissy spoke of contributions as alms, and he explained the motivations of contributors as petitions or gifts of thanksgiving. He made clear that the acts of his bienfaiteurs were known in heaven. At the same time, his appeals referenced the material needs of humanity and tracked the practical changes that donations made in the lives of those who received aid. His letters showed the permeability between ideas of charity motivated by religious belief and of bienfaisance focused on material conditions.

De Boissy's letters publicized the charitable association's business dealings, but they also conveyed to the reader the material difference that donations made in the lives of those the charity helped. Each letter ended with a reference to the men who had been released from their debts and restored to their families. Over the course of 1787, de Boissy reported that 60,503 livres were raised to meet the organization's goals, and some 920 men were released from prison. In the last letter of the year, de Boissy thanked the contributors by speaking for those the charity had helped: "May we be permitted to testify, on behalf of these fathers and mothers of families, our gratitude to the souls who are sensitive to suffering humanity, and to be the interpreters of these children . . . who cannot yet unite with the authors to bless their liberators and their benefactors."[41] The donor-oriented approach and the tone of de Boissy's correspondence that spoke on behalf of the recipients reflected the paternalism that bienfaisance often perpetuated. For the donors, his letters emphasized the importance of fellow feeling. De Boissy's letters underscored the human impact of his charity on the "sensitive souls" who contributed funds and documented the number of men, women, and children who benefited from his subscribers. Broadcasting the success of his organization by specifying down to the livre how much he had raised seemed to propel the organization forward, as readers continued to contribute donations collected by the newspaper.

Bienfaisance took on many forms in the affiches. To some extent, bienfaisance offered a new material and empathic vocabulary for charitable efforts that had long existed in France. The church, hospitals, municipal administrators, and private organizations mobilized resources and galvanized others to act by writing letters that accounted for their commitments. Their letters aimed to educate the public, identify the needs of institutions, and provide innovations to ameliorate the conditions of those in need. Through their support for Old Regime institutions, the affiches, to a certain extent, undergirded the status quo.[42] Although the discussions of bienfaisance did not question existing institutions outright, they did suggest actionable possibilities for change.

Education and Bienfaisance

In the information press, correspondence on education articulated the urgency of social reform. Writers who discussed bienfaisance took a special interest in intellectual and moral education, holding to the notion that virtue and usefulness were traits that anyone could learn and practice.[43] New schools were proposed in the press, and writers debated the feasibility and impact of new educational programs.[44] Such calls for education identified the students they hoped to reach, such as the poor, children with disabilities, and young girls, whom letter writers believed were in need of support and instruction. In suggesting new educational programs, the writers envisioned philanthropic efforts on a grander scale.

Letters to the editor concerning educational programs emphasized the opportunities for social advancement and moral instruction they provided to children. In a letter printed in Paris in January 1781, Claude Antoine, comte de Thélis proposed the establishment of a system of national schools that would provide both moral and intellectual instruction to children of twelve or thirteen years of age: "Our principal goal is to work for the reformation of public morals [mœurs], giving the children of the people a Christian and patriotic education." His primary aim in addressing the paper was to raise funds; he asked his fellow readers of the paper to contribute twelve livres to the school. But in writing to the newspaper he also noted the limitations for economic advancement the children faced, and he sought to improve the situation of young people within the limits of the social hierarchy of the Old Regime. He thought a school was the solution, which he argued would "do good for the entire nation."[45] Requests for support for new philanthropic societies in the information press often prompted the reader to consider the circumstances of those who would benefit; they argued that bienfaisance was both patriotic and charitable.[46] The correspondence on the founding of bienfaisant societies was one of the few occasions when writers to the affiches made appeals to the nation.

Letters celebrating schools appeared throughout the 1780s. A letter printed in January 1787 recounted the invitation to the royal court of Valentin Haüy and blind schoolchildren from his school, when the students and their teacher had an audience at court where they presented a book to the royal family.[47] The writer, who identified himself as a "philanthropist," was present at court that day, and he noted the skills the children had learned, the quality of their education, and the dedication of their teachers. Haüy, the influential founder of the school, also wrote two letters to the *Journal de Paris* in 1787 to advertise his educational endeavors.[48] By underscoring in their correspondence that all children could learn, the information press suggested the possibility of mobility through education.

In a similar vein, correspondence in the provincial affiches publicized schools for the blind and for the "deaf-mute." A member of a philanthropic society in Angers dedicated to the support of education for the deaf explained that the students could learn "to speak, to develop through reflection the natural laws of morality engraved in their hearts, to know by representative signs the positive laws, and finally to express in writing what they thought and what they felt." The support for their education expanded beyond basic proficiency in communication and considered their comprehension and expression of natural laws. The writer emphasized that the students possessed the ability to communicate their thoughts and feelings, and not just as ends in themselves. Their education also equipped them to enter into professions. The letter offered the example of a successful deaf printer named Mame, whom the writer described as "already trained in his art" after just a few years.[49] This letter to the *Affiches d'Angers* illustrated a vision of intellectual and moral education that equipped children to communicate, to think for themselves, and to enter a profession. Moreover, the writer made clear that even the newspaper's readers with false impressions about the ability of deaf children to learn could influence the opinion of others. He wrote to the paper to correct such false impressions, to offer proof, and to make a compelling case for the education of deaf children.

Letter writers concerned with bienfaisance participated in the growing conversation in France about who education was for. By illustrating that students were capable of abstract thought and of entering a profession, the writer to the *Affiches d'Angers* underscored principles that philosophers such as Condillac and Diderot had proposed. Although provincial vocational schools such as the one in Angers are less studied, Paris experienced a flourishing of such institutions after mid-century. In the capital, the first free school for deaf children, the National Institute for Deaf-Mutes, was opened in 1760 by the Abbé de l'Epée, and later run by the Abbé Sicard. L'Epée was perhaps best known for his implementation of sign language among his students, which enabled them to communicate effectively and fostered a sense of community that was previously inaccessible to them.[50] For the Abbé de l'Epée and other reformers, language itself was a tool for social reform.[51] By focusing their efforts on the moral and intellectual instruction of children, the press presented a vision for the future with greater social mobility. The explanations for such programs also presented education as a normative—and increasingly, as a patriotic—good. Moreover, education was a topic that interested many letter writers as parents and caregivers. For example, in Compiègne a father expressed his concern with the education of his children. A governess's letter on the role of parents and educators in the instruction of children appeared in the *Affiches de Dijon*.[52] Through education, bienfaisance took on more expansive forms in projects to include children and to make their lives visible in the press.

Bienfaisant programs in education also cultivated new visions of the nation. Writers described those who participated in social welfare projects as the embodiment of a new national character trait, which people of all estates could carry out. What is more, they intended to cultivate the children targeted in such bienfaisant initiatives in this value. The discussions of bienfaisance in the affiches prompted writers' reflections on the nature of citizenship and public virtue.

Model Benefactors and Public Virtue

The affiches cultivated their readers' interest in bienfaisance by showing what philanthropic and charitable institutions looked like, what kind of work they did, and what reforms they could offer. They invited readers to suggest improvements, and they solicited donations. In addition, the discussions of bienfaisance in the information press introduced readers to bienfaisance by presenting models of *bienfaiteurs* and *bienfaitrices*. In letters about exemplary benefactors, authors outlined the characteristics of public virtue, demonstrated the importance of the social action of model citizens, and encouraged the newspaper-reading public to participate by following their example. Bienfaisance took a range of forms, but the language of feeling was key. Writers described individuals moved to act out of the sensitivity of their souls, out of love for humanity, out of a desire to be useful. Their discussions followed the literary model of the anecdote, a short narrative with a plausible historical basis, which highlighted larger cultural values.[53] In discussions of bienfaisance, writers found virtue among all social groups, and in doing so articulated who the beneficent citizen could be.

Some of the depictions of model benefactors looked to figures with well-established duties. The letters documenting bienfaisant actions by nobles relied on the trope that a seigneur should care for his tenants as a matter of long-standing custom. One such account describing the role of the nobility in bienfaisance appeared in the *Affiches des Trois-Évêchés et Lorraine*. In the letter an anonymous marquis in the "Village de F . . ." saved one of his tenants, a *vigneron*, from the collection of debts he could not pay. The letter writer exclaimed, "I cannot express to you the feeling that this act of humanity has made on these good villagers." The *vigneron* and his family fell to their knees before the marquis to show their gratitude, but the nobleman shied away from their thanks. He answered instead, "Go, my friends, try to live happier, and you will find in me a protector."[54] A similar unsigned letter recounted an act of bienfaisance where the writer observed a generous man pay the rent for a family. Without his help, debt collectors at the door would have seized the family's furniture. The writer believed that the public had to know about what had transpired, but he asked for the editor to print it anonymously so that the writer would not face the reproach of the benefactor.[55] The anonymity of the donors and writers were a common trend in such letters. Like these examples suggest, some of the letters may have been fictive accounts that drew on familiar tropes. The timing of landlords who stepped in at the most fortuitous moment echoed the depictions of benevolent gentlemen in popular novels.

The depiction of the anonymous landlords resonated with the paternalistic and material orientation of bienfaisance articulated by Voltaire. But the stories in the affiches also reflected the changing relationships between seigneurs and tenants in the late eighteenth century. The prevalence of absentee landlords grew in the eighteenth century, in ways that had reduced the authority of seigneurs in some regions and that had allowed for greater cooperation with the peasantry in others. In some cases, peasants remained on the same farms even as absentee landlordship grew.[56] The letters depicting beneficent landlords show that some writers used the information press as a space for the recuperation of the image of seigneurialism, even as the authority that many landlords exercised over their estates waned.

The use of anonymity in letters depicting the nobility also underscored the more widely shared attitude that benefactors ought to carry out their duties humbly and eschew recognition for their good work. One especially thorough account of a noble benefactor appeared in the *Journal de Paris* in response to a particularly severe epidemic in Savigny. The doctor who composed the letter wrote, "By their nature, the following facts should be consigned to the annals of bienfaisance, and your *Journal* is their storehouse." In the letter that followed, the doctor recounted the dedication of "Madame la Marquise de M***," an anonymous local noblewoman who had worked tirelessly for the people of her community. Already forty people in the community had succumbed to an epidemic, but the marquise continued to care for those affected by it. She had opened her home to their care by transforming her chateau kitchen into a hospital kitchen, which she also equipped as a pharmacy. The marquise visited the sick night and day, taking on the most arduous of hospital tasks. The doctor argued that all people should be consecrated to the service of those suffering from maladies. He noted that while her service "honored her sex and her rank," her actions spoke most of all to "a new trait of the national character." By framing her actions not as a product of her duty but rather as an illustration of what anyone in the nation might do, the doctor invited readers of all ranks to imagine themselves in her shoes. Because the marquise's response so clearly typified what he called the new national character, the doctor believed that "its publication could be useful, because there is nothing as persuasive as an example."[57] The doctor found in this woman's example a figure worthy of emulation, and he situated the information press as the venue to share such cases.

As the letters concerning anonymous nobles suggested, bienfaisance often involved acts of generosity and care, but the anonymity and empathy of the benefactor were key. In making their case to the editors to print their letters, writers made claims about the virtues of those who enacted bienfaisance. While virtue was understood in gendered and socially differentiated terms, letters to the editor made clear that many could embody it. In this way, letters in the information press reflected a popular genre known as *annales de la bienfaisance*. The *annales* were books that gathered together accounts of philanthropic acts into a published compendium. Filled with cases of good works performed by virtuous benefactors, they underscored that bienfaisance was enacted not only by men and women of noble birth but also by figures from the working classes.[58] Writers to the affiches routinely described the newspapers as the depot for such "traits de bienfaisance." In finding benefactors from all social positions, the affiches suggested that reform was the work of all. Social distinctions did not fall away in their letters to the editor, but public virtue could be enacted by everyone.

Cases of bienfaisance among the working classes described virtuous men and women making swift decisions and acting as benefactors given the means they had. In some cases, the benefactor acted on behalf of his or her own family. For example, when an orphaned young man raised by a traiteur and his wife enlisted in the army to save his adopted parents from their debts, the traiteur who had raised the young man was celebrated in the press as a *bienfaiteur*.[59] In a similar manner, in the *Affiches d'Angers* an anonymous writer who identified himself as "a subscriber" related the courageous and beneficent action of a peasant woman who saved others in the village of Les Ponts-de-Cé from a rabid dog. The dog bit her as she kept it at bay from the children in the village. Like the letters documenting the quick responses to fires, the bienfaisance performed by figures from the working classes emphasized spontaneity and self-sacrifice.

Letters profiling model benefactors also underscored the responsibility of the affiches and their readers to enact bienfaisance. Presenting the young woman who defended her neighbors from a rabid dog as a figure to emulate, the writer asked that the paper publish her "act of courage," which the author found all the more admirable for the way in which she suffered after the attack. The writer solicited donations to alleviate her misery and provide for her children. The editors seconded the call for financial support and offered to collect funds on her behalf. Alongside the monetary request, the author also made a case to the editor that the paper was the record keeper for such good works: "Your pages have for a long time, sir, been the respectable depository in which are recorded these beautiful deeds, worthy of being transmitted to posterity, and of being proposed as models to the present generation."[60] As letters depicting model benefactors illustrated, writers and editors understood the affiches as a repository for such work. The paper functioned as a catalog of actions taken, a gallery of those who enacted bien-faisance, and as a bookkeeper of funds raised on their behalf.

The notion of the affiches as the site for bienfaisance was vividly conveyed by a letter in the *Affiches du Dauphiné* concerning a group of market women who prevented a poor farmer from attacking a thief. Seeing the thief steal from the farmer and responding spontaneously to the farmer's distress, the market women physically restrained and disarmed him to prevent an alterca-tion with the thief and the arrest of the farmer. In an act of compassion, one woman named Jeanne Pascal gave the farmer the sum he had lost. When the other women witnessed her sacrifice, they raised funds among themselves to repay her.[61] The story emphasized the social nature of bienfaisance, because one woman's action had inspired the other market women to act benefi-cently too. The writer told the editor that the nature of the community response and the act of generosity of one woman in particular had inspired them to write the letter and asked the editor to print the act of bienfaisance, since it would be "the only reward she and her companions will receive, and they deserve it."[62] Letters like this one suggested that anyone moved by fel-low feeling could enact bienfaisance. Moreover, such accounts underscored that the peasantry were not merely victims in such narratives but could also become the benefactors.

While some of the letters depicting model benefactors were dramatic human interest stories, most writers considered how to practice bienfaisance in their everyday lives. This was the case for a group of journeymen who were celebrated in the press as *bienfaiteurs*. As one anonymous writer to the *Journal de Paris* explained in his letter, after thirty years of work, a journey-man engraver was afflicted by a mysterious paralysis over the entire left side of his body. The writer explained that the "accident had reduced him to the most terrible misery." Noting the virtue, good manners, and morals of their unfortunate brother, his fellow *compagnons graveurs* raised enough money from their own labor to support their friend. The anonymous writer who shared this story argued that the editors should print the letter so that the example of the men's action would become less rare. The writer asserted that "acts of bienfaisance have always merited the highest praise," and the newspaper would be privileged "to encourage good people to imitate them" by their publication.[63] By sharing examples of philanthropic action in daily life, writers and editors sought to motivate readers to recognize needs in their own community and to act on them.

The information press published letters that profiled benefactors from a range of positions in society whom the writers deemed worthy of emulation. Appeals to good citizenship and the public good, mixed with references to piety and virtue, were especially evident in the letters that described *rosières* festivals. The *rosière*, or rose-girl, was the "queen of virtue" chosen from a group of single women known for their chastity and integrity in eighteenth-century spring festivals. While the tradition supposedly began in Salency, *rosière* festivals gained popularity in the 1760s and 1770s through enactments in the countryside, literature, and plays. Such festivals celebrated a partic-ular vision of country life and feminine virtue, and they held widespread appeal among social elites.[64] By 1780 the festivals were widely adopted. Even the small village of Saint-Aupre had a lively festival, where some two thou-sand guests attended the festivities and the marquis Joseph-Marrie de Barral crowned the *rosière*.[65]

Letters to the editor that documented virtue prizes reinforced gender and social hierarchies, but they also became a space to reconsider the meaning of citizenship. In a letter describing a prize competition similar to the *rosières*, Cantuel de Blémeur, the curé of Saint-Séverin in Paris, described a founda-tion run by his parish each year since 1751 and organized to celebrate the morals (mœurs) of the young women in the parish. Like many other writers, he characterized his work as bienfaisance and wrote to the press "for the encouragement of so many religious and beneficent citizens, friends and apostles of virtue by their good works and their examples." For the priest, virtue, citizenship, bienfaisance, and religion were intertwined.

The competition at Saint-Séverin functioned as a lottery that all young women in the parish could enter, and a prize of 100 livres was awarded to the five young women who won. He explained the selection process, which included an evaluation of the morals, piety, and conduct of each of the young women who entered the contest. The curé assured his readers that the reputations of all the young women were kept private so as not to dishonor any of them, but he noted that a young woman could be removed from the list on the basis of a religious leader's evaluation. The winners were selected by a drawing held in the presence of witnesses. The judges awarded five prizes to the young women at a celebration their parents attended to honor "morals, religion, and *la patrie.*" The priest submitted his letter "in the sweet hope that such an interesting example will be followed in the Capital with the same zeal as it multiplies in the Provinces." He asked for the paper to print his letter about the parish lottery with the aim of inspiring other par-ishes to reward their own "true citizens."[66] Depictions of virtue as they were articulated in prize competitions such as the one for the Saint-Séverin parish reinforced traditional mores. At the same time, the writers who pitched such competitions in the press also raised questions about what it meant to be a citizen, and they fused patriotism to piety and moral conduct.

Through the correspondence on bienfaisance, the idea that any individual could be virtuous, in ways appropriate to their social position, circulated widely. Letter writers discussed prize competitions that were awarded according to one's demonstration of bienfaisance. For example, the intendant in Perpignan nominated three men from nearby villages for a prize in recognition of their moral character and acts of bravery in rescuing others.[67] The correspondence about such contests put forward models of public virtue much as the letters on bienfaisance did, and the writers made clear the social positions of the recipients of virtue prizes. Peasants, craftsmen, and domestic servants appeared in the press as people with agency worthy of recognition.

In a similar manner, one nomination letter for an annual virtue prize written by a lawyer appeared in the *Journal de Paris* and then later in the *Affiches du Dauphiné* and the *Affiches de Montpellier*. He nominated a servant woman who had demonstrated remarkable commitment. The nominated woman, La Blonde, had been in the employ of the Migeon family for some twenty years. When the merchant Migeon died, he left his wife, aged thirty, and their two young children destitute, in the words of the lawyer, "without bread." La Blonde refused to abandon the family and stayed with them; despite Madame Migeon's encouragement to seek new employment, La Blonde demurred. After all, she argued, "who will take care of the family if I leave it?" She continued to serve the family, but within months the widow Migeon fell ill, consumed with grief. La Blonde sold everything she had to pay the family's bills. After the widow's death, La Blonde didn't want to leave the children, so she offered to continue to care for them. After sharing La Blonde's story, the writer enclosed the attestations of ten men familiar with the events that had transpired.

La Blonde's self-sacrifice was central to the narrative of bienfaisance presented in the paper, but the writer also encouraged fellow feeling by drawing the reader's attention to the precipitous fall of a bourgeois family and to the welfare of children. The writer asked that the paper publish this letter for two reasons: first, because "your *Journal* has become more interesting and more valuable since you have made it your duty to transmit to public veneration good deeds which, without you, might be ignored," and second, to nominate La Blonde for a virtue prize.[68] Like the *rosières*, letters concerning prize competitions were a way to idealize the status quo, but the motif was also a way of highlighting social tensions and critiquing arbitrary power.[69] Letters held up the conduct of the benefactor as an example, and in doing so they highlighted the material and social conditions of journeymen, domestic servants, widows, and orphans. Their letters asked the reader to empathize with them. By featuring marginalized figures as the agents in the stories, letter writers pushed against social hierarchies.

The letters explaining why men and women participated in bienfaisance relied less on appeals to one's duty as a member, for example, of the nobility and clergy, and instead they made the argument that empathy and fellow feeling compelled all people to action. The role of emotion in discussions of bienfaisance marked an important shift away from the early modern conceptualization of compassion that had reinforced social difference. In the seventeenth century, compassion was the attitude of a spectator, who looked on attentively but remained an observer.[70] By contrast, the emotional accounts of eighteenth-century bienfaisance depicted a reader who was moved to tears but also to action, whether to write about the event or to emulate it.[71] The applied nature of beneficent models in the affiches relied on the power of an example to influence the reader. The information press supplied such models in abundance. The figures who enacted bienfaisance were portrayed as courageous men and women who jumped into action motivated by a sense of fellow feeling. Such benefactors simultaneously maintained an archetypal element that was not overly contextualized. In doing so, the letters to the editor about bienfaisance allowed readers to imagine themselves in a similar situation.

The editors of the affiches published letters to the editor on a multitude of topics, but most of all on bienfaisance. For the writers of the affiches, the newspaper served an important function: it kept them informed, afforded a space for debate, and offered avenues for the amelioration of daily life. In their correspondence, writers conveyed that change was possible at the local level. Those who situated their discussions of bienfaisance in a letter to the editor expressed the sense that by writing to the paper, they could be a part of such change. The depictions of bienfaisance in their letters revealed that writers had differing motivations, vantage points, and approaches to philanthropy and charity. While many of those who undertook bienfaisance were associated with institutions who were traditionally responsible for such work, such as parish priests, doctors, or the nobility, the language they used to explain their actions and their motivations emphasized that compassion should guide people to action. Above all, bienfaisance was the work of good citizens, of men and women of virtue. As the writers emphasized, social reform and spontaneous bienfaisance alike served humanity.

In formulating a model benefactor on whom readers could pattern their own philanthropic efforts, writers depicted agents of change from all positions in society. Bienfaisance often supported established organizations, and some letter writers characterized the people from the peasantry or the working classes they aimed to help in paternalistic terms. But writers also suggested changes of social consequence, such as the expansion of education and the amelioration of local problems. Descriptions of model benefactors asserted the universality of virtue as a quality that anyone could possess, and bienfaisance as a practice anyone could adopt. Writers offered examples of virtuous character, of fellow feeling, and of honest conduct in daily life. Moreover, the discussion of bienfaisance suggested that *bienfaiteurs* and *bienfaitrices* came from all social ranks. Such representations mattered, for even among those who merely read the affiches without writing a letter, they could begin to see images of people like themselves as agents in the newspaper.

Making the case for bienfaisance in the press was both a public act and a personal one, for it relied on empathy. The majority of the published letters on charity and philanthropy encouraged the reader to emulate the individuals about whom they read by acting locally to care for those who were victims of circumstance—of theft, fire, illness, hunger—but were otherwise like the readers. They encouraged fellow feeling explicitly, by casting those they helped as like themselves (*leurs semblables*), and arguing that those with sensitive souls would act to support them. Through the forum of letters to the editor, private citizens formulated ways to participate in shaping their society. By forging affective ties among readers, the information press prompted writers to consider the public good. The debates over the projects and participants involved in bienfaisance were part of a wider conversation about the formulation of civil society.

Letters to the editor that explained social welfare projects and encouraged other readers to participate serve as a powerful reflection of the ways in which members of a more expansive writing public made sense of the current events within their community and sought to change their social environments. Indeed, imagining a completely new society, like the one that the Revolution would introduce, remained largely unexplored before 1789. Nevertheless, writers discussed public service frequently, and their correspondence in the newspapers showed that many sought to enact change, both through written critique and direct action. The practice of imagining and enacting local, material changes in the affiches equipped readers with habits of mind they would soon put to new uses.

CHAPTER 7

Communicating the Revolution

Joly, a lieutenant colonel of the Garde Citoyenne in Plancy-sur-Aube, wrote to his local newspaper in Troyes in December 1789 to suggest that he was living through a remarkable moment in history. He argued that all of the paper's readers had a role to play in the Revolution "taking place among us," and so he called on all "citoyens éclairés" reading the paper to dedicate themselves to the public good. Joly believed that the Revolution could only attain a salutary end by the efforts and sacrifices of its citizens, so he wrote a letter to the editor. He linked the patriotic actions in the small town where he lived to the efforts of the National Assembly that he admired. He reasoned that it was only natural that patriotism and ardent zeal would lead the affiches' readers to support the Revolution.[1] In less than a year of revolution, the letters published in the information press had become a forum for political discussions like Joly's. In much the same way as they had participated in balloon launches, potato harvests, or beneficent recipe sharing, writers emphasized that they had a role to play in the unfolding Revolution. The information press that had generally avoided politics now ushered it in. As they navigated their experiences of the Revolution, writers relied on norms they had been building for two decades. Appeals to the public good remained the framework for justifying one's letter. Like so much of the explanations for acting beneficently, the politics of the Revolution were made local and personal.

Joly's correspondence was emblematic of the optimism that had for two decades appeared in the letters to the affiches. The new practices of dialogue honed by writers in the information press and the pervasive habits they had built in order to argue for practical, incremental changes at the local level had prepared the writing public to participate in the Revolution. At the same time, the media landscape the information press inhabited had changed utterly, as hundreds of new, uncensored publications entered the marketplace in 1789 and thereafter. The affiches, once the only licensed general information newspapers for a given town, by and large adapted to the Revolution and continued to publish at least until 1791.

This chapter traces the experiences of writers who participated in the Revolution via the affiches. As censorship fell away, writers voiced their political opinions openly in the general information newspapers. The forum of letters to the editor in the early years of the Revolution continued to publish lively correspondence concerning the arts and sciences, agriculture, and bienfaisance. But even more so, letter writers continued to bring to bear the habits of mind to question, to debate, and to establish their own authority to speak on new questions concerning the Revolution. Writers debated the meaning of the revolutionary events in which they participated. Deputies in the National Assembly used the press to foster conversation with their constituents. Writers raised questions about the impacts of national policies on their particular town. Taken as a whole, the letters to the editor reveal both the widespread engagement of the writing public with the Revolution and the contested, negotiated responses to the events in which they participated.

The letters to the editor published in the early years of the Revolution reveal the lived experiences of writers who navigated far greater access to information. In the prerevolutionary information press, debates over who had published a particular pamphlet, book, or letter to the editor had become matters of personal and public concern. In the eighteenth century, honor had become a salient signifier as social distinctions had become less legible.[2] During the Revolution such preoccupations would only intensify. The writers to the affiches in 1790 and 1791 increasingly noted that their letter was in response to a rumor and concerned their personal reputation. When the letters dwindled sharply in the autumn of 1791, as the deputies attempted to regulate the press, the crisis over authority and personal honor had reached a fever pitch.

Letter writers adapted the repertories of establishing authority they had honed together in the affiches in the 1770s and 1780s to the new social and political realities of revolution. Through the letters to the editor, many writers who would not hold public office learned to become revolutionaries.

Previous scholarship on the history of the revolutionary press has focused on what Hugh Gough has called the "campaigning journalist," an individual writer who participated in revolutionary events and used his newspaper in the service of his political campaigns.[3] Historians have devoted monographs to the best-known journalist revolutionaries who worked in this campaigning style, especially Camille Desmoulins, Jacques Pierre Brissot, Jean-Paul Marat, and Jacques-René Hébert.[4] While most of the "campaigning journalists" were affiliated with the Cordeliers and Jacobin clubs, conservative journalists and their newspapers are also well studied. Historians of the conservative press have shown that editors likewise invited their partisan readers to respond to newspaper content, and readers participated enthusiastically.[5] Many of these journalists held public office, and their lives and writings have been well documented.

As the new revolutionary newspapers found a clear journalistic voice, the information press remained more varied, informed by the personal and at times contradictory responses to the events unfolding before the writing public. As they continued to publish letters to the editor, the affiches show the ways that readers processed the early years of the Revolution. Writers continued to debate one another in the shared venue of the affiches, even as newspapers across the political spectrum began to publish. This chapter focuses on writers who, for the most part, were not prominent revolutionaries but nevertheless shaped the early years of the Revolution.

The Evolution of the Revolutionary Affiches

News of the Revolution of 1789 arrived in the French information press in a piecemeal fashion. For the first time in the domestic newspapers, editorial opinions appeared that ranged from the radical to the archconservative, and readers' responses to the events of the Revolution were just as varied. As censorship began to fall away in 1788–89, editors ventured into political coverage by running columns on key events and printing letters from their readers on political matters. From July 5, 1788, censorship effectively ended on pamphlets, when Loménie de Brienne, the king's chief finance minister, issued a decree inviting the public to share their opinions on the procedures that would guide the Estates General. Censorship of newspapers collapsed over the ensuing months as printers began to comment on the preparations for the Estates General. On May 19, 1789, the crown tried to reassert its power to regulate political news by authorizing the *Journal de Paris*, the *Mercure*, and the *Gazette de France* to print reports on the Estates General approved by a royal censor.[6] Provincial affiches were permitted to reprint the reports published in the Parisian papers. Between May 20 and 23, the deputies took up the question of press freedom, but after discussing the possibility of publishing their own periodical, they ultimately decided not to do so. In his study of the revolutionary press, Hugh Gough suggests that it was this decision by the deputies that marked a turning point after which newspaper producers assumed they could print freely.[7]

From this point, letter writers to the affiches spoke for the first time in a free press. In the *Journal de Paris*, letters in the form of proposed *cahiers de doléances* and correspondence written in anticipation of the calling of the Estates General began appearing in April and May. On April 1 a future deputy from the Third Estate who identified himself by the initials C. D. described the local elections in Senlis and asserted that "distinctions in rank necessary for the social order will merge within the unanimity of our sentiments."[8] In his discussion of the *cahiers* drawn up by each estate, he reflected the widespread optimism felt by many that reform was possible. Throughout the late spring, writers began to test the waters on political subjects. Despite their cautious tone, early accounts expressed excitement about the calling of the Estates General. The discussion of the fiscal crisis and the mobilization for the election of deputies permeated the information press in Caen, Metz, Orleans, Poitiers, Rennes, Rouen, Toulouse, and Troyes. Correspondence concerning local and regional government, taxation, privilege, and the future of the nation increased notably in late 1788 and into 1789.[9]

At the same time as the range of opinions in the affiches grew, the newspapers printed fewer letters to the editor. Across a sample of the newspapers published in Amiens, Angers, Arras, Caen, Dijon, Marseille, Paris, Rouen, and Troyes, the total letters published in 1789, 1790, and 1791 were 423, 289, and 190, respectively, as compared to the 424 total letters published in 1788 and 306 total letters in 1786. Beginning in May 1789, editors dedicated more of their newspapers to covering the Estates General and, after June 17, to the National Assembly. The *Journal de Paris* did so on a daily basis. The coverage of political news in the Assembly often took up the first page or two of the short four-page newspapers. Everywhere readers were eager to learn more about the events transpiring in the Assembly and the transformations undertaken by the people of Paris and other metropolitan centers. In order to make room for expanding columns on political news, the rest of the newspaper's contents—including letters to the editor—were condensed or cut.

Moreover, newspapers proliferated in 1789. One hundred and forty new periodicals were published that year in Paris alone.[10] Each paper took a political position that could hew more closely to their readers' interests. Many of them also included correspondence from their readers. Letters did not cease to appear in the affiches in 1789, but they quickly became but one element in a dynamic body of conversations about the Revolution. As editors grew increasingly confident that censorship had fallen for good, they printed correspondence that reflected their own views and those of their readers.

Old Regime Continuities

By the summer of 1789, censorship had entirely collapsed, and the affiches freely printed letters on political matters. The Revolution garnered sustained attention in the press, but politics was by no means the only topic people wrote about. Letters concerning bienfaisance, agriculture, the sciences, and arts and letters, which had formed the majority of content prior to 1789, persisted during the period of 1789–91. In a quantitative analysis of a sample of four newspapers, discussions of politics composed just over a third of the correspondence published between 1789 and 1791.[11] For the majority of writers to the affiches, their correspondence remained preoccupied with implementing practical, incremental social and technological improvements at the local level.

Writers continued to share their work in the sciences via the information press. Much as chapter 4 illustrated, engineers and amateur scientists wrote letters to the editor to publicize their new inventions and to invite critiques from the public. They announced the new inventions as useful technical breakthroughs. The projects pitched in the press included a pump to extract the water in wells, a mechanism to improve the efficiency of mills, and a table to enable clerks to write as fast as one could speak.[12] Other contributions on scientific topics were more observational in nature, covering the different readings gleaned from thermometers, documenting the behavior of squirrels, or relaying the success of a putty used to waterproof cellars.[13] In Amiens, for example, Buissart corresponded with his fellow *physiciens* over the accuracy of hygrometers in the affiches.[14] Debates concerning the sciences persisted into the 1790s.

Agriculture also remained a prominent topic in the letters to the editor. Letter writers focused on how to mitigate the grain shortages that were widely reported in the countryside in 1789. As early as January, letters suggesting recipes for bread that could compensate for the shortage of grains appeared. Potatoes—even the frozen ones—one writer assured, could be used to make bread.[15] Reports on frozen grains and the related shortages continued into the summer. A letter from Tessier mailed from the experimental royal farm at Rambouillet reported that despite the hardship of the winter, the writer firmly believed conditions were improving: the fields seeded in

March, April, and May looked healthy and abundant.[16] In the countryside surrounding Dijon, writers to the affiches discussed the local 1,200-livre prize at stake for the farmer who brought the most wheat to market over the 1789–90 winter.[17] Reports on mitigating diseases in livestock also persisted into the Revolution.[18] The interest of the writing public in agricultural questions was sustained throughout the period.

Letters documenting bienfaisance also continued to appear in the newspaper throughout the early years of the Revolution, where writers raised awareness for groups in need of assistance, solicited the support of their fellow readers, and provided examples of model bienfaiteurs and bienfaitrices. Some of the published contributions served as documentation of donations to beneficent organizations, such as an association in Marseille to support poor sailors and their families, or M. de Boissy's Compagnie de MM. de Charité in Paris.[19] Others focused on the bienfaisance enacted by priests or landlords, such as the seigneur of Thoste in Burgundy, who provided for the subsistence of some fifty-six poor families in the region.[20] Letters to the editor concerning bienfaisance remained as prevalent in 1789 as they had been before the Revolution.

During the winter of 1789–90, the information press also continued the prerevolutionary trend of portraying bienfaisance as good citizenship, and writers even portrayed the royal family as good citizens who enacted bienfaisance. Letters detailing the queen's charity in a sympathetic light appeared throughout the period of 1789–91.[21] Such accounts painted a portrait of the royal family as model benefactors who were aware of and responsive to the needs of the people. In August 1789, a writer noted that when Versailles experienced grain shortages, and lines stretched between thirty and forty people deep at the bakeries, the king and queen ordered that they did not want any pastries for themselves or their households.[22] In the affiches the royal family were cast as responsive and bienfaisante, and letters to the editor concerning the royal family reflected a generally favorable opinion of them that persisted until their attempted flight in June 1791.

In 1790 and 1791 bienfaisance appeared in letters to the editor less frequently. Letters documenting model benefactors decreased, and in their place writers covered organizations. Such groups used the newspaper page to display transparency in the receiving and spending of donations. At least in Paris, this decline in beneficent letters reflected the influence of Dominique-Joseph Garat as an editor of the Journal de Paris; he did not share the other editors' penchant for philanthropic subjects.[23] In most of the affiches, the editorial leadership did not change in this period. The shift in their coverage of bienfaisance after 1790 likely reflected the space constraints editors faced as they adapted their weekly newspapers to a more competitive marketplace.

The history of the information press after 1789 is, in part, one of continuity, for writers expressed many of the same preoccupations with literature, the sciences and arts, agriculture and bienfaisance that they had in previous years. Politics were a growing part, but not the only part, of the conversation. After all, many of the revolutionary affiches were published by the editors who had held the Old Regime privilège to publish the paper. The editorial responses once censorship had fallen varied. While some editors became staunch supporters of the Revolution, others viewed events in Paris warily and maintained a more conservative approach to the coverage of political events by refusing to print opinion pieces. Jean Milcent, for example, eventually gave up his affiches in Rouen and moved to Paris to focus instead on the arts.[24] André Villot in Dijon adapted his coverage to suit the political climate of the moment and continued to publish into the Directory.[25] While their politics varied, in the early years of the Revolution the editors maintained the publication of letters from their readers. Writers throughout France continued to turn to the affiches to debate issues that were of importance to them.

Writing Revolutionary Events

To read the letters to the editor in this period is to trace the political education of a wide spectrum of figures who participated in revolutionary events. In their letters, writers processed the experience of rapid political and social change. The experience for them was both exciting and disconcerting, and they highlighted the contingent nature of the early months of the Revolution. Moreover, the letters to the affiches show that members of the general public debated what particular moments meant, and they brought that contentiousness to the press. They shared a concern with offering a personal, up-close record of what they had witnessed. Writers did not always reach the same conclusions about the significance of revolutionary *journées*, especially in the summer of 1789.

Revolutionary events appeared in the affiches after the storming of the Bastille on July 14. In Paris especially, writers focused on the presence of street crowds, which they generally depicted as immense and uncontrollable. On August 5, a letter signed "L. C. D. L." recounted the day when the Bastille was taken. According to the writer, caught up in the moment, the crowd tried to destroy nearby buildings, and they succeeded in breaking doors and windows. Such looting incidents do not appear in the standard accounts of the Bastille; the heavy rain on the evening of July 14 forced most of those involved to take shelter or go home. Nevertheless, the letter asserting that looting had taken place praised the chevalier de Laizer, who led his soldiers to defend the neighborhood and set up guards "to avoid disorder and pillaging that was beginning to reach its height."[26] Whether the letter was authored by de Laizer himself is plausible but unknown. While the letter provided no evidence that looting actually transpired, it articulated an anxiety about spontaneous collective action. Descriptions in the papers of being swept up into a massive crowd gave an impression of the summers' events as unsettling and powerful. While historians have found that the symbol of the Bastille was clarified by the press that summer as events unfolded, the vantage point of the affiches reveals a more iterative process as letters writers considered its significance.[27]

The July 22 murder of the two Old Regime officials, the controller-general of finances, Joseph Foullon de Doué, and his son-in-law, the intendant of Paris, Louis-Bénigne-François Bertier de Sauvigny, that occurred the week following the Bastille's fall was outlined in detail by another anonymous letter published on July 25. The writer described the crowd that convened on the Place de Grève before the Hôtel de Ville, the site of executions under the Old Regime: "The tumultuous movements spread in an immense crowd that filled the square. Monsieur the Mayor, accompanied by many Electeurs, came down to the multitude and endeavored to calm them. The calm did not last long; new cries of death could be heard."[28] The eyewitness accounts of the events of July 14, but especially those of July 22, communicated the shock that the deputies and many Parisians felt. The letters to the editor published in the immediate aftermath of these events show writers who struggled in the moment with how to interpret crowd action.

Letters published after the taking of the Bastille also portrayed the revolutionary crowds as knowledgeable, legitimate, and well organized. On July 17 a letter appeared in the *Journal de Paris* comparing the emergence from the crowd of capable political speakers to the birth of a fully armed Minerva springing from Jupiter's brain.[29] One of the earliest depictions of collective action was printed in the *Journal de Paris* on July 19, portraying a peaceful crowd of women with a clear agenda. A M. Jacquinot, the secretary of the St-Etienne-du-Mont district where the events transpired, wrote a letter describing the women's actions. The market women of the Place Maubert were invited to participate in the mass at the Église Sainte-Geneviève, where they placed a bouquet adorned with ribbons near the shrine of Saint Geneviève's relics. They refused any gifts, and instead demanded "bread and liberty for the people."[30] Market women such as the Dames des Halles used "liberty" as a demand that referenced specific marketplace issues that affected their business, such as the freedom to sell in public spaces, or the freedom to rent from multiple shelter providers.[31] Women's collective action also tended to center around the neighborhood where they lived and worked. Their political and commercial agency within the neighborhood space was widely accepted throughout the eighteenth century.[32] Jacquinot's account made clear that the market women of the Place Maubert acted politically and that they had the moral authority to do so. The depictions published in July of revolutionary crowds in the information press show the avid interest of the writing public in the collective action they witnessed and in which they participated. Swept up in the Revolution that summer, writers shared competing reactions to what the events meant.

Over the summer of 1789, letter writers emphasized the significance of the moment through which they were living. Their accounts conveyed a sense that the Revolution harbored possibilities for imagining new communities. An anonymous letter in August called for the institution of a *fête nationale* to celebrate the unparalleled events of the past month and proposed a grand meal that would bring everyone together without regard for social difference:

I would like all the inhabitants of the good city of Paris to set their tables in public and take their meals in front of their houses. The rich and the poor would be united and all ranks combined. The streets, adorned with tapestries, littered with leaves and flowers, and it would be forbidden to drive through by carriage or horse. All the National Guard on foot would easily maintain order everywhere. The capital, from one end to the other, would form an immense family; we would see a million people sitting at the same table; the health of the King would be carried by the sound of all the bells, by the noise of a hundred cannon shots, the salvos of the musketry, and at the same moment in all the neighborhoods of Paris; and on that day, the nation will have its "grand couvert."[33]

The *grand couvert* was the name of the ceremonial public dinners the king and queen held at court, but this letter also prefigured a practice in revolutionary Paris, especially after 1792, of *le banquet républicain* or *banquet fraternel*, which are well known for the songs written and performed there.[34] The writer's vision for the future reflected the tenor of the Revolution in 1789, which celebrated the monarchy and the Revolution together. The writer also looked to newly formed revolutionary groups for leadership by depicting the emergence of the National Guard as a capable and patriotic police force.

Moreover, the celebratory nature of the letter proposing a fraternal banquet echoed sonically—with convivial conversation, toasts to the king, the ringing of bells, and the volley of artillery. The proposal also reimagined the use of public space, where the street would become a banquet hall and social rank would fall away. This letter was published on August 30, after the night of August 4 when the deputies of the Constituent Assembly renounced all manner of Old Regime privileges. As chapter 2 has shown, writers had for some time performed in the press other forms of self-description than social position. By the summer of 1789, some were prepared to dispense with distinctions based on social position entirely.

Writers such as the proposer of the *fête nationale* articulated a hopeful vision of the future. Their perspective differed in scope from the practical, local, and incremental changes that writers prior to the Revolution invariably articulated in their letters to the editor. Compared to the prerevolutionary correspondence, the writers who published with the affiches in 1789 and thereafter were more willing both to commend and, as we will see, to criticize the Revolution and its leaders. The portrayals of the revolutionary crowd in the wake of the taking of the Bastille reveal the rather contentious views that persisted in the affiches. The range of opinions expressed in the press show that for many, a transformation in political attitudes did not predate the Revolution but instead was shaped by their participation in it.

As the Revolution spread beyond Paris that summer, letters from the provinces documented the rumors of bands of brigands that circulated in late July and August.[35] The Great Fear traveled by word of mouth, spreading in waves throughout the kingdom in a matter of days beginning in mid-July.[36] In fact, the word "brigand" characterized all manner of people deemed undesirable; the flexibility of the term may have helped the rumor spread, as its meaning could adapt to various regions and social groups.[37] Some villages received news that groups of brigands were arriving from multiple directions, which seemed to give the rumors greater local credence and urgency.[38] While the Great Fear spread orally, it was also covered in the information press, which tracked its movement.

Throughout July and August, rumors regarding the stockpiling of grain circulated. Oral and print cultures were again linked, as writers used the information press to denounce accusations and clear their names. One letter cosigned by *procureurs-syndics* in the department of Senlis in northern France tried to dispel rumors by disparaging those who were quick to believe such unfounded claims: "Credulity avidly adopts anything that malignity invents." Having conducted interviews and inspected the region for stockpiling, the writers reported, "There is not a single grain of wheat, nor traces, nor the possibility that it had been deposited here."[39] In a similar letter to the editor,

Guy le Gentil, the marquis de Paroy, who served as a deputy for the nobility in the Estates General, went so far as to offer an award of 1,000 écus to anyone who could prove the calumnious rumors that he was stockpiling grain.[40] In Normandy a series of letters to the editor concerned the circulation of rumors over the grain supply in Dieppe.[41] Letters emphasizing loyalty to the Revolution and declaring that the writer was not stockpiling goods were common throughout July and August. Denials of grain hoarding published in the newspapers that summer are significant because they show that some nobles took the rumors that aristocrats were hoarding grain seriously enough to deny them. However, the letters stopped far short of describing these cases as symptoms of a generalized plot. In the face of the rumors that circulated in 1789, the information press adapted their long-standing practices to new purposes. They tried to provide a truthful and public record—to offer evidence that would be of use to their readers.

Taking Part in the Revolution

The total number of letters to the editors of the Parisian and provincial information press declined over the autumn of 1789, but the letters that did appear showed writers' avid interest in taking part in the Revolution. In much the same style as the writers to the affiches under the Old Regime had done, letter writers explored systemic challenges in personal terms. One vivid example of this process of making revolutionary participation personal was patriotic gift giving.

Inspired by the delegation of women giving their jewelry before the Constituent Assembly the previous summer, many of the letters to the information press composed during the first winter concerned contributions to la Patrie.[42] Thus, "a young Parisian lady who desires the general good of the Nation" asked the deputies of the Constituent Assembly to accept her gift to the nation of 2,000 livres. Referring to herself in the third person, she wrote, "Her wish would have been to present them herself to this august Assembly; but, wishing to remain unrecognized, she finds herself deprived of this honor."[43] In a similar letter to the Marseillaise newspaper, in which the author identified herself only as "L . . . ," a woman reflected on the act of patriotic gift giving, which had "warmed my imagination" and prompted the reflections she enclosed. By remarking on how reading about other patriotic gifts had influenced her own, Madame L. spoke to the information press's long-standing efforts to encourage emulation by providing noteworthy examples. The affiches still expressed their dedication to sharing useful information, and the well-being of the nation became part of that conversation.

Yet Madame L. proposed a somewhat different approach to gift giving by focusing not on a gift to the nation but rather on French commerce. After considering how she might participate in supporting the Revolution in the form of a gift, she decided she could not bear to give up her wedding ring. She instead proposed purchasing in the future only goods made in France, which she marked by the privation of "English carriages, English heads-carves, English ribbons, English washbowls, and English hardware of any kind." Henceforth she would serve her guests only on French plates and silver, and her cupboard would be devoid of English linens, knits, and buttons. As she saw it, stimulating French commerce, "to make our manufactories work, to establish new ones, and in doing so to nourish the large number of workmen who want for bread by lack of work," would benefit the Revolution more than her wedding ring would.[44] As citizen-consumers, she conveyed that all had a role to play in supporting the Revolution.

Writers linked their support for the Revolution to the National Assembly and to the king in their descriptions of revolutionary participation. Nau Deville, a self-described "citizen-soldier" and member of the District committee of Saint-Germain-l'Auxerrois, recounted the intensity of his sentiments at a dinner party at the archbishop's residence. The Voluntary Company of the Battalion of Saint-Germain-l'Auxerrois, the Third Company, and the Committee Saint-Germain-l'Auxerrois, as he told it, had all been invited to partake in the festivities. After a mass at the church of Saint-Germain-l'Auxerrois, where the royal family habitually attended mass when in residence at the Tuileries Palace, the guests proceeded to the archbishop's residence for a dinner party for some five or six hundred guests. Although in the church they had entered and exited according to their rank or order, at the dinner all such "order was broken," and guests sat without concern for rank as a "family of Citizens." After a moment of silence devoted to God, the quiet was broken by a general toast to the health of the king, and "cries of long live the King, long live our General, long live the Nation, rang out through the hall." Nau Deville remarked that "it seemed we were intoxicated: indeed, we are. It is the intoxication of patriotism."[45] As his account illustrated, readers expressed a nascent patriotism, along with the feeling that they were being swept up in the moment of social transformation. A writer from Grenoble echoed such sentiments in his description of a public reading of the king's speech before the National Assembly on February 4, which was met with cries of joy that echoed through the streets of Grenoble.[46] The fusion of personal affinity for the revolution with support for the king and the nation was inscribed throughout the letters to the affiches.

In contrast to the elation of patriotic banquets, some writers emphasized the uneven emotional and physical impacts of the Revolution. One account by the doctor and founder of French psychiatry, Philippe Pinel, focused on the impact that the uncertainty of revolution had on public health. As editor of the *Gazette de santé* until it merged with the *Journal de médecine, chirurgie et pharmacie* in 1789, Pinel had cultivated a dialogue with the readers of his paper; during the Revolution he pursued his work on mental health in new professional venues.[47] In his letter to the editors of the *Journal de Paris*, he described how the social body and individuals alike had experienced in the preceding decades "all the infirmities of a social order ready to expire, or, to use Rousseau's expression from 1760, of a constitution which threatened France with a coming deterioration." He saw the last decades of the Old Regime as those of a society in decay, where "the slackening in all places of society and the fatal progress of personal interest had frozen all hearts, constantly saddened and discouraged by the idea of arbitrary power." In Pinel's interpretation, the political and social limits of the Old Regime were borne upon the bodies of people in the form of chronic illnesses.

By January 1790 Pinel declared that France had taken on a new outlook, which began with the events in Paris and in the provinces in the summer of 1789. In describing the symptoms in the bodies of his patients, Pinel also explored the impact of the Revolution on the collective social body. He tracked what he saw as the health benefits of the Revolution on individual patients, in whom he witnessed "a calm serenity and sometimes a more or less ardent enthusiasm," and he heard from many that since the coming of the Revolution they felt better. As far as he was concerned, the changes of 1789 had reset the balance of nature and, "as if by virtue of electricity," reanimated the body and soul.[48] The metaphor of the Revolution as an electric shock echoed the treatments of Franz Mesmer and the parlor experiments with electric currents that were so prevalent in the years preceding the Revolution. Pinel's letter was popular; it was reprinted in the *Esprit des Journaux*.

At the same time, Pinel documented the vast range of effects of the Revolution on the bodies of men and women. While he found that illness in the capital had declined overall, some people suffered profoundly. He noted one man who was so tormented by "panicked terrors" that he had committed suicide.[49] Long interested in treating mental illness, Pinel would be appointed to Bicêtre Hospital in 1793 and to Pitié-Salpêtrière in 1795. As Pinel's letter to the editor underscored, the Revolution had come to shape every aspect of lived experience. Particularly concerned with the constitution of human bodies, Pinel turned to the body politic in order to measure the health of the nation, and in general, he found revolution beneficial to the body and the soul. Even so, he pointed out the potential harms that social change and ensuing instability could present for individuals.

Nau Deville, the district member who described patriotism as a form of intoxication, and Pinel, the doctor who documented the bodily impact of political change, both praised the Revolution. And yet their accounts also acknowledged the ambivalence and uncertainty the Revolution harbored. The leaders of the Revolution were no more immune to the physical and psychological strain of revolution than were the observers in the press. Maximilien Robespierre's physical bouts of illness, brought on by personal and political conflict in mid-1790, November 1792, September 1793, and February, April, and June 1794 are one well-documented example.[50] Letters to the editor such as Pinel's were no doubt motivated by the authors' desire to publicize their life's work and burnish their reputations, and, as Nina Gelbart has suggested, to offer a semblance of order in a time of disorder—to search for a new equilibrium that would remedy individual and social health.[51] At the same time, Pinel's description highlighted the emotional and physical impact of the Revolution on those who experienced it.

Over the first year of the Revolution, the information press had served as a key site for conversations among readers about what the unfolding Revolution meant for them. Writers' correspondence about their participation confirmed that the Revolution was a surprise for most people. The early years of the Revolution were a period of political education, as people responded to contingent events. The writing public's experience was consistent with what historians have previously found for the political formation that transpired in the Revolution's early years among the deputies in the Constituent Assembly.[52] Letters to the editor showed that the writing public adapted long-practiced habits to new uses: they invoked the paper as an important locus for useful knowledge, they offered material evidence that their fellow readers could evaluate, and they shared noteworthy examples for emulation. In short, while it is unlikely that the readers of the information press imagined the Revolution before it began, once it had begun, the repertoires on which they had long relied for all manner of practical discussions were put to political uses.

Public Policy and the Information Press

Over the next two years, the affiches took on the role of communicating the Revolution by publishing letters from the deputies of the Constituent

Assembly, and by printing letters from people who sought information about the local impacts of the Assembly's policies. Deputies themselves wrote letters to the editor that functioned as brief, unofficial reports, which they sent to the editor. For example, the conservative deputy Abbé de Bonneval wrote to his constituents via the *Journal de Paris* to counter a report that said he had not been allowed to speak in the Constituent Assembly, when in fact he had indeed been permitted; he explained he had only declined to speak voluntarily so that decisions could be made more quickly. In a similar manner, the more moderate deputy Jacques-Guillaume Thouret wrote on behalf of the Constitutional Committee to correct an unreliable copy of a decree circulated in the press; he said the errors confused the document's original meaning.[53] Provincial affiches also published letters to the editor written by deputies. The Abbé Grégoire wrote to correct the editor of the affiches in Dijon.[54] Jean-Jacques Duval d'Eprémesnil's letter to the *Gazette de France* was republished by the affiches in Grenoble.[55] In some cases, the editor initiated correspondence with the deputy, as the editor of the affiches in Arras, Barbe-Thérèse Lefebvre Marchand, did in her letter to Louis Marie, marquis d'Estourmel. Estourmel wrote back to the paper the week after Marchand asked him to comment on poor relief in the department of Pas-de-Calais in the wake of the closure of monasteries. He assured her that funds would go to the department to support local poor relief, and he emphasized that he knew the needs of those in the department.[56] Indeed, a major aim of the letters from the deputies was communicating what the decisions made in the Constituent Assembly meant for people living in their department.

Some deputies wrote letters to the editor on a more regular basis to clarify their positions, combat rumors, and express a continued affinity for their hometown. The deputy Charles-François Bouche wrote to the *Journal de Paris* to declare his affiliation as president of the Feuillant club in 1791.[57] The affiches in Amiens published letters to the editor from the deputy Jean-Charles Laurendeau. In his letters in 1790 and 1791 he clarified his policy positions, including his support for the Civil Constitution of the Clergy. He described his activities in the Assembly, but he also declared his willingness to return to "live and die among my *concitoyens*" in Amiens as soon as his duties as a deputy concluded.[58] Laurendeau's published missive illustrated how a deputy could use a letter to the editor in an effort to shore up support among his constituents in the provinces. To an extent, the deputies' letters functioned in a similar manner to those addressed to editors by intendants under the Old Regime, who had asked that the papers print clarifications or announcements from time to time. But letters from the deputies were also doing something new: by addressing the readers of general information newspapers, they expressed their interest in appealing to and developing public opinion. In Rennes, Nantes, Brest, Angers, Montauban, and Agen, correspondence from deputies to their constituents led directly to the founding of more newspapers.[59]

For readers of the information press, the newspaper remained a trustworthy channel to clarify how the Revolution would change their lives and livelihoods. In their assessments of the impact of the Constituent Assembly's decrees, writers expressed the sense of confidence and investment in local change that they had communicated for decades in the affiches. In their letters, writers conveyed that they had the right to criticize and discuss changes that affected them. Writers solicited clarification on how new laws might apply in their department, and they directed these inquiries to the information press. For example, Malardot, a lawyer from Dijon, wrote in to the affiches to discuss the impact of tax reforms. His letter consisted of an analysis of the law and its ramifications, and in particular the financial burden for the general public.[60] In a similar manner in Amiens, a debate around the personal impacts of the Revolution emerged in the affiches between two men: Leroux, who held the office of *arpenteur royal* before the Revolution, and Breton. Breton made clear in his letter that all surveyors had to acquire the revolutionary government's certification, even if they had held a royal office before the Revolution. Breton asserted that the privileges that Leroux claimed "are of the Old Regime," and Leroux could claim no exclusive right to a suppressed office.[61] Breton's letter was part of a local dispute over an office he wanted, but his defense of why Leroux was no longer entitled to this post reflected the impact of the Revolution at the local level. His justification relied on a critique of privilege and the conviction that the Constituent Assembly's authority on the question of public offices was paramount. In bringing this dispute to the affiches, he sought to settle the issue in the court of public opinion too.

Parish priests were among those who wrote to the information press to clarify how the Constituent Assembly's decision to nationalize church land, and later to require a constitutional oath, would affect their lives and their parishioners. A letter to the èditor of the *Affiches de Normandie* by Dupuys, the parish priest in Salmonville-la-Sauvage, a village northeast of Rouen, asked how the decision that church property be placed at the disposal of the nation would affect the rights of priests and the local peasantry to the fruits of trees on their land. The harsh winter had killed many of the trees, and the priest wanted to inquire about who was responsible for replanting those that had died.[62] An English doctor named Davis also wrote to the paper to propose a method for parceling the nationalized church property that was inspired by the administration of city lands in London.[63] Parish priests and villagers wrote letters to the editor in Arras the following year concerning the impacts of the Civil Constitution of the Clergy. Both juring and nonjuring clergy used their letters to clarify the record and make the case for their decision before the public.[64] The revolutionary affiches allowed for writers to speak more directly than ever before to the local impacts of the policy decisions made in Paris.

For those who disagreed with local administrative decisions, writers turned to the information press to settle their complaint in the court of public opinion. For example, a contributor identified only as "one of your subscribers" wrote to question the local Commune's mandate that the newspaper no longer publish prices for commodities sold in Dijon. The decision was made, according to the writer, out of fear that mentioning prices might lead to an increase in the cost of grain. According to the writer, the opposite had happened: the prices had increased since the paper stopped listing them. Disagreeing with the Commune, the writer argued that for the sake of the poor in the country, the prices should appear in the newspaper.[65] The anonymous writer from Dijon did not make an argument about his rights as a citizen, but he did suggest that the paper had a responsibility to the public. Notably, the writer's rhetoric relied on local contexts rather than appeals to the nation. When it came to what the author anticipated to be convincing, local and material explanations that writers had long practiced in the affiches prevailed.

Some writers used their letters to assert the importance of the expansion of rights. They directed their letters at specific policies debated in the Constituent Assembly. By 1791 especially, writers were more willing than ever before to take positions on the political agenda. They wrote opinion pieces calling for free expression and freedom from surveillance in the theater.[66] Emphasizing the fraternity among all Frenchmen, an anonymous writer to the *Affiches de Montpellier* supported full rights of citizenship for Jews two weeks before the Constituent Assembly voted on civil rights for the Sephardim.[67] M. Benjamin, a colonel in the National Guard in Dimont, wrote to the editors of the *Journal de Paris* a year later to call for active citizenship for all Jews in the weeks before the Assembly voted.[68] The increase in letters that took a political position signaled that the information press was seen by its contributors as a space where their opinions would be heard. Letter writers wanted to participate in politics, and the editors made space in their pages for such participation.

It is noteworthy that writers turned to the affiches in order to discuss politics, because the information press was only one of the possible venues where such debates could take place. By 1791 political factions and newspapers that reflected their positions had established themselves in Paris and in the provinces. The proliferation of newspapers printing on a daily schedule since 1789 had provided Parisian and provincial readers with more options for reading material that aligned with their political preferences. Nevertheless, many deputies and members of the public turned to the generally more moderate affiches to present their political opinions. The information press remained a trusted venue where information could be collected, debated, and shared.

Rumor, Reputation, and the Information Press

Writers continued to turn to the affiches as a reliable record keeper over 1790 and 1791, but the tenor of their letters to the editor began to change. A dramatic increase of pamphlets and brochures had accompanied the end of censorship in 1789, and such proliferation grew in the ensuing months and years.[69] Many revolutionary publications were anonymous or pseudonymous in nature, which made it difficult for the reader to determine who had written what. Counterfeit versions of popular titles proliferated. Jacques Hébert's *Le Père Duchesne*, which took to inserting the word "veritable" in its title, serves as one familiar example of the lack of regulation that allowed impersonators to flourish.[70] In letters to the editors of the affiches, writers expressed their wish to "détromper le public"—to disabuse readers of rumor and to correct the record. In one such letter, the officers of the Enghien regiment wrote from Gap to the *Affiches du Dauphiné* to demand a correction that only the "honesty and impartiality" of the affiches could offer.[71] In their letters, writers situated the affiches as a truthful record keeper, and they called on the editors to print their correspondence because they claimed it would benefit the public. For writers whose reputation was at stake, the information press was a longstanding channel to settle confusion and garner public attention.

Efforts to correct the record came from letter writers who declared and denied their affiliations with prominent clubs. Letters of affiliation declared membership to the Société des Amis des Noirs and the Jacobins.[72] In Dijon the sculptor Daujon and the joiner Nefliez wrote to the affiches to note their surprise in seeing their names on the list of members of the Société des Amis de la Paix, which met at the home of the carpenter Tussat. They disavowed membership in the conservative club, saying they were not at present nor would they ever be members, and they asked the paper to print a letter to that effect. Labrosse, a *procureur*, Boquet, a *limonadier* and *épicier*, and the

Abbé Colas each wrote letters to the affiches the previous April and May to disavow membership in the same club.[73] The departmental council banned Tussat's club on December 29, 1790, less than a week before Daujon's and Nefliez's letter was published.[74] Letters asserting affiliation and nonaffiliation rested on the widely shared premise that the information press was a source of reliable information. They made claims about the affiches as the storehouse of useful, truthful knowledge. The prevalence of correspondence aimed at correcting the record further underscored the ways that many contributors understood the role of the affiches.

In letters responding to rumor, the most frequent request was to print a denial of what the writer claimed were false attributions of authorship. Letter writers disavowed authorship of pamphlets, newspapers, and even letters to the editor.[75] For example, the inspector Havas swore in his letter to the editor that he was in no way involved with the "direction, editing, profits or losses" of the *Chronique de Normandie*.[76] Charles-François, marquis de Bonnay, denied being an editor of the royalist pamphlet *Les Actes des Apôtres*, which the police had recently visited.[77] An anonymous writer disparaged the "new and dangerous fraud" by printers who used his pamphlet's title to publish work that was not his, an act he described as "literary brigandage."[78] Similar letters to the editor had appeared before the Revolution, but they increased in frequency as the number of revolutionary newspapers in France burgeoned.

Other writers instead wrote to the affiches to claim a particular publication. For example, Joseph-Antoine Cerutti wrote to the *Journal de Paris* in what he claimed was his third attempt to get the editors' attention. Someone was printing his manuscript about the criminal code without his permission. As he saw it, this was an act of "typographic brigandage" that amounted to calumny and theft, both of which, he argued, undermined the freedom of the press.[79] Calumny was an attack that harmed one's reputation, but it did not necessarily have to be false. Calumnious attacks on the personal honor of the deputies of the Constituent Assembly also intensified during these years. Unable to tolerate assaults on their honor, the deputies devised a series of crimes of speech and opinion.[80] In calling the misattribution of authorship calumny, Cerutti called on the press to consider his personal honor. By describing false claims of authorship as calumnious attacks, writers argued that such attributions were direct and intentional affronts to their reputation.

Much of the recourse for calumny under the Old Regime, such as duels, *lettres de cachet*, and libel suits, were available only to social elites, but even they turned to the press to rebuff attacks on their honor. François Henri, comte de Virieu and deputy in the Constituent Assembly, wrote a letter to disavow the "absurd calumnies" printed about him in the press, and he declared his love of liberty.[81] Armand-Désiré de Vignerot du Plessis-Richelieu, duc d'Aiguillon and one of the leaders of the night of August 4, 1789, wrote to the *Journal de Paris* to defend himself against direct and calumnious attacks and to declare his "attachment to the Constitution and my ardent zeal for the defense of the rights of the people," which he said in no way weakened his profound respect for the king.[82] In response to rumors he had heard, the deputy Claude-Emmanuel de Pastoret wrote to the *Journal de Paris* in response to calumnious rumors about his patriotism in order to affirm his constant support for the sovereignty of the people and the Constitution.[83] The deputy Michel Louis Etienne Regnaud wrote to the *Journal de Paris* to respond to a rumor about whether he had been at the opera earlier in the month.[84] Deputies wrote to the information press throughout 1790 and 1791 in order to counter reputational attacks.

Less prominent figures likewise responded to rumors they deemed harmful to their personal honor or the honor of their town. Abraham Locquet, an administrator for the Somme department and a justice of the peace for the Canton d'Hornoy, wrote to the affiches in Amiens to disavow the claims of "infamous calumniators" that he was coordinating those in his department to stop paying the *champart*. He declared his loyalty to the National Assembly and his intent to follow their decrees to the letter.[85] A M. Soret wrote to the *Affiches de l'Orléanois* to counter claims made in the *Feuille du Jour* earlier that month that, in his opinion, disparaged the municipal elections in Orléans.[86] In short, writers took it on themselves to settle attacks on their honor. They too situated the readers of the information press as judges in the disputes over their reputation.

Writers also took to the newspapers to reject calumnious claims and settle disputes when they had little other remedy. In Dijon, for example, two parties brought their complaint to the editor of the affiches. Beline, the captain in the Picardie regiment, wrote to combat what he saw as "injurious charges" that a man named Renaudin had spread against him. Beline claimed Renaudin's son had asked to join the regiment while Beline was away from the home, so his wife had registered and paid the young man for his enlistment.[87] Renaudin responded with a letter of his own, in which he argued that the captain had not followed proper procedure of inquiring with the young man's parents before enlisting him. He stated that his own son was too young, and Beline knew it. Unable to find a resolution elsewhere, Renaudin brought his complaint to the paper, where he wrote, "I leave it to the public to weigh in the balance the fairness of Beline's conduct and mine."[88]

Published disputes such as this one showed writers turned to the newspaper in order to convince others to listen and judge the evidence for themselves. The increasing concern about personal honor in the revolutionary affiches was emblematic of the preoccupation with authority that writers had formulated in the Old Regime press. In the *Journal de Paris*, for example, writers increasingly rejected rumors that concerned them by writing to the paper. Before the Revolution, writers showed little interest in calumny, and in 1789 letters raising issues of personal honor made up 1.4 percent of the total letters published. Over the year 1790, the proportion reached 14.5 percent of all letters published and rose to 26.5 percent between January and September 1791.[89] While similar letters had appeared in the prerevolutionary affiches, the proportion of letters concerned with reputation intensified during the Revolution, especially in 1791.

Over the spring and summer of 1791, the total number of letters to the editor published in the information press declined. The growing volume of calumnious attacks in the press and elsewhere heightened the stakes of participation in the pages of the affiches for letter writers and for those who published the newspapers. Editors rarely commented directly on the claims of calumny that they printed. In one exceptional case, Justine Giroud included an editorial note after a letter to the editor where the writer claimed a previous letter in her affiches was calumnious. For her part, she asserted the claims were not calumny at all but rather sarcasm. Nevertheless, she said that she would be more careful in the future to preserve the tone of moderation that characterized her paper.[90] In most cases, however, editors simply published the letters from writers who wished to dispute calumny or rumor. From the vantage point of the letters to the editor, the culture of calumny was a revolutionary phenomenon that extended far beyond social elites to the broader writing public. Their correspondence underscored the urgency expressed by writers to educate newspaper readers and correct false claims.

For their part, deputies debated what freedom of the press ought to include throughout this period, and they expressed concerns about the threat that false claims posed to the public order. Article 11 of the Declaration of Rights of Man and of the Citizen addressed the issue of public order and free speech directly. But personal honor and public opinion remained urgent issues for the deputies from 1789 to 1793.[91] Writers expressed similar concerns in their letters to the editor, where they feared that false news would lead astray or divide the newspaper's readers.[92]

A de facto press freedom remained in place until August 1791. Yet even in this period of toleration between 1789 and 1791, newspapers that the authorities believed would pose a threat to public order were suppressed. The *Gazette de Paris* and the *Journal général de la cour et de la ville*, two archconservative newspapers, were convicted of libel in civil cases in 1790. On the opposite end of the political spectrum, Marat's press was impounded, and he was nearly arrested by the Châtelet in January 1790 for the inflammatory content he had printed in his *Ami du peuple*. In the first six months of 1790 alone, four libel suits were brought against Camille Desmoulins. Many suits over press freedom were brought before the Châtelet. When the Châtelet was replaced in the autumn of 1790 with a new revolutionary court system, prosecutions against the press ceased until 1791 after the massacre at the Champs de Mars on July 17 and the subsequent passage of the sedition law of July 18.[93] Fearing that radical papers that wrote of resistance to the law presented a threat to the public order, the deputies enacted constitutional provisions on August 22 and 23, 1791, which permitted prosecution for published calumnious attacks against the probity or intentions of public officials.[94] The Constituent Assembly passed the Constitution on September 3 and then disbanded at the end of September. The newly elected deputies of the Legislative Assembly took their seats. Though the laws curbing press freedom were not fully enforced, they seemed to have had a chilling effect on the editors and letter writers of the affiches. In August and September the information press stopped regularly printing letters. Perhaps the risk of prosecution was sufficient to suppress the letters to the editor, at least in the short term.

During the Revolution, the letters to the editor in Paris and in the provinces provided a locus for information sharing, critique, and debate through which readers voiced their opinions on agriculture, commerce, medicine, bienfaisance, the sciences, and the arts. As the system of censorship began to fall away in 1788 and 1789, writers brought to the affiches their opinions on politics and current events. The habits of mind that writers had cultivated in the forum of letters to the editor over the previous two decades equipped them to imagine change on a new level and to communicate it compellingly. The self-confidence that had bolstered Old Regime responses to reform as it related to scientific experimentation, social welfare, or agricultural innovation were now brought to bear on a more expansive scale. Once given the opportunity, writers voiced their political opinions boldly, bringing their practical approach to a range of social problems they now believed demanded their participation.

The affiches continued to provide room for debate through letters to the editor, at least until the autumn of 1791. In the early months of 1789, writers commented on the same wide range of subjects so typical of the Old Regime information press, expressing a spirit of optimism about the human capacity to modify the sciences and society. They articulated the desire to figure out intellectual puzzles, and they shared a general commitment to implementing local changes. The writers also refashioned the information press as a responsive site for the discussion of politics. Deputies in the Constituent Assembly wrote to those who had elected them via the affiches. Writers who wanted to know just how policies in the Assembly would impinge on their own lives wrote letters to the editor. Their correspondence vividly conveyed the political education of the writing public.

The spike in letters concerning personal reputation in 1791 showed how much communication had changed in the early years of the Revolution. In the wake of the summer of 1791, with the king's flight to Varennes and the massacre at the Champs de Mars, political uncertainty and the prevalence of calumnious attacks in the press took on a new significance for readers. The personal stakes of participation in the press had risen, both for editors and for those who wrote letters to them. The vibrant forum of letters to the editor that had shaped the affiches for more than two decades dwindled in the late summer and early autumn of 1791.

Moreover, press freedom had increased the number of newspapers that readers could choose from over the early years of the Revolution, and the affiches faced direct competition for the first time in their history. Many revolutionary newspapers printed letters from their readers as the affiches did. After 1791 the editors of some of the newspapers, such as the *Journal de Paris* and the *Affiches de Toulouse*, would renew the printing of letters from their readers. The *Journal de Provence*'s founding editor, Ferréol Beaugeard, welcomed the Revolution and adapted his paper to make room for political news, but the number of letters declined in 1791; only three letters appeared in the paper that summer.[95] Other newspapers, such as the *Affiches de l'Orléanois* and the *Affiches d'Angers*, abandoned the publication of letters to the editor. Some newspapers ceased to publish altogether, such as the *Affiches de Montpellier*, which ended its run in 1791.

The style of conversations fostered in the information press likely found new revolutionary venues. A proliferation of social organizations provided spaces for debate and facilitated more efficient responses from those in authority than the newspapers ever had. In Paris the neighborhood districts and, after the spring of 1790, section meetings, organized ostensibly for the election of local and national representatives, continued to meet spontaneously and provide for local administrative needs.[96] Political cafés became vibrant spaces where information was read, announced, and debated. And there was a great proliferation of popular clubs, which began as gatherings for deputies to the National Assembly to discuss policy but grew into networks that spread throughout the provinces and the Atlantic world to unite partisans around a shared ideological position and policy agenda.[97] In just three years, 1,500 clubs had formed throughout France; by 1791 every department had at least one. Clubs also served to connect the provincial town to a national community.[98] The forum of letters to the editor had provided space for debate and motivated projects for social change and scientific inquiry. Clubs, sections, and cafés moved into the discursive space the information press had occupied, providing a new means of sociability and facilitating accountability from both the local administration and the national government. The habits of mind that writers had forged in the affiches were applied in new sites to implement practical, social, and political changes.

Conclusion

In 1777 a dentist named Catalan who worked
in Paris on the rue Dauphine summed up the goals of the information press
as he saw them: "To encourage emulation, to do justice to merit, to instruct
the Public about discoveries useful to humanity, this is the law that you, your-
selves, have imposed."[1] For many readers, the information press served as a
venue for instruction, as a space for debate framed by a responsive readership, and as a source of inspiration that readers could emulate. As writers
often put it, "all that was useful to humanity" fit within the purview of the
paper.

Catalan captured the aims that editors themselves had set for the information press. Between 1770 and 1788, editors launched affiches in towns and
cities throughout France, and in the prospectuses announcing the appearance of their newspapers, they frequently requested correspondence from
their subscribers. Licensing, censorship, postal systems, and the interests of
the editors themselves shaped the content that appeared on the newspaper
page. Nevertheless, the public engagement with the affiches was extensive;
readers accessed the newspaper by subscriptions delivered via the post and
through social spaces such as reading rooms, booksellers' shops, and cafés.
By inviting and publishing letters from their readers, editors fostered an epistolary reciprocity that played a major role in defining the general information newspapers.

Thousands of participants, representing a wide and diverse readership, wrote to the affiches in the two decades before the Revolution. Some of the writers in question were published authors, or were already or would soon become public officials. But in a great many cases, their only foray into print was their letter to the editor. The relatively low cost of writing a letter to one's local paper permitted writers, men and women who lacked the resources or social networks to publish a book or pamphlet, to see their ideas in print. And for the historian, listening to such voices offers a substantially new perspective on how the Enlightenment and the Revolution were experienced.

The affiches invited men and women from a spectrum of social positions into conversations with one another. By comparison with the men and women of the age who authored books or who participated in salons or academies, those who addressed letters to the editor constituted an expansive range of writers. Moreover, by publishing anonymous and pseudonymous letters in addition to signed ones, the editors opened up their papers to an even wider array of participants. For thousands of letter writers in Paris and the provinces, the affiches afforded them a new venue to share their opinions.

There is ample evidence, moreover, that letter writers learned from one another. The processes of citation and attribution in the affiches extended to books, newspapers, and other letter writers. Writers referenced periodicals as often as they did books. Rather than returning to the same titles repeatedly, they mentioned a capacious body of texts that pointed the readers toward a wider world of print beyond the newspaper page. References to books, periodicals, and other letters functioned as signposts, and they shaped the way that readers interpreted the information press. The letter writers also commented from time to time on the experience of reading itself—where, and how, and for what purposes they had confronted specific texts. Through such activity, they situated the forum of letters as a virtual space for reading together.

The discussions of popular science, agronomy, and bienfaisance in the press vividly conveyed how writers interacted with the information press, in such a way—as Catalan had described it—as to inspire emulation, recognize merit, and share useful and humane knowledge. Taken together, such letters reveal that writers responded to both the spectacular and the material, to suggestions of both dramatically new innovations and of relatively minor adjustments to the manner in which men and women interacted with their world. While popular attitudes toward knowledge ranged from the dramatic to the banal, what united them was a preoccupation with the utility of innovation. Hot-air balloons, electricity, medicinal remedies, and new fodder crops were all celebrated by letter writers because they were, above all, useful.

The published correspondence underscored the general fascination with the intellectual and cultural questions of the day. In letters to the editor the circulation of knowledge took on new, participatory forms. Experts used the affiches to foster public interest in new scientific questions. It was around some of the most visually arresting experiments that the conversation converged. The uncertainty about precisely how ballooning or electricity worked prompted more correspondence from savants who ran precise, well-documented experiments. But the writing public was not satisfied just to observe and read along; they wanted to take part and debate. In their responses, contestation was a defining feature of the press.

Writers concerned with farming in particular attempted to address a wider audience that spanned social distinctions. In their effort to increase knowledge about new agricultural products and techniques, they relied on information that they themselves had tested. In so doing, they formulated new claims to authority that opened up debates over land management, new crops, and crop diseases. Agriculture concerned writers and readers throughout the kingdom, and the information press was a space in which all could share useful knowledge, instruct the reader, and encourage emulation.

In their discussions of bienfaisance the letter writers advocated change based on a common sense of feeling. The frequent references to the "sensitive souls" among the prospective readers underscored their reliance on the empathy of the reader to motivate action. The changes they suggested were usually material and local, but the cumulative effect of such mundane proposals had the potential, nevertheless, to change people's lives. The correspondence about bienfaisance in the affiches fostered a questioning of the way things existed at present and afforded a space to act on that questioning, even—and perhaps particularly—on relatively minor issues. Writing a letter on bienfaisance afforded writers on the margins a means of claiming the authority to speak in the paper.

From the vantage point of the letters published in the affiches, the concept of Enlightenment was not a fixed doctrine or ideology but rather a psychology and an epistemology about the capacity of people like themselves to change the conditions of daily life, even if only in small steps. The optimism conveyed in letters concerning a new discovery stimulated public imagination, generating ideas that would put new knowledge to use. Some ideas were practical ones, suitable for immediate implementation. Others were suggestions that inadvertently delineated the limits of the writer's understanding of underlying scientific or social processes. But the majority of the suggestions for improvement shared in their pages entailed local and attainable efforts aimed at the amelioration of the material circumstances of people's day-to-day lives.

The letters to the editor of the late Old Regime continued to appear into the period of the French Revolution. The capacious nature of the affiches, as well as the wide range of participants and of opinions expressed, still endured after 1789, even as political debates, with the collapse of state censorship, came also to be included. Indeed, many of the conversations about agricultural reform, bienfaisance, the sciences, and the arts persisted at least until 1791. Such continuities suggest that political participation in the affiches was only a new manifestation of the larger debates that had come to define the information press, as newspapers focused on the amelioration of daily life and the questioning of established norms in an incremental, small-scale fashion.

The cultural and intellectual changes of the late Old Regime did not in themselves cause the Revolution, but the practices of reading, comparing, and critiquing that guided the letters to the editor prepared writers to act once the Revolution had begun. Through the pages of the affiches, writers had formulated new habits of mind, which they adapted to new political purposes after 1789. The information press changed too, responding to a new media market and press freedom. Through their letters, men and women, most of whom would never hold political office, could now share their political opinions as they had once shared ideas on the sciences, agriculture, and bienfaisance.

Penning a letter to the editor could also move a writer to consider his or her place within society in new ways. Participation via the letters to the editor was exciting for writers, who recorded in their diaries or private letters the thrill of seeing their letter in print. For approximately half of the writers, the inclusion of one's actual name and profession served as the basis of self-presentation. The other half of the writers adopted different modes of self-assertion, by submitting an unsigned letter, writing under a pen name, indicating only their initials, or describing themselves simply as "a subscriber." The editors of the affiches made room for all such contributions by publishing signed and unsigned letters alike. In doing so, the letters became a creative field for the experimentation with public personae and the consideration of one's subjectivity.

The dialogical character of the papers stimulated new forms of correspondence. Correspondence in the affiches drew on the epistolary norms of reciprocity in letters exchanged between individuals, where the reception of a letter invited a response from the recipient. Writers might openly appeal for feedback from the editors and from fellow readers, asking them to judge for themselves the merits of the letter. Editors often actively called for letters to the editor on particular subject matter to include in their pages. Their *notes du rédacteur* at the end of letters offered comments, corrections, or suggestions for further reading. And they arranged the pages themselves to invite conversation. They might also cut and paste into their own newspapers interesting letters garnered from other affiches. Such processes of cutting and pasting, and of replying and contesting, generated a dense web of exchange.

More than merely the solitary musings of individuals, the letters to the editor constituted a form of social media—an ongoing discussion between readers and newspaper editors, and among readers themselves. Taken together, the letters formed a complex and multitudinous conversation between interlocutors who would not otherwise have interacted with one another. Even the readers who did not write letters to the editor could see people like themselves participating in the paper. In bringing a more capacious group of voices to the fore, the affiches had the potential to transform people's reflections and perceptions about the world in which they lived, to modify, as it were, the very nature of the conversation.

Potential contributors to the information press relied on a variety of arguments to justify the publication of their letters. The merits and clarity of their ideas no doubt mattered, but the cases they made to the editor to publish their letters were likewise significant. Some writers referenced their qualifications or expertise as the basis for publication, but credentials were not a prerequisite for publication. For many, the case they made relied on empirical or emotional grounds. Writers explained that they had seen an event happen and were thus particularly equipped to explain it. Others wrote to the paper to share the results of an experiment that had produced interesting results, even if they could not explain why it did so. Writers also styled their letters to the editor in affective terms by emphasizing the empathy that had prompted their action. In all cases, the writers wanted to participate in the conversation. In their efforts to garner the attention of the affiches' editors and readers, they developed repertoires for claiming the authority to speak.

At the same time, writers found assessing all of the opinions by known and unknown correspondents disconcerting. They weighed the truth of letters that appeared in the paper, and they wrote in to correct the record when they encountered information they deemed false or confusing. Evaluating the credibility of the claims they found in the paper presented challenges to the writing public. The affiches allowed for compelling stories to spread, at times, before they were substantiated. It was the very lack of consensus that animated the contestation in the letters over scientific and social questions. For writers, determining whether one could trust what a letter writer whom one had never met had to say grew even more complex with the coming of the French Revolution, when hundreds of journalists began publishing papers of their own. In their efforts to deal with such uncertainty, writers learned how to participate in an eighteenth-century sphere of sociability. Letter writers represented themselves as useful and civic-minded. Through the affiches, they devised ways of communicating with strangers.

Interest in social relations would only grow in the wake of the Revolution. With the advent of statistics and the social sciences, society itself would become an object that one could visualize and comprehend. Letters to the editor published in the affiches were one early venue in which readers began to glimpse society, and through the act of writing their own letters, men and women imagined themselves as participants in a social body. The forum of letters to the editor opened up a social and critical space that readers accessed from their writing desks and dressing tables, their cafés and living rooms. In writing back to the paper, they fashioned a public with one another.

APPENDIX A

Key, Figure 1.1, Reprinted Content in the Affiches, 1770–1788

Newspapers Cited in Network Plot

NEWSPAPER NAME	UNIQUE IDENTIFIER NUMBER LISTED IN NETWORK NODE
Affiches	
Affiches d'Aix	1
Affiches d'Angers	2
Affiches du Beauvaisis (Compiègne)	4
Affiches de la Basse-Normandie (Caen)	5
Affiches de Dijon	6
Affiches du Dauphiné (Grenoble)	7
Journal de Provence (Marseille)	8
Affiches des Trois-Évêchés et Lorraine (Metz)	9
Affiches de l'Orléanois	10
Journal général de France (Paris)	11
Journal de Paris	12
Affiches du Poitou (Poitiers)	13
Affiches de Toulouse	14
Affiches de Troyes	15
Affiches de Normandie (Rouen)	16
Affiches de Picardie et Soissonnais (Amiens)	17
Affiches de Bordeaux	18
Affiches de Montpellier	19

(Continued)

NEWSPAPER NAME	UNIQUE IDENTIFIER NUMBER LISTED IN NETWORK NODE
Journal de Lyon	52
Affiches de Reims	65
Affiches de Rennes	67
Periodicals with subject matter–specific coverage	
Gazette d'agriculture	21
Gazette de santé	22
Gazette de France	23
Mercure de France	24
Éphémérides du citoyen	25
L'Année littéraire	26
Courrier lyrique et amusant	27
Journal politique et littéraire	28
Journal polytype des sciences et des arts	29
Journal de littérature nationale & étrangère	30
Journal militaire	31
Gazette des tribunaux	33
Journal de la langue française	34
Courrier de l'Europe	35
Regional newspapers cited as reprints[1]	
Feuilles d'Auvergne	42
Affiches de Bretagne	44
Affiches de Chartres	45
Almanach de Compiègne	46
Journal de Franche-Comté	47
Feuille de Flandres (Lille)	49
Journal de Guyenne	48
Affiches de La Rochelle	50
Affiches de Limoges	51
Affiches de Mans (généralité de Tours)	53
Affiches de Meaux	54
Affiches de Moulins	56
Affiches de Nantes	66
Journal de Nîmes	57
Affiches de Paris	58
Affiches de Roussillon	59
Affiches de Senlis	60
Affiches de Sens	61
Affiches de Tours	62
Affiches de Touraine	64
Journal de Verdun	63

NEWSPAPER NAME	UNIQUE IDENTIFIER NUMBER LISTED IN NETWORK NODE
Periodicals published abroad	
Journal de Luxembourg	81
Morning Herald	82
Journal de Genève	83
The Spectator	84

1 Some of the affiches in this group are no longer extant; others were not included in the study owing to time, funding, and access constraints on data collection.

Books Cited in the Affiches Sampled in Chapter 3, Alphabetized by Title

Authors are listed as N/A when the author of the book was not mentioned in the letter and a search of the book title in the Bibliothèque nationale de France catalog did not yield a conclusive author name.

Table B.1

BOOK TITLE	BOOK AUTHOR
Abrégé de l'histoire du théâtre françois	Mouhy, Charles de Fieux
Acta sanctorum	Henschen, Godfrey
Actes imprimés	Morelli Fernandez, Marie-Madeleine
Adèle & Théodore	Genlis, Stéphanie-Félicité du Crest, Madame de
Agaricus bulbosus vernus	Bulliard, Pierre
Aîles de l'amour	Beffroy de Reigny, Louis Abel
Alexandrine, ou l'amour est une vertu, par Mlle. de S . . .	Colleville, Anne-Hyacinthe de
Almanach de Gotha	N/A
Almanach de Liège	N/A
Almanach de Troyes	Simon
Almanach général & historique de la province de Dauphiné	N/A
Ami des hommes, ou, traité de la population	Mirabeau, Victor de Riquetti
Ami des pauvres, ou l'économe politique . . . avec deux mémoires intéressans sur les maîtrises et sur les fêtes	Faiguet de Villeneuve, Joachim

(continued)

Table B.1   (continued)

BOOK TITLE	BOOK AUTHOR
Annales modernes	N/A
Annales politiques, civiles et littéraires	Linguet, Simon-Nicolas-Henri
Année littéraire	Cousin Jacques
Antiquités d'Anjou	Hiret
Antiquités de France par Des-Rues	Des-Rues
Architecture pratique	Bullet
Aristotelis parva naturalia	Aristotle
Arlequin Mahomet, ou le cabriolet volant	L'Estandoux, Jean-François Cailhava de
Art de nager démontré par figures, avec des avis pour se baigner utilement	Thévenot, Melchisédech
Art poétique	N/A
Atlas portatif	Grenet, l'Abbé
Aveugle de Palmyre	Desfontaines
Aveugles juges des couleurs	Voltaire
Avis au public	N/A
Avis important aux personnes qui veulent réparer la perte de leurs dents	Dubois de Chémant, Nicolas
Bacco in Toscana	Redi, Francesco
Bembus sive de animorum essentia	Thomaeus, Nicholas Leonicus
Berceau de l'histoire-naturelle	N/A
Bibliotheca Pinelliana	Morelli, Jacopo
Bibliothèque françoise	Goujet, Abbé
Bibliothèque latine de moyen âge	Fabricius
Bonheur dans les campagnes	Lezay-Marnésia, Paul Adrien François Marie de
Boniface Pointu & sa famille	Guillemain de Saint-Victor, Louis
Brave homme de campagne	N/A
Britannicus	Racine, Jean
Calcul pour les années & portions de tems des pensions de toute nature & pour les intérêts à tous deniers	Garnier
Caliste	Mauprié
Candide	Voltaire
Cantique	Venance, Dougados
Castor & Pollux	Rameau, Jean-Philippe
Catalogue (imprimé à Saint-Brieuc)	N/A
Cause des esclaves-nègres portée au tribunal de la politique, de la justice, de la religion	Frossard, Benjamin-Sigismond
Chants guerriers de l'amazone de Vienne	Chiabréra
Chasse	N/A
Chasse aux palombes	Andichon, Henri d'
Chef-d'œuvres dramatiques, par M. Marmontel	Marmontel, Jean-François
Chevaliers romaines	Auguste

BOOK TITLE	BOOK AUTHOR
Chymie expérimentale et raisonnée	Beaumé
Clarissa, or the History of a Young Lady	Richardson, Samuel
Clytemnestre	N/A
Comment. intorno all'istoria della volgar poesia	Creseimbani
Commentaire sur le code criminel d'Angleterre	Blackstone, William, trans. Gabriel-François Coyer
Conoissance des tems de 1763	N/A
Considérations intéressantes sur les affaires présentes	N/A
Considérations sur l'esprit & les mœurs	Chevalier
Considérations sur l'état présent de la colonie française de Saint-Domingue, ouvrage politique et législatif	Hilliard d'Auberteuil, Michel-René
Considérations sur la guerre actuelle des turcs	Volney, Constantin-François de Chasseboeuf comte de
Contemporaines	Rétif de La Bretonne, Nicolas-Edme
Contes de Voltaire	Voltaire
Copie d'un lettre de Henri le grand adressée à M. Malicorne, conseiller	Henri IV
Copie d'une lettre du prince de Condé	N/A
Cornelii Taciti de moribus Germanorum et de vita Agricolæ	Brotier, Gabriel
Costume des acteurs	N/A
Courrier des planètes	Beffroy de Reigny, Louis Abel
Courtisanes	Molière
D'in-promptu	N/A
De doctrina temporum	Pétau
De l'Alcade de Zalamea	Calderon de la Barca, Pedro
De l'esprit des loix	Montesquieu, Charles-Louis de Secondat baron de
De l'importance de la morale et des opinions religieuses	Necker, Jacques
De la fonte des mines et des fonderies, etc. traduit de l'allemand de Christophe-André Schlutter	Hellot, Jean
De la morale naturelle	Necker, Jacques
De laudibus Stiliconis	Claudian
De litteratorum infelicitate	Valeriano, Pierio
De naturali vinorum historiá	Baccio, André
Délibérations & mémoires de l'Académie d'agriculture	N/A
Delle antichità italiche	Carli-Rubbi, Gian Rinaldo comte de
Description des moyens employés pour mesurer la base de Hounslow-Heath	Musschenbrock
Description des P.S.	Winckelmann, Johann Joachim
Description générale et particulières de cette Province	Courtépée
Devoirs du prince réduits à un seul principe, ou discours sur la justice	Moreau, Jacob-Nicolas

(continued)

Table B.1   (continued)

BOOK TITLE	BOOK AUTHOR
Dictionnaire	N/A
Dictionnaire anglais des grands hommes	Carver, Jonathan
Dictionnaire de chymie	Macquer, Pierre Joseph
Dictionnaire de l'Académie	N/A
Dictionnaire de l'encyclopédie	N/A
Dictionnaire de la poésie italienne	Affò, Irénée
Dictionnaire de la voierie	Prost de Royer, Antoine-François
Dictionnaire de Monet	Monet
Dictionnaire de musique	N/A
Dictionnaire de Nicot	Nicot
Dictionnaire de synonymes	N/A
Dictionnaire de trévoux	Le Clerc, Laurent-Josse
Dictionnaire des hommes illustres, rédigé par une société de gens de lettres	N/A
Dictionnaire des origines	Origny, Pierre-Adam d'
Dictionnaire diplomatique	N/A
Dictionnaire encyclopédique	N/A
Dictionnaire lyrique	Dubreuil, Jean
Dictionnaire raisonné universel d'histoire naturelle	Valmont de Bomare
Dictionnaire, par Bayle	Bayle, Pierre
Dictionnaires	la Croix du Maine and du Duverdier
Didon à Énée (Héroïde)	N/A
Dimanche grec	N/A
Diodore de Sicile	N/A
Diogène à Paris	Balainvilliers
Diptyque Quirinien	Cange
Discours	Rousseau, Jean-Jacques
Discours à l'Académie françoise	Duclos
Discours d'Hincmar	Eginhard
Discours de M. Turlin	Turlin
Discours destiné à être prononcé à la distribution des prix de l'Université de Nancy	M. le Principal du Collège
Dissertation couronné (1734)	Eginhard
Dissertation de magnitudine terrae parmi P. van Musschenbroek Physica experimentalis & gemoetricae dissertatione	Musschenbroek, Pieter van
Dissertation sur la musique moderne	Rousseau, Jean-Jacques
Dissertations sur la cause du froid en Canada	N/A
Du jugement de Midas	Grétry, André
Écueil des mœurs	Molière
Éléments de littérature	Marmontel, Jean-François
Éloge de la ville de Moukden	K'ien-Loung

BOOK TITLE	BOOK AUTHOR
Éloge historique, ou vie abrégée de Madame de Chantal	N/A
Éloge philosophique de l'impertinence	Maimeux, Joseph de
Embarras des richesses	Allainval, Léonor-Jean-Christin Soulas d'
Émile, ou de l'éducation	Rousseau, Jean-Jacques
Encyclopédie	Diderot, Denis, and Jean le Rond d'Alembert
Encyclopédie de Genève	N/A
Encyclopédie poétique	Gaigne, Alexis Toussaint de
Encyclopédie raisonnée des charades	N/A
Énéide	Virgile
Enfant prodigue	N/A
Entretiens sur l'état de la musique grecque, chez les frères de Bure	Barthélemy, Jean-Jacques
Épitre à Virginie	Tibullus, Albius
Époques de la nature	Buffon, Georges-Louis Leclerc comte de
Esprit de Fontenelle, par Prémonval	Prémonval
Esprit de la ligue	Belleforest & Auberi
Essai	Pannelier, Pierre-Lucien
Essai & expériences	Macbride
Essai historique	Le Roux, Philibert-Joseph
Essai sur Hyder-Ali	Roche-Tilhac, Jean-Charles Poncelin de La
Essai sur l'histoire de la société civile	Ferguson, Adam
Essai sur la musique ancienne et moderne	Borde, Jean-Benjamin de La
Essai sur la putréfaction	Shaw
Essai général de tactique	Guibert, Jacques-Antoine-Hippolyte de
Essai sur les plantes usuelles de la Jamaïque	Wright, William
Essais historiques sur Paris	Fréron, Louis-Marie Stanislas
Essais sur l'hygrométrie	Saussure, Horace-Bénédict de
Essais sur Paris	Saint-Foix, Germain-François Poullain de
État de la France, avec des mémoires sur l'ancien gouvernement	Boulainviliers, Henri comte de
Étrennes de cousin	Beffroy de Reigny, Louis Abel
Étrennes du Parnasse	N/A
Étrennes mignonnes	N/A
Étrennes nationales pour l'année 1788	N/A
Étrennes nationales, curieuses et instructives, enrichies de figures, d'anecdotes historiques et d'une infinité de traits remarquables	N/A
Études de la nature	Bernardin de Saint-Pierre, Henri
Expériences & observations sur différentes espèces d'air	Priestley
Exposition du calcul astronomique	Lalande, Joseph Jérôme Lefrançois de
Fables de la Fontaine	La Fontaine, Jean de

(continued)

Table B.1 (continued)

BOOK TITLE	BOOK AUTHOR
Fausse Agnès	Destouches
Favole di Giovanni Gherardo de Rossi	Rossi, Giovanni Gherardo de
Fête de village	Dorvigny
Fiers-fat	N/A
Fluxions de Newton	N/A
Fille travestie, ou le stratagème extravagant	N/A
France littéraire	N/A
Franche Comté ancienne & moderne	Joly, Joseph-Romain
Frères rivaux	La Font, Joseph de
Gazette des tribunaux	N/A
General Advertiser	N/A
George Dandin ou le mari confondu	Molière
Grammaire française	Ramée, Pierre de la
Grammaire latine	Ramée, Pierre de la
Grammarithmes, ou expressions littérales de tous les nombres	Archange de Charleroy
Guide de ceux qui veulent bâtir	Camus de Mézières, Nicolas Le
Guide des voyageurs étrangers à Paris	Thiéry, Luc-Vincent
Henriade	Voltaire
Heure du berger, ou l'horloge de Cythère	N/A
Hist. critica philosophiae	Brucker, Johann Jakob
Hist. lit. de Cave	Alcuini
Histoire de l'Allemagne	Risbeck, baron de
Histoire d'Henri III	Varillas
Histoire de Charlemagne	Gaillard, Gabriel-Henri
Histoire de France	Velly, Paul-François
Histoire de l'Académie (1712)	Saint Pierre, Charles-Irénée Castel de
Histoire de l'Académie de 1748	N/A
Histoire de l'art	N/A
Histoire de l'Eglise d'Aix	Alibert
Histoire de l'ordre du Saint-Esprit	Saint-Foix, Germain-François Poullain de
Histoire de la dernière guerre	N/A
Histoire de la maison de France	Sainte-Marthe
Histoire de la poésie	Massieu, l'Abbé
Histoire de la Rochelle	Arcère
Histoire de nos rois	Hiret
Histoire de Russie	Levesque, Pierre-Charles
Histoire des animaux	Buffon, Georges-Louis Leclerc comte de
Histoire des empereurs	Gordon
Histoire du concile de Trente	N/A
Histoire du règne de l'empereur Charles-Quint	Robertson, William

BOOK TITLE	BOOK AUTHOR
Histoire du Russie	N/A
Histoire ecclésiastique	N/A
Histoire gén. des voyages	N/A
Histoire générale d'Italie	Targe, Jean-Baptiste
Histoire naturelle	Pliny
Histoire naturelle	Buffon, Georges-Louis Leclerc comte de
Histoire naturelle des quadrupedes ovipares des lézards	Cépède, le comte de la
Histoire physique, morale, civile, & politique de la Russie	Le Clerc
Histoires	Livius, Titus
Historie véritable des temps fabuleux	Guérin du Rocher, Pierre Marie Stanislas
Honnête homme	Maydieu, Jean
Idées sur la cause & le traitement des maladies véné-riennes, &c.	Birague
Iliade	Homer
Infelix literatus	Spitzel, Gottlieb
Intermede	N/A
Introduction à la vie de Charles-Quint, par M. Robertson	Robertson
Introduction à la vie de Lycurgue	Plutarque
Iphigénie en Aulide	Gluck, Christoph Willibald
Iphigénie en Tauride	Cherubini
Jardin anglois, ou variétés tant originales que traduites	Le Tourneur, Pierre-Prime-Félicien
Journal astronomique	N/A
Journal de Monsieur	Royou, l'Abbé
Journal de physique, de chimie, d'histoire naturelle et des arts	Rozier, François
Journal des sçavans	N/A
Journal du voyage de Michel de Montaigne en Italie	Montaigne, Michel de
Journal encyclopédique	N/A
Julie, ou la nouvelle Héloïse	Rousseau, Jean-Jacques
Kniga Stephennaia	N/A
Koran	
Lamentations de Jérémie, paraphrasées à l'occasion de la peste de Naples, & les sept Psaumes de David	Médicis, Jean Gaston de
Lanval & Viviane	N/A
Leçons de physique expérimentale	Nollet, l'Abbé
Léopold de Brunswick	N/A
Lettre sur la richesse & les impôts actuels, comparés au temps de Louis XII	Hocquart de Coubron
Lettres d'un fermier américain	St. John de Crèvecœur, J. Hector
Lettres écrites de Suisse, d'Italie, de Sicile et de Malte, par M. ***	Roland de la Platière, Jean-Marie

(continued)

Table B.1   (continued)

BOOK TITLE	BOOK AUTHOR
Lettres persanes	Montesquieu, Charles-Louis de Secondat baron de
Lettres physiques & morales	Luc, J. A. de
Lettres sur l'Egypte	Savary
Lettres sur l'Italie, par Roland de la Platière	Roland de la Platière, Jean-Marie
Lettres sur les spectacles, avec une histoire des ouvrage pour & contre les théâtres	Desprez de Boissy, Charles
Lévite d'Ephraïm	N/A
Libellus Petri Bertranai de jurisdictione ecclesiasticá adversùs Petr. De Cugneris	N/A
Luminare minus ut proeeffet nocti	N/A
Lunes	Beffroy de Reigny, Louis Abel
Magia universalis naturae & artis	Schott, Gaspar
Magisterium naturae & artis	Lana de Terzi, Francesco
Maison rustique	N/A
Mariages samnites	Grétry, André
Médecin malgré lui	Molière
Médecine domestique ou traité complet des moyens de se conserver en santé	Buchan, William traduit de l'Anglais par J. D. Duplanil
Mélanges d'opuscules mathématiques	Delorthe, G. A.
Mélanges tirés d'une grande bibliothèque	Contant d'Orville, André-Guillaume
Mémoire de l'influence de l'air sur les plaies	Champeau
Mémoire de M. William Wright	Wright, William
Mémoire des médecins d'Arras	N/A
Mémoire des savans étrangers	N/A
Mémoire per le belle arti	N/A
Mémoire physique et médicinal, montrant des rapports évidens entre les phénomènes de la baguette divinatoire, du magnétisme et de l'électricité . . .	Thouvenel, Pierre
Mémoire sur la différente réfrangibilité de rayons hétérogènes	Marat, Jean-Paul
Mémoire sur les anti-septiques	Boissieu
Mémoire sur un rouet	Bernières de
Mémoires américains	N/A
Mémoires de l'Académie	N/A
Mémoires de l'Académie des inscriptions & belles-lettres	N/A
Mémoires de littéraire & d'histoire	N/A
Mémoires de M. de la Faye	de la Faye
Mémoires de Madame de Staal	Launay, Madame de Staal, Marguerite Jeanne Cordier de
Mémoires de Peiresc (1770)	N/A
Mémoires du Général Gordon	Gordon
Mémoires historique d'Amelot de la Houssaye	Amelot de la Houssaye, Abraham Nicolas

BOOK TITLE	BOOK AUTHOR
Mémoires littéraires	Palissot
Mémoires pour servir à l'histoire de l'empire russien sous Pierre le Grand	Voltaire
Mémoires sur les substances septiques & antiseptiques	Pringle
Mémorial pittoresque de la France	Bellavoine, L.
Mercure	Panckoucke
Mérope	Voltaire
Messager boiteux	N/A
Messiade	Klopstock, Friedrich Gottlieb
Métamorphoses	Ovide
Métanée ou la pénitence	Auger, Émond
Metanœologie: sur le suget de l'archicongrégation des pénitens de l'annonciation de Nostre Dame et de toutes telles autres devotieuses assemblées, en l'église sainte	Auger, Émond
Méthode des fluxions, et les suites infinies	Newton, Isaac
Michel & Jacqueline	N/A
Mille et une nuits	Galland, Antoine
Moïse considéré comme législateur et comme moraliste	Pastoret, Claude-Emmanuel de
Molière a la nouvelle salle, ou, les audiences de Thalie	La Harpe, Jean François de
Monarchie (de la) prussienne sous Frédéric le Grand	Mirabeau, Honoré-Gabriel Riqueti comte de
Mont-Glonne, ou recherches historiques sur l'origine des celtes, angevins &c.	Robin, Claude
Mort marié	Sedaine, Michel Jean
Nécrologe des hommes célèbres de France	N/A
Notes sur les traités de droit françois	Bannelier
Nouveaux elemens de la science de l'homme	Barthez, Paul-Joseph
Nouveaux mémoires ou observations sur l'Italie et sur les Italiens, par deux gentilshommes suédois	Grosley, Pierre-Jean
Nouveaux synonimes	N/A
Nouvelle Omphale	Grimm, Friedrich Melchior baron von
Nouvelles de la république des lettres	Pahin de la Blancherie
Nouvelles éphémérides économiques	Mirabeau, Victor de Riquetti marquis de
Nouvelles observations microscopiques, par Néedham	Needham, John Turberville
Objet moral	N/A
Observations générales sur les hôpitaux	Iberti
Observations sur la rage, consignées dans les recherches sur cette maladie	Andry, Charles-Louis-François
Observations sur les fosses d'aisance	MM. Laborie, Cadet le jeune, & Parmentier
Observations sur les loix criminelles	Boucher-d'Argis, André-Jean-Baptiste
Observations sur plusieurs maladies de bestiaux	Tessier, Alexandre Henri
Odyssée	Homer

(continued)

Table B.1   (continued)

BOOK TITLE	BOOK AUTHOR
Œuvre miséricordieuse	Saint-Foix, Germain-François Poullain de
Œuvres complètes	Rousseau, Jean-Jacques
Œuvres complètes d'Antoine-Raphel Mengs, premier peintre du roi d'Espagne	Bodoni, Giambattista
Œuvres complètes de Gilbert	Gilbert, Nicolas-Joseph-Laurent
Œuvres complètes de M. Colardeau	Colardeau, Charles Pierre
Œuvres complètes de M. de Saint-Foix	Saint-Foix, Germain-François Poullain de
Œuvres morales de Plutarque	Plutarque
Opinion d'un citoyen sur le mariage & sur la dot	N/A
Opuscules sur la langue françoise, par divers académiciens (1754)	N/A
Orpheline angloise, ou histoire de Charlotte Summers	N/A
Ossian	Macpherson, James
Ouvrage de médecine	Barthez, Paul-Joseph
Ouvrage sur l'Amérique (Saggio di storia americana o sia storia naturale, civile, e sacra . . . nell' America meridionale, descritta dall'abate Filippo Salvadore Gilii)	Gilii, Filippo Salvadore
Ouvrages philosophiques	Alembert, Jean le Rond d'
Parnasse françois	Titon du Tillet, Evrard
Parthénice	Spignoli, Baptiste, traduit du latin en français, par Jacq. de Mortières
Paul et Virginie	Bernardin de Saint-Pierre, Henri
Paysan magistrat, drame en cinq actes, imité de l'espagnol de Calderon, traduite par M. Linguet	N/A
Pédagogue d'armes: pour instruire un prince chrétien à bien entreprendre & heureusement achever une bonne guerre, pour être victorieux de tous les ennemis de son état & de l'église catholique	Auger, Émond
Pensées sur les femmes, & sur le mariage, dédiées aux hommes, par un vieux militaire	N/A
Perfidies à la mode	Nougaret, Pierre-Jean-Baptiste
Petites-maisons du Parnasse	Beffroy de Reigny, Louis Abel
Physique occulte	de Vallemont
Pièces fugitives en vers et en prose élégie aux mânes d'Adélaïde	N/A
Poemata didascalica	Strozzi
Poème d'Électre	N/A
Poème des jardins	N/A
Poésie dévotionnel	Métivier
Poésies de Gaspar vicomte	N/A
Portefeuille	N/A
Portefeuille de l'académie & son histoire littéraire	Warren & Dobson
Pratique des devoirs des curés, traduite en françois, de l'italien, du P. Paul Segneri	Segneri, Paolo

BOOK TITLE	BOOK AUTHOR
Précis sur la vertu anthelminthique ou vermifuge par excellence de l'huile empyreumatique, découverte par l'habile & le célébré M. Chabert, directeur & inspecteur général des écoles royales vétérinaires de France, &c.	Chabert
Premier livre des bâtiments de France	Androuet du Cerceau
Principes de géométrie	Delorthe, G. A.
Principes de morale, de politique et de droit public puisés dans l'histoire de notre monarchie, ou Discours sur l'histoire de France (1777–89)	Moreau, Jacob-Nicolas
Proclus sur le Timée de Platon	Proclus
Prodromo overo saggio di alcune inventioni nuove, premesso all'arte maestra	Lana de Terzi, Francesco
Prospectus d'un armement de six frégates & deux corvettes	N/A
Prospectus de l'Encyclopédique	Alembert, Jean le Rond d'
Prospectus de M. le Prince	Leprince de Beaumont, Jeanne-Marie
Provinciales de royaume, pendant l'année 1787	Beaujour de
Quatuors d'airs connus	Davaux
Questions sur l'édit des hypothèques	Corail de Sainte-Foy
Quête du blé, ou voyage	Venance, Dougados
Quinti sectani satyrae	Sergardi, Louis
Rapport fait par ordre de l'Académie des sciences sur les effets des vapeurs méphitiques	Portal, Antoine
Recherches historiques & politiques sur les États Unis de l'Amérique	Brissot de Warville, Jacques-Pierre
Recherches philosophiques sur les grecs	Pauw, Cornelius de
Recherches sur la nature et les causes de la richesse des nations	Smith, Adam
Recherches sur la pouzzolane, sur la théorie de la chaux, et sur la cause de la dureté du mortier	Faujas de Saint-Fond, Barthélemy
Recherches sur une loi générale de la nature, ou mémoire sur la fusibilité & la dissolubilité des corps relativement à leur masse, &c.	N/A
Recueil de divers écrits	LeBeuf, Jean
Recueil de fables italiennes	Rossi, Jean-Gérard de
Recueil des actes de la société royale d'Upsal	N/A
Recueil des mémoires sur les chinois	N/A
Recueil manuscrit	Perrier, Nicolas
Réflexions détachées sur les traités d'éducation	Beguillet, Edme
Réflexions ou sentences et maximes morales	Rochefoucauld, François de La
Réflexions philosophiques sur l'origine de la civilisation et sur les moyens de remédier aux abus qu'elle entraîne	Delacroix, Jacques-Vincent
Réflexions sur la poésie, la musique & la peinture	Fontenelle, Bernard Le Bovier de
Réflexions sur le progrès des sciences en Europe	Bartoli, Daniello
Relazione del fulmine caduto nel conduttore della pubblica Specola di Padova	Toaldo, Giuseppe

(Continued)

Table B.1   (continued)

BOOK TITLE	BOOK AUTHOR
Remarques diététiques sur l'usage de la poire	Pinel
Remarques diverses sur la prononciation & l'orthographe	Harduin, Alexandre-Xavier
Résumé des principaux objets présentés & discutés dans les assemblées provinciales du royaume, pendant l'année 1787	Beaujour
Résumé des principaux objets présentés & dissertés dans les assemblées le société encyclopédique	N/A
Révolutions de Tahiti	Roche-Tilhac, Jean-Charles Poncelin de La
Rime degli Arcadi	Crescimbeni, Giovanni Mario
Romance de Sapho	N/A
Rudiment	N/A
Saisons	Saint-Lambert, Jean-François de
Sganarelle	Molière
Soirée d'été	Parisau
Soirées amusantes, ou entretiens sur les jeux à gages dont s'amusent les jeunes personnes	N/A
Solitaires de Normandie	Piis, Pierre-Antoine-Augustin de
Sonnet de Zappe	N/A
Sposa colerica	Chiavacci
Stances à Parthémie	Racine, Jean
Statique des végétaux, et celles des animaux	Hales, Stephen, traduit par Buffon
Storia e regione d'ogni poesia	Quadrio
Sucre spirituel	Auger, Émond
Suite de la lithologie	Nictié
Sur la bonhomie	N/A
Sur Moses Mendelssohn, sur la réforme politique des juifs	Mirabeau, Honoré-Gabriel Riqueti comte de
Système de la différente réfrangibilité	Marat, Jean-Paul
Table géographique	Gordon
Tablettes dramatiques de M. de Mouhy	Voltaire
Tartuffe	Molière
Théogonie d'Hésiode	Carli-Rubbi, Gio Rinaldo, Comte
Théologie	Courayer, Pierre François le
Théorie & nouveaux procédés pour la fermentation & l'amélioration de tous les vins blancs & des cidres	Maupin
Théorie de l'art	N/A
Théorie des comètes	N/A
Théorie des sentiments moraux	Smith, Adam
Timocrate	N/A
Tractatus de lamiis et pythonicis	Bertrandi
Tractatus tractatuum	N/A
Tragédie de Mustapha	Mallet, David
Tragédie françoise	N/A
Traité d'horlogerie	N/A

BOOK TITLE	BOOK AUTHOR
Traité de commerce avec l'Angleterre	N/A
Traité de la distillation des liqueurs	Hornot, Antoine
Traité de la police	La Mare, Nicolas de
Traité des couleurs & vernis	N/A
Traité des donations entre-vifs et testamentaires, pt II	Ricard, Jean-Marie
Traité des dispositions conditionnelles	N/A
Traité des eaux minérales, tome 5	N/A
Traité des loups-garoux	Grillandus, Paul
Traité des nègres	N/A
Traité des successions	Le Brun, Denis
Traité général des grains	Béguillet, Edme
Traité physique et historique de l'aurore boréale	Mairan
Traité universel des drogues simples	Lemery, Nicolas
Traités de Pierius Valerianus, de Tollius & de Spizelius	N/A
Transactions philosophiques de la société royale de Londres	N/A
Transactions philosophiques de Londres, vol. XIII, n. 147, pour l'année 1683	Tyon
Trésor du Parnasse, ou élite de poésies fugitives	N/A
Trois âges de l'opéra	Grétry, André-Ernest-Modeste
Troisième exhortation	Fléchier, Valentin Esprit
Varia historiae libri	Aelinius, Claudius
Vers à ma mère	N/A
Veuve de Malabar	Lemierre, Antoine-Marin
Vie du Capitaine Cook	Kippis
Vie du chancelier	Mallet, David
Vieux militaire, ou du mari confiant	N/A
Voyage à la Sainte Baume	Strozzi
Voyage dans les parties intérieures de l'Amérique septentrionale	Carver, Jonathan
Voyage de France, géographique, &c.	M. M. L. R.
Voyage en Provence	Bérenger
Voyage fait par ordre du roi en 1771 & 1772	Verdun, de Borda, & Pingré
Voyage pittoresque de Paris	Dézallier d'Argenville, Antoine-Nicolas
Voyage sur les côtes de l'Arabie heureuse	Rooke, Henri
Voyageur françois	Fontenai, Abbé de
Vrai pasteur, ode	Miramond de
Zaïre	Voltaire
Zémire & Azor	Grétry, André

Notes

Introduction

1. *Affiches du Beauvaisis*, February 12, 1786, 3–4. The affiches under investigation in this book are referenced in the notes by their shortened titles. The full titles are listed in the bibliography with the corresponding dates for each full title. All translations from the affiches are my own unless otherwise indicated.

2. In using the "information press" to describe the genre of provincial newspapers titled *Affiches, annonces, et avis divers*, and the Parisian *Journal général de France* and the *Journal de Paris*, my book follows Gilles Feyel's definition of "presse d'information." Gilles Feyel, *L'annonce et la nouvelle: La presse d'information en France sous l'Ancien Régime, 1630–1788* (Oxford: Voltaire Foundation, 2000), 1–7.

3. There are noteworthy exceptions authored by historians of the press. Jack Censer dedicates a chapter to the history of the affiches in *The French Press in the Age of Enlightenment* (London: Routledge, 1994), 54–86. Hugh Gough discusses the affiches in *The Newspaper Press in the French Revolution* (New Fetter Lane, UK: Routledge, 1988). Gilles Feyel also devotes part of his study of the Old Regime press to the affiches in *L'annonce et la nouvelle*, 929–1274.

4. On the uncensored press in Old Regime and revolutionary France, and its discursive links to revolutionary politics, see especially Jeremy D. Popkin, *News and Politics in the Age of Revolution: Jean Luzac's Gazette de Leyde* (Ithaca: Cornell University Press, 1989); Jack R. Censer, *Prelude to Power: The Parisian Radical Press, 1789–1791* (Baltimore: Johns Hopkins University Press, 1976); Nina Rattner Gelbart, *Feminine and Opposition Journalism in Old Regime France: Le Journal des dames* (Berkeley: University of California Press, 1987). Their work demonstrates the role that journalists played in shaping revolutionary politics via their newspapers. Studies of the counterrevolutionary press also focused on their political impact on the press by tracing the interactions of editors with their readers. See Harvey Chisick, *The Production, Distribution and Readership of a Conservative Journal of the Early French Revolution: The Ami du Roi of the Abbé Royou* (Philadelphia: American Philosophical Society, 1992); Laurence Coudart, *La Gazette de Paris: Un journal royaliste pendant la Révolution française (1789–1792)* (Paris: L'Harmattan, 1995); W. J. Murray, *The Right-Wing Press in the French Revolution: 1789–92* (Woodbridge, UK: Boydell, 1986).

5. Timothy Tackett, "Paths to Revolution: The Old Regime Correspondence of Five Future Revolutionaries," *French Historical Studies* 32, no. 4 (2009): 531–54; Timothy Tackett, *Becoming a Revolutionary: The Deputies of the French National Assembly and the Emergence of a Revolutionary Culture (1789–1790)* (Princeton: Princeton University Press, 1996), 48–116; Robert H. Blackman, *1789: The French Revolution Begins* (Cambridge: Cambridge University Press, 2019), 72–114.

6. Sophia Rosenfeld, "Thinking about Feeling, 1789–1799," *French Historical Studies* 32, no. 4 (2009): 697–706; Lynn Hunt, "The Experience of Revolution," *French Historical Studies* 32, no. 4 (2009): 671–78.

7. Lindsey Porter, *Popular Rumour in Revolutionary Paris, 1792–1794* (Manchester, UK: Palgrave Macmillan, 2017); Tabetha Leigh Ewing, *Rumour, Diplomacy and War in Enlightenment Paris* (Oxford: Oxford University Studies in the Enlightenment, 2014); Timothy Tackett, *The Coming of the Terror in the French Revolution* (Cambridge, MA: Belknap Press of Harvard University Press, 2015); Peter R. Campbell, Thomas Kaiser, and Marisa Linton, eds., *Conspiracy in the French Revolution* (Manchester, UK: Manchester University Press, 2007). Sophia Rosenfeld's historiographical essay on the cultural history of the French Revolution has underscored the need to treat the late Old Regime, the Enlightenment, and the Revolution within a shared framework. She highlights recent scholarly work on the history of lived experience and the history of communication as two of the most promising new directions in the field. Sophia Rosenfeld, "The French Revolution in Cultural History," *Journal of Social History* 52, no. 3 (January 2019): 558–61.

8. See especially Roger Chartier, Alain Boureau, and Cécile Dauphin, *Correspondence: Models of Letter-Writing from the Middle Ages to the Nineteenth Century* (Princeton: Princeton University Press, 1997); Dena Goodman, *Becoming a Woman in the Age of Letters* (Ithaca: Cornell University Press, 2009).

9. Lindsay A. H. Parker, *Writing the Revolution: A French Woman's History in Letters* (New York: Oxford University Press, 2013); Tackett, "Paths to Revolution."

10. Antoine-Gaspard Boucher d'Argis, "Lettre missive," vol. 9, p. 426, and "Lettre circulaire," vol. 3, p. 467, in *Encyclopédie, ou dictionnaire raisonné des sciences, des arts et des métiers, etc.*, ed. Denis Diderot and Jean le Rond d'Alembert (University of Chicago: ARTFL Encyclopédie Project, Autumn 2017, ed. Robert Morrissey and Glenn Roe), available at http://encyclopedie.uchicago.edu/.

11. Dena Goodman, *The Republic of Letters: A Cultural History of the French Enlightenment* (Ithaca: Cornell University Press, 1994), 137.

12. Carla Alison Hesse, *The Other Enlightenment: How French Women Became Modern* (Princeton: Princeton University Press, 2001), xii.

13. Dena Goodman, "Letter Writing and the Emergence of Gendered Subjectivity in Eighteenth-Century France," *Journal of Women's Studies* 17, no. 2 (2005): 9–37.

14. Antoine Lilti suggests that celebrity in the eighteenth century was a manifestation of such an affective public sphere, where people formed connections with those they had never met. Antoine Lilti, *The Invention of Celebrity*, trans. Lynn Jeffress (Malden: Polity Press, 2017), 8–11, 271–75.

15. The first page of each edition contained a list of advertisements. Colin Jones has suggested the affiches offered an equal footing among readers as consumers. Colin Jones, "The Great Chain of Buying: Medical Advertisement, the Bourgeois Public Sphere, and the Origins of the French Revolution," *American Historical Review* 101, no. 1 (1996): 13–40.

16. Jürgen Habermas, *The Structural Transformation of the Public Sphere* (Cambridge, MA: MIT Press, 1989), 31–56.

17. Harvey Chisick, "Public Opinion and Political Culture in France during the Second Half of the Eighteenth Century," *English Historical Review* 117, no. 470

(February 2002): 48–77; Thierry Rigogne, *Between State and Market: Printing and Book-selling in Eighteenth-Century France* (Oxford: Oxford University Studies in the Enlightenment, 2007), 165–72; Daniel Roche, *The People of Paris: An Essay in Popular Culture in the Eighteenth Century*, trans. Marie Evans with Gwynne Lewis (Berkeley: University of California Press, 1987), 197–233.

18. Pablo Piccato, "Public Sphere in Latin America: A Map of the Historiography," *Social History* 35, no. 2 (May 2010): 165–92; Marwan M. Kraidy and Marina R. Krikorian, "The Revolutionary Public Sphere: The Case of the Arab Uprisings," *Communication and the Public* 2, no. 2 (July 2017): 111–19; Michael Warner, *The Letters of the Republic: Publication and the Public Sphere in Eighteenth-Century America* (Cambridge, MA: Harvard University Press, 1992); Michael Warner, *Publics and Counterpublics* (Brooklyn: Zone Books, 2005); John L. Brooke, "Consent, Civil Society, and the Public Sphere in the Age of Revolution and the Early American Republic," in *Beyond the Founders: New Approaches to the Political History of the Early American Republic*, ed. Jeffery Pasley, Andrew Robertson, and David Waldstreicher (Chapel Hill: University of North Carolina Press, 2004), 207–50.

19. James B. Given, *Inquisition and Medieval Society: Power, Discipline, and Resistance in Languedoc* (Ithaca: Cornell University Press, 2001); Michael Alan Sizer, "Making Revolution Medieval: Revolt and Political Culture in Late Medieval Paris" (PhD diss., University of Minnesota, 2008). On the chronological challenges to Habermas's public sphere, see Jill Maciak Walshaw's compelling analysis in *A Show of Hands for the Republic: Opinion, Information, and Repression in Eighteenth-Century Rural France* (Rochester: University of Rochester Press, 2014), 14–16.

20. See especially Sarah Maza, *The Myth of the French Bourgeoisie* (Cambridge, MA: Harvard University Press, 2003); David Garrioch, *The Formation of the Parisian Bourgeoisie, 1690–1830* (Cambridge, MA: Harvard University Press, 1997).

21. Keith Michael Baker, "Public Opinion as Political Invention,'" in *Inventing the French Revolution*, ed. Keith Michael Baker (Cambridge: Cambridge University Press, 1990), 167–200; Keith Michael Baker, "Defining the Public Sphere in Eighteenth-Century France: Variations on a Theme by Habermas," in *Habermas and the Public Sphere*, ed. Craig Calhoun (Cambridge, MA: MIT Press, 1992), 181–211; Mona Ozouf, "'Public Opinion' at the End of the Old Regime," in "Rethinking French Politics in 1788," Supplement, *Journal of Modern History* 60 (September 1988): S1–S21.

22. Sarah Maza, *Private Lives and Public Affairs: The Causes Célèbres of Prerevolutionary France* (Berkeley: University of California Press, 1993); Jeffrey S. Ravel, *The Contested Parterre: Public Theater and French Political Culture, 1680–1791* (Ithaca: Cornell University Press, 1999).

23. James Van Horn Melton, *The Rise of the Public in Enlightenment Europe* (Cambridge: Cambridge University Press, 2001); Isabel Hull, *Sexuality, State, and Civil Society in Germany, 1700–1815* (Ithaca: Cornell University Press, 1996).

24. Walshaw, *Show of Hands*; Chisick, "Public Opinion and Political Culture," 71.

25. Maza, *Private Lives and Public Affairs*; Meghan K. Roberts, *Sentimental Savants: Philosophical Families in Enlightenment France* (Chicago: University of Chicago Press, 2016); Garrioch, *Formation of the Parisian Bourgeoisie*.

26. Robert Darnton, "The High Enlightenment and the Low-Life of Literature in Pre-Revolutionary France," *Past and Present* 51 (May 1971): 81–115.

27. Roger Chartier, *The Cultural Origins of the French Revolution*, trans. Lydia G. Cochrane (Durham: Duke University Press, 1991), 67–91.

28. Jeremy Caradonna, *The Enlightenment in Practice: Academic Prize Contests and Intellectual Culture in France, 1670–1794* (Ithaca: Cornell University Press, 2012), 1–13, 94.

29. Lauren R. Clay, *Stagestruck: The Business of Theater in Eighteenth-Century France and Its Colonies* (Ithaca: Cornell University Press, 2013).

30. Chisick, "Public Opinion and Political Culture," 66.

31. Benedict Anderson, *Imagined Communities: Reflections on the Origin and Spread of Nationalism* (London: Verso, 2006), 25–64. The idea of the "textual community" was coined by Brian Stock in *The Implications of Literacy: Written Language and Models of Interpretation in the Eleventh and Twelfth Centuries* (Princeton: Princeton University Press, 1983), 88–92.

32. Lynn Hunt, *Inventing Human Rights* (New York: W. W. Norton, 2008), 35–112.

33. Antoine Lilti emphasizes these dual and interlocking meanings of sociability as the study of a practice, and as a historical concept shaped by eighteenth-century theories of natural law. Antoine Lilti, *The World of Salons: Sociability and Worldliness in Eighteenth-Century Paris*, trans. Lydia G. Cochrane (Oxford: Oxford University Press, 2015), 6.

34. Maurice Agulhon, *La sociabilité méridionale: Confréries et associations en Provence orientale à la fin du XVIIIe siècle*, 2 vols. (Aix en Provence: La Pensée universitaire, 1966).

35. Daniel Gordon, *Citizens without Sovereignty: Equality and Sociability in French Thought, 1670–1789* (Princeton: Princeton University Press, 1994), 4–5. On the significance of literary spaces as laboratories of sociability, see Gregory S. Brown, *Literary Sociability and Literary Property in France, 1775–1793: Beaumarchais, the Société des Auteurs Dramatique, and the Comédie Française* (Aldershot, UK: Ashgate, 2006).

36. Meghan K. Roberts, "Philosophes Mariés and Epouses Philosophiques: Men of Letters and Marriage in Eighteenth-Century France," *French Historical Studies 35*, no. 3 (Summer 2012): 509–39; Anne Goldgar, *Impolite Learning: Conduct and Community in the Republic of Letters, 1680–1760* (New Haven: Yale University Press, 1995), 54–114.

37. Louis, chevalier de Jaucourt, "Sociabilité," in Diderot and d'Alembert, *Encyclopédie*, 15:250–51.

38. On the significance of optimism and the idea of progress, see Anton M. Matytsin, "Whose Light Is It Anyway? The Struggle for Light in the French Enlightenment," in *Let There Be Enlightenment: The Religious and Mystical Sources of Rationality*, ed. Anton M. Matytsin and Dan Edelstein (Baltimore: Johns Hopkins University Press, 2019), 64–66; J. B. Shank, *The Newton Wars and the Beginning of the French Enlightenment* (Chicago: University of Chicago Press, 2008), 35.

39. Clifford Siskin and William Warner, eds., *This Is Enlightenment* (Chicago: University of Chicago Press, 2010), 1–34.

40. Caradonna, *Enlightenment in Practice*, 12.

41. Margaret C. Jacob, *Living the Enlightenment: Freemasonry and Politics in Eighteenth-Century Europe* (New York: Oxford University Press, 1991); Caradonna, *Enlightenment in Practice*; Charles W. J. Withers, *Placing the Enlightenment: Thinking Geographically about the Age of Reason* (Chicago: University of Chicago Press, 2008).

42. The twentieth-century work in this field was pioneered by Ernst Cassirer and Peter Gay, who envisioned a particular unity among the philosophes. Ernst Cassirer, *The Philosophy of the Enlightenment* (Princeton: Princeton University Press, 1951); Peter Gay, *The Enlightenment: An Interpretation*, 2 vols. (New York: Knopf, 1966). Scholarly work on skepticism has brought such unitary conceptions of the Enlightenment into question. See, for example, Anton Matytsin, *The Specter of Skepticism in the Age of Enlightenment* (Baltimore: Johns Hopkins University Press, 2016); R. H. Popkin, "Skepticism in the Enlightenment," *Studies on Voltaire and the Eighteenth Century* 26 (1963): 1321–35; Giorgio Tonelli, "The 'Weakness' of Reason in the Age of Enlightenment," in *Scepticism in the Enlightenment*, ed. Richard H. Popkin, Ezequiel de Olaso, and Giorgio Tonelli (Dordrecht: Kluwer, 1997), 217–44. Dan Edelstein elucidates "the Enlightenment" as a historically specific story, born out of the Quarrel of the Ancients and the Moderns between 1680 and 1720. Edelstein, *The Enlightenment: A Genealogy* (Chicago: University of Chicago Press, 2010). Maria Teodora Comsa et al. focused on the participants within self-referential circles of correspondence, suggesting that the Enlightenment was a rather elite and closed endeavor. Maria Teodora Comsa, Melanie Conroy, Dan Edelstein, Chloe Summers Edmondson, and Claude Willan, "The French Enlightenment Network," *Journal of Modern History* 88, no. 3 (2016): 495–534. In opposition to much of the historiography of the Enlightenment, Jonathan Israel has argued for an intellectual strain of "radical" Enlightenment that he attributes largely to Spinoza, and which he believed animated the Atlantic revolutions. See Jonathan Irvine Israel, *Radical Enlightenment: Philosophy and the Making of Modernity, 1650–1750* (Oxford: Oxford University Press, 2001); Israel, *Enlightenment Contested: Philosophy, Modernity, and the Emancipation of Man, 1670–1752* (Oxford: Oxford University Press, 2006); Israel, *Democratic Enlightenment: Philosophy, Revolution, and Human Rights, 1750–1790* (Oxford: Oxford University Press, 2011).

43. J. G. A. Pocock, "Historiography and Enlightenment: A View of Their History," *Modern Intellectual History* 5, no. 1 (2008): 83–96.

44. Recent scholarship has underscored the dynamic and rich relationship between religion and eighteenth-century philosophy. See especially David Jan Sorkin, *The Religious Enlightenment: Protestants, Jews, and Catholics from London to Vienna* (Princeton: Princeton University Press, 2008); Ulrich L. Lehner, *The Catholic Enlightenment: The Forgotten History of a Global Movement* (Oxford: Oxford University Press, 2016); Jonathan Sheehan, *The Enlightenment Bible* (Princeton: Princeton University Press, 2005); Jeffrey D. Burson, *The Rise and Fall of Theological Enlightenment: Jean-Martin de Prades and Ideological Polarization in Eighteenth-Century France* (South Bend: University of Notre Dame Press, 2010). Margaret Jacob has shown that both well-known thinkers and rather unknown figures shared a secular mindset through which they encountered the world before them on its own terms. Margaret C. Jacob, *The Secular Enlightenment* (Princeton: Princeton University Press, 2019). See also Franco Venturi, *Utopia and Reform in the Enlightenment* (Cambridge: Cambridge University Press, 1971); John Marshall, *Toleration and Early Enlightenment Culture* (Cambridge: Cambridge University Press, 2006). The Radical Enlightenment continues to garner new scholarly attention in the history and philosophy of Europe and the Americas. Margaret C. Jacob, *The Radical Enlightenment: Pantheists, Freemasons, and Republicans* (London: Allen & Unwin, 1981); Steffen Ducheyne, *Reassessing the Radical Enlightenment* (New

York: Routledge, 2017). Historians have also explored the contemporary opposition to the Enlightenment and its role in the formation of the "Right" in modern society. See especially Darrin McMahon, *Enemies of the Enlightenment: The French Counter-Enlightenment and the Making of Modernity* (Oxford: Oxford University Press, 2001). Others have instead emphasized the more pragmatic orientation of Enlightenment philosophy and literature. See, for example, Giles Gunn, *The Pragmatist Turn: Religion, the Enlightenment, and the Formation of American Literature* (Charlottesville: University of Virginia Press, 2017); Dennis C. Rasmussen, *The Pragmatic Enlightenment: Recovering the Liberalism of Hume, Smith, Montesquieu, and Voltaire* (Cambridge: Cambridge University Press, 2014). The term "Artisanal Enlightenment" was coined by Paola Bertucci to indicate the role of making and of makers (savants and craftsmen) in shaping eighteenth-century ideas of improvement and progress. Paola Bertucci, *Artisanal Enlightenment: Science and the Mechanical Arts in Old Regime France* (New Haven: Yale University Press, 2017). Historians of science and the Enlightenment have revealed both the role of the sciences in the making of the Enlightenment and the role of the Enlightenment in shaping scientific institutions and practices. See especially Jessica Riskin, *Science in the Age of Sensibility: The Sentimental Empiricists of the French Enlightenment* (Chicago: University of Chicago Press, 2002); Daniel Roche, *Le siècle des lumières en province: Académies et académiciens provinciaux, 1680–1789*, 2 vols. (Paris: Mouton, 1978); Shank, *Newton Wars*. Much of the scholarship on the Enlightenment now adopts a comparative or transnational approach, including several of the titles that appear above. See also John Robertson, *The Case for the Enlightenment: Scotland and Naples, 1680–1760* (Cambridge: Cambridge University Press, 2005); Susan Manning and Francis D. Cogliano, eds., *The Atlantic Enlightenment* (Aldershot, UK: Ashgate, 2008); Caroline Winterer, *American Enlightenments: Pursuing Happiness in the Age of Reason* (New Haven: Yale University Press, 2016).

45. Jeffrey Burson, "Reflections on the Pluralization of Enlightenment and the Notion of Theological Enlightenment as Process," *French History* 26, no. 4 (2012): 524–25.

46. Daniel Brewer, *The Enlightenment Past: Reconstructing Eighteenth-Century French Thought* (Cambridge: Cambridge University Press, 2008); Jean-Marie Goulemot, *La littérature des Lumières* (Paris: Armand Colin, 2005).

47. Elizabeth Losh and Jacqueline Wernimont, eds., *Bodies of Information: Intersectional Feminism and Digital Humanities* (Minneapolis: University of Minnesota Press, 2018); Mark Vareschi, *Everywhere and Nowhere: Anonymity and Mediation in Eighteenth-Century England* (Minneapolis: University of Minnesota Press, 2018); Glenn Roe, "A Sheep in Wolff's Clothing: Émilie du Châtelet and the Encyclopédie," *Eighteenth-Century Studies* 51, no. 2 (Winter 2018): 179–96; Lara Putnam, "The Transnational and the Text-Searchable: Digitized Sources and the Shadows They Cast," *American Historical Review* 121, no. 2 (April 2016): 377–402.

48. See especially Kate Davison, "Early Modern Social Networks: Antecedents, Opportunities, and Challenges," *American Historical Review* 124, no. 2 (April 2019): 456–82; Maximilian Schich, Chaoming Song, Yong-Yeol Ahn, Alexander Mirsky, Mauro Martino, Albert-László Barabási, and Dirk Helbing, "A Network Framework of Cultural History," *Science* 345, no. 6196 (August 1, 2014): 558–62; Christopher N. Warren, Daniel Shore, Jessica Otis, Lawrence Wang, Mike Finegold, and Cosma Shalizi,

"Six Degrees of Francis Bacon: A Statistical Method for Reconstructing Large Historical Social Networks," *Digital Humanities Quarterly* 10, no. 3 (2016), http://www.digitalhumanities.org/dhq/vol/10/3/000244/000244.html.

49. John F. Padgett, "Open Elite? Social Mobility, Marriage, and Family in Florence, 1282–1494," *Renaissance Quarterly* 63, no. 2 (2010): 357–411.

50. Comsa et al., "French Enlightenment Network," 495–97.

51. Emma Rothschild, "Isolation and Economic Life in Eighteenth-Century France," *American Historical Review* 119, no. 4 (October 2014): 1055–82.

1. The Production and Distribution of the Information Press

1. *Journal de Paris*, March 10, 1782, 274.

2. Gough, *Newspaper Press*, 2–3.

3. Theophraste Renaudot first devised the *bureau d'adresse*. In addition to publishing foreign and domestic political news each Saturday in the *Gazette*, he published *Nouvelles ordinaires*, which covered political news west of Paris, and *Feuille du Bureau d'Adresse*, which published advertisements for unemployed persons looking for work and want ads for those seeking workers. Stephen Auerbach, "'Encourager le commerce et répandre les lumières': The Press, the Provinces and the Origins of the Revolution in France: 1750–1789" (PhD diss., Louisiana State University Agricultural and Mechanical College, 2004), 35–38.

4. Gilles Feyel traces the history of the *privilège* of the *Gazette* in further detail in *L'annonce et la nouvelle*, 1015–21.

5. Gilles Feyel, "Denis Rabiot de Meslé" and "Louis Le Bas de Courmont," in *Dictionnaire des journalistes, 1600–1789*, 2 vols., ed. Jean Sgard (Oxford: Voltaire Foundation, 1999), http://dictionnaire-journalistes.gazettes18e.fr/journaliste/663-denis-rabiot-de-mesle, http://dictionnaire-journalistes.gazettes18e.fr/journaliste/470-lou is-le-bas-de-courmont.

6. Michelle Gasc, "La naissance de la presse periodique locale à Lyon: Les *Affiches de Lyon, annonces et avis divers*," *Etudes sur la presse au XVIIIe siècle* 3 (1978): 64–65.

7. There were exceptions to this pattern of early newspaper launches, for example in Orléans, where a local paper began in 1764. The average number of affiches per *généralité* was between one and two. The northwest and the north published the highest concentration of papers. Gilles Feyel, "La presse provinciale au XVIIIe siècle: Géographie d'un réseau," *Revue Historique* 272, no. 2 (1984): 359.

8. Feyel, *L'annonce et la nouvelle*, 1021.

9. Gilles Feyel, "La presse provinciale sous l'ancien régime," in *La presse provinciale au XVIIIe siècle*, ed. Jean Sgard (Grenoble: Centre de Recherches sur les Sensibilités, Université des Langues et Lettres de Grenoble, 1983), 16–18.

10. Feyel, *L'annonce et la nouvelle*, 1032.

11. Feyel, "La presse provinciale sous l'ancien régime," 20.

12. Smaller towns were less likely to have an affiche of their own. Among the next fifty smaller cities, just 14 percent had their own newspaper. The number of newspapers in towns with five to eight thousand residents was even more striking—just 5 percent of such towns had weekly affiches. Gilles Feyel, "La presse provinciale au XVIIIe siècle," 363–66.

13. Colin Jones, "Great Chain of Buying," 17–18; Marc Martin, *La presse régionale: Des affiches aux grands quotidiens* (Paris: Fayard, 2002), 24.

14. Philip Stewart, "Affiches de Paris," in *Dictionnaire des journaux, 1600–1789*, ed. Jean Sgard (Oxford: Voltaire Foundation, 1999), http://dictionnaire-journaux.gazet tes18e.fr/journal/0049-affiches-de-paris-3.

15. Feyel, "La presse provinciale sous l'ancien régime," 20.

16. Auerbach, "'Encourager le commerce,'" 53–54.

17. Gilles Feyel, *La presse en France des origines à 1944: Histoire politique et matérielle* (Paris: Ellipses, 1999), 30.

18. Denis Diderot, "Journaliste," in Diderot and d'Alembert, *Encyclopédie*, 8:897–98.

19. Christian Albertan, "Jean Milcent," in Sgard, *Dictionnaire des journalistes*, http://dictionnaire-journalistes.gazettes18e.fr/journaliste/576-jean-milcent.

20. Jean Sgard, "Louis Couret de Villeneuve," in Sgard, *Dictionnaire des journalistes*, http://dictionnaire-journalistes.gazettes18e.fr/journaliste/200-louis-couret-de-villeneuve.

21. Gilles Feyel, "René Jouyneau-Desloges," and Albert Ronsin, "Jean François Blouet," in Sgard, *Dictionnaire des journalistes*, http://dictionnaire-journalistes.gazet tes18e.fr/journaliste/424-rene-jouyneau-desloges, http://dictionnaire-journalistes. gazettes18e.fr/journaliste/082-jean-francois-blouet.

22. Henri Duranton, "Aimé Delaroche," and Nicole Brondel, "Antoine Cadet de Vaux," in Sgard, *Dictionnaire des journalistes*, http://dictionnaire-journalistes.gazet tes18e.fr/journaliste/216-aime-delaroche, http://dictionnaire-journalistes.gazettes 18e.fr/journaliste/136-antoine-cadet-de-vaux.

23. There were limits to widows' rights as printers; they were prohibited from training apprentices. Jane McLeod, "Printer Widows and the State in Eighteenth-Century France," in *Women and Work in Eighteenth-Century France*, ed. Daryl M. Hafter and Nina Kushner (Baton Rouge: Louisiana State University Press, 2015), 115.

24. Jean Sgard, "Justine Souverant, veuve Giroud," in Sgard, *Dictionnaire des journalistes*, http://dictionnaire-journalistes.gazettes18e.fr/journaliste/346-justine-souverant-veuve-giroud.

25. Gilles Feyel, "Affiches de Rennes," in Sgard, *Dictionnaire des journaux*, http:// dictionnaire-journaux.gazettes18e.fr/journal/0059-affiches-de-rennes.

26. Louis Eugène Ferdinand Pouy, *Recherches historiques sur l'imprimerie et la librairie à Amiens, avec une description de livres divers imprimés dans cette ville* (Amiens: Typographie de Lemer ainé, 1861), 90–91.

27. For the affiches in Arras, see "Prospectus," *Affiches d'Artois*, 4.

28. Feyel, *L'annonce et la nouvelle*, 1028–30.

29. The writers of Grub Street were made famous by Robert Darnton in *The Literary Underground of the Old Regime* (Cambridge, MA: Harvard University Press, 1982).

30. Claude Labrosse and Pierre Rétat, *Naissance du journal révolutionnaire, 1789* (Lyon: Presses universitaires de Lyon, 1989), 187.

31. Eugène Hatin, *Bibliographie historique et critique de la presse périodique Française, ou, Catalogue systématique et raisonné de tous les écrits périodiques de quelque valeur publiés ou ayant circulé en France depuis l'origine du journal jusqu'à nos jours* (Paris: Firmin Didot frères, fils et cie, 1866), 17–21, 62–77.

32. Censer, *French Press*, 198–201; Elizabeth Andrews Bond, "Diffusion du genre dans la presse régionale Française: L'exemple des 'affiches,'" in *Nouvelles formes du*

discours journalistique au dix-huitième siècle, trans. Samuel Baudry, ed. Denis Reynaud and Samuel Baudry (Lyon: Presses universitaires de Lyon, 2018), 77–80.

33. The complete titles of the affiches are listed in the bibliography with the corresponding dates when they appeared.

34. For example, the affiches published in Metz appeared first as the *Affiches de Lorraine et des Affiches des Trois-Évêchés* (1769–73), then as both *Affiches, annonces et avis divers pour les Trois-Évêchés et la Lorraine* and as *Affiches, annonces et avis divers pour la Lorraine et les Trois-Évêchés* until 1790, when the paper took on the name of *journal* and revised the title to reflect the new revolutionary department to which it belonged. Denise Koszul, "Affiches des Evêchés 1," in Sgard, *Dictionnaire des journaux*, http://dictionnaire-journaux.gazettes18e.fr/journal/0069-affiches-des-eveches-1.

35. Sean Takats, *The Expert Cook in Enlightenment France* (Baltimore: Johns Hopkins University Press, 2011), 17–18.

36. Marc Martin, *La presse régionale*, 28–29.

37. Feyel, *La presse en France*, 35.

38. Censer, *French Press*, 54–86; Feyel, *L'annonce et la nouvelle*, 1103–89.

39. Feyel, *La presse en France*, 26.

40. For example, in the *Affiches du Poitou*, readers addressed their letters directly to Jouyneau-Desloges, the editor of the paper.

41. Some signed off with more formal flourishes such as "Your very humble servant" or "Your very humble and obedient servant." Abbreviated formulations such as "V.T.H.S." appeared frequently.

42. Feyel, "La presse provinciale sous l'ancien régime," 37.

43. Kathryn Shevelow's work has emphasized the dialogic newspaper in the eighteenth-century British context. Kathryn Shevelow, *Women and Print Culture: The Construction of Femininity in the Early Periodical* (London: Routledge, 1989), 44.

44. *Journal général de France*, June 8, 1784, 330; *Affiches des Trois-Évêchés et Lorraine*, July 3, 1783, 213; *Affiches de Toulouse*, January 22, 1783, 18.

45. *Affiches du Poitou*, November 30, 1786, 190.

46. *Affiches de Rennes*, May 25, 1785, 176–77.

47. *Affiches de la Basse-Normandie*, April 9, 1786, 2.

48. Will Slauter, *Who Owns the News? A History of Copyright* (Palo Alto: Stanford University Press, 2019), 87–112. Elizabeth Andrews Bond, "Circuits of Practical Knowledge: The Network of Letters to the Editor in the French Provincial Press, 1770–1788," *French Historical Studies* 39, no. 3 (2016): 551–61.

49. *Affiches du Dauphiné*, February 22, 1782, 173, May 24, 1782, 14–16.

50. Robert Darnton, *Censors at Work: How States Shaped Literature* (New York: W. W. Norton, 2014), 28.

51. The history of the clandestine book trade and the clandestine press is rich and extensive. On the press, see, for example, Jeremy D. Popkin, *News and Politics*; Simon Burrows, *French Exile Journalism and European Politics, 1792–1814* (Suffolk, UK: Royal Historical Society, 2000). On the clandestine book trade, see, for example, Robert Darnton, *The Forbidden Best-Sellers of Pre-Revolutionary France* (New York: W. W. Norton, 1995); Mark Curran, *The French Book Trade in Enlightenment Europe I: Selling Enlightenment* (New York: Bloomsbury, 2018).

52. Feyel, *La presse en France*, 45.

53. Colin Jones, "Great Chain of Buying," 35–36.

54. The first case was against the Basoche, the guild of legal clerks in Toulouse, who claimed Baour promoted disunity. The second was brought by the procureurs. Robert Alan Schneider, *Public Life in Toulouse, 1463–1789: From Municipal Republic to Cosmopolitan City* (Ithaca: Cornell University Press, 1989), 332–36; Marie-Thérèse Blanc-Rouquette, *La presse et l'information à Toulouse* (Toulouse: Faculté des Lettres de Toulouse, 1967), 131–165.

55. Georges Minois, *Censure et culture sous l'ancien régime* (Paris: Fayard, 1995), 266.

56. Thomas Jefferson recorded the entire affair in his personal papers. Thomas Jefferson, *The Papers of Thomas Jefferson*, vol. 8: *February 1785 to October 1785*, ed. Julian P. Boyd (Princeton: Princeton University Press, 2018), 242.

57. Minois, *Censure et culture*, 263–70.

58. Allan A. Tulchin, "Weekly Enlightenment: The *Affiches de Bordeaux*, 1758–1765," *French Historical Studies* 42, no. 2 (April 2019): 175–202.

59. The *Mercure*, the *Journal des sçavans*, and other papers such as the *Observateur hollandaise* were censored by the *chancellerie*. The *Journal des sçavans* editorial committee met twice a week in the chancellor's office. Some seventeen censors worked for the *Journal* during their careers. Forty-one censors worked on the *Mercure*. Raymond Birn, *Royal Censorship of Books in Eighteenth-Century France* (Stanford: Stanford University Press, 2012), 36–41.

60. Feyel has devoted the most attention to such cases of disputes in *L'annonce et la nouvelle*, 1022–32.

61. Feyel, "La presse provinciale sous l'ancien régime," 13.

62. In most towns the lieutenant general of the police served as the weekly censor. See, for example, the last page of each *numéro* of the *Affiches d'Angers*, *Affiches de la Basse-Normandie*, *Affiches de Normandie*, and *Affiches de l'Orléanois*.

63. Feyel, *La presse en France*, 43–44.

64. Feyel, *L'annonce et la nouvelle*, 1070.

65. Darnton, *Censors at Work*, 30. An array of tacit permissions, tolerances, simple permissions, and permissions of the police were created for works that did not meet either the quality standards or the content standards required for an official approbation.

66. Edoardo Tortarolo, *The Invention of Free Press: Writers and Censorship in Eighteenth Century Europe* (Dordrecht: Springer Netherlands, 2016), 60. Jack Censer and Charles Walton have both characterized censorship in this period as tolerant. Censer, *French Press*, 145, 54; G. Charles Walton, *Policing Public Opinion in the French Revolution: The Culture of Calumny and the Problem of Free Speech* (Oxford: Oxford University Press, 2009), 25–26.

67. Tortarolo, *Invention of Free Press*, 59.

68. Daniel Roche, "La censure," in *Le livre triumphant, Histoire de l'édition française*, vol. 2, ed. Roger Chartier and Henri-Jean Martin (Paris: Promodis, 1984), 78–83.

69. Darnton, *Censors at Work*, 36.

70. Jay Caplan, *Postal Culture in Europe, 1500–1800* (Oxford: Voltaire Foundation, 2016), 180.

71. Lindsay A. H. Parker, *Writing the Revolution*, 67.

72. Caplan, *Postal Culture*, 84, 180; Guy Arbellot, Bernard Lepetit, Jacques Bertrand, *Routes et communications*, ed. Serge Bonin and Claude Langlois, vol. 1,

Atlas de la Révolution française (Paris: Editions de l'Ecole des hautes études en sciences sociales, 1987), 38.

73. Arbellot et al., *Routes et communications*, 42.

74. By 1792, in addition to the twelve routes with daily departures, the remaining three routes from Paris included departures to Bordeaux and Nantes, which occurred six days a week, and to Toulouse three times a week. Arbellot et al., *Routes et communications*, 38.

75. Caplan, *Postal Culture*, 177.

76. Feyel, *La presse en France*, 21.

77. Recipients assumed a significant cost, and many people kept an account of expenses related to their correspondence. The cost of receiving a letter was so high that Jean-Jacques Rousseau took out a notice in the *Mercure de France* in 1762 asking the public to stop sending him fan mail and excerpts of their own literary work. The request seemed to have had little effect, as the correspondence he received only grew in the years that followed. Claude Labrosse, *Lire au XVIIIe siècle: La Nouvelle Héloïse et ses lecteurs* (Lyon: Presses universitaires de Lyon, 1985), 23–32.

78. Vincent Denis, "Les Parisiens, la police et les numérotages des maisons, du XVIIIe siècle à l'Empire," *French Historical Studies* 38, no. 1 (February 2015): 83–103.

79. The cost for the remaining newspapers under study were as follows: 7 livres, 10 sous for the affiches in Metz, Amiens, Aix, and Poitiers, and 7 livres, 4 sous for Compiègne.

80. "Prospectus," *Affiches d'Artois*, 4.

81. Archives départmentales de l'Aube, 48 H 465. More than twenty subscription envelopes printed and preaddressed to the notary Jean-François Delion in 1778 are held in a carton of his notarial records.

82. Bibliothèque universitaire, Aix-en-Provence, 34784. A receipt for subscription in 1777 was bound with the pages of the *Affiches d'Aix*. The printed form included a space to fill in the subscriber's name, the amount paid, and the date.

83. Feyel, "La presse provinciale sous l'ancien régime," 16–18; Marc Martin, *La presse régionale*, 37.

84. Colin Jones, "Great Chain of Buying," 18.

85. Feyel, *La presse en France*, 32. For example, in Metz the cost for an annual subscription to a reading room in the 1770s was 18 livres.

86. Vivian R. Gruder, *The Notables and the Nation: The Political Schooling of the French, 1787–1788* (Cambridge, MA: Harvard University Press, 2007), 200.

87. Gruder, *The Notables and the Nation*, 199; Paul Benhamou, "La lecture publique des journaux," *Dix-huitième Siècle* 24 (1992): 294.

88. See, for example, *Affiches de Picardie et Soissonnais*, December 15, 1786, 101–2.

89. Feyel, *La presse en France*, 32.

90. Roger Chartier, *Lectures et lecteurs dans la France d'Ancien Régime* (Paris: Seuil, 1987).

91. Thierry Rigogne, "Readers and Reading in Cafés, 1660–1800," *French Historical Studies* 41, no. 3 (August 2018): 473–94.

92. Roche, *People of Paris*, 197–233.

93. Walshaw, *Show of Hands*, 32–33.

94. Daniel Roche, *France in the Enlightenment*, trans. Arthur Goldhammer (Cambridge, MA: Harvard University Press, 1998), 134–35.

95. Martyn Lyons traced the locations and activities of the *veillées d'hiver* of the nineteenth century, and he found that most of the stories shared were recited from memory, not read aloud. Martyn Lyons, *Reading Culture and Writing Practices in Nineteenth-Century France* (Toronto: University of Toronto Press, 2008), 139–50. Robert Mandrou contended that peasants read *bibliothèques bleues* aloud at such winter gatherings. Robert Mandrou, *A History of French Civilization* (New York: Random House, 1964), as cited in Lyons, 139. Eugène Bougeâtre found that almanacs were present in nineteenth-century *veillées d'hiver*. Bougeâtre, *La vie Rurales dans le Mantois et le Vexin au XIX siècle* (Cergy-Pontoise: Ed. du Valhermeil, 1996), 176.

96. *La Feuille Villageoise* 1, no. 4 (1790), 50. For a thorough study on *La Feuille Villageoise*, see Melvin A. Edelstein, *La Feuille Villageoise: Communication et modernisation dans les régions rurales pendant la Révolution* (Paris: Bibliothèque nationale, 1977).

97. Colin Jones, "Great Chain of Buying," 18; Jeremy D. Popkin, *News and Politics*, 84; Auerbach, "Encourager le commerce," 23; Morag Martin, *Selling Beauty: Cosmetics, Commerce, and French Society, 1750–1830* (Baltimore: Johns Hopkins University Press, 2009), 55.

2. The Writers, Self-Presentation, and Subjectivity

1. Siméon-Prosper Hardy, *Mes loisirs, ou Journal d'événemens tels qu'ils parviennent à ma connoissance,* Bibliothèque nationale de France manuscrit: Français 6683, 260–61 (March 3, 1780). For further background on Gaucher, see A. V. Arnault et al., *Biographie nouvelle des contemporains,* 20 vols. (Paris: Librairie historique et des arts et métiers d'Emile Babeuf, 1822), 8:18.

2. Chartier et al., *Correspondence*, 142.

3. Among the performances at the Opéra-Comique that used letters to advance the plot were *Le Déserteur* (1769), *Richard Cœur de Lion* (1784), and *Sargines, ou l'Elève de l'amour* (1788).

4. Goodman, *Becoming a Woman*, 161–246.

5. See, for example, Emma Rothschild, *The Inner Life of Empires: An Eighteenth-Century History* (Princeton: Princeton University Press, 2011), 170–85.

6. James Livesey, *Civil Society and Empire* (New Haven: Yale University Press, 2009), 133–35.

7. Altman's formulation of the masked and transparent self in epistolary culture is based on published volumes of missive letters between two fictional writers. Nevertheless, her observations about the self for fictional letters held true for letters to the editor. Janet Gurkin Altman, *Epistolarity: Approaches to a Form* (Columbus: Ohio State University Press, 1982), 186.

8. Out of a total of 6,909 letters, 3,467 were signed. Of the 6,909 total letters, 2,593 letters indicated a social position or profession.

9. Of the 4,424 letters to the *Journal de Paris* and the *Journal général de France*, 2,278 were signed. Of the 2,485 letters to the provincial affiches, 1,189 were signed.

10. My schema is an adapted version of Harvey Chisick and Yossi Trilnik's list of professions and social positions for the subscribers of the monarchist revolutionary newspaper, the *Ami du Roi*. Chisick, *Production, Distribution and Readership*, 231–46.

11. See, for example, *Journal général de France*, September 23, 1784, 538, December 18, 1784, 711.

12. Doyle's study of ennoblement includes an investigation of the affiches, which published advertisements for venal offices. William Doyle, *Venality: The Sale of Offices in Eighteenth-Century France* (Oxford: Oxford University Press, 1996), 152–95.

13. Christy Pichichero, *The Military Enlightenment: War and Culture in the French Empire from Louis XIV to Napoleon* (Ithaca: Cornell University Press, 2017), 141–45.

14. Maza has argued that by the late eighteenth century, "bourgeois" was a label one gave to others who were an object of ridicule. This may explain why so few letter writers adopted this self-description. Maza, *Myth of the French Bourgeoisie*, 21–23.

15. Caradonna, *Enlightenment in Practice*, 40–87.

16. Some provincial administrators contributed to the affiches regularly, as was the case for Denis Louis Joseph Robin de Scévole and his letters to the editor of the *Affiches du Poitou*. Elizabeth Andrews Bond, "Science, Technology, and Reform in the French Countryside: The Role of Provincial Officials in the Eighteenth-Century Press," *French History and Civilization* 7 (2017): 39–50.

17. Elizabeth Andrews Bond, "Reading the Transnational in the Provincial Press: Letters to the Editor in French Journaux and Affiches, 1770–1791," *Perspectives on Europe* 44, no. 2 (2014): 88–93.

18. *Affiches de Troyes*, January 1, 1784, 5–7. A true *manœuvre* would be unlikely to have functional literacy at this time. It is possible that the writer minimized his own professional position by signing his letter as a day laborer.

19. Julia V. Douthwaite, *The Frankenstein of 1790 and Other Lost Chapters from Revolutionary France* (Chicago: University of Chicago Press, 2012), 8; Roxana Fialcofschi, "Le 'Journal de Paris' et les arts visuels, 1777–1788" (PhD diss., Université Lumière Lyon 2, 2010).

20. *Journal de Paris*, April 4, 1781, 397, January 27, 1786, 110–11.

21. *Affiches de Montpellier*, August 13, 1785, 56; *Journal de Paris*, September 23, 1779, 1082, July 4, 1780, 759, December 25, 1782, 1468.

22. For letters by locksmiths, see *Journal de Paris*, August 27, 1777, 2–3, October 13, 1783, 1181, for the master bookbinder, see *Journal de Paris*, March 30, 1787, 389, and a master joiner, *Journal de Paris*, November 28, 1780, 1359.

23. For clockmakers, see *Affiches des Trois-Évêchés et Lorraine*, December 18, 1783, 403–4; *Affiches de Dijon*, August 19, 1777, 130. A letter circulated by the Parisian tanner Jean-Antoine de Rubigny de Berteval appeared in the *Affiches de Montpellier*, March 3, 1787, 174–75; *Affiches du Poitou*, April 5, 1787, 54; *Affiches de Dijon*, April 17, 1787, 94–95. Master tanners were quite wealthy, while their workers were very poor. Rubigny in particular was a successful tanner, prolific writer, and future revolutionary.

24. *Journal de Paris*, May 24, 1783, 604–5, August 16, 1785, 945.

25. Letters signed by *laboureurs* appeared in *Affiches de Troyes*, February 19, 1783, 30–31; *Journal général de France*, July 9, 1785, 381–82, July 30, 1785, 366. On the definition of a *laboureur*, see Cynthia A. Bouton, *The Flour War: Gender, Class, and Community in late Ancien Régime French Society* (State College: Pennsylvania State University Press, 1993), 49.

26. Steven Laurence Kaplan, *Provisioning Paris: Merchants and Millers in the Grain and Flour Trade during the Eighteenth Century* (Ithaca: Cornell University Press, 1984), 206–13.

27. *Affiches de Troyes*, April 2, 1783, 55–56, April 6, 1785, 54–55.

28. *Affiches du Poitou*, October 4, 1781, 159–60; *Journal de Paris*, March 3, 1784, 285, April 21, 1784, 492.

29. The *agriculteur* wrote a letter to the *Affiches du Dauphiné*, January 28, 1785, 167–68. *Cultivateurs* wrote letters published in *Affiches du Poitou*, March 31, 1774, 54; *Affiches de Dijon*, August 26, 1777, 134; *Affiches du Dauphiné*, February 3, 1786, 168. The future revolutionary and deputy in the Constituent Assembly, Etienne Chevalier, wrote two letters to the *Journal de Paris* describing himself as a "cultivateur from Argenteuil," January 3, 1785, 10, August 10, 1785, 916–17.

30. *Affiches du Poitou*, March 2, 1780, 33.

31. See, for example, *Affiches des Trois-Évêchés et Lorraine*, January 4, 1786, 1–2; *Journal général de France*, December 1, 1785, 579; *Journal de Paris*, May 8, 1786, 518–19.

32. For letters by a countess, see, for example, *Affiches de Normandie*, February 4, 1786, 38–39; *Journal de Paris*, September 18, 1782, 1064; by a marquise, *Affiches d'Angers*, October 9, 1788, 171–72; by a baroness, *Journal général de France*, May 14, 1785, 231.

33. See, for example, *Affiches de l'Orléanois*, November 14, 1777, 189–90; *Affiches des Trois-Évêchés et Lorraine*, August 1, 1782, 139; *Journal de Paris*, December 3, 1779, 1373.

34. *Affiches du Poitou*, December 21, 1775, 214–15, March 11, 1779, 38–39, April 8, 1779, 54–55, May 20, 1779, 79–80.

35. Robert J. Griffin, *The Faces of Anonymity: Anonymous and Pseudonymous Publication from the Sixteenth to the Twentieth Century* (New York: Palgrave Macmillan, 2003), 1–17.

36. Mary Louise Roberts, *Disruptive Acts: The New Woman in Fin-de-Siècle France* (Chicago: University of Chicago Press: 2002), 70.

37. *Journal de Paris*, September 17, 1780, 1059, November 15, 1780, 1302–3; De Rousset was a *maîtresse de pension*, *Affiches d'Aix*, April 26, 1778, 126–28.

38. Guillaume-François Rouelle was an apothecary known for his early work in chemistry on the base. *Journal de Paris*, November 15, 1779, 1300–1301.

39. *Journal de Paris*, May 8, 1779, 514–15. The postpartum complications were described as "spilt milk," a commonly used designation for postpartum death from unknown cause. For further discussion of Weisse's petition to the Royal Society of Medicine, see G. Steinheil, ed., *Commentaires de la Faculté de Médecine de Paris, 1777 à 1786*, vol. 2 (Paris: Faculty of Medicine of Paris, 1903), 34–35.

40. *Journal de Paris*, January 16, 1777, 2.

41. *Journal de Paris*, September 16, 1779, 1054–55. She also published in the *Mercure de France*, where she signed some but not all of her works. Katherine Astbury, "Madame de Laisse," *Dictionnaire Siefar*, last modified May 3, 2011, http://siefar.org/dictionnaire/fr/Madame_de_Laisse.

42. *Affiches de Dijon*, May 25, 1779, 88, June 15, 1779, 103.

43. Ralph A. Leigh, "Editorial Notes" for Marie Thérèse Levasseur [née Renout], "Marie Thérèse Levasseur [née Renout] to *Le Journal de Paris*: Tuesday, 11 May 1779," in *Electronic Enlightenment Scholarly Edition of Correspondence*, ed. Robert McNamee et al., University of Oxford, available at https://www.e-enlightenment.com/.

44. *Journal de Paris*, September 5, 1778, 990; *Journal général de France*, September 16, 1778, 147.

45. Beaumesnil was the stage name of Henriette Adélaïde Villard. *Journal de Paris*, December 27, 1778, 1457.

46. *Journal de Paris*, August 31, 1780, 991.

47. *Affiches de Normandie*, April 25, 1787, 141–42; Clay, *Stagestruck*, 110–12.

48. Fialcofschi, "Le 'Journal de Paris,'" 86.

49. Annie Duprat, *'Les affaires d'État sont mes affaires de cœur,' Lettres de Rosalie Jullien, une femme dans la Révolution, 1775–1810* (Paris: Belin, 2017), 60–63, 67–68, 208; Lindsay A. H. Parker, *Writing the Revolution*, 145.

50. *Journal général de France*, February 15, 1787, 78–79.

51. Hesse, *Other Enlightenment*, xii.

52. John Shovlin, "Nobility," in Doyle, *Oxford Handbook of the Ancien Régime*, 120.

53. Of the 6,909 letters published, 573 letters (8.3 percent) were signed with a pen name.

54. Shalev has argued that anonymous and pseudonymous writing began as a response to censorship, as "political debate unfolded more easily under mediation that would not expose writers to the severity of the censor." Eran Shalev, "Ancient Masks, American Fathers: Classical Pseudonyms during the American Revolution and Early Republic," *Journal of the Early Republic* 23, no. 2 (2003): 154.

55. The "hermit of the Sennar forest" was a known pen name of Marie-Jean-Antoine-Nicolas de Caritat, marquis de Condorcet. Anne-Marie Chouilhet, "Condorcet," in Sgard, *Dictionnaire des journalistes*, http://dictionnaire-journalistes.gazetes18e.fr/journaliste/190-jean-antoine-de-condorcet.

56. The "Lexovien" asked the editor to publish some word puzzles he sent to the paper. *Affiches de Normandie*, November 4, 1786, 355.

57. *Journal de Paris*, July 4, 1779, 754, July 7, 1779, 767.

58. Fialcofschi, "Le 'Journal de Paris,'" 83–84. Kergolé was the invention of the artist Antoine Renou. Nicole Brondel and Paul Benhamou, "Antoine Renou," in Sgard, *Dictionnaire des journalistes*, http://dictionnaire-journalistes.gazettes18e.fr/journaliste/679-antoine-renou.

59. As Shalev has argued for the American context, pseudonymity possesses an inherent element of deception. Shalev, "Ancient Masks," 154.

60. *Affiches de Toulouse*, March 6, 1782, 39–40.

61. Of the 6,909 letters under study, 327 were signed by "un/e abonné/e." Approximately 25.7 percent (1,773 letters) of the 6,909 letters in the entire corpus were unsigned.

62. Regarding the anonymous letters published in *Journal de Paris* discussed above, see Dorothy Medlin, "André Morellet, the *Journal de Paris*, and *Le Publiciste*, 1795–1807," in *Correspondence; Dialogue; History of Ideas*, SVEC (Oxford: Voltaire Foundation, 2005), 183–97; *Affiches de Dijon*, June 15, 1779, 102–3, September 13, 1785, 183.

63. *Affiches des Trois-Évêchés et Lorraine*, May 13, 1779, 151.

64. *Affiches du Dauphiné*, February 27, 1778, 175, January 30, 1784, 164, December 7, 1787, 138, April 25, 1788, 236.

65. Of the 6,909 letters under study, 769 were signed with initials.

66. *Affiches de l'Orléanois*, July 17, 1777, 121.

67. *Affiches des Trois-Évêchés et Lorraine*, July 1, 1779, 202.

68. All letters published in the *Journal de Paris*, *Affiches du Poitou*, *Affiches des Trois-Évêchés et Lorraine*, and *Affiches de Dijon* during the three years sampled were evaluated, with two exceptions: the *Affiches de Dijon* was not published during 1774, and the *Journal de Paris* was not founded until 1777.

69. Richmond Pugh Bond, *New Letters to the Tatler and Spectator* (Austin: University of Texas Press, 1959), 17.

70. See especially Coudart, *La Gazette de Paris*; Jean Paul Bertaud, *Les amis du Roi: Journaux et journalistes royalistes en France de 1789 à 1792* (Paris: Perrin, 1984); Chisick, *Production, Distribution and Readership.*

71. Gelbart, *Feminine and Opposition Journalism.*

72. Some of Moysant's papers are held in the manuscripts collection of the Bibliothèque municipale de Caen, 214 In-folio 122. Correspondence concerning Baour's printing business are held in the Bibliothèque municipale de Toulouse, MS 1873.

73. There are two letters mentioned in the published private correspondence of Felix Faulcon, the Poitevin who would become a deputy during the French Revolution. See G. Debien, *Correspondence de Félix Faulcon* (Poitiers: Société des Archives Historiques du Poitou, 1953), 133. In 1789 the paper published his signature. In 1784 his letter was printed unsigned.

The Bibliothèque municipale de Troyes has three manuscript letters, one of which was an ad written on October 22, 1784, by a M. Michelin publicizing his *Annales*, which was couriered to the editor by Courtalon. This letter was not published in the *Affiches de Troyes*, but letters by the same Michelin did appear in the *affiches* in Reims and Marseille in 1782. Bibliothèque municipale de Troyes, MS 4°2795.

One manuscript letter was a transcribed copy of a letter from the *Affiches de l'Orléanois* by a doctor Paul to the *Affiches de Reims* from Monday, September 25, 1780, which had first appeared in the *Affiches de Champagne* on August 9, 1780. A marginal note on the manuscript indicates that the letter was for the *Almanach de Troyes*. Bibliothèque municipale de Troyes, MS 4°2795.

P.-J. Grosley also wrote several letters to the *Mercure de France* and to the *Affiches de Troyes*. Manuscript copies of his letters remain in the Bibliothèque municipale de Troyes. Most of his letters include a note indicating the date when they appeared in the paper. Bibliothèque municipale de Troyes, MS 4°2795.

74. In his research into extant manuscript letters to Addison and Steele, Richmond Pugh Bond was able to verify the identity of only one writer among the letters. Bond, *New Letters to the Tatler and Spectator*, 22.

75. For further discussion of similarities to American letter-printing practices, see Chad Reid, "'Widely Read by American Patriots': The *New-York Weekly Journal* and the Influence of Cato's Letters on Colonial America," in *Periodical Literature in Early America*, ed. Mark Kamrath and Sharon M. Harris (Knoxville: University of Tennessee Press, 2005), 113.

76. *Journal de Paris*, February 12, 1788, 194.

3. Reading Together, Book References, and Interacting with Print

1. *Journal de Paris*, August 18, 1779, 937.

2. Of the letters in this sample, 377 referenced book titles, and 387 cited a periodical. A simple difference of proportions test shows the difference between the percentage of letters with book references and those with newspaper citations was statistically indistinguishable ($Z = .4159$, $p = .67448$). That is, based on this sample of three years, it is likely that writers cited periodicals and book titles in the information press at equivalent rates. This test does not account for other factors that may have influenced citation styles, such as editorial practices, repeated authorship, and regional variation.

3. *Affiches de Dijon*, May 25, 1779, 88. This letter was a reprinted copy from the *Journal de Paris*, May 16, 1779, 545–46.

4. Robert Darnton, "Reading, Writing, and Publishing in Eighteenth-Century France: A Case Study in the Sociology of Literature," *Daedalus* 100, no. 1 (1971): 238.

5. Elizabeth Andrews Bond, "Mapping the Media Landscape in Old Regime France," *Current Research in Digital History* 1 (2018), https://doi.org/10.31835/crdh.2018.11.

6. During the American Revolution, the London-based *Courier de l'Europe* supported French intervention in support of American independence, parliamentary systems of government, and freedom of the press. Hélène Maspero-Clerc, "Une 'gazette anglo-française' pendant la guerre d'amérique: Le 'Courier de l'Europe' (1776–1788)," *Annales historiques de la Révolution française* 48, no. 226 (1976): 572–94.

7. As noted earlier in the chapter, 24.1 percent of the 1,567 letters published in the three-year sample (1777, 1782, and 1788) referenced one or more book titles.

8. Simon Burrows, *The French Book Trade in Enlightenment Europe II: Enlightenment Bestsellers* (London: Bloomsbury Academic, 2018), 79–82. On the history of the schema in the eighteenth and nineteenth centuries, see Edward Edwards, *Memoirs of Libraries: Including a Handbook of Library Economy*, 2 vols. (London: Trübner, 1859).

9. The classics in this field include Daniel Mornet, "Les enseignements des bibliothèques privées (1750–1780)," *Revue d'histoire littéraire de la France* 17, no. 3 (1910): 449–96; François Furet, "La 'librairie' du royaume de France au 18e siècle," in *Livre et société dans la France du XVIIIe siècle*, ed. G. Bollème et al. (Paris: Mouton, 1965), 1:3–32; Robert Darnton, *The Corpus of Clandestine Literature in France, 1769–1789* (New York: W. W. Norton, 1995). Recent reassessments of bookseller catalogs have revised both the counts of books sold and the impact of their distribution in France. Curran, *French Book Trade*; Burrows, *French Book Trade*; Alicia Montoya, "Middlebrow, Religion, and the European Enlightenment: A New Bibliometric Project, MEDIATE (1665–1820)," *French History and Civilization* 7 (2017): 66–79.

10. The catalogs also reflected the mentalities of the day, for example, history subcategories included categories for "histoire de l'Orient" and "histoire profane." The catalog subheadings thus are not neutral labels but rather an illustration of how eighteenth-century booksellers and their readers conceptualized a wide array of subject matter. On the implications of taxonomies of print on taxonomies of thought, see especially Burrows, *French Book Trade*, 79–82.

11. In this chapter I follow the Parisian booksellers' schema for subcategories as it is used by the French Book Trade in Enlightenment Europe Project. Simon Burrows, Mark Curran, Vincent Hiribarren, Sarah Kattau, and Henry Merivale, "The French Book Trade in Enlightenment Europe Project, 1769–1794," last modified May 6, 2014, http://fbtee.uws.edu.au/stn/.

12. Silvie Caucanas and Rémy Cazals, *Venance Dougados et son temps. André Chénier. Fabre d'Eglantine. Actes du colloque de Carcassonne, 5–7 mai 1994* (Carcassone: Les Audois, 1995).

13. Works on "great men" chronicled the acts of exemplary figures who embodied the values and virtues of the age. Lilti, *The Invention of Celebrity*, 87–92.

14. P. Giles, *Plutarch's Lives* (Cambridge: Cambridge University Press, 2014), xi–xii.

15. On the interest in collecting and interpreting Roman medals, see, for example, *Affiches de Picardie et Soissonnais*, May 20, 1775, 79–80. A letter on the Roman amphitheater in Arles appeared in *Journal général de France*, April 12, 1787, 175.

16. Between 1750 and 1810, sixty-four collectors of coins and antiquities operated in the Rhone valley alone. Some of the coins were unearthed locally. The

correspondence and gift-giving networks consisted of serious collectors such as Esprit-Claude-François Calvet and young amateurs whom they helped build their own collections. L. W. B. Brockliss, *Calvet's Web: Enlightenment and the Republic of Letters in Eighteenth-Century France* (Oxford: Oxford University Press, 2002), 198–200.

17. Karen E. Carter, *Creating Catholics: Catechism and Primary Education in Early Modern France* (South Bend: University of Notre Dame Press, 2011), 23–57.

18. Fearing trial for heresy, Le Courayer lived in England from 1728 until his death. His exile and correspondence with British clergy influenced his theology. Colin Haydon, "Le Courayer, Pierre-François (1681–1776)," in *Oxford Dictionary of National Biography*, ed. Lawrence Goldman (Oxford: Oxford University Press, 2006).

19. On this subject see, especially, Daniel Mornet, *Les origines intellectuelles de la révolution française (1715–1787)* (Paris: A. Colin, 1933); Bollème et al., *Livre et société dans la France du XVIIIe siècle*; Darnton, *Forbidden Best-Sellers*; Curran, *French Book Trade*.

20. Beffroy de Reigny wrote letters to affiches throughout the kingdom to advertise his own publications. Four of the references to his titles in the press were ones that he himself wrote and signed. *Affiches de Normandie*, April 16, 1788, 127; *Affiches de Toulouse*, May 7, 1788, 79; *Affiches de Picardie et Soissonnais*, May 17, 1788, 88; *Journal de Lyon*, May 28, 1788, 135–36.

21. I compared digital copies of the full order lists at the Société Typographique de Neuchâtel placed by the printer-booksellers Michel-Vincent Chevrier in Poitiers, Louis-Pierre Couret de Villeneuve in Orléans, and Jean-Baptiste Capel in Dijon to the books mentioned in letters published in the affiches they edited in Poitiers, Orléans, and Dijon, respectively. Darnton's digital copies of the book orders placed with the Société Typographique de Neuchâtel are available on his website. Robert Darnton, "Booksellers / Literary Demand," *A Literary Tour de France*, September 1, 2014, http:/ / www.robertdarnton.org/ literarytour/ booksellers.

22. Dan Edelstein, Robert Morissey, and Glenn Roe, "To Quote or Not to Quote: Citation Strategies in the *Encyclopédie*," 74, no. 2 (April 2013): 224–27.

23. Ira O. Wade, *The Intellectual Development of Voltaire*, 2nd ed. (Princeton: Princeton University Press, 2016), 40–43. According to Rancière, poets of the previous century were seen as animating a new generation of literature, an idea that Voltaire himself highlighted in his definition of the *littérateur*. Jacques Rancière, *Mute Speech: Literature, Critical Theory, and Politics* (New York: Columbia University Press, 2011), 33–36.

24. "Preface" to Karl Enenkel, Jan L. de Jong, and Janine de Landtsheer, eds., with Alicia Montoya, *Recreating Ancient History: Episodes from the Greek and Roman Past in the Arts and Literature of the Early Modern Period* (Leiden: Brill, 2001), viii–xiii.

25. Leah Price, "Reading: The State of the Discipline," *Book History* 7 (2004): 314. Studies of women's reading communities underscore the connections between community and individual reading practice. See Janice A. Radway, *Reading the Romance: Women, Patriarchy, and Popular Literature* (Chapel Hill: University of North Carolina Press, 1991); Barbara Hochman, *Getting at the Author: Reimagining Books and Reading in the Age of American Realism* (Amherst: University of Massachusetts Press, 2001); Mary Kelley, *Learning to Stand and Speak* (Chapel Hill: Omohundro Institute of Early American History and Culture and the University of North Carolina Press, 2012).

26. *Journal de Provence*, January 26, 1782, 227–28.

27. *Affiches de Troyes*, February 19, 1783, 30.

28. *Journal de Paris*, October 16, 1788, 1239.

29. *Journal de Paris*, September 20, 1778, 1050–51. He explained that the issue published on the 14th had been read to him, and it concerned him enough that he had sent a response to the paper.

30. *Affiches d'Angers*, February 24, 1775, 32.

31. *Journal de Paris*, February 19, 1782, 198.

32. *Journal de Paris*, October 28, 1778, 1206.

33. *Affiches de Reims*, February 12, 1776, 30–31.

34. *Journal de Paris*, March 16, 1788, 334–35.

35. *Journal de Paris*, March 19, 1788, 346.

36. *Journal de Paris*, June 13, 1788, 722.

37. Hunt, *Inventing Human Rights*, 41.

38. *Affiches du Dauphiné*, May 30, 1788, 22; *Journal général de France*, May 13, 1788, 231–32.

39. Robert Darnton, *The Great Cat Massacre and Other Episodes in French Cultural History* (New York: Basic Books, 1984), 215–56; Labrosse, *Lire au XVIIIe siècle*, 23–32.

40. *Journal de Paris*, June 5, 1788, 689.

41. Hunt, *Inventing Human Rights*, 40–54.

42. *Journal de Paris*, August 9, 1778, 882–83.

43. *Journal de Paris*, December 8, 1778, 1380.

44. William M. Reddy, *The Navigation of Feeling: A Framework for the History of Emotions* (Cambridge: Cambridge University Press, 2001), 155–72.

45. Barbara Rosenwein, *Generations of Feeling: A History of Emotions, 600–1700* (Cambridge: Cambridge University Press, 2016), 3.

46. Ute Frevert, "Defining Emotions: Concepts and Debates over Three Centuries," in *Emotional Lexicons: Continuity and Change in the Vocabulary of Feeling, 1700–2000*, ed. Ute Frevert et al. (Oxford: Oxford University Press, 2014), 14.

47. *Journal général de France*, January 29, 1788, 50.

48. Daniel Rosenberg argues that it was this very "logic of progress" that gave the *Encyclopédie* its urgency and significance. Daniel Rosenberg, "An Eighteenth-Century Time Machine: The 'Encyclopedia' of Denis Diderot," *Historical Reflections/Réflexions Historiques* 25, no. 2 (1999): 246–50.

49. *Journal de Paris*, October 30, 1782, 1232.

50. *Journal général de France*, March 13, 1782, 43.

51. *Affiches de Rennes*, November 21, 1787, 70.

52. See, for example, *Affiches de Reims*, October 4, 1773, 319–20; *Journal de Paris*, January 11, 1778, 42; *Journal général de France*, April 7, 1785, 167.

53. *Journal général de France*, March 27, 1788, 150.

54. *Journal de Paris*, February 21, 1788, 233.

55. Jonathan Sheehan, "From Philology to Fossils: The Biblical Encyclopedia in Early Modern Europe," *Journal of the History of Ideas* 64, no. 1 (January 2003): 41–42.

56. Ann Blair, *Too Much to Know: Managing Scholarly Information before the Modern Age* (New Haven: Yale University Press, 2010), 2–9.

57. *Journal général de France*, November 6, 1788, 535–36.

58. Eltjo Buringh and Jan Luiten Van Zanden, "Charting the 'Rise of the West': Manuscripts and Printed Books in Europe, a Long-Term Perspective from the Sixth through Eighteenth Centuries," *Journal of Economic History* 69, no. 2 (June 2009): 417.

59. Richard Yeo, "A Solution to the Multitude of Books: Ephraim Chambers's Cyclopaedia (1728) as 'the Best Book in the Universe,'" *Journal of the History of Ideas* 64, no. 1 (January 2003): 61–65.

60. Literacy estimates rely largely on the ability of people at the time to sign a legal document, such as a marriage certificate. The estimates are complicated by the fact that reading was taught before writing, and in some cases completely separate from writing. Simon Burrows, "Books, Philosophy, Enlightenment," in *The Oxford Handbook of the French Revolution*, ed. David Andress (Oxford: Oxford University Press, 2015), 79.

61. Roche, *People of Paris*, 200–214.

62. Blair, *Too Much to Know*, 62–172.

63. Ann Blair, "Reading Strategies for Coping with Information Overload ca. 1550–1700," *Journal of the History of Ideas* 64, no. 1 (January 2003): 19–28.

64. Of the 441 unique titles cited in 1778, 1782, and 1788, eighty-six were works of poetry.

65. *Journal de Paris*, October 14, 1778, 1149.

66. *Journal de Paris*, August 22, 1778, 933–34. The writer noted that the poem captured "maternal pain in its every expression."

67. *Affiches de Picardie et Soissonnais*, August 12, 1775, 126.

68. *Affiches de l'Orléanois*, June 12, 1778, 100; *Journal de Paris*, August 11, 1778, 889–90.

69. *Journal de Paris*, September 6, 1778, 993–94.

70. *Journal de Paris*, December 6, 1782, 1381.

71. *Journal général de France*, October 30, 1782, 175.

72. *Affiches du Beauvaisis*, October 14, 1787, 162.

73. *Journal de Provence*, January 4, 1782, 221–22.

74. John R. Iverson, "Putting Voltaire's *Henriade* in the Hands of the Young," *French Review* 76, no. 3 (2003): 522–24.

75. *Journal de Paris*, September 7, 1778, 998–99.

76. *Journal de Paris*, July 11, 1788, 842.

77. *Affiches de Dijon*, July 3, 1787, 138–39; *Journal général de France*, July 10, 1787, 327. The letter was probably by Pierre Laureau de Saint-André, writer and future revolutionary elected to the Legislative Assembly.

78. The gender of this writer is unknown. *Affiches des Trois-Évêchés et Lorraine*, June 26, 1788, 204–5.

79. *Journal de Paris*, August 17, 1778, 915.

80. *Affiches de Normandie*, January 25, 1786, 27.

81. Roger Chartier, "Laborers and Voyagers," in *The Book History Reader*, ed. David Finkelstein and Alistair McCleery (London: Routledge, 2002), 47–59.

82. Antoine Lilti, *World of Salons*, 157.

83. *Journal de Paris*, March 19, 1780, 328.

84. Abigail Williams, *The Social Life of Books: Reading Together in the Eighteenth-Century Home* (New Haven: Yale University Press, 2017), 11–24.

85. *Journal de Paris*, September 18, 1782, 1063.

86. *Journal de Paris*, March 13, 1783, 301.

87. *Journal de Paris*, December 31, 1782, 1488.

88. Penny Brown, *A Critical History of French Children's Literature, 1600–1830* (New York: Routledge, 2008), 86–88.

89. Jennifer J. Popiel, *Rousseau's Daughters: Domesticity, Education, and Autonomy in Modern France* (Durham: University of New Hampshire Press, 2008), 112–39.

90. Williams, *Social Life of Books*, 37–43, 58–62.

91. *Journal général de France*, January 29, 1788, 50.

92. Chartier, *Cultural Origins of the French Revolution*, 83.

93. *Affiches de Toulouse*, July 9, 1788, 115.

4. Popular Science and Public Participation

1. *Affiches de Toulouse*, November 19, 1783, 191.

2. The letters analyzed in this chapter include all of the 1,287 letters to the editor published in fourteen provincial newspapers in Angers, Amiens, Dijon, Grenoble, Lyon, Marseille, Montpellier, Metz, Orléans, Poitiers, Reims, Rennes, Toulouse, and Troyes, and in two Parisian newspapers, the *Journal général de France* and the *Journal de Paris*. Of these letters, 462 (approximately 35.9 percent) concerned science and medicine.

3. Charles Gillispie, *The Montgolfier Brothers and the Invention of Aviation, 1783–1784* (Princeton: Princeton University Press, 1983), 15–17.

4. Mi Gyung Kim, *The Imagined Empire: Balloon Enlightenments in Revolutionary Europe* (Pittsburgh: University of Pittsburgh Press, 2017), 55.

5. The "chapeau au ballon" was also called the Lunardi hat, after the Italian aeronaut who first took flight in September 1784. Paul Keen, *Literature, Commerce, and the Spectacle of Modernity, 1750–1800* (Cambridge: Cambridge University Press, 2012), 63–74.

6. Robert Darnton, *Mesmerism and the End of the Enlightenment in France* (Cambridge, MA: Harvard University Press, 1968), 20.

7. Darnton, *Mesmerism*, 22.

8. I have not translated *physicien* because it was not synonymous with "physicist" in the eighteenth century. *Physiciens'* work encompassed natural philosophy that would later become known as "physics," but it was also a more expansive descriptor of a professional thinker working in the sciences. In this approach, I follow Riskin's distinction in *Science in the Age of Sensibility*, 140.

9. *Affiches du Dauphiné*, September 19, 1783, 85–86.

10. Pilatre de Rozier was a celebrated aeronaut who later died in a ballooning accident as he attempted to cross the English Channel.

11. *Affiches du Dauphiné*, October 31, 1783, 109–10.

12. Kim, *Imagined Empire*, 148–49.

13. *Affiches d'Angers*, December 12, 1783, 207.

14. *Affiches de Dijon*, December 23, 1783, 32.

15. *Affiches d'Angers*, February 20, 1784, 35.

16. *Affiches de Dijon*, January 13, 1784, 43.

17. *Affiches des Trois-Évêchés et Lorraine*, January 1, 1784, 4.

18. Bernadette Bensaude-Vincent, "A Public for Science: The Rapid Growth of Popularization in Nineteenth-Century France," trans. Liz Libbrecht, *Réseaux: The French Journal of Communication* 3, no. 11 (1995): 78.

19. Roche, *France in the Enlightenment*, 241–47.

20. Roche, *Le siècle des lumières en province*, 136–255. The history of the academies is extensive. See, for example, Roger Chartier, "L'Académie de Lyon au XVIIIe siècle,

1700–1793, étude de sociologie culturelle," *Nouvelles études Lyonnaises* (1969): 133–250; Michel Taillefer, *Une académie interprète des Lumières: L'Académie des sciences, inscriptions et belles lettres de Toulouse au XVIIIe siècle* (Paris, 1984).

21. Jacques de Flesselles was from a recently ennobled family and worked as a reform-minded intendant from 1762 to 1784. In 1789 he was the *prévôt des marchands* of Paris. He was killed on July 14, 1789. Charles Coulston Gillispie, *Science and Polity in France at the End of the Old Regime* (Princeton: Princeton University Press, 1981), 23–24, 35.

22. *Journal de Lyon*, February 5, 1784, 41.

23. Roche, *France in the Enlightenment*, 242–44.

24. Caradonna, *Enlightenment in Practice*, 2, 180–201.

25. *Affiches de Picardie et Soissonnais*, June 26, 1784, 103.

26. The editor published three letters on the same day that concerned such themes in the *Affiches du Dauphiné*, October 3, 1783, 94–95.

27. *Journal de Paris*, October 26, 1783, 1231; *Affiches du Dauphiné*, November 7, 1783, 116.

28. *Affiches des Trois-Évêchés et Lorraine*, January 15, 1784, 18.

29. *Affiches d'Angers*, April 2, 1784, 60.

30. *Affiches du Dauphiné*, October 3, 1783, 95.

31. *Affiches de Toulouse*, April 28, 1784, 71.

32. Geoffrey Wawro, *The Franco-Prussian War: The German Conquest of France in 1870–1871* (Cambridge: Cambridge University Press, 2003), 274.

33. *Affiches du Dauphiné*, February 6, 1784, 167.

34. *Affiches du Poitou*, February 19, 1784, 29–30. This letter was one of several that Denis Louis Joseph Robin de Scévole wrote to the *Affiches du Poitou*.

35. *Affiches de Montpellier*, December 20, 1783, 139.

36. *Journal de Paris*, December 8, 1783, 1404–5; *Affiches des Trois-Évêchés et Lorraine*, December 18, 1783, 403–4; Darnton, *Mesmerism*, 23.

37. Colin Jones, "Great Chain of Buying," 14.

38. *Journal de Paris*, October 3, 1783, 1141; *Affiches d'Angers*, October 10, 1783, 170–71; *Affiches de Toulouse*, October 15, 1783, 171; *Affiches du Poitou*, October 16, 1783, 165–66; *Affiches du Dauphiné*, October 17, 1783, 102–3; *Affiches des Trois-Évêchés et Lorraine*, October 23, 1783, 342–43.

39. Darnton, *Mesmerism*, 36.

40. Larry Stewart, "The Laboratory, the Workshop, and the Theater of Experiment," in *Science and Spectacle in the European Enlightenment*, ed. Bernadette Bensaude-Vincent and Christine Blondel (Hampshire, UK: Ashgate, 2008), 12.

41. Mary Fairclough has argued that imagery and ideas related to electricity were used to signal that which was mysterious or opaque in *Literature, Electricity and Politics, 1740–1840: 'Electrick communication every where'* (London: Palgrave, 2017), 2–3.

42. The *conseils souverains* were the courts of last appeal in four provinces in France where a parlement did not have jurisdiction. Jessica Riskin discussed the organization of the Conseil d'Artois and the significance of Vissery's trial in depth in *Science in the Age of Sensibility*, 139–84.

43. Antoine-Joseph Buissart was a close friend of Maximilien Robespierre. Peter McPhee, *Robespierre: A Revolutionary Life* (New Haven: Yale University Press, 2012), 34–37.

44. Riskin, *Science in the Age of Sensibility*, 176–84.

45. Riskin, *Science in the Age of Sensibility*, 174–76.

46. Robespierre's success was touted in the *Mercure de France* in an account that was possibly written by Buissart. McPhee, *Robespierre*, 34.

47. *Affiches de Toulouse*, September 24, 1783, 158.

48. *Affiches de Troyes*, August 13, 1783, 132–33.

49. Paola Bertucci, "Enlightening Towers: Public Opinion, Local Authorities, and the Reformation of Meteorology in Eighteenth Century Italy," in *Playing with Fire: Histories of the Lightning Rod*, ed. Peter Heering, Oliver Hochadel, and David J. Rhees (Philadelphia: American Philosophical Society, 2009), 26–32.

50. *Affiches de Montpellier*, November 8, 1783, 113.

51. *Affiches de Dijon*, October 6, 1778, 161. Louis-Bernard Guyton, baron de Morveau was a chemist who participated in the design of the first system of chemical nomenclature. Frederic Lawrence Holmes, *Lavoisier and the Chemistry of Life: An Exploration of Scientific Creativity* (Madison: University of Wisconsin Press, 1987), 316–19. After serving as a deputy in the Legislative Assembly and the National Convention, he retired to focus on setting up a corps of balloonists for the revolutionary army. He piloted one of the balloons in the battle of Fleurus in 1794. Richard P. Hallion, *Taking Flight: Inventing the Aerial Age, from Antiquity through the First World War* (New York: Oxford University Press, 2003), 63–65.

52. Bertucci, "Enlightening Towers," 27.

53. *Affiches de Troyes*, February 12, 1783, 27.

54. J. L. Heilbron, *Electricity in the 17th and 18th Centuries: A Study of Early Modern Physics* (Berkeley: University of California Press, 1979), 353.

55. Paola Bertucci, "Therapeutic Attractions: Early Applications of Electricity to the Art of Healing," in *Brain, Mind and Medicine: Essays in Eighteenth-Century Neuroscience*, ed. Harry Whitaker, C. U. M. Smith, and Stanley Finger (Boston: Springer, 2007), 277.

56. Riskin, *Science in the Age of Sensibility*, 196.

57. Paola Bertucci, "Revealing Sparks: John Wesley and the Religious Utility of Electrical Healing," *British Journal for the History of Science* 39, no. 3 (2006): 341–62.

58. *Affiches du Dauphiné*, March 12, 1784, 191–92; *Affiches de Toulouse*, March 17, 1784, 47–48. Louis Filiol de Raimond was *directeur des postes* in Besançon from 1775 until 1790, a position he inherited from his mother, Adélaïd Poulain du Clos, and would pass to his wife, Mélanie Suzanne Isnard. Susan Bachrach, *Dames Employées: The Feminization of Postal Work in Nineteenth-Century France* (Philadelphia: Haworth Press, 1984), 9–10.

59. Michael Brian Schiffer, *Draw the Lightning Down: Benjamin Franklin and Electrical Technology in the Age of Enlightenment* (Berkeley: University of California Press, 2003), 67–69.

60. Carra would become a leading Girondin during the Revolution. On his efforts to establish himself as a *physicien*, see Stefan Lemny, *Jean-Louis Carra, 1742–1793: Parcours d'un révolutionnaire* (Paris: L'Harmattan, 2000), 117–26.

61. *Journal de Paris*, May 11, 1784, 572. Carra's letter also appeared in *Affiches des Trois-Évêchés et Lorraine*, May 13, 1784, 154–55; *Affiches de Montpellier*, July 1, 1784, 47.

62. *Affiches du Dauphiné*, December 10, 1784, 136–37.

63. The references made by Jal de Muntel to the experiments in Bertholon's book are so brief that the mechanisms for the experiments in the volume are unclear.

64. *Affiches du Dauphiné*, September 10, 1784, 82–83.

65. Among the 462 letters published in 1783–84 that covered scientific subject matter, 293 letters were signed by the author.

66. *Affiches du Dauphiné*, December 19, 1783, 139; *Journal de Paris*, January 20, 1784, 89.

5. Agricultural Reform and Local Innovation

1. *Affiches du Poitou*, May 25, 1786, 82.

2. Peter M. Jones, *Agricultural Enlightenment: Knowledge, Technology, and Nature, 1750–1840* (Oxford: Oxford University Press, 2016), 83.

3. Liana Vardi, *The Physiocrats and the World of the Enlightenment* (Cambridge: Cambridge University Press, 2012), 114–15.

4. Elizabeth Fox-Genovese, *The Origins of Physiocracy: Economic Revolution and Social Order in Eighteenth-Century France* (Ithaca: Cornell University Press, 1976), 9–10.

5. Vardi, *Physiocrats*, 3, 239 (quotation); George Weulersse, *Le Mouvement physiocratique en France (de 1756 à 1770)*, vol. 2 (Paris: Alcan, 1910), 120–50.

6. Vardi, *Physiocrats*, 9.

7. Dan Edelstein, *The Terror of Natural Right: Republicanism, the Cult of Nature, and the French Revolution* (Chicago: University of Chicago Press, 2009), 109; Michael Sonenscher, "Property, Community, and Citizenship," in *The Cambridge History of Eighteenth-Century Political Thought*, ed. Mark Goldie and Robert Wokler (Cambridge: Cambridge University Press, 2006), 466–68.

8. Pierre Claude Reynard, "Charting Environmental Concerns: Reactions to Hydraulic Public Works in Eighteenth-Century France," *Environment and History* 9, no. 3 (2003): 255.

9. Caradonna, *Enlightenment in Practice*, 196–97, 234–35.

10. Bond, "Science, Technology, and Reform," 41–44.

11. *Affiches du Poitou*, November 30, 1780, 189.

12. *Affiches du Poitou*, April 5, 1781, 53. Jacques Dumoustier de la Fond was mayor of Loudun when he wrote this letter. In 1789 he became a revolutionary and deputy in the Constituent Assembly.

13. *Affiches de Troyes*, May 26, 1784, 82–83.

14. John Shovlin, "Political Economy and the French Nobility," in *The French Nobility in the Eighteenth Century: Reassessments and New Approaches*, ed. Jay Smith (State College: Pennsylvania State University Press, 2006), 124–28; John Shovlin, *The Political Economy of Virtue: Luxury, Patriotism, and the Origins of the French Revolution* (Ithaca: Cornell University Press, 2007), 66–71; Roberts, *Sentimental Savants*, 152–60.

15. *Affiches de l'Orléanois*, November 16, 1787, 187.

16. His own letter was a test of the treatise by Abbé Adam, professor at the Université de Caen. *Affiches de Toulouse*, April 27, 1785, 67–68.

17. *Affiches du Poitou*, October 25, 1787, 169–70.

18. Liana Vardi, "Imagining the Harvest in Early Modern Europe," *American Historical Review* 101, no. 5 (December 1996): 1387–96.

19. *Affiches de Troyes*, June 30, 1784, 103.

20. *Affiches de l'Orléanois*, March 6, 1778, 43–44.

21. *Affiches du Poitou*, June 14, 1787, 93.

22. *Affiches de Troyes*, March 26, 1783, 53.

23. Geoffrey Parker, "Crisis and Catastrophe: The Global Crisis of the Seventeenth Century Reconsidered," *American Historical Review* 113, no. 4 (October 2008): 1053–79.

24. Sherry Johnson, "El Niño, Environmental Crisis, and the Emergence of Alternative Markets in the Hispanic Caribbean, 1760s–70s," *William and Mary Quarterly* 62, no. 3 (July 2005): 365–410; Richard H. Grove, "The Great El Niño of 1789–93 and Its Global Consequences: Reconstructing an Extreme Climate Event in World Environmental History," *Medieval History Journal* 10, nos. 1–2 (2007): 75–98.

25. See, for example, *Journal de Paris*, August 6, 1788, 950, February 2, 1789, 148–49.

26. Kaplan, *Provisioning Paris*, 7; Daniel Roche, *A History of Everyday Things: The Birth of Consumption in France, 1600–1800* (Cambridge: Cambridge University Press, 2000), 221–49.

27. Kaplan, *Provisioning Paris*, 41–79; E. C. Spary, *Feeding France: New Sciences of Food, 1760–1815* (Cambridge: Cambridge University Press, 2014), 55–88.

28. Steven L. Kaplan, *Bread, Politics and Political Economy in the Reign of Louis XV*, 2 vols. (The Hague: Martinus Nijhoff, 1976), 252–488; David Andress, *French Society in Revolution, 1789–1799* (Manchester: Manchester University Press, 1999), 16–18; Bouton, *Flour War*, 79–119.

29. Peter Jones, *Agricultural Enlightenment*, 84.

30. James Livesey, *Provincializing Global History: Money, Ideas and Things in the Languedoc, 1680–1830* (New Haven: Yale University Press, 2020), 124–39; Peter Jones, *Agricultural Enlightenment*, 85–91.

31. Roberts, *Sentimental Savants*, 142.

32. Shovlin, *Political Economy of Virtue*, 87.

33. *Affiches du Poitou*, August 23, 1787, 134.

34. Spary, *Feeding France*, 9–12.

35. Peter Jones, *Agricultural Enlightenment*, 57.

36. James Livesey, "Botany and Provincial Enlightenment in Montpellier: Antoine Banal Père and Fils, 1750–1800," *History of Science* 43 (2005): 60–61.

37. Fredrik Albritton Jonsson, *Enlightenment's Frontier: The Scottish Highlands and the Origins of Environmentalism* (New Haven: Yale University Press, 2013), 123–24.

38. On methods of clearing land, see, for example, *Journal général de France*, August 16, 1785, 395. For a discussion of letting fields lie fallow, see *Affiches du Poitou*, June 7, 1787, 89–90, June 14, 1787, 93–94.

39. *Journal général de France*, May 17, 1785, 234–35.

40. Peter Jones, *Agricultural Enlightenment*, 95–97.

41. *Journal général de France*, January 31, 1786, 54–55.

42. *Journal général de France*, August 9, 1785, 381–82.

43. Jonsson, *Enlightenment's Frontier*, 220.

44. Roche, *History of Everyday Things*, 223–24, 242–49.

45. Spary, *Feeding France*, 79–80.

46. *Journal général de France*, August 2, 1785, 370–71.

47. André Bourde, *The Influence of England on the French Agronomes, 1750–1789* (Cambridge: Cambridge University Press, 2013), 210.

48. *Journal général de France*, January 10, 1786, 15; *Affiches du Poitou*, September 28, 1786, 155.

49. Spary, *Feeding France*, 64.

50. *Affiches d'Aix*, February 24, 1777, 32.

51. Bond, "Science, Technology, and Reform," 8.

52. *Affiches des Trois-Evêchés et Lorraine*, January 18, 1787, 19–20.

53. *Affiches de l'Orléanois*, February 23, 1770, 31–32. François-George Mustel was a Norman nobleman who cultivated potatoes on his estate after the Seven Years' War. He published his experiments with potato flour in bread and presented his findings to the agricultural society in Rouen. André Dubuc, "La culture de la pomme de terre en Normandie avant et depuis Parmentier," *Annales de Normandie* 3 (1953): 50–68.

54. *Affiches des Trois-Évêchés et Lorraine*, January 4, 1781, 5–6.

55. *Affiches de Toulouse*, March 16, 1785, 43–44.

56. Spary, *Feeding France*, 63–72.

57. See, for example, *Journal général de France*, June 16, 1773, 95–96; *Affiches de Dijon*, January 12, 1790, 43.

58. *Affiches du Beauvaisis*, March 26, 1786, 4.

59. *Affiches du Dauphiné*, September 6, 1782, 74–75.

60. Steven Laurence Kaplan, *The Bakers of Paris and the Bread Question, 1700–1775* (Durham: Duke University Press, 1996), 30–32; Bouton, *Flour War*, 38–39, 79–87.

61. *Affiches des Trois-Évêchés et Lorraine*, October 13, 1782, 245.

62. See, for example, *Affiches de l'Orléanois*, January 10, 1783, 10–11. For a further discussion of *maladie rouge*, see "Maladie Rouge," in *Nouveau dictionnaire d'histoire naturelle: Appliquée aux arts, à l'agriculture, à l'économie rurale et domestique, à la médecine, etc.*, vol. 19 (Paris: Deterville, 1818), 608–9.

63. *Affiches de Picardie et Soissonnais*, January 28, 1775, 15–16.

64. *Journal général de France*, August 13, 1785, 389–90.

65. *Affiches de l'Orléanois*, October 12, 1787, 166.

66. *Affiches du Poitou*, October 18, 1787, 165.

67. *Journal général de France*, May 11, 1786, 222.

68. On the practical ethos of the agricultural Enlightenment, see especially André Bourde, *Agronomie et agronomes en France au XVIIIe siècle*, 3 vols. (Paris: S.E.V.P.E.N., 1967), 30.

69. *Affiches des Trois-Évêchés et Lorraine*, October 27, 1782, 282–83. Lottinger's activity in the Royal Society is discussed in Pierre-Théophile Barrois, *Histoire de la Société Royale de Médecine: Avec les mémoires de médecine et de physique* (Paris: Imprimerie de Philippe Denys, 1780), 15. The D. Casbois referenced by the editors is mentioned by Michaud, *Biographie universelle ancienne et moderne: Histoire par ordre alphabétique de la vie publique et privée de tous les hommes*, vol. 7 (Paris: Desplaces, 1843), 107–8.

70. *Affiches de l'Orléanois*, September 2, 1785, 150–51, September 9, 1785, 155–56, September 16, 1785, 159.

71. *Affiches des Trois-Évêchés et Lorraine*, April 5, 1787, 107–8.

72. *Journal général de France*, June 24, 1786, 298.

73. *Journal général de France*, December 6, 1785, 587.

74. *Affiches du Poitou*, October 27, 1785, 169.

75. Two affiches published this particular letter, which is cited at the beginning of the chapter. *Affiches du Poitou*, May 25, 1786, 82; *Affiches de Toulouse*, August 9, 1786,

136–37. Maupin's correspondence also appeared in newspapers in Angers, Marseille, Metz, Orléans, and Paris. Maupin published on agriculture, and especially vineyard cultivation. Michaud, *Biographie universelle ancienne et moderne*, 27:332.

76. *Affiches de l'Orléanois*, August 5, 1785, 135–36.

77. *Journal général de France*, July 30, 1785, 366. The major distinctions between the three fields were the amount of lime used to treat the seeds, and whether he mixed the soil with water or manure.

78. Broussonet is known for his work as a natural philosopher and a revolutionary. Charles Gillispie, *Science and Polity in France* (Princeton: Princeton University Press, 2004), 67–70, 101–11, 168–70.

79. *Journal général de France*, September 10, 1785, 438.

80. Livesey, "Botany and Provincial Enlightenment," 70–71.

81. E. C. Spary, *Utopia's Garden: French Natural History from Old Regime to Revolution* (Chicago: University of Chicago Press, 2000), 132–33.

82. *Affiches du Poitou*, November 4, 1773, 174–75.

83. Popiel, *Rousseau's Daughters*, 18–19; Lesley H. Walker, *A Mother's Love: Crafting Feminine Virtue in Enlightenment France* (Lewisburg: Bucknell University Press, 2008), 37–57.

84. *Affiches de Troyes*, May 5, 1784, 69–70.

85. Roberts, *Sentimental Savants*, 13–40.

86. *Affiches de l'Orléanois*, January 7, 1774, 5.

87. *Affiches d'Angers*, September 15, 1775, 147; *Affiches de l'Orléanois*, September 22, 1775, 155.

88. *Affiches du Poitou*, September 13, 1787, 145.

6. Bienfaisance, Fellow Feeling, and the Public Good

1. *Affiches du Poitou*, March 20, 1777, 45–46.

2. Elizabeth Andrews Bond and Robert M. Bond, "Topic Modelling the French Pre-Revolutionary Press," in *Digitizing Enlightenment*, ed. Simon Burrows and Glenn Roe (Liverpool: Oxford University Studies in the Enlightenment, 2020), 254–60.

3. Théophraste Renaudot founded the *Gazette de France*, the first weekly newspaper in France, and served as France's minister of the poor. When he founded the *Gazette* in 1631, he opened a *bureau d'adresse et de rencontre* to match up those searching for employment with those looking for workers. Renaudot began the bureau to resolve the problem of unemployment, but over time it grew to include low-interest loans, a pawnshop of personal and household goods, and the sale of land and royal offices. Renaudot occasionally published a *Feuille du Bureau d'Adresse* to advertise goods for sale in the shop, effectively making him the inventor of classified papers in France. In addition to its employment functions, Renaudot's bureau also offered medical assistance to the poor of Paris. See Christopher Todd, "French Advertising in the Eighteenth Century," *Studies on Voltaire and the Eighteenth Century* 266 (1989): 523; Howard M. Solomon, *Public Welfare, Science, and Propaganda in Seventeenth-Century France: The Innovations of Théophraste Renaudot* (Princeton: Princeton University Press, 1972), 43–47.

4. Cissie C. Fairchilds, *Poverty and Charity in Aix-en-Provence, 1640–1789* (Baltimore: Johns Hopkins University Press, 1976), 147–58; Jean Pierre Gutton, *La société et les*

pauvres: L'exemple de la généralité de Lyon, 1534–1789 (Lyon: Bibliothèque de la Faculté des lettres et sciences humaines de Lyon, 1971), 326–42; Kathryn Norberg, *Rich and Poor in Grenoble, 1600–1814* (Berkeley: University of California Press, 1985), 159–266.

5. Paul Hazard, *European Thought in the Eighteenth Century: From Montesquieu to Lessing* (New Haven: Yale University Press, 1954), 170–71.

6. *Journal de Provence*, October 19, 1781, 152–54.

7. R. S. Ridgway, *Voltaire and Sensibility* (McGill–Queen's University Press, 1973), 46–52.

8. Julia Douthwaite, "Is Charity for Schmucks? The Legitimacy of Bienfaisance, ca. 1760–82 and ca. 2013–15," *Eighteenth Century: Theory and Interpretation* 57, no. 1 (2016): 12–14; Emma Barker, "From Charity to Bienfaisance: Picturing Good Deeds in Late Eighteenth-Century France," *Journal for Eighteenth-Century Studies* 33, no. 3 (2010): 285–311; Colin Jones, *Charity and Bienfaisance: The Treatment of the Poor in the Montpellier Region, 1740–1815* (Cambridge: Cambridge University Press, 1982), 3.

9. Michel Vovelle, *Piété baroque et déchristianisation en Provence au XVIIIe siècle: Les attitudes devant la mort d'après les clauses des testaments* (Paris: Plon, 1973), 285–300, 610–14.

10. Barbara Diefendorf, *From Penitence to Charity: Pious Women and the Catholic Reformation in Paris* (New York: Oxford University Press, 2004), 203–38; Susan E. Dinan, *Women and Poor Relief in Seventeenth-Century France: The Early History of the Daughters of Charity* (Aldershot, UK: Ashgate, 2006), 62–117; Rachel G. Fuchs, "The Right to Life: Paul Strauss and the Politics of Motherhood," in *Gender and the Politics of Social Reform in France, 1870–1914*, ed. Elinor Ann Accampo, Rachel Ginnis Fuchs, and Mary Lynn Stewart (Baltimore: Johns Hopkins University Press, 1995), 81–105; Adam J. Davis and Bertrand Taithe, "From the Purse and the Heart: Exploring Charity, Humanitarianism, and Human Rights in France," *French Historical Studies* 34, no. 3 (Summer 2011): 413–32.

11. Natalie Zemon Davis, "Poor Relief, Humanism, and Heresy: The Case of Lyon," *Studies in Medieval and Renaissance History* 5 (1968): 217–75.

12. *Journal de Paris*, August 20, 1777, 2.

13. *Journal de Provence*, January 27, 1784, 135.

14. Catherine Duprat, *'Pour l'amour de l'humanité': Le temps des philanthropes, la philanthropie parisienne des lumières à la monarchie de Juillet* (Paris: Editions du C.T.H.S., 1993), 52–57.

15. *Affiches de Dijon*, June 3, 1777, 87–88.

16. See, for example, *Affiches du Dauphiné*, May 25, 1781, 15.

17. *Journal de Paris*, March 13, 1777, 2–3. The doctor's recipe she praises is likely the work of Adrian Helvetius, court doctor to Louis XIV who introduced ipecac; Adrian was the grandfather of the philosophe Claude Adrien Helvétius.

18. Mary Fissel, "Popular Medical Writing," in *Oxford History of Popular Print Culture*, ed. Joan Raymond (Oxford: Oxford University Press, 2011), 418–31; Elaine Leong, *Recipes and Everyday Knowledge: Medicine, Science, and the Household in Early Modern England* (Chicago: University of Chicago Press, 2018), 2–9.

19. See, for example, *Journal de Paris*, October 17, 1779, 1184–85.

20. *Journal de Paris*, November 22, 1781, 1313.

21. *Journal de Paris*, April 5, 1787, 415.

22. E. Claire Cage, *Unnatural Frenchmen: The Politics of Priestly Celibacy and Marriage, 1720–1815* (Charlottesville: University of Virginia Press, 2015), 32–34.

23. Timothy Tackett, *Religion, Revolution, and Regional Culture in Eighteenth-Century France: The Ecclesiastical Oath of 1791* (Princeton: Princeton University Press, 1986), 291–92.

24. *Affiches du Poitou*, March 20, 1777, 45.

25. *Affiches de Troyes*, October 29, 1783, 178.

26. *Journal de Lyon*, October 15, 1788, 339.

27. Roberts, *Sentimental Savants*, 32–35.

28. *Affiches de l'Orléanois*, October 24, 1777, 177.

29. Anne-Marie Mercier-Faivre, "Naissance du genre nécrologique dans la presse française," in *Nouvelles formes du discours journalistique au XVIIIe siècle: Lettres au rédacteur, nécrologies, querelles médiatiques*, ed. Samuel Baudry and Denis Reynaud (Lyon: Presses universitaires de Lyon, 2018), 139–58.

30. Lilti, *Invention of Celebrity*, 71–73.

31. *Journal de Paris*, February 4, 1781, 140.

32. *Journal de Paris*, February 6, 1781, 149.

33. *Journal de Paris*, September 29, 1787, 1176; *Affiches du Dauphiné*, October 5, 1787, 101.

34. *Journal de Paris*, March 15, 1781, 296–97.

35. *Affiches de Troyes*, March 13, 1782, 40; June 9, 1784, 91.

36. *Affiches des Trois-Évêchés et Lorraine*, December 13, 1781, 396–97.

37. *Journal de Provence*, April 2, 1782, 284–85.

38. *Affiches du Dauphiné*, November 1, 1776, 110; *Affiches de Reims*, January 22, 1776, 20.

39. *Journal de Paris*, April 6, 1787, 418, April 15, 1787, 461–62, April 25, 1787, 502.

40. *Journal de Paris*, May 25, 1787, 633–34, December 31, 1787, 1579.

41. *Journal de Paris*, December 31, 1787, 1579.

42. Censer has argued that the desire to preserve the social status quo was a guiding principle for the affiches. Censer, *French Press in the Age of Enlightenment*, 54–63.

43. Adrian O'Connor, *In Pursuit of Politics: Education and Revolution in Eighteenth-Century France* (Manchester: Manchester University Press, 2017), 27–35.

44. See, for example, *Affiches de Bordeaux*, December 26, 1771, 211–12; *Affiches du Dauphiné*, April 19, 1776, 203.

45. *Journal de Paris*, January 5, 1781, 18–19. Claude Antoine de Thélis published a book on the same subject in 1779 titled *Plan d'éducation nationale en faveur des pauvres enfans de la campagne*.

46. See, for example, *Journal de Lyon*, November 26, 1788, 387–89.

47. *Journal de Paris*, January 1, 1787, 3.

48. *Journal de Paris*, January 8, 1787, 31, November 11, 1787, 1354–55. On Haüy's life and work, see especially Pierre Henri, *La vie et l'œuvre de Valentin Haüy* (Paris: Presses universitaires de France, 1984); Zina Weygand, *The Blind in French Society from the Middle Ages to the Century of Louis Braille* (Stanford: Stanford University Press, 2009), 57–172.

49. *Affiches d'Angers*, March 4, 1787, 75–76.

50. Anne T. Quartararo, *Deaf Identity and Social Images in Nineteenth-Century France* (Washington, DC: Gallaudet University Press, 2008), 36–48; Renate Fischer, "Abbé de l'Epée and the Living Dictionary," in *Deaf History Unveiled: Interpretations from the New Scholarship*, ed. John V. Van Cleve (Washington, DC: Gallaudet University Press, 1993), 13–26.

51. Sophia A. Rosenfeld, *A Revolution in Language: The Problem of Signs in Late Eighteenth-Century France* (Stanford: Stanford University Press, 2001), 123–74.

52. *Affiches du Beauvaisis*, February 17, 1788, 25–27; *Affiches de Dijon*, April 26, 1785, 102–3.

53. Ravel, *Contested Parterre*, 203; Lionel Gossman, "Anecdote and History," *History and Theory* 42, no. 2 (May 2003): 143–68.

54. *Affiches des Trois-Évêchés et Lorraine*, March 15, 1781, 84.

55. *Affiches de Dijon*, February 6, 1787, 54–55.

56. William Doyle, "Was There an Aristocratic Reaction in Pre-Revolutionary France?" *Past and Present* 57, no. 1 (November 1972): 97–122. On the potential for conflict between seigneurs and the peasantry, see Peter McPhee, *Revolution and Environment in Southern France: Peasants, Lords, and Murder in the Corbières, 1780–1830* (Oxford: Oxford University Press, 1999), 12–39. By contrast, Hoffman found that peasants remained on the same farms, suggesting cooperation. Philip T. Hoffman, *Growth in a Traditional Society: The French Countryside, 1450–1815* (Princeton: Princeton University Press, 1996), 187–92.

57. *Journal de Paris*, May 13, 1781, 338.

58. Marisa Linton, *The Politics of Virtue in Enlightenment France* (New York: Palgrave Macmillan, 2001), 184–86.

59. *Affiches du Dauphiné*, October 6, 1780, 90. This letter was reprinted from the *Affiches de Picardie et Soissonnais*, September 16, 1780, 151.

60. *Affiches d'Angers*, December 20, 1787, 228.

61. This episode is discussed at greater length in Bond, "Circuits of Practical Knowledge," 549–51.

62. *Affiches du Dauphiné*, May 25, 1787, 14–15.

63. *Journal de Paris*, August 7, 1781, 883.

64. Maza, *Private Lives and Public Affairs*, 68–111.

65. *Affiches du Dauphiné*, November 24, 1780, 117–18.

66. *Journal de Paris*, September 12, 1777, 3.

67. *Journal général de France*, January 19, 1788, 35–36.

68. *Journal de Paris*, June 4, 1787, 681–82; *Affiches du Dauphiné*, June 15, 1787, 28;ʹ *Affiches de Montpellier,* June 30, 30–31.

69. On the *rosières* festivals, stories, and plays as a critique of arbitrary power, see Maza, *Private Lives and Public Affairs*, 71–81.

70. Katherine Ibbett, *Compassion's Edge: Fellow-Feeling and Its Limits in Early Modern France* (Philadelphia: University of Pennsylvania Press, 2018), 156–68.

71. David Denby, *Sentimental Narrative and the Social Order in France, 1760–1820* (Cambridge: Cambridge University Press, 1994), 76–79.

7. Communicating the Revolution

1. *Affiches de Troyes*, December 30, 1789, 221–22.

2. The recent historiography of the nobility, and of the Old Regime society of orders more broadly, underscores the significance of honor in the late eighteenth century. John Shovlin, "Nobility," and Gail Bossenga, "Estates, Orders and Corps," in Doyle, *Oxford Handbook of the Ancien Régime*, 116–20, 145–61.

3. Gough, *Newspaper Press*, 36.

4. On Desmoulins, see Hervé Leuwers, *Camille et Lucile Desmoulins: Un rêve de république* (Paris: Fayard, 2018); Jean-Paul Bertaud, *Camille et Lucile Desmoulins: Un couple dans la tourmente* (Paris: Presses de la Renaissance, 1986); Jacques Janssens, *Camille Desmoulins: Le premier républicain de France* (Paris: Perrin, 1973). On Brissot, see Eloise Ellery, *Brissot de Warville: A Study in the History of the French Revolution* (Boston: Houghton Mifflin, 1915); Suzanne d'Huart, *Brissot: La gironde au pouvoir* (Paris: Robert Laffont, 1986). On Marat, see Jean Massin, *Marat* (Paris: Livre Club Diderot, 1975); Gérard Walter, *Marat* (Paris: A. Michel, 1933); Lise Andriès and Jean-Claude Bonnet, *La Mort de Marat* (Paris: Flammarion, 1986); Charlotte Goëtz, *"Plumes de Marat" et "Plumes sur Marat": Pour une bibliographie générale* (Brussels: Pôle Nord, 2006). On Hébert, see Louis Jacob, *Hébert le Père Duchesne, chef des sans-culottes* (Paris: Gallimard, 1960); Gérard Walter, *Hébert et le 'Père Duchesne'* (Paris: J. B. Janin, 1946).

5. Royalist journalists invited responses from their readers. Coudart studied the 2,838 manuscript letters readers sent to the *Gazette de Paris*. Coudart, *La Gazette de Paris*, 167–74. Other studies of the conservative press show that conservative journalists designed and produced papers that garnered public interest and support. See especially Chisick, *Production, Distribution and Readership*, 158–207; Bertaud, *Les amis du roi*; Murray, *Right-Wing Press*.

6. Gough, *Newspaper Press*, 16, 22.

7. Historians of the revolutionary press have studied the newspapers as a whole, by focusing on the evolution in newspaper production, regulation, distribution, and content over the revolutionary decade. See Gough, *Newspaper Press*; Jeremy Popkin, *Revolutionary News: The Press in France, 1789–1799* (Durham: Duke University Press, 1990); Censer, *Prelude to Power*; Labrosse and Rétat, *Naissance du journal révolutionnaire*.

8. *Journal de Paris*, April 1, 1789, 411.

9. Bond and Bond, "Topic Modelling," 164–79.

10. Labrosse and Rétat, *Naissance du journal révolutionnaire*, 19–25.

11. To measure quantitatively the prevalence in political content over time, I sampled 260 letters published between June and August in 1788–91 in four newspapers: the *Journal de Paris*, *Affiches de Dijon*, *Affiches de Normandie*, and *Journal de Provence*. The rest of the chapter treats all of the affiches that published during 1789–91.

12. *Journal de Provence*, March 3, 1789, 211–15; *Affiches de Dijon*, February 3, 1789, 54–55; *Journal de Paris*, August 1, 1790, 866.

13. *Affiches de Dijon*, March 3, 1789, 71–72; *Journal de Paris*, February 11, 1789, 187–89; *Journal de Provence*, January 3, 1789, 12–13.

14. *Affiches de Picardie et Soissonnais*, January 8, 1791, 6–7.

15. *Affiches de Dijon*, January 5, 1790, 39.

16. *Journal de Paris*, June 1, 1789, 688–89.

17. *Affiches de Dijon*, March 17, 1789, 78–79, April 27, 1790, 103, June 1, 1790, 123, June 8, 1790, 126.

18. *Journal de Provence*, May 28, 1789, 94–95.

19. *Journal de Provence*, January 31, 1789, 111–12; *Journal de Paris*, August 7, 1789, 984–85.

20. *Affiches de Dijon*, December 15, 1789, 26.

21. In one such letter, de Boissy described the queen as "the most august mother, the model of tender mothers." *Journal de Paris*, December 22, 1789, 1671–72.

22. *Journal de Paris*, August 16, 1789, 1032–33.

23. William J. Murray, "Un Philosophe en Révolution: Dominique-Joseph Garat et le *Journal de Paris*," in *La plume et le sabre: Volume d'hommages offerts à Jean-Paul Bertaud*, ed. Michel Biard, Annie Crépin, and Bernard Gainot (Paris: Publications de la Sorbonne, 2002), 89–100.

24. Milcent returned to Paris in 1792, but historians disagree about why he may have done so. Dubuc contends that Milcent was affiliated with the Jacobins, and he moved to the capital to participate in popular politics. Albertan has questioned whether enough evidence exists to make such a claim. In any case, once in Paris, Milcent returned to his involvement with the Opéra. Christian Albertan, "Jean Milcent," in Sgard, *Dictionnaire des journalistes*, http://dictionnaire-journalistes. gazettes18e.fr/journaliste/576-jean-milcent; A. Dubuc, "Le Journal de Normandie avant et durant les Etats généraux," *Actes du congrès des sociétés savantes de lyon* 1, no. 1 (1964): 385–404.

25. Villot's political position changed over time. He declared his support of the Revolution in 1788 and 1789 and became a member of the Jacobin club in 1792; by 1795 his new publication, *L'original*, was Thermidorian in tone. Whether such positions reflected his convictions or were merely an effort to keep up with a changing market remains unknown. Jean Sgard, "André Villot," in Sgard, *Dictionnaire des journalistes*, http://dictionnaire-journalistes.gazettes18e.fr/journaliste/805-andre-villot.

26. Jacques Léon Godechot, *The Taking of the Bastille, July 14th, 1789* (New York: Scribner, 1970), 243–49; *Journal de Paris*, August 5, 1789, 977.

27. Historians of the Revolution have argued that the press, crowd, and orators shaped the meaning of the fall of the Bastille in the days immediately following the event. Jeremy Popkin, *Revolutionary News*, 125–28; Hans-Jürgen Lüsebrink and Rolf Rechardt, *The Bastille: A History of a Symbol of Despotism and Freedom*, trans. Norbert Schürer (Durham: Duke University Press, 1997), 47–85; William Sewell, "Historical Events as Transformations of Structures: Inventing Revolutions at the Bastille," *Theory and Society* 25 (1996): 841–81.

28. *Journal de Paris*, July 25, 1789, 923–25.

29. *Journal de Paris*, July 17, 1789, 892–93.

30. *Journal de Paris*, July 19, 1789, 901.

31. Katie Jarvis, *Politics in the Marketplace: Work, Gender, and Citizenship in Revolutionary France* (Oxford: Oxford University Press, 2018), 77–80, 81–103.

32. David Garrioch, "Parisian Women and the October Days," *Social History* 24, no. 3 (October 1999): 231–49.

33. *Journal de Paris*, August 30, 1789, 1088–89.

34. Maurice Agulhon, *Les mots de la république* (Toulouse: Presses universitaires du Mirail-Toulouse, 2007), 19; Laura Mason, *Singing the French Revolution: Popular Culture and Politics, 1787–1799* (Ithaca: Cornell University Press, 1996), 98–103; Frédéric Derne, "La chanson, 'arme' révolutionnaire et chambre d'écho de la société en Auvergne," *Annales historiques de la Révolution française* 341 (July–September 2005): 4–5.

35. On rumors of brigandage, see, for example, *Journal de Paris*, July 30, 1789, 949, August 28, 1789, 1081.

36. Georges Lefebvre's analysis of the spread of rumors is the foundational treatment of the events of the Great Fear. Lefebvre, *The Great Fear of 1789: Rural Panic in Revolutionary France* (New York: Schocken Books, 1989), 59–122. Historians question

the extent to which people in the countryside actually feared what Lefebvre described as an "aristocratic plot," a belief that aristocrats acted together to hoard grain and starve the peasantry. But Lefebvre's study of the communication of rumors in general remains sound. On the lack of evidence for widespread belief in an aristocratic plot to stockpile grain, see, for example, Clay Ramsay, *The Ideology of the Great Fear: The Soissonnais in 1789* (Baltimore: Johns Hopkins University Press, 1992). Timothy Tackett also gives little credence to a widespread belief in an aristocratic plot. Vertical social ties were much stronger in 1789 than they were by the subsequent panics of 1791 in the wake of the king's flight to Varennes. Timothy Tackett, "Collective Panics in the Early French Revolution, 1789–1791: A Comparative Perspective," *French History* 17, no. 2 (2003): 149–71. John Markoff, however, has found an increase in antiseigneurial riots in the months of 1789 predating the Great Fear. Markoff, *The Abolition of Feudalism: Peasants, Lords, and Legislators in the French Revolution* (University Park: Pennsylvania State University Press, 1996), 240–56.

37. Ramsay, *Ideology of the Great Fear*, 138–48.

38. Henri Dinet, "Les peurs du Beauvaisis et du Valois," *Mémoires de la Fédération des Sociétés Historiques et Archéologiques de Paris* 23–24 (1975): 385.

39. *Journal de Paris*, July 9, 1789, 856–57.

40. *Journal de Paris*, August 14, 1789, 1020–21.

41. *Affiches de Rouen*, July 26, 1789, 303–4, September 2, 1789, 315–16.

42. *Affiches de Dijon*, October 13, 1789, 201; *Affiches de Normandie*, October 21, 1789, 382–83, November 7, 1789, 409–10, November 18, 1789, 423–24; *Journal de Provence*, November 10, 1789, 246–47; *Affiches de Picardie et Soissonnais*, September 11, 1790, 266. On the history of patriotic gift giving, see Charles Walton, "Between Trust and Terror: Patriotic Giving in Revolutionary France," in *Experiencing the French Revolution*, ed. David Andress (Oxford: Voltaire Foundation, 2013), 47–67.

43. *Journal de Paris*, September 11, 1789, 1153.

44. *Journal de Provence*, November 3, 1789, 221–22.

45. *Supplément du Journal de Paris*, February 11, 1790, i.

46. *Journal de Paris*, February 22, 1790, 212.

47. Jan Goldstein, *Console and Classify: The French Psychiatric Profession in the Nineteenth Century* (Cambridge: Cambridge University Press, 1987), 64–119; Dora B. Weiner, "A Provincial Doctor Faces the Paris Establishment: Philippe Pinel, 1778–1793," in *Enlightenment, Passion, Modernity: Historical Essays in European Thought and Culture*, eds. Mark Micale and Robert L. Dietle (Palo Alto: Stanford University Press, 2000): 66–87.

48. *Journal de Paris*, January 18, 1790, 71.

49. *Journal de Paris*, January 18, 1790, 72.

50. McPhee, *Robespierre*, 206–12.

51. In her study of Pinel, Nina Gelbart argued that he and other doctors understood the Revolution as the outcome, or *événement*, of the malady of the Old Regime. They sought to restore the social body to health. Nina Rattner Gelbart, "The French Revolution as Medical Event: The Journalistic Gaze," *History of European Ideas* 10, no. 4 (1989): 417–21.

52. Tackett, *Becoming a Revolutionary*, 77–116, 149–75; Gruder, *The Notables and the Nation*, 11–33; Robert H. Blackman, *1789: The French Revolution Begins* (Cambridge: Cambridge University Press, 2019), 180–217.

53. *Journal de Paris*, December 17, 1789, 1647, January 30, 1790, 119-20.

54. *Affiches de Dijon*, June 30, 1789, 140-41. Grégoire also authored letters to the editor in 1793 on the question of the king's trial and death sentence. Alyssa Goldstein Sepinwall, *The Abbé Grégoire and the French Revolution: The Making of Modern Universalism* (Berkeley: University of California Press, 2005), 125-28.

55. *Affiches du Dauphiné*, October 14, 1790, 550. Duval d'Eprémesnil was a staunchly conservative deputy elected by the nobility.

56. *Affiches d'Artois*, September 16, 1791, 236, September 26, 1791, 264.

57. *Journal de Paris*, July 27, 1791, 839.

58. *Affiches de Picardie et Soissonnais*, July 2, 1791, 117. See also *Affiches de Picardie et Soissonnais*, May 29, 1790, 202, February 12, 1791, 30-31.

59. The deputies' use of the press to shore up political capital with their constituents merits further scholarly attention. Gough cites local studies of the press over the *longue durée* that mention the newspapers founded to circulate the deputies' correspondence in the region. Gough, *Newspaper Press*, 31-32; G. Rouanet, "La Correspondance de Bretagne," *Annales révolutionnaires* 10 (1918): 542-49; Nicole Coisel, Marie-Pierre Omnès, Alexis Le Bihan, and Yves Le Gallo, *Bibliographie de la presse française politique et d'information générale* (Paris: Bibliothèque nationale, 1973), 10; Jean-Joseph Lebon, *La presse montalbanaise des origines au début du dix-neuvième siècle* (Toulouse: Mémoire de maitrise, 1972), 91-92, 108-9.

60. *Affiches de Dijon*, January 19, 1790, 46-47.

61. *Affiches de Picardie et Soissonnais*, September 24, 1791, 165. Leroux's letter claiming rights to his post based on his status as the *arpenteur royal* was published two weeks prior. *Affiches de Picardie et Soissonnais*, September 10, 1791, 157-58. Breton responded to the Constituent Assembly's decree of March 17, 1791, and its effect on land surveying in the department. As the decree did not indicate a reimbursement price for the prerevolutionary office of land surveyor, he explained that some officials tried to hold their posts based on the previous legal precedents (set in 1690 and 1702).

62. *Affiches de Normandie*, January 5, 1790, 11-12.

63. *Affiches de Normandie*, May 11, 1790, 247-48.

64. *Affiches d'Artois*, February 1, 1791, 76, February 22, 1791, 127-28, March 11, 1791, 166-67, March 15, 1791, 195-96, June 17, 1791, 418-19.

65. *Affiches de Dijon*, January 19, 1790, 47. Rebecca Spang has argued that protests arguing for a single price for goods reflected the popular desire that as one nation, the money of all citizens should be treated equally. Rebecca Spang, *Stuff and Money in the French Revolution* (Cambridge, MA: Harvard University Press, 2015), 158.

66. *Journal de Paris*, September 5, 1791, 1013-14.

67. *Affiches de Montpellier*, January 13, 1790, 147. Deputies confirmed the right to vote and hold public office to "Portuguese, Spanish, and Avignonese Jews" on January 28, 1790.

68. *Supplément au Journal de Paris*, September 15, 1791, i. The Constituent Assembly voted on September 27, 1791, to grant civil rights to all Jews in France. This decree expanded active citizenship to those within the Ashkenazi majority who met the monetary eligibility requirements and took a civic oath to the Constitution. On the struggle for Jewish rights and equality during the Revolution, and the limits of the deputies'

universalism, see especially Ronald Schechter, *Obstinate Hebrews: Representations of Jews in France, 1715–1815* (Berkeley: University of California Press, 2003), 150–93.

69. On the growth of pamphlet literature, see especially Kenneth Margerison, *Pamphlets and Public Opinion: The Campaign for a Union of Orders in the Early French Revolution* (West Lafayette: Purdue University Press, 1998), 51–80, 90–124; Paul R. Hanson, "Monarchist Clubs and the Pamphlet Debate over Political Legitimacy in the Early Years of the French Revolution," *French Historical Studies* 21, no. 2 (1998): 299–324.

70. Jeremy Popkin, *Revolutionary News*, 152–54.

71. *Affiches du Dauphiné*, May 20, 1790, 255–56.

72. *Journal de Paris*, January 13, 1790, i–ii, May 19, 1790, 560.

73. *Affiches de Dijon*, January 4, 1791, 4, April 13, 1790, 95, April 20, 1790, 99, May 25, 1790, 119.

74. Lüsebrink and Rechardt, *Bastille*, 140–43.

75. See, for example, *Affiches de l'Orléanois*, November 18, 1791, 1060; *Journal de Paris*, April 21, 1790, 448, July 5, 1790, 754.

76. *Affiches de Normandie*, July 9, 1791, 925–26.

77. *Journal de Paris*, April 23, 1790, 455.

78. *Journal de Paris*, February 4, 1789, 156.

79. *Journal de Paris*, May 6, 1789, 572. Cerutti would become a deputy in the Legislative Assembly in 1791.

80. Charles Walton has shown that such a preoccupation with personal honor was prevalent among social elites even before the Revolution, and the concerns with one's reputation reconfigured in violent forms during the Revolution. Walton, *Policing Public Opinion*, 147–58.

81. *Affiches du Dauphiné*, April 10, 1790, 181.

82. *Supplément du Journal de Paris*, May 27, 1790, i–iii.

83. *Journal de Paris*, February 24, 1791, i.

84. *Supplément du Journal de Paris*, December 18, 1790, i.

85. *Affiches de Picardie et Soissonnais*, July 2, 1791, 116.

86. *Affiches de l'Orléanois*, November 29, 1791, 1096.

87. *Affiches de Dijon*, July 12, 1791, 146.

88. *Affiches de Dijon*, July 26, 1791, 154–55.

89. Of the letters in the sample published in 1789, 4 of the 280 concerned calumny. In 1790 that proportion increased to 26 of the 179 letters published. Between January and September 1791, 22 of the 83 letters to the editor covered calumny.

90. *Affiches du Dauphiné*, February 16, 1790, 80.

91. Walton, *Policing Public Opinion*, 3–13, 97–136.

92. See, for example, *Affiches du Dauphiné*, May 6, 1790, 231.

93. Gough, *Newspaper Press*, 48–50.

94. Alma Söderhjelm, *Le Régime de la presse pendant la Révolution française*, vol. 1 (Helsingfors: Imprimerie Hufvudstadsbladet, 1900), 145–48. Popkin suggests that the politics of the Revolution in the following months prevented the new regulations from taking full effect. Jeremy Popkin, *Revolutionary News*, 170. For Walton, such provisions were significant precedent, even though they were not immediately enforced. Factionalism, the challenges of establishing new courts, the absence of provisions for how to enforce such limits on the press, and the lack of clarity in the penal code

about how to categorize such crimes all delayed the enforcement of the constitutional provisions. Walton, *Policing Public Opinion*, 123–28.

95. Beaugeard supported the federalist movement in Marseille and was later arrested in 1798; he survived the Revolution but relocated to Lyon in 1800, where he worked as a lawyer and abandoned his career in journalism entirely. Guy Martinet, "La vie politique à Marseille en 1795 et en 1796: Lettres inédites du journaliste Ferréol Beaugeard à Paul Cadroy, membre du Conseil des Cinq-Cents," *Provence Historique* 64 (1966), 126–27; René Gérard, *Un journal de province sous la Révolution: Le "Journal de Marseille" de Ferréol Beaugeard (1781–1797)* (Paris: Société des Etudes Robespierristes, 1964).

96. The revolutionary sections, which first organized to vote deputies into the Estates General, continued to meet to resolve local administrative issues. David Garrioch, "The Local Experience of Revolution: The Gobelins/Finistère Section in Paris," *French History and Civilization* 1 (2005), 20–29, https://h-france.net/rude/wp-content/uploads/2017/08/Vol1_Garrioch2.pdf.

97. On the formation of political clubs among deputies, see Jean Boutier, Philippe Boutry, and Serge Bonin, *Les sociétés politiques*, vol. 6 of *Atlas de la Révolution française*, ed. Claude Langlois and Serge Bonin (Paris: L'École des Hautes Études en Sciences Sociales, 1992). On the formation of political clubs in the provinces, see Michael L. Kennedy, *The Jacobin Clubs in the French Revolution: The First Years* (Princeton: Princeton University Press, 1982). On the network formation among political clubs, see Micah Alpaugh, "The British Origins of the French Jacobins: Radical Sociability and the Development of Political Club Networks, 1787–1793," *European History Quarterly* 44 (2014): 593–619.

98. The clubs were largely urban organizations. All towns with more than 4,000 residents, 97 percent of those with 3,000 to 4,000 residents, and 87 percent of those with 2,000 to 3,000 residents had at least one club in town between 1789 and 1794. The larger the town, the greater role the clubs took in the administrative hierarchy. Boutier et al., *Les sociétés politiques*, 16, 38.

Conclusion

1. *Journal de Paris*, December 6, 1777, 3. Louis-Sébastien Mercier commented on Catalan's establishment on the rue Dauphine and his skill as a *chirurgien-dentiste*. Louis-Sébastien Mercier, *Le Tableau de Paris, Nouvelle Edition, corrigée & augmentée*, vol. 5 (Amsterdam, 1783), 75.

BIBLIOGRAPHY

Author's Note

In researching this book I visited repositories throughout France. In Paris I worked with the collections of the Bibliothèque nationale de France-Mitterrand, the Bibliothèque nationale de France-Arsenal, and the Bibliothèque de l'Institut d'histoire de la Révolution française. I also studied the newspapers and related print and manuscript sources in the municipal libraries in Aix-en-Provence, Amiens, Caen, Dijon, Lyon, Marseille, Poitiers, Toulouse, and Troyes, and in the Archives départementales du Calvados, the Archives départementales de l'Aube, and the Archives départementales de la Haute-Garonne. The special collections in the university libraries of the Université Toulouse 1 Capitole, the Université d'Aix, and Princeton University enabled me to analyze longer print runs of rare newspapers. I also consulted the digital collections of the Bibliothèque municipale de Reims, the Bibliothèque municipale de Rennes, and the Archives départementales de l'Hérault.

The primary focus of this book was the study of the newspaper collections, and whenever possible I examined paper copies of the full run of the paper. In each library and archive I also searched for print and manuscript sources that spoke to the editors' decision-making, especially as it concerned the publication of letters from their readers. Few such sources remain, but the extant records cited in this book are listed in the bibliography.

The newspapers that constitute the major sources of this book are listed in the bibliography first by shortened title, as they are referenced in the notes. The full title with the corresponding dates when that particular title was used are listed below. Some of the newspapers continued to publish after 1791 under new titles, which are not considered part of this study and are not given here.

I. Primary Newspaper Sources

Affiches d'Aix

    Annonces, affiches, avis divers d'Aix (1769–73)
    Affiches de Provence, feuille hebdomadaire d'Aix (1778–88)

Affiches d'Angers

Affiches d'Angers, capitale de l'apanage de Monseigneur le Comte de Provence, et de la province d'Anjou (1773–74)
Affiches, annonces et avis divers d'Angers, capitale de l'apanage de Monsieur, fils de France, frère du Roi (1774–89)
Affiches d'Angers ou Journal national de la province d'Anjou (1789–91)

Affiches d'Artois (Arras)

Annonces, affiches, nouvelles et avis divers, pour la province d'Artois, le Boulonnois et le Calaisis (1788–89)
Affiches d'Artois, du Boulonnois et Calaisis (1789–90)
Journal général du département du Pas-de-Calais (1790–91)

Affiches de Bordeaux

Annonces, affiches, et avis divers (1758–59)
Annonces, affiches, nouvelles et avis divers de/pour la ville de Bordeaux (1759–64)
Annonces, affiches, et avis divers pour la ville de Bordeaux (1764–74)
Affiches de Bordeaux, annonces, etc. (1774–84)

Affiches de Dijon

Annonces et affiches. Dijon (1770–71)
Affiches de Bourgogne (1776–83)
Affiches, annonces et avis divers de Dijon, ou Journal de la Bourgogne (1783–85)
Affiches de Dijon, ou Journal de Bourgogne (1785–90)
Affiches de Dijon, ou Journal du département de la Côte d'Or (1790–91)

Affiches de la Basse-Normandie (Caen)

Affiches, annonces et avis divers de la Basse-Normandie (1786–87)
Affiches de la Basse-Normandie (1787–88)
Affiches ou Journal et avis divers de la Basse-Normandie (1788–91)

Affiches de l'Orléanois

Annonces, affiches, nouvelles et avis divers de l'Orléanois, contenant généralement tout ce qui peut intéresser cette province (1764–73)
Annonces, affiches et avis divers, etc. (1773–82)
Affiches de l'Orléanois, annonces (1782–83)

Journal de l'Orléanois ou Annonces, affiches et avis divers (1783–88)
Journal général de l'Orléanois (1788–90)
Journal général du département du Loiret (1790–91)

Affiches de Montpellier

Annonces, affiches et avis divers. Feuille hebdomadaire de Montpellier (1770–76)

Affiches de Normandie (Rouen)

Annonces, affiches, et avis divers de la Haute et Basse Normandie (1762–84)
Journal de Normandie (1785–91)

Affiches de Picardie et Soissonnais (Amiens)

Affiches de Picardie et Soissonnois (1770–74)
Affiches, annonces et avis de Picardie, Artois, Soissonnais (1774–90)
Affiches du département de la Somme (1790–91)

Affiches de Reims

Affiches, annonces et avis divers de Reims et Généralités de Champagne (1772–78)
Affiches de Reims et Généralité de Champagne (1778–81)
Journal de Champagne (1781–91)

Affiches de Rennes

Affiches de Rennes, feuille hebdomadaire pour la Bretagne (1784–91)

Affiches de Toulouse

Affiches et annonces de Toulouse (1775–77)
Affiches ou Journal local de Toulouse et Haut-Languedoc (1777–78)
Affiches, annonces, avis divers, etc. de Toulouse et du Haut-Languedoc (1781–85)
Affiches et annonces, de Toulouse, etc. (1785–86)
Affiches de Toulouse et du Haut-Languedoc (1787–89)
Journal universel, et affiches de Toulouse et du Languedoc (1789–90)

Affiches de Troyes

Annonces, affiches et avis divers de Troyes, capitale de la Champagne (1782–83)

Journal de Troyes et Champagne Méridionale (1783–90)
Journal du département de l'Aube, et districts voisins (1790–91)

Affiches des Trois-Évêchés et Lorraine (Metz)

Affiches de Lorraine et des Affiches des Trois-Évêchés (1769–73)
Affiches, annonces et avis divers pour les Trois-Évêchés et la Lorraine (1773–78)
Affiches des Évêchés et Lorraine (1778–90)
Journal des départements de la Moselle, de la Meurthe, de la Meuse, des Ardennes et des Vosges (1790–91)

Affiches du Beauvaisis (Compiègne)

Affiches du Beauvaisis, du Soissonais etc. (1786–88)
Affiches de Compiègne et du Beauvaisis (1788)

Affiches du Dauphiné (Grenoble)

Affiches, annonces et avis divers du Dauphiné (1774–77)
Affiches du Dauphiné, annonces, etc. (1777–90)
Affiches de la ci-devant province de Dauphiné, annonces, etc. (1790–91)

Affiches du Poitou (Poitiers)

Annonces, affiches, nouvelles et avis divers de la province du Poitou (1773–77)
Affiches de Poitou (1777–81)
Affiches de Poitou, Province de l'Apanage de Monseigneur le Comte d'Artois (1781–82)
Annonces, affiches, nouvelles et avis divers, de la Province du Poitou, Apanage de Monseigneur, Comte d'Artois (1782)
Annonces et affiches de la Province du Poitou, Apanage de Monseigneur, Comte d'Artois (1782–87)
Affiches du Poitou, Apanage de Monseigneur, Comte d'Artois (1787–90)
Journal du Poitou (1790–91)

La Feuille Villageoise (1790–95)

Journal de Lyon

Journal de Lyon, ou annonces et variétés littéraires, pour servir de suite aux petites affiches de Lyon (1784–87)
Journal de Lyon et des provinces de la Généralité (1787–90)
Journal de Lyon et des provinces voisines (1790)

Journal de Lyon et du Département du Rhône et Loire. (1790–91)

Journal de Paris (1777–91)

Journal de Provence (Marseille)

> *Journal de Provence. Dédié à Monseigneur le Prince de Beauvau par M. Beaugeard* (1781–83)
> *Journal de Provence dédié à Monseigneur le Prince de Beauvau. Affiches, annonces et avis* (1783–91)

Journal général de France (Paris)

> *Annonces, affiches, et avis divers* (1751–77)
> *Annonces, affiches et avis divers, ou Journal général de France* (1777–83)
> *Journal général de France* (1783–90)

II. Manuscript Sources

Archives départementales de l'Aube, 48 H 465
Bibliothèque municipale de Caen, 214 In-folio 122
Bibliothèque municipale de Toulouse, MS 1873
Bibliothèque municipale de Troyes, MS 4°2795
Bibliothèque nationale de France, Mitterrand, MS fr. 6683

III. Other Print Sources

Arnault, A. V., et al. *Biographie nouvelle des contemporains,* vol. 8. Paris: Librairie historique et des arts et métiers d'Emile Babeuf, 1822.

Barrois, Pierre-Théophile. *Histoire de la Société Royale de Médecine: Avec les mémoires de médecine et de physique.* Paris: Imprimerie de Philippe Denys, 1780.

Diderot, Denis, and Jean le Rond d'Alembert, eds. *Encyclopédie, ou dictionnaire raisonné des sciences, des arts et des métiers, etc.* University of Chicago: ARTFL Encyclopédie Project (Autumn 2017 Edition), edited by Robert Morrissey and Glenn Roe, http://encyclopedie.uchicago.edu/.

Edwards, Edward. *Memoirs of Libraries: Including a Handbook of Library Economy.* 2 vols. London: Trübner, 1859.

Jefferson, Thomas. *The Papers of Thomas Jefferson,* vol. 8: *February 1785 to October 1785,* edited by Julian P. Boyd. Princeton: Princeton University Press, 2018.

Kant, Immanuel. "An Answer to the Question: What Is Enlightenment? (1784)." In *Practical Philosophy,* 11–22. Edited by Mary J. Gregor, with an introduction by Allen W. Wood. Cambridge: Cambridge University Press, 1996.

Mercier, Louis-Sébastien. *Le Tableau de Paris, nouvelle édition, corrigée & augmentée,* vol. 5. Amsterdam, 1783.

Musset-Pathay, V. D. *Bibliographie agronomique.* Paris, 1810.

Mustel, Nicolas-Alexandre. *Traité théorique et pratique de la végétation, contenant plus-ieurs expériences nouvelles et démonstratives sur l'économie végétale et sur la culture des arbres.* Paris, 1781.

Steinheil, G., ed. *Commentaires de la Faculté de Medecine de Paris, 1777 à 1786,* vol. 1. Paris: Faculté de Médecine de Paris, 1903.

IV. Secondary Sources

Accampo, Elinor Ann, Rachel Ginnis Fuchs, and Mary Lynn Stewart, eds. *Gender and the Politics of Social Reform in France, 1870–1914.* Baltimore: Johns Hopkins University Press, 1995.

Adams, David, and Adrian Armstrong, eds. *Print and Power in France and England, 1500–1800.* Aldershot, UK: Ashgate, 2006.

Agulhon, Maurice. *Les mots de la république.* Toulouse: Presses universitaires du Mirail-Toulouse, 2007.

———. *La sociabilité méridionale. Confréries et associations en Provence orientale à la fin du XVIIIe siècle.* 2 vols. Aix-en-Provence: La Pensée universitaire, 1966.

Albert, Pierre, and Christine Leteinturier. *La presse française.* Paris: Secrétariat général du gouvernement, La Documentation française, 1983.

Alpaugh, Micah. "The British Origins of the French Jacobins: Radical Sociability and the Development of Political Club Networks, 1787–1793." *European History Quarterly* 44 (2014): 593–619.

Altman, Janet Gurkin. *Epistolarity: Approaches to a Form.* Columbus: Ohio State University Press, 1982.

Anderson, Benedict R. *Imagined Communities: Reflections on the Origin and Spread of Nationalism.* London: Verso, 2006.

Andreani, Roland. *La presse départementale en révolution: 1789–1799.* La Garenne-Colombes: Editions de l'Espace européen, 1992.

Andress, David. *French Society in Revolution, 1789–1799.* Manchester: Manchester University Press, 1999.

———, ed. *The Oxford Handbook of the French Revolution.* Oxford: Oxford University Press, 2015.

Andrews, Elizabeth. "Between Auteurs and Abonnés: Reading the *Journal de Paris,* 1787–1789." *Proceedings of the Western Society for French History* 37 (2009): 135–47. http://hdl.handle.net/2027/spo.0642292.0037.009.

Andriès, Lise, and Jean-Claude Bonnet. *La Mort de Marat.* Paris: Flammarion, 1986.

Arbellot, Guy, Bernard Lepetit, and Jacques Bertrand. *Routes et Communications. Atlas de la Révolution française,* vol. 1, edited by Serge Bonin and Claude Langlois. Paris: Editions de l'Ecole des hautes études en sciences sociales, 1987.

Auerbach, Stephen. "'Encourager le commerce et répandre les lumières': The Press, the Provinces and the Origins of the Revolution in France: 1750–1789." PhD diss., Louisiana State University and Agricultural and Mechanical College, 2004.

Bachrach, Susan. *Dames Employées: The Feminization of Postal Work in Nineteenth-Century France.* Philadelphia: Haworth Press, 1984.

Baker, Keith Michael. "Defining the Public Sphere in Eighteenth-Century France: Variations on a Theme by Habermas." In *Habermas and the Public Sphere*, edited by Craig Calhoun, 181–211. Cambridge, MA: MIT Press, 1992.

———. "Public Opinion as Political Invention." In *Inventing the French Revolution*, edited by Keith Michael Baker, 167–200. Cambridge: Cambridge University Press, 1990.

Baker, Keith Michael, Colin Lucas, François Furet, and Mona Ozouf, eds. *The French Revolution and the Creation of Modern Political Culture*. Oxford: Pergamon Press, 1987.

Bannet, Eve Tavor. *Empire of Letters: Letter Manuals and Transatlantic Correspondence, 1680–1820*. Cambridge: Cambridge University Press, 2005.

Barker, Emma. "From Charity to Bienfaisance: Picturing Good Deeds in Late Eighteenth-Century France." *Journal for Eighteenth Century Studies* 33, no. 3 (2010): 285–311.

Barker, Hannah, and Simon Burrows. *Press, Politics and the Public Sphere in Europe and North America, 1760–1820*. Cambridge: Cambridge University Press, 2002.

Basu, Anupam, Jonathan Hope, and Michael Witmore. "The Professional and Linguistic Communities of Early Modern Dramatists." In *Community-Making in Early Stuart Theatres: Stage and Audience*, edited by Anthony W. Johnson, Roger D. Sell, and Helen Wilcox, 63–94. London: Routledge, 2019.

Baudry, Samuel, and Denis Renaud, eds. *Nouvelles formes du discours journalistique au XVIIIe siècle: Lettres au rédacteur, nécrologies, querelles médiatiques*. Lyon: Presses universitaires de Lyon, 2018.

Beaurepaire, Pierre-Yves, Silvia Marzagalli, and Guillaume Balavoine. *Atlas de la Révolution française: Circulation des hommes et des idées, 1770–1804*. Paris: Autrement, 2010.

Beebee, Thomas O. *Epistolary Fiction in Europe, 1500–1850*. Cambridge: Cambridge University Press, 1999.

Bellanger, Claude. *Histoire générale de la presse Française*, vol. 1. Paris: Presses universitaires de France, 1969.

Benhamou, Paul. "Essai d'inventaire des instruments de lecture publique des gazettes." In *Les Gazettes européennes de langue française (XVIIe–XVIIIe siècles)*, edited by Henri Duranton, Claude Labrosse, and Pierre Rétat, 121–29. Saint-Etienne: Publications de l'Université de Saint-Etienne, 1992.

———. "La lecture publique des journaux." *Dix-Huitième Siècle* 24 (1992): 283–95.

Bensaude-Vincent, Bernadette. "A Public for Science: The Rapid Growth of Popularization in Nineteenth-Century France." Translated by Liz Libbrecht. *Réseaux: The French Journal of Communication* 3, no. 11 (1995): 75–92.

Bertaud, Jean Paul. *Les amis du Roi: Journaux et journalistes royalistes en France de 1789 à 1792*. Paris: Perrin, 1984.

———. *Camille et Lucile Desmoulins: Un couple dans la tourmente*. Paris: Presses de la Renaissance, 1986.

———. *La presse et le pouvoir de Louis XIII à Napoléon Ier*. Paris: Perrin, 2000.

Bertucci, Paola. *Artisanal Enlightenment: Science and the Mechanical Arts in Old Regime France*. New Haven: Yale University Press, 2017.

——. "Enlightening Towers: Public Opinion, Local Authorities, and the Reformation of Meteorology in Eighteenth Century Italy." In *Playing with Fire: Histories of the Lightning Rod*, edited by Peter Heering, Oliver Hochadel, and David J. Rhees, 25–44. Philadelphia: American Philosophical Society, 2009.

——. "Revealing Sparks: John Wesley and the Religious Utility of Electrical Healing." *British Journal for the History of Science* 39, no. 3 (2006): 341–62.

——. "Therapeutic Attractions: Early Applications of Electricity to the Art of Healing." In *Brain, Mind and Medicine: Essays in Eighteenth-Century Neuroscience*, edited by Harry Whitaker, C. U. M. Smith, and Stanley Finger, 271–83. Boston: Springer, 2007.

Birn, Raymond. *Royal Censorship of Books in Eighteenth-Century France*. Stanford: Stanford University Press, 2012.

Blackman, Robert H. *1789: The French Revolution Begins*. Cambridge: Cambridge University Press, 2019.

Blair, Ann. "Reading Strategies for Coping with Information Overload, ca. 1550–1700." *Journal of the History of Ideas* 64, no. 1 (January 2003): 11–28.

——. *Too Much to Know: Managing Scholarly Information before the Modern Age*. New Haven: Yale University Press, 2010.

Blanc-Rouquette, Marie-Thérèse. *La presse et l'information à Toulouse*. Toulouse: Faculté des Lettres de Toulouse, 1967.

Bollème, G., J. Ehrard, F. Furet, D. Roche, and J. Roger, eds. *Livre et société dans la France du XVIIIe siècle*, vol. 1. Paris: Mouton, 1965.

Bond, Elizabeth Andrews. "Circuits of Practical Knowledge: The Network of Letters to the Editor in the French Provincial Press, 1770–1788." *French Historical Studies* 39, no. 3 (2016): 535–65.

——. "Diffusion du genre dans la presse régionale Française: L'exemple des 'affiches.'" Translated by Samuel Baudry. In *Nouvelles formes du discours journalistique au dix-huitième siècle*, edited by Denis Reynaud and Samuel Baudry, 77–96. Lyon: Presses universitaires de Lyon, 2018.

——. "Mapping the Media Landscape in Old Regime France." *Current Research in Digital History* 1 (2018), https://doi.org/10.31835/crdh.2018.11.

——. "Reading the Transnational in the Provincial Press: Letters to the Editor in French Journaux and Affiches, 1770–1791." *Perspectives on Europe* 44, no. 2 (2014): 88–93.

——. "Science, Technology, and Reform in the French Countryside: The Role of Provincial Officials in the Eighteenth-Century Press." *French History and Civilization* 7 (2017): 39–50.

Bond, Elizabeth Andrews, and Robert M. Bond. "Topic Modelling the French Pre-Revolutionary Press." In *Digitizing Enlightenment*, edited by Simon Burrows and Glenn Roe, 247–76. Liverpool: Oxford University Studies in the Enlightenment, 2020.

Bond, Richmond Pugh. *New Letters to the Tatler and Spectator*. Austin: University of Texas Press, 1959.

Bots, Hans, Jean Sgard, and Katholieke Universiteit Nijmegen. *La diffusion et la lecture des journaux de langue française sous l'ancien régime*. Amsterdam: APA-Holland University Press, 1988.

Bougeâtre, Eugène. *La vie Rurales dans le Mantois et le Vexin au XIX siècle*. Cergy-Pontoise: Editions du Valhermeil, 1996.

Bourde, André. *Agronomie et agronomes en France au XVIIIe siècle*. 3 vols. Paris: S.E.V.P.E.N., 1967.

———. *The Influence of England on the French Agronomes, 1750–1789*. Cambridge: Cambridge University Press, 2013.

Boutier, Jean, Philippe Boutry, and Serge Bonin. *Les sociétés politiques. Atlas de la Révolution française*, vol. 6, edited by Claude Langlois and Serge Bonin. Paris: L'École des Hautes Études en Sciences Sociales, 1992.

Bouton, Cynthia A. *The Flour War: Gender, Class, and Community in late Ancien Régime French Society*. State College: Pennsylvania State University Press, 1993.

Bouyssy, M. T., J. Brancolini, J.-L. Flandrin, M. Flandrin, A. Fontana, F. Furet, and D. Roche. *Livre et société dans la France du XVIIIe siècle*, vol. 2. Paris: Mouton, 1970.

Brake, Laurel, Bill Bell, and David Finkelstein, eds. *Nineteenth-Century Media and the Construction of Identities*. Houndsmills, UK: Palgrave, 2000.

Brant, Clare. *Eighteenth-Century Letters and British Culture*. Basingstoke, UK: Palgrave Macmillan, 2006.

———. "'I Will Carry You with Me on the Wings of Immagination': Aerial Letters and Eighteenth-Century Balloning." *Eighteenth-Century Life* 35, no. 1 (2011): 168–87.

———. "The Progress of Knowledge in the Regions of Air? Divisions and Disciplines in Early Ballooning." *Eighteenth-Century Studies* 45, no. 1 (2011): 71–86.

———. "The Tribunal of the Public: Eighteenth-Century Letters and the Politics of Vindication." In *Gender and Politics in the Age of Letter Writing, 1750–2000*, edited by Caroline Bland and Máire Cross, 15–28. Aldershot, UK: Ashgate, 2003.

Brewer, Daniel. *The Enlightenment Past: Reconstructing Eighteenth-Century French Thought*. Cambridge: Cambridge University Press, 2008.

Brockliss, L. W. B. *Calvet's Web: Enlightenment and the Republic of Letters in Eighteenth-Century France*. Oxford: Oxford University Press, 2002.

———. *French Higher Education in the Seventeenth and Eighteenth Centuries: A Cultural History*. Oxford: Clarendon Press, 1987.

Brooke, John L. "Consent, Civil Society, and the Public Sphere in the Age of Revolution and the Early American Republic." In *Beyond the Founders: New Approaches to the Political History of the Early American Republic*, edited by Jeffery Pasley, Andrew Robertson, and David Waldstreicher, 207–50. Chapel Hill: University of North Carolina Press, 2004.

Brown, Gregory S. *Literary Sociability and Literary Property in France, 1775–1793: Beaumarchais, the Société des Auteurs Dramatique, and the Comédie Française*. Aldershot, UK: Ashgate, 2006.

Brown, Penny. *A Critical History of French Children's Literature, 1600–1830*. New York: Routledge, 2008.

Buringh, Eltjo, and Jan Luiten Van Zanden. "Charting the 'Rise of the West': Manuscripts and Printed Books in Europe, a Long-Term Perspective from the Sixth through Eighteenth Centuries." *Journal of Economic History* 69, no. 2 (June 2009): 409–45.

Burrows, Simon. *Blackmail, Scandal, and Revolution: London's French Libellistes, 1758–92.* Manchester: Manchester University Press, 2006.

———. *The French Book Trade in Enlightenment Europe II: Enlightenment Bestsellers.* New York: Bloomsbury, 2018.

———. *French Exile Journalism and European Politics, 1792–1814.* Suffolk, UK: Royal Historical Society, 2000.

Burrows, Simon, Mark Curran, Vincent Hiribarren, Sarah Kattau, and Henry Merivale. "The French Book Trade in Enlightenment Europe Project, 1769–1794." Last modified May 6, 2014. http://fbtee.uws.edu.au/stn/.

Burson, Jeffrey D. "Reflections on the Pluralization of Enlightenment and the Notion of Theological Enlightenment as Process." *French History* 26, no. 4 (2012): 524–37.

———. *The Rise and Fall of Theological Enlightenment: Jean-Martin de Prades and Ideological Polarization in Eighteenth-Century France.* South Bend: University of Notre Dame Press, 2010.

Cage, E. Claire. *Unnatural Frenchmen: The Politics of Priestly Celibacy and Marriage, 1720–1815.* Charlottesville: University of Virginia Press, 2015.

Calhoun, Craig J. *Habermas and the Public Sphere.* Cambridge, MA: MIT Press, 1992.

Campbell, Peter R., Thomas Kaiser, and Marisa Linton, eds. *Conspiracy in the French Revolution.* Manchester: Manchester University Press, 2007.

Caplan, Jay. *Postal Culture in Europe, 1500–1800.* Oxford: Voltaire Foundation, 2016.

Caradonna, Jeremy L. *The Enlightenment in Practice: Academic Prize Contests and Intellectual Culture in France, 1670–1794.* Ithaca: Cornell University Press, 2012.

Carter, Karen E. *Creating Catholics: Catechism and Primary Education in Early Modern France.* South Bend: University of Notre Dame Press, 2011.

Cassirer, Ernst. *The Philosophy of the Enlightenment.* Princeton: Princeton University Press, 1951.

Caucanas, Silvie, and Rémy Cazals. *Venance Dougados et son temps. André Chénier. Fabre d'Eglantine. Actes du colloque de Carcassone, 5–7 mai 1994.* Carcassone: Les Audois, 1995.

Censer, Jack R. *The French Press in the Age of Enlightenment.* London: Routledge, 1994.

———. *Prelude to Power: The Parisian Radical Press, 1789–1791.* Baltimore: Johns Hopkins University Press, 1976.

Censer, Jack Richard, and Jeremy D. Popkin. *Press and Politics in Pre-Revolutionary France.* Berkeley: Universtiy of California Press, 1987.

Chartier, Roger. "L'Académie de Lyon au XVIIIe siècle, 1700–1793, étude de sociologie culturelle." *Nouvelles études lyonnaises* (1969): 133–250.

———. *Lectures et lecteurs dans la France d'Ancien Régime.* Paris: Seuil, 1987.

———. *The Cultural Origins of the French Revolution.* Translated by Lydia G. Cochrane. Durham: Duke University Press, 1991.

———. *Histoires de la lecture: Un bilan de recherches.* Paris: Distribution Distique, 1995.

———. "Labourers and Voyagers: From the Text to the Reader." In *The Book History Reader,* edited by David Finkelstein and Alistair McCleery, 47–58. London: Routledge, 2002.

Chartier, Roger, Alain Boureau, and Cécile Dauphin. *Correspondence: Models of Letter-Writing from the Middle Ages to the Nineteenth Century.* Princeton: Princeton University Press, 1997.

Chartier, Roger, and Hans-Jürgen Lüsebrink. *Colportage et lecture populaire: Imprimés de large circulation en Europe, XVIe–XIXe siècles*. Paris: Distribution Distique, 1996.

Chartier, Roger, and Henri-Jean Martin. *Le livre triumphant: Histoire de l'édition française*, vol. 2. Paris: Promodis, 1984.

Chartier, Roger, and Alain Paire. *Pratiques de la lecture*. Marseille: Rivages, 1985.

Chisick, Harvey. *The Limits of Reform in the Enlightenment: Attitudes toward the Education of the Lower Classes in Eighteenth-Century France*. Princeton: Princeton University Press, 1981.

——. *The Production, Distribution and Readership of a Conservative Journal of the Early French Revolution: The Ami du Roi of the Abbé Royou*. Philadelphia: American Philosophical Society, 1992.

——. "Public Opinion and Political Culture in France during the Second Half of the Eighteenth Century." *English Historical Review* 117, no. 470 (February 2002): 48–77.

Chisick, Harvey, Ilana Zinguer, and Ouzi Elyada. *The Press in the French Revolution*. Oxford: Voltaire Foundation at the Taylor Institution, 1991.

Clay, Lauren R. *Stagestruck: The Business of Theater in Eighteenth-Century France and Its Colonies*. Ithaca: Cornell University Press, 2013.

Coisel, Nicole, Marie-Pierre Omnès, Alexis Le Bihan, and Yves Le Gallo. *Bibliographie de la presse française politique et d'information générale*. Paris: Bibliothèque nationale, 1973.

Colley, Linda. *Britons: Forging the Nation, 1707–1837*. New Haven: Yale University Press, 1992.

Comsa, Maria Teodora, Melanie Conroy, Dan Edelstein, Chloe Summers Edmondson, and Claude Willan. "The French Enlightenment Network." *Journal of Modern History* 88, no. 3 (2016): 495–534.

Coudart, Laurence. *La Gazette de Paris: Un journal royaliste pendant la Révolution française (1789–1792)*. Paris: L'Harmattan, 1995.

Curran, Mark. *The French Book Trade in Enlightenment Europe I: Selling Enlightenment*. New York: Bloomsbury, 2018.

Dagenais, Simon. "L'almanach de Mathieu Laensbergh: L'émergence d'une marque (XVIIe–XIXe siècles)." PhD diss., Université du Québec à Montréal, 2016.

Darnton, Robert. "Booksellers/Literary Demand." In *A Literary Tour de France*, September 1, 2014, http://www.robertdarnton.org/literarytour/booksellers.

——. *Censors at Work: How States Shaped Literature*. New York: W. W. Norton, 2014.

——. *The Corpus of Clandestine Literature in France, 1769–1789*. New York: W. W. Norton, 1995.

——. *The Forbidden Best-Sellers of Pre-Revolutionary France*. New York: W. W. Norton, 1995.

——. *The Great Cat Massacre and Other Episodes in French Cultural History*. New York: Basic Books, 1984.

——. "The High Enlightenment and the Low-Life of Literature in Pre-Revolutionary France." *Past and Present* 51 (May 1971): 81–115.

——. *The Literary Underground of the Old Regime*. Cambridge, MA: Harvard University Press, 1982.

———. *Mesmerism and the End of the Enlightenment in France*. Cambridge, MA: Harvard University Press, 1968.

———. *Poetry and the Police: Communication Networks in Eighteenth-Century Paris*. Cambridge: Belknap Press of Harvard University Press, 2010.

———. "Reading, Writing, and Publishing in Eighteenth-Century France: A Case Study in the Sociology of Literature." *Daedalus* 100, no. 1 (1971): 214–56.

———. "Writing News and Telling Stories." *Daedalus* 104, no. 2 (Spring 1975): 175–94.

David, Marcel. *Fraternité et Révolution française, 1789–1799*. Paris: Aubier, 1987.

Davidson, Cathy. *Revolution and the Word: The Rise of the Novel in America*. New York: Oxford University Press, 1986.

Davis, Adam J., and Bertrand Taithe. "From the Purse and the Heart: Exploring Charity, Humanitarianism, and Human Rights in France." *French Historical Studies* 34, no. 3 (Summer 2011): 413–32.

Davis, Natalie Zemon. "Poor Relief, Humanism, and Heresy: The Case of Lyon." *Studies in Medieval and Renaissance History* 5 (1968): 217–75.

Davison, Kate. "Early Modern Social Networks: Antecedents, Opportunities, and Challenges." *American Historical Review* 124, no. 2 (April 2019): 456–82.

Dean, Ann C. *The Talk of the Town: Figurative Publics in Eighteenth-Century Britain*. Lewisburg: Bucknell University Press, 2007.

Debien, G. *Correspondence de Félix Faulcon*. Poitiers: Société des Archives Historiques du Poitou, 1953.

Denby, David. *Sentimental Narrative and the Social Order in France, 1760–1820*. Cambridge: Cambridge University Press, 2006.

Denis, Vincent. "Les Parisiens, la police et les numérotages des maisons, du XVIIIe siècle à l'Empire." *French Historical Studies* 38, no. 1 (February 2015): 83–103.

Derne, Frédéric. "La chanson, 'arme' révolutionnaire et chambre d'écho de la société en Auvergne." *Annales historiques de la Révolution française* 341 (July–September 2005): 25–51.

D'Huart, Suzanne. *Brissot: La Gironde au pouvoir*. Paris: Robert Laffont, 1986.

DiCaprio, Lisa. *The Origins of the Welfare State: Women, Work, and the French Revolution*. Champaign: University of Illinois Press, 2007.

Diefendorf, Barbara. *From Penitence to Charity: Pious Women and the Catholic Reformation in Paris*. New York: Oxford University Press, 2004.

Dijk, Suzanna van. "Traces de femmes: Présence féminine dans le journalisme français du XVIIIe siècle." PhD thesis, APA-Holland University Press, 1988.

Dinan, Susan E. *Women and Poor Relief in Seventeenth-Century France: The Early History of the Daughters of Charity*. Aldershot, UK: Ashgate, 2006.

Dinet, Henri. "Les peurs du Beauvaisis et du Valois." *Mémoires de la Fédération des Sociétés Historiques et Archéologiques de Paris* (1975): 23–24.

Dingli, Laurent. *Robespierre*. Paris: Flammarion, 2004.

Douthwaite, Julia V. *The Frankenstein of 1790 and Other Lost Chapters from Revolutionary France*. Chicago: University of Chicago Press, 2012.

———. "Is Charity for Schmucks? The Legitimacy of Bienfaisance, ca. 1760–82 and ca. 2013–15." *Eighteenth Century: Theory and Interpretation* 57, no. 1 (2016): 1–21.

Doyle, William, ed. *The Oxford Handbook of the Ancien Régime*. Oxford: Oxford University Press, 2012.

———. *Venality: The Sale of Offices in Eighteenth-Century France.* Oxford: Oxford University Press, 1996.

———. "Was There an Aristocratic Reaction in Pre-Revolutionary France?" *Past and Present* 57, no. 1 (November 1972): 97–122.

Dubuc, André. "La culture de la pomme de terre en Normandie avant et depuis Parmentier." *Annales de Normandie* 3, no. 1 (1953): 50–68.

———. "Le Journal de Normandie avant et durant les Etats Généraux." *Actes du congrès des sociétés savantes de lyon* 1, no. 1 (1964): 385–404.

Ducheyne, Steffen. *Reassessing the Radical Enlightenment.* New York: Routledge, 2017.

Duprat, Annie. *'Les affaires d'État sont mes affaires de cœur': Lettres de Rosalie Jullien, une femme dans la Révolution, 1775–1810.* Paris: Belin, 2017.

Duprat, Catherine. *'Pour l'amour de l'humanité': Le temps des philanthropes: La philanthropie parisienne des lumières à la monarchie de Juillet.* Paris: Editions du C.T.H.S., 1993.

Duranton, Henri, Claude Labrosse, and Pierre Rétat. *Les Gazettes Européennes de langue Française (XVII–XVIIIe siècles).* Saint-Etienne: Publications de l'Université de Saint-Etienne, 1992.

Earle, Rebecca. *Epistolary Selves: Letters and Letter-Writers, 1600–1945.* Aldershot, UK: Ashgate, 1999.

Edelstein, Dan. *The Terror of Natural Right: Republicanism, the Cult of Nature, and the French Revolution.* Chicago: University of Chicago Press, 2009.

———. *The Enlightenment: A Genealogy.* Chicago: University of Chicago Press, 2010.

Edelstein, Dan, Robert Morrissey, and Glenn Roe. "To Quote or Not to Quote: Citation Strategies in the Encyclopédie." *Journal of the History of Ideas* 74, no. 2 (2013): 213–36.

Edelstein, Melvin A. *La Feuille Villageoise: Communication et modernisation dans les régions rurales pendant la Révolution.* Paris: Bibliothèque nationale, 1977.

Eisenstein, Elizabeth L. *Divine Art, Infernal Machine: The Reception of Printing in the West from First Impressions to the Sense of an Ending.* Philadelphia: University of Pennsylvania Press, 2011.

Ellery, Eloise. *Brissot de Warville: A Study in the History of the French Revolution.* Boston: Houghton Mifflin, 1915.

Enenkel, Karl, Jan L. de Jong, and Jeanine de Landtsheer, eds., with Alicia Montoya. *Recreating Ancient History: Episodes from the Greek and Roman Past in the Arts and Literature of the Early Modern Period.* Leiden, Netherlands: Brill, 2001.

Erickson, Bonnie H. "Social Networks and History." *Historical Methods* 30, no. 3 (1997): 149–57.

Ewing, Tabetha Leigh. *Rumour, Diplomacy and War in Enlightenment Paris.* Oxford: Oxford University Studies in the Enlightenment, 2014.

Fairchilds, Cissie C. *Poverty and Charity in Aix-en-Provence, 1640–1789.* Baltimore: Johns Hopkins University Press, 1976.

Fairclough, Mary. *Literature, Electricity and Politics, 1740–1840: 'Electrick communication every where.'* London: Palgrave, 2017.

Farge, Arlette. *Subversive Words: Public Opinion in Eighteenth-Century France.* University Park: Pennsylvania State University Press, 1995.

Feyel, Gilles. *L'annonce et la nouvelle: La presse d'information en France sous l'Ancien Régime, 1630–1788*. Oxford: Voltaire Foundation, 2000.

——. *La distribution et la diffusion de la presse, du XVIIIe siècle au IIIe millénaire*. Paris: Panthéon-Assas, 2002.

——. *La presse en France des origines à 1944: Histoire politique et matérielle*. Paris: Ellipses, 1999.

——. "La presse provinciale au XVIIIe siècle: Géographie d'un réseau." *Revue Historique* 272, no. 2 (1984): 353–74.

——. "La presse provinciale sous l'Ancien Regime." In *La presse provinciale au XVIIIe siècle*, edited by Jean Sgard, 3–47. Grenoble: Centre de Recherches sur les Sensibilités, Université des Langues et Lettres de Grenoble, 1983.

Fialcofschi, Roxana. "Le 'Journal de Paris' et les arts visuels, 1777–1788." PhD diss., Université Lumière Lyon 2, 2010.

Fissel, Mary. "Popular Medical Writing." In *Oxford History of Popular Print Culture, Beginnings to 1660*, edited by Joan Raymond, 418–31. Oxford: Oxford University Press, 2011.

Flynn, Elizabeth A., and Patrocinio P. Schweickart, eds. *Gender and Reading: Essays on Readers, Texts, and Contexts*. Baltimore: Johns Hopkins University Press, 1986.

Forrest, Alan. *The French Revolution and the Poor*. Oxford: Basil Blackwell, 1981.

Fox-Genovese, Elizabeth. *The Origins of Physiocracy: Economic Revolution and Social Order in Eighteenth-Century France*. Ithaca: Cornell University Press, 1976.

Freedman, Jeffrey. *Books without Borders in Enlightenment Europe: French Cosmopolitan and German Literary Markets*. Philadelphia: University of Pennsylvania Press, 2012.

Frevert, Ute. "Defining Emotions: Concepts and Debates over Three Centuries." In *Emotional Lexicons: Continuity and Change in the Vocabulary of Feeling, 1700–2000*, edited by Ute Frevert, Christian Bailey, Pascal Eitler, Benno Gammerl, Bettina Hitzer, Margrit Pernau, Monique Scheer, Anne Schmidt, and Nina Verheyen, 1–31. Oxford: Oxford University Press, 2014.

Furet, François, and Jacques Ozouf. *Lire et écrire: L'alphabétisation des Français de Calvin à Jules Ferry*. 2 vols. Paris: Éditions de Minuit, 1977.

Garrioch, David. *The Formation of the Parisian Bourgeoisie, 1690–1830*. Cambridge, MA: Harvard University Press, 1996.

——. "From Christian Friendship to Secular Sentimentality: Enlightenment Re-evaluations." In *Friendship: A History*, edited by Barbara Caine, 163–212. London: Equinox, 2009.

——. "From Religious to Secular Sociability: Confraternities and Freemasonry in Eighteenth-Century Paris." In *Sociability and Its Discontents: Civil Society, Social Capital, and Their Alternatives in Early Modern Europe*, edited by Nick Terpstra, Mark Jurdjevic, and Nicholas Eckste, 313–26. Turnhout: Brepols, 2009.

——. "The Local Experience of Revolution: The Gobelins/Finistère Section in Paris." *French History and Civilization* 1 (2005): 20–29.

——. "Mutual Aid Societies in Eighteenth-Century Paris." *French History and Civilization* 4 (2011): 22–33.

——. "Parisian Women and the October Days." *Social History* 24, no. 3 (October 1999): 231–49.

Garrioch, David, Harold Love, Ian Morrison, Brian McMullin, and Meredith Sherlock, eds. *The Culture of the Book.* Melbourne: Bibliographical Society of Australia and New Zealand, 1999.

Gasc, Michelle. "La naissance de la presse periodique locale à Lyon: *Les Affiches de Lyon, Annonces et Avis Divers.*" *Etudes sur la presse au XVIIIe siècle* 3 (1978): 61–79.

Gay, Peter. *The Enlightenment: An Interpretation.* 2 vols. New York: Knopf, 1966.

Gelbart, Nina Rattner. *Feminine and Opposition Journalism in Old Regime France: Le Journal des dames.* Berkeley: University of California Press, 1987.

——. "The French Revolution as Medical Event: The Journalistic Gaze." *History of European Ideas* 10, no. 4 (1989): 417–27.

Gérard, René. *Un journal de province sous la Révolution: Le 'Journal de Marseille' de Ferréol Beaugeard (1781–1797).* Paris: Société des études robespierristes, 1964.

Giles, P. *Plutarch's Lives.* Cambridge: Cambridge University Press, 2014.

Gillispie, Charles. *The Montgolfier Brothers and the Invention of Aviation, 1783–1784.* Princeton: Princeton University Press, 1983.

——. *Science and Polity in France at the End of the Old Regime.* Princeton: Princeton University Press, 1981.

Giraud, Jacqueline, Pierre Rétat, and Henri Duranton. *Le Journalisme d'Ancien Régime: Questions et propositions: Table Ronde CNRS, 12–13 juin 1981.* Lyon: Presses universitaires de Lyon, 1982.

Given, James B. *Inquisition and Medieval Society: Power, Discipline, and Resistance in Languedoc.* Ithaca: Cornell University Press, 2001.

Godechot, Jacques Léon. *The Taking of the Bastille, July 14th, 1789.* New York: Scribner, 1970.

Goëtz, Charlotte. "*Plumes de Marat*" et "*Plumes sur Marat*": Pour une bibliographie générale. Brussels: Pôle Nord, 2006.

Goldgar, Anne. *Impolite Learning: Conduct and Community in the Republic of Letters, 1680–1760.* New Haven: Yale University Press, 1995.

Goldstein, Jan. *Console and Classify: The French Psychiatric Profession in the Nineteenth Century.* Cambridge: Cambridge University Press, 1987.

——. "Enthusiasm or Imagination? Eighteenth-Century Smear Words in Comparative National Context." *Huntington Library Quarterly* 60, nos. 1–2 (1997): 29–49.

Goodman, Dena. *Becoming a Woman in the Age of Letters.* Ithaca: Cornell University Press, 2009.

——. "Letter Writing and the Emergence of Gendered Subjectivity in Eighteenth-Century France." *Journal of Women's Studies* 17, no. 2 (2005): 9–37.

——. "Old Media: Lessons from Letters." *French Historical Studies* 36, no. 1 (2013): 1–17.

——. "L'ortografe des Dames: Gender and Language in the Old Regime." *French Historical Studies* 25 (Spring 2002): 191–223.

——. *The Republic of Letters: A Cultural History of the French Enlightenment.* Ithaca: Cornell University Press, 1994.

Goodman, Dena, and Elizabeth Goldsmith. *Going Public: Women and Publishing in Early Modern France.* New York: Cornell University Press, 1995.

Gordon, Daniel. *Citizens without Sovereignty: Equality and Sociability in French Thought, 1670–1789.* Princeton: Princeton University Press, 1994.

Gossman, Lionel. "Anecdote and History." *History and Theory* 42, no. 2 (May 2003): 143–68.

Gough, Hugh. *The Newspaper Press in the French Revolution*. New Fetter Lane, UK: Routledge, 1988.

Goulemot, Jean-Marie. *La littérature des Lumières*. Paris: Armand Colin, 2005.

Griffin, Robert J. *The Faces of Anonymity: Anonymous and Pseudonymous Publication from the Sixteenth to the Twentieth Century*. New York: Palgrave Macmillan, 2003.

Grove, Richard H. "The Great El Niño of 1789–93 and Its Global Consequences: Reconstructing an Extreme Climate Event in World Environmental History." *Medieval History Journal* 10, nos. 1–2 (2007): 75–98.

Gruder, Vivian R. *The Notables and the Nation: The Political Schooling of the French, 1787–1788*. Cambridge, MA: Harvard University Press, 2007.

Guenée, Bernard. *L'opinion publique à la fin du Moyen Age d'après la "Chronique de Charles VI" du religieux de Saint-Denis*. Paris: Perrin, 2002.

Gunn, Giles. *The Pragmatist Turn: Religion, the Enlightenment, and the Formation of American Literature*. Charlottesville: University of Virginia Press, 2017.

Gutton, Jean Pierre. *La société et les pauvres: L'exemple de la généralité de Lyon, 1534–1789*. Lyon: Bibliothèque de la Faculté des Lettres et sciences humaines de Lyon, 1971.

Habermas, Jürgen. *The Structural Transformation of the Public Sphere: An Inquiry into a Category of Bourgeois Society*. Cambridge, MA: MIT Press, 1989.

Haine, W. Scott. *The World of the Paris Café: Sociability among the French Working Class, 1789–1914*. Baltimore: Johns Hopkins University Press, 1996.

Hallion, Richard P. *Taking Flight: Inventing the Aerial Age, from Antiquity through the First World War*. New York: Oxford University Press, 2003.

Hanson, Paul R. "Monarchist Clubs and the Pamphlet Debate over Political Legitimacy in the Early Years of the French Revolution." *French Historical Studies* 21, no. 2 (1998): 299–324.

Hart, Jim Allee. *Views on the News: The Developing Editorial Syndrome, 1500–1800*. Carbondale: Southern Illinois University Press, 1970.

Hatin, Eugène. *Bibliographie historique et critique de la presse périodique Française, ou, Catalogue systématique et raisonné de tous les écrits périodiques de quelque valeur publiés ou ayant circulé en France depuis l'origine du journal jusqu'à nos jours*. Paris: Firmin Didot frères, fils et cie., 1866.

——. *Manuel théorique et pratique de la liberté de la presse: Histoire, législation, doctrine et jurisprudence, bibliographie, 1500–1868*. 2 vols. Paris: Librairie Pagnerre, 1868.

Haydon, Colin. "Le Courayer, Pierre-François (1681–1776)." In *Oxford Dictionary of National Biography*, edited by Lawrence Goldman. Oxford: Oxford University Press, 2006.

Haynes, Christine. *Lost Illusions: The Politics of Publishing in Nineteenth-Century France*. Cambridge, MA: Harvard University Press, 2010.

Hazard, Paul. *European Thought in the Eighteenth Century: From Montesquieu to Lessing*. New Haven: Yale University Press, 1954.

Heilbron, J. L. *Electricity in the 17th and 18th Centuries: A Study of Early Modern Physics*. Berkeley: University of California Press, 1979.

Henri, Pierre. *La vie et l'œuvre de Valentin Haüy*. Paris: Presses universitaires de France, 1984.

Hesse, Carla Alison. *The Other Enlightenment: How French Women Became Modern.* Princeton: Princeton University Press, 2001.

——. *Publishing and Cultural Politics in Revolutionary Paris, 1789–1810.* Berkeley: University of California Press, 1991.

Hochadel, Oliver. "The Sale of Shocks and Sparks: Itinerant Electricians in the German Enlightenment." In *Science and Spectacle in the European Enlightenment,* edited by Bernadette Bensaude-Vincent and Christine Blondel, 89–102. Aldershot, UK: Ashgate, 2008.

Hochman, Barbara. *Getting at the Author: Reimagining Books and Reading in the Age of American Realism.* Amherst: University of Massachusetts Press, 2001.

Hoffman, Philip T. *Growth in a Traditional Society: The French Countryside, 1450–1815.* Princeton: Princeton University Press, 1996.

Holmes, Lawrence. *Lavoisier and the Chemistry of Life: An Exploration of Scientific Creativity.* Madison: University of Wisconsin Press, 1987.

Hull, Isabel. *Sexuality, State, and Civil Society in Germany, 1700–1815.* Ithaca: Cornell University Press, 1996.

Hunt, Lynn. "The Experience of Revolution." *French Historical Studies* 32, no. 4 (2009): 671–78.

——. *Inventing Human Rights.* New York: W. W. Norton, 2008.

Ibbett, Katherine. *Compassion's Edge: Fellow-Feeling and Its Limits in Early Modern France.* Philadelphia: University of Pennsylvania Press, 2018.

Israel, Jonathan I. *Democratic Enlightenment: Philosophy, Revolution, and Human Rights, 1750–1790.* Oxford: Oxford University Press, 2011.

——. *Enlightenment Contested: Philosophy, Modernity, and the Emancipation of Man, 1670–1752.* Oxford: Oxford University Press, 2006.

——. *Radical Enlightenment: Philosophy and the Making of Modernity, 1650–1750.* Oxford: Oxford University Press, 2001.

Iverson, John R. "Putting Voltaire's *Henriade* in the Hands of the Young." *French Review* 76, no. 3 (2003): 522–33.

Jacob, Louis. *Hébert le Père Duchesne, chef des sans-culottes.* Paris: Gallimard, 1960.

Jacob, Margaret C. *Living the Enlightenment: Freemasonry and Politics in Eighteenth-Century Europe.* New York: Oxford University Press, 1991.

——. *The Radical Enlightenment: Pantheists, Freemasons, and Republicans.* London: Allen & Unwin, 1981.

——. *The Secular Enlightenment.* Princeton: Princeton University Press, 2019.

Janssens, Jacques. *Camille Desmoulins: Le premier républicain de France.* Paris: Perrin, 1973.

Jarvis, Katie. *Politics in the Marketplace: Work, Gender, and Citizenship in Revolutionary France.* Oxford: Oxford University Press, 2018.

Johnson, Sherry. "El Niño, Environmental Crisis, and the Emergence of Alternative Markets in the Hispanic Caribbean, 1760s–70s." *William and Mary Quarterly* 62, no. 3 (July 2005): 365–410.

Jones, Colin. *Charity and Bienfaisance: The Treatment of the Poor in the Montpellier Region, 1740–1815.* Cambridge: Cambridge University Press, 1982.

——. "The Great Chain of Buying: Medical Advertisement, the Bourgeois Public Sphere, and the Origins of the French Revolution." *American Historical Review* 101, no. 1 (1996): 13–40.

——. "Pulling Teeth in Eighteenth-Century Paris." *Past and Present* 166 (2000): 100–145.

Jones, Peter. *Agricultural Enlightenment: Knowledge, Technology, and Nature, 1750–1840.* Oxford: Oxford University Press, 2016.

——. "The Challenge of Land Reform in Eighteenth and Nineteenth-Century France." *Past and Present* 216 (2012): 107–42.

——. "Making Chemistry the 'Science' of Agriculture, c. 1760–1840." *History of Science* 54, no. 2 (2016): 169–94.

——. "Paysans et seigneurs dans la France de 1789: La construction d'une arène politique locale dans une terre adjacente de Provence." In *Peuples en Révolution d'aujourd'hui à 1789,* edited by C. Belmonte and C. Peyrard, 11–24. Aix-en-Provence: Presses universitaires de Provence, 2014.

Jonsson, Fredrik Albritton. *Enlightenment's Frontier: The Scottish Highlands and the Origins of Environmentalism.* New Haven: Yale University Press, 2013.

Kaplan, Steven L. *The Bakers of Paris and the Bread Question, 1700–1775.* Durham: Duke University Press, 1996.

——. *Bread, Politics and Political Economy in the Reign of Louis XV.* 2 vols. The Hague: Martinus Nijhoff, 1976.

——. *Provisioning Paris: Merchants and Millers in the Grain and Flour Trade during the Eighteenth Century.* Ithaca: Cornell University Press, 1984.

Keen, Paul. *Literature, Commerce, and the Spectacle of Modernity, 1750–1800.* Cambridge: Cambridge University Press, 2012.

Kelley, Mary. *Learning to Stand and Speak.* Chapel Hill: Omohundro Institute of Early American History and Culture and the University of North Carolina Press, 2012.

Kennedy, Emmet. *A Cultural History of the French Revolution.* New Haven: Yale University Press, 1989.

Kennedy, Michael L. *The Jacobin Clubs in the French Revolution, 1793–1795.* Princeton: Princeton University Press, 1982.

Kim, Mi Gyung. *The Imagined Empire: Balloon Enlightenments in Revolutionary Europe.* Pittsburgh: University of Pittsburgh Press, 2017.

Kraidy, Marwan M., and Marina R. Krikorian. "The Revolutionary Public Sphere: The Case of the Arab Uprisings." *Communication and the Public* 2, no. 2 (July 2017): 111–19.

Kwass, Michael. *Contraband: Louis Mandrin and the Making of a Global Underground.* Cambridge, MA: Harvard University Press, 2014.

Labrosse, Claude. *Lire au XVIIIe siècle: La Nouvelle Héloïse et ses lecteurs.* Lyon: Presses universitaires de Lyon, 1985.

Labrosse, Claude, and Pierre Rétat. *Naissance du journal révolutionnaire, 1789.* Lyon: Presses universitaires de Lyon, 1989.

Labrosse, Claude, Pierre Rétat, and Henri Duranton. *L'instrument périodique: La fonction de la presse au XVIIIe siècle.* Lyon: Presses universitaires de Lyon, 1985.

Lamy, Jérôme. *L'observatoire de Toulouse aux XVIIIe et XIXe siècles: Archéologie d'un espace savant.* Rennes: Presses universitaires de Rennes, 2007.

Lebon, Jean-Joseph. *La presse montalbanaise des origines au début du dix-neuvième siècle.* Toulouse: Mémoire de maitrise, 1972.

Lefebvre, Georges. *The Great Fear of 1789: Rural Panic in Revolutionary France.* New York: Schocken Books, 1989.

Lehner, Ulrich L. *The Catholic Enlightenment: The Forgotten History of a Global Movement.* Oxford: Oxford University Press, 2016.

Leigh, Ralph A. "Editorial Notes" for Marie Thérèse Levasseur [née Renout], "Marie Thérèse Levasseur [née Renout] to La Gazette de Leyde: Tuesday, 11 May 1779." In *Electronic Enlightenment Scholarly Edition of Correspondence,* edited by Robert McNamee et al., University of Oxford, available at https://www.e-enlightenment.com/.

Lemercier, Claire. "Analyse de réseaux et histoire." *Revue d'histoire moderne et contemporaine 52,* no. 2 (2005): 88–112.

———. *Quantitative Methods in the Humanities: An Introduction.* Charlottesville: University of Virginia Press, 2019.

Lemny, Stefan. *Jean-Louis Carra, 1742–1793: Parcours d'un révolutionnaire.* Paris: L'Harmattan, 2000.

Leong, Elaine. *Recipes and Everyday Knowledge: Medicine, Science, and the Household in Early Modern England.* Chicago: University of Chicago Press, 2018.

Le Roy Ladurie, Emmanuel. *Histoire humaine et comparé du climat: Disettes et révolutions, 1740–1860.* Paris: Fayard, 2006.

Leuwers, Hervé. *Camille et Lucile Desmoulins: Un rêve de république.* Paris: Fayard, 2018.

Lilti, Antoine. *The Invention of Celebrity.* Translated by Lynn Jeffress. Malden: Polity Press, 2017.

———. *The World of Salons: Sociability and Worldliness in Eighteenth-Century Paris.* Translated by Lydia G. Cochrane. Oxford: Oxford University Press, 2015.

Linton, Marisa. *The Politics of Virtue in Enlightenment France.* New York: Palgrave Macmillan, 2001.

———. "Virtue Rewarded? Women and the Politics of Virtue in 18th-Century France. Part I." *History of European Ideas 26,* no. 1 (2000): 35–49.

———. "Virtue Rewarded? Women and the Politics of Virtue in 18th-Century France. Part II." *History of European Ideas 26,* no. 1 (2000): 51–65.

Livesey, James. "Botany and Provincial Enlightenment in Montpellier: Antoine Banal Pére and Fils, 1750–1800." *History of Science 43* (2005): 57–76.

———. *Civil Society and Empire.* New Haven: Yale University Press, 2009.

———. *Provincializing Global History: Money, Ideas and Things in the Languedoc, 1680–1830.* New Haven: Yale University Press, 2020.

———. "A Revolutionary Career? François de Neufchâteau Does Well by Doing Good, 1774–1799." *French History 18,* no. 2 (2004): 173–95.

Losh, Elizabeth, and Jacqueline Wernimont, eds. *Bodies of Information: Intersectional Feminism and Digital Humanities.* Minneapolis: University of Minnesota Press, 2018.

Lüsebrink, Hans-Jürgen. "Horizons médiatiques et ouvertures interculturelles dans la presse au dix-huitième siècle." In *Enlightenment, Revolution and the Periodical*

Press, edited by Hans-Jürgen Lüsebrink and Jeremy D. Popkin, 22–32. Oxford: Voltaire Foundation, 2004.

Lüsebrink, Hans-Jürgen, and Rolf Reichardt. *The Bastille: A History of a Symbol of Despotism and Freedom*. Translated by Norbert Schürer. Durham: Duke University Press, 1997.

Lynn, Michael R. *The Sublime Invention: Ballooning in Europe, 1783–1820*. London: Pickering & Chatto, 2010.

Lyons, Martyn. *Reading Culture and Writing Practices in Nineteenth-Century France*. Toronto: University of Toronto Press, 2008.

Machor, James L., and Philip Goldstein, eds. *Reception Study: From Literary Theory to Cultural Studies*. New York: Routledge, 2001.

Mandrou, Robert. *A History of French Civilization*. New York: Random House, 1964.

Manning, Susan, and Francis D. Cogliano, eds. *The Atlantic Enlightenment*. Aldershot, UK: Ashgate, 2008.

Margerison, Kenneth. *Pamphlets and Public Opinion: The Campaign for a Union of Orders in the Early French Revolution*. West Lafayette: Purdue University Press, 1998.

Marion, Marcel. *Dictionnaire des Institutions*. Paris: Picard, 1923.

——. *Recherches sur les bibliothèques privées à Paris au milieu du XVIIIe siècle (1750–1759)*. Paris: Bibliothèque nationale, 1978.

Markoff, John. *The Abolition of Feudalism: Peasants, Lords, and Legislators in the French Revolution*. University Park: Pennsylvania State University Press, 1996.

Marshall, John. *Toleration and Early Enlightenment Culture*. Cambridge: Cambridge University Press, 2006.

Martin, Marc. *La presse régionale: Des affiches aux grands quotidiens*. Paris: Fayard, 2002.

Martin, Morag. *Selling Beauty: Cosmetics, Commerce, and French Society, 1750–1830*. Baltimore: Johns Hopkins University Press, 2009.

Martinet, Guy. "La vie politique à Marseille en 1795 et en 1796: Lettres inédites du journaliste Ferréol Beaugeard à Paul Cadroy, membre du Conseil des Cinq-Cents." *Provence historique* 64 (1966): 126–176.

Mason, Laura. *Singing the French Revolution: Popular Culture and Politics, 1787–1799*. Ithaca: Cornell University Press, 1996.

Maspero-Clerc, Hélène. "Une 'gazette anglo-française' pendant la guerre d'amérique: Le 'Courier de l'Europe' (1776–1788)." *Annales historiques de la Révolution française* 48, no. 226 (1976): 572–94.

Massin, Jean. *Marat*. Paris: Livre Club Diderot, 1975.

Matytsin, Anton M. *The Specter of Skepticism in the Age of Enlightenment*. Baltimore: Johns Hopkins University Press, 2016.

——. "Whose Light Is It Anyway? The Struggle for Light in the French Enlightenment." In *Let There Be Enlightenment: The Religious and Mystical Sources of Rationality*, edited by Anton M. Matytsin and Dan Edelstein, 62–85. Baltimore: Johns Hopkins University Press, 2019.

Maza, Sarah. *The Myth of the French Bourgeoisie*. Cambridge, MA: Harvard University Press, 2003.

——. *Private Lives and Public Affairs: The Causes Célèbres of Prerevolutionary France.* Berkeley: University of California Press, 1993.

McLeod, Jane. *Licensing Loyalty: Printers, Patrons, and the State in Early Modern France.* University Park: Pennsylvania State University Press, 2011.

——. "Printer Widows and the State in Eighteenth-Century France." In *Women and Work in Eighteenth Century France,* edited by Daryl M. Hafter and Nina Kushner, 113–29. Baton Rouge: Louisiana State University Press, 2015.

McMahon, Darrin. *Enemies of the Enlightenment: The French Counter-Enlightenment and the Making of Modernity.* Oxford: Oxford University Press, 2001.

McPhee, Peter. *Liberty or Death.* New Haven: Yale University Press, 2016.

——. *Revolution and Environment in Southern France, 1780–1830: Peasants, Lords, and Murder in the Corbières.* Oxford: Oxford University Press, 1999.

——. *Robespierre: A Revolutionary Life.* New Haven: Yale University Press, 2012.

Medlin, Dorothy. "André Morellet, the *Journal de Paris,* and *Le Publiciste,* 1795–1807." In *Correspondence; Dialogue; History of Ideas,* 3–94. Oxford: Voltaire Foundation, 2005.

Melton, James Van Horn. *The Rise of the Public in Enlightenment Europe.* Cambridge: Cambridge University Press, 2001.

Mercier-Faivre, Anne-Marie. "Naissance du genre nécrologique dans la presse française." In *Nouvelles formes du discours journalistique au XVIIIe siècle: Lettres au rédacteur, nécrologies, querelles médiatiques,* edited by Samuel Baudry and Denis Reynaud, 139–58. Lyon: Presses universitaires de Lyon, 2018.

Michaud, Louis-Gabriel. *Biographie universelle ancienne et moderne: Histoire par ordre alphabétique de la vie publique et privée de tous les hommes.* Paris: Desplaces, 1843.

Minois, Georges. *Censure et culture sous l'ancien régime.* Paris: Fayard, 1995.

Montoya, Alicia. "Middlebrow, Religion, and the European Enlightenment: A New Bibliometric Project, MEDIATE (1665–1820)." *French History and Civilization* 7 (2017): 66–79.

Mornet, Daniel. "Les enseignements des bibliothèques privées (1750–1780)." *Revue d'histoire littéraire de la France* 17, no. 3 (1910): 449–96.

——. *Les origines intellectuelles de la Révolution française (1715–1787).* Paris: A. Colin, 1933.

Motte, Claude, and Marie-Christine Vouloir, eds. "Des villages de Cassini aux communes d'aujourdhui." cassini.ehess.fr/cassini/fr/html/1_navigation.php.

Multigraph Collective (Scholarly Group). *Interacting with Print: Elements of Reading in the Era of Print Saturation.* Chicago: University of Chicago Press, 2018.

Murray, W. J. *The Right-Wing Press in the French Revolution: 1789–92.* Woodbridge, UK: Boydell, 1986.

——. "Un philosophe en Révolution: Dominique-Joseph Garat et le *Journal de Paris.*" In *La plume et le sabre: Volume d'hommages offerts à Jean-Paul Bertaud,* edited by Michel Biard, Annie Crépin, and Bernard Gainot, 89–99. Paris: Publications de la Sorbonne, 2002.

Norberg, Kathryn. *Rich and Poor in Grenoble, 1600–1814.* Berkeley: University of California Press, 1985.

Nord, David Paul. *Communities of Journalism: A History of American Newspapers and Their Readers.* Urbana: University of Illinois Press, 2001.

O'Connor, Adrian. *In Pursuit of Politics: Education and Revolution in Eighteenth-Century France*. Manchester: Manchester University Press, 2017.

Ozouf, Mona. "'Public Opinion' at the End of the Old Regime." In "Rethinking French Politics in 1788," Supplement, *Journal of Modern History* 60 (September 1988): S1–S21.

Padgett, John F. "Open Elite? Social Mobility, Marriage, and Family in Florence, 1282–1494." *Renaissance Quarterly* 63, no. 2 (2010): 357–411.

Parker, Geoffrey. "Crisis and Catastrophe: The Global Crisis of the Seventeenth Century Reconsidered." *American Historical Review* 113, no. 4 (October 2008): 1053–79.

Parker, Lindsay A. H. *Writing the Revolution: A French Woman's History in Letters*. New York: Oxford University Press, 2013.

Pettegree, Andrew. *The Invention of News: How the World Came to Know about Itself.* New Haven: Yale University Press, 2014.

Piccato, Pablo. "Public Sphere in Latin America: A Map of the Historiography." *Social History* 35, no. 2 (May 2010): 165–92.

Pichichero, Christy. *The Military Enlightenment: War and Culture in the French Empire from Louis XIV to Napoleon*. Ithaca: Cornell University Press, 2017.

Pocock, J. G. A. "Historiography and Enlightenment: A View of Their History." *Modern Intellectual History* 5, no. 1 (2008): 83–96.

Popiel, Jennifer J. *Rousseau's Daughters: Domesticity, Education, and Autonomy in Modern France*. Durham: University of New Hampshire Press, 2008.

Popkin, Jeremy D. *News and Politics in the Age of Revolution: Jean Luzac's Gazette de Leyde*. Ithaca: Cornell Univiversity Press, 1989.

——. *Press, Revolution, and Social Identities in France, 1830–1835*. University Park: Pennsylvania State University Press, 2002.

——. *Revolutionary News: The Press in France, 1789–1799*. Durham: Duke University Press, 1990.

——. *The Right-Wing Press in France, 1792–1800*. Chapel Hill: University of North Carolina Press, 1980.

Popkin, Jeremy D., and Jack R. Censer. "Some Paradoxes of the Eighteenth-Century Periodical." In *Enlightenment, Revolution and the Periodical Press: Studies on Voltaire and the Eighteenth Century*, edited by Hans-Jürgen Lüsebrink and Jeremy D. Popkin, 3–21. Oxford: Voltaire Foundation, 2004.

——, eds. *Press and Politics in Pre-Revolutionary France*. Berkeley: University of California Press, 1987.

Popkin, R. H. "Skepticism in the Enlightenment." *Studies on Voltaire and the Eighteenth Century* 26 (1963): 1321–35.

Porter, Lindsey. *Popular Rumour in Revolutionary Paris, 1792–1794*. Manchester: Palgrave Macmillan, 2017.

Poster, Carol, and Linda C. Mitchell. *Letter-Writing Manuals and Instruction from Antiquity to the Present: Historical and Bibliographic Studies*. Columbia: University of South Carolina Press, 2007.

Pouy, Louis Eugène Ferdinand. *Recherches historiques sur l'imprimerie et la librairie à Amiens, avec une description de livres divers imprimés dans cette ville*. Amiens: Typographie de Lemer ainé, 1861.

Powell, Maushag N. *Performing Authorship in Eighteenth-Century English Periodicals*. Lewisburg: Bucknell University Press, 2012.

Price, Leah. "Reading: The State of the Discipline." *Book History* 7 (2004): 303–20.

Putnam, Lara. "The Transnational and the Text-Searchable: Digitized Sources and the Shadows They Cast." *American Historical Review* 121, no. 2 (April 2016): 377–402.

Quartararo, Anne T. *Deaf Identity and Social Images in Nineteenth-Century France.* Washington, DC: Gallaudet University Press, 2008.

Radway, Janice A. *Reading the Romance: Women, Patriarchy, and Popular Literature.* Chapel Hill: University of North Carolina Press, 1991.

Ramsay, Clay. *The Ideology of the Great Fear: The Soissonnais in 1789.* Baltimore: Johns Hopkins University Press, 1992.

Rancière, Jacques. *Mute Speech: Literature, Critical Theory, and Politics.* New York: Columbia University Press, 2011.

Rasmussen, Dennis C. *The Pragmatic Enlightenment: Recovering the Liberalism of Hume, Smith, Montesquieu, and Voltaire.* Cambridge: Cambridge University Press, 2014.

Ravel, Jeffrey S. *The Contested Parterre: Public Theater and French Political Culture, 1680–1791.* Ithaca: Cornell University Press, 1999.

Reader, Bill, Guido Stempel III, and Douglas K. Daniel. "Age, Wealth, Education Predict Letters to the Editor." *Newspaper Research Journal* 25, no. 4 (2004): 55–66.

Reader, Bill. "The Enlightenment Ethics of DIY Culture." In *Ethics and Entertainment,* edited by Howard Good and Sandra Borden, 226–44. Jefferson: McFarland, 2010.

——. "Letters to the Editor Policy." In *Community Journalism: Relentlessly Local,* edited by Jock Lauterer, 151–55. Chapel Hill: University of North Carolina Press, 2006.

Reddy, William M. *The Navigation of Feeling: A Framework for the History of Emotions.* Cambridge: Cambridge University Press, 2001.

Reid, Chad. "'Widely Read by American Patriots': The *New-York Weekly Journal* and the Influence of Cato's Letters on Colonial America." In *Periodical Literature in Eighteenth-Century America,* edited by Mark Kamrath and Sharon M. Harris, 109–42. Knoxville: University of Tennessee Press, 2005.

Rentet, Thierry. "Network Mapping: Ties of Fidelity and Dependency among the Major Domestic Officers of Anne de Montmorency." *French History* 17, no. 2 (2003): 109–26.

Rétat, Pierre. *La révolution du journal: 1788–1794.* Paris: Editions du Centre national de la recherche scientifique, 1989.

Rétat, Pierre, and Jeanne-Marie Métivier. *Les gazettes européennes de langue française: Répertoire.* Paris: Bibliothèque nationale de France, 2002.

Rétat, Pierre, and Jean Sgard. *Presse et histoire au XVIIIè siècle: L'année 1734.* Paris: Éditions du CNRS, 1978.

Reynard, Pierre Claude. "Charting Environmental Concerns: Reactions to Hydraulic Public Works in Eighteenth-Century France." *Environment and History* 9, no. 3 (2003): 251–73.

Ridgway, R. S. *Voltaire and Sensibility.* Montreal: Queen's University Press, 1973.

Rigogne, Thierry. *Between State and Market: Printing and Bookselling in Eighteenth-Century France.* Oxford: Oxford University Studies in the Enlightenment, 2007.

——. "Readers and Reading in Cafés, 1660–1800." *French Historical Studies* 41, no. 3 (August 2018): 473–94. doi: https://doi.org/10.1215/00161071-6682124.

Riskin, Jessica. *Science in the Age of Sensibility: The Sentimental Empiricists of the French Enlightenment.* Chicago: University of Chicago Press, 2002.

Roche, Daniel. *Le siècle des lumières en province: Académies et académiciens provinciaux, 1680–1789.* 2 vols. Paris: Mouton, 1978.

———. *The People of Paris: An Essay in Popular Culture in the Eighteenth Century.* Translated by Marie Evans with Gwynne Lewis. Berkeley: University of California Press, 1987.

———. *France in the Enlightenment.* Translated by Arthur Goldhammer. Cambridge, MA: Harvard University Press, 1998.

———. *A History of Everyday Things: The Birth of Consumption in France, 1600–1800.* Translated by Brian Pearce. Cambridge: Cambridge University Press, 2000.

Roberts, Mary Louise. *Disruptive Acts: The New Woman in Fin de Siècle France.* Chicago: University of Chicago Press, 2002.

Roberts, Meghan K. "Philosophes Mariés and Epouses Philosophiques: Men of Letters and Marriage in Eighteenth-Century France." *French Historical Studies* 35, no. 3 (Summer 2012): 509–39.

———. *Sentimental Savants: Philosophical Families in Enlightenment France.* Chicago: University of Chicago Press, 2016.

Robertson, John. *The Case for the Enlightenment: Scotland and Naples, 1680–1760.* Cambridge: Cambridge University Press, 2005.

Roe, Glenn. "A Sheep In Wolff's Clothing: Émilie du Châtelet and the Encyclopédie." *Eighteenth-Century Studies* 51, no. 2 (Winter 2018): 179–96.

Roe, Glenn, Clovis Gladstone, and Robert Morissey. "Discourses and Disciplines in the Enlightenment: Topic Modeling the French Encyclopédie." *Frontiers in Digital Humanities* 2 (2016), https://doi.org/10.3389/fdigh.2015.00008.

Rosenberg, Daniel. "An Eighteenth-Century Time Machine: The 'Encyclopedia' of Denis Diderot." *Historical Reflections/Réflexions Historiques* 25, no. 2 (1999): 227–50.

Rosenfeld, Sophia A. "The French Revolution in Cultural History." *Journal of Social History* 52, no. 3 (January 2019): 555–65.

———. *A Revolution in Language: The Problem of Signs in Late Eighteenth-Century France.* Stanford: Stanford University Press, 2001.

———. "Thinking about Feeling, 1789–1799." *French Historical Studies* 32, no. 4 (2009): 697–706.

Rosenwein, Barbara. *Generations of Feeling: A History of Emotions, 600–1700.* Cambridge: Cambridge University Press, 2016.

Rothschild, Emma. *The Inner Life of Empires: An Eighteenth-Century History.* Princeton: Princeton University Press, 2011.

———. "Isolation and Economic Life in Eighteenth-Century France." *American Historical Review* 119, no. 4 (October 2014): 1055–82. https://doi.org/10.1093/ahr/119.4.1055.

Rouanet, G. "La *Correspondance de Bretagne*." *Annales révolutionnaires* 10 (1918): 542–49.

Schechter, Ronald. *Obstinate Hebrews: Representations of Jews in France, 1715–1815.* Berkeley: University of California Press, 2003.

Schich, Maximilian, Chaoming Song, Yong-Yeol Ahn, Alexander Mirsky, Mauro Martino, Albert-László Barabási, and Dirk Helbing. "A Network Framework of Cultural History." *Science* 345, no. 6196 (August 1, 2014): 558–62.

Schiffer, Michael Brian. *Draw the Lightning Down: Benjamin Franklin and Electrical Technology in the Age of Enlightenment.* Berkeley: University of California Press, 2003.

Schneider, Robert Alan. *Public Life in Toulouse, 1463–1789: From Municipal Republic to Cosmopolitan City.* Ithaca: Cornell University Press, 1989.

Sepinwall, Alyssa Goldstein. *The Abbé Grégoire and the French Revolution: The Making of Modern Universalism.* Berkeley: University of California Press, 2005.

Sewell, William. "Historical Events as Transformations of Structures: Inventing Revolutions at the Bastille." *Theory and Society* 25 (1996): 841–81.

Sgard, Jean, ed. *Dictionnaire des journalistes, 1600–1789.* 2 vols. Oxford: Voltaire Foundation, 1999. dictionnaire-journalistes.gazettes18e.fr.

——. *Dictionnaire des journaux, 1600–1789.* Oxford: Voltaire Foundation, 1999. http://dictionnaire-journaux.gazettes18e.fr.

Sgard, Jean, and Anne-Marie Chouillet. "La presse provinciale et les lumières." In *La presse provinciale au XVIIIIe siècle*, edited by Jean Sgard, 49–64. Grenoble: Centre de recherches sur les sensibilités, Université des langues et lettres de Grenoble, 1983.

Shalev, Eran. "Ancient Masks, American Fathers: Classical Pseudonyms during the American Revolution and Early Republic." *Journal of the Early Republic* 23, no. 2 (2003): 151–72.

Shami, Seteney Khalid. *Publics, Politics and Participation: Locating the Public Sphere in the Middle East and North Africa.* New York: Social Science Research Council, 2009.

Shank, J. B. *The Newton Wars and the Beginning of the French Enlightenment.* Chicago: University of Chicago Press, 2018.

Sheehan, Jonathan. *The Enlightenment Bible.* Princeton: Princeton University Press, 2005.

——. "From Philology to Fossils: The Biblical Encyclopedia in Early Modern Europe." *Journal of the History of Ideas* 64, no. 1 (January 2003): 41–60.

Shevelow, Kathryn. *Women and Print Culture: The Construction of Femininity in the Early Periodical.* London: Routledge, 1989.

Shovlin, John. "Political Economy and the French Nobility." In *The French Nobility in the Eighteenth Century: Reassessments and New Approaches*, edited by Jay Smith, 111–40. State College: Pennsylvania State University Press, 2006.

——. *The Political Economy of Virtue: Luxury, Patriotism, and the Origins of the French Revolution.* Ithaca: Cornell University Press, 2007.

Siskin, Clifford, and William Warner, eds. *This Is Enlightenment.* Chicago: University of Chicago Press, 2010.

Sizer, Michael Alan. "Making Revolution Medieval: Revolt and Political Culture in Late Medieval Paris." PhD diss., University of Minnesota, 2008.

Slauter, Will. "The Paragraph as Information Technology." *Annales HSS* 67, no. 2 (2012): 253–78.

——. *Who Owns the News? A History of Copyright.* Palo Alto: Stanford University Press, 2019.

Smith, Jay. *The French Nobility in the Eighteenth Century: Reassessments and New Approaches.* State College: Pennsylvania State University Press, 2006.

Söderhjelm, Alma. *Le Régime de la presse pendant la Révolution française*, vol. 1. Helsing-fors: Imprimerie Hufvudstadsbladet, 1900.

Solomon, Howard M. *Public Welfare, Science and Propaganda in Seventeenth Century France: The Innovations of Théophraste Renaudot.* Princeton: Princeton University Press, 1972.

Sonenscher, Michael. "Property, Community, and Citizenship." In *The Cambridge History of Eighteenth-Century Political Thought*, edited by Mark Goldie and Robert Wokler, 465–94. Cambridge: Cambridge University Press, 2006.

Sorkin, David Jan. *The Religious Enlightenment: Protestants, Jews, and Catholics from London to Vienna.* Princeton: Princeton University Press, 2008.

Spang, Rebecca. *Stuff and Money in the French Revolution.* Cambridge, MA: Harvard University Press, 2015.

Spary, E. C. *Eating the Enlightenment: Food and the Sciences in Paris.* Chicago: University of Chicago Press, 2012.

———. *Feeding France: New Sciences of Food, 1760–1815.* Cambridge: Cambridge University Press, 2014.

———. *Utopia's Garden: French Natural History from Old Regime to Revolution.* Chicago: University of Chicago Press, 2000.

Stewart, Larry. "The Laboratory, the Workshop, and the Theater of Experiment." In *Science and Spectacle in the European Enlightenment*, edited by Bernadette Bensaude-Vincent and Christine Blondel, 11–24. Hampshire, UK: Ashgate, 2008.

Stock, Brian. *The Implications of Literacy: Written Language and Models of Interpretation in the Eleventh and Twelfth Centuries.* Princeton: Princeton University Press, 1983.

Stuber, Martin. "Journal and Letter: The Interaction between Two Communications Media in the Correspondence of Albrecht Von Haller." In *Enlightenment, Revolution and the Periodical Press*, edited by Hans-Jürgen Lüsebrink and Jeremy D. Popkin, 114–41. Oxford: Voltaire Foundation, 2004.

Stuber, Martin, and Lothar Krempel. "Las redes académicas de Albrecht von Haller y la Sociedad Económica: un análisis de redes a varios niveles." *REDES: Revista hispana para el análisis de redes sociales* 24, no. 7 (June 2013): 1–24.

Tackett, Timothy. *Becoming a Revolutionary: The Deputies of the French National Assembly and the Emergence of a Revolutionary Culture (1789–1790).* Princeton: Princeton University Press, 1996.

———. "Collective Panics in the Early French Revolution, 1789–1791: A Comparative Perspective." *French History* 17, no. 2 (2003): 149–71.

———. *The Coming of the Terror in the French Revolution.* Cambridge, MA: Belknap Press of Harvard University Press, 2015.

———. "Paths to Revolution: The Old Regime Correspondence of Five Future Revolutionaries." *French Historical Studies* 32, no. 4 (2009): 531–54.

———. *Priest and Parish in Eighteenth-Century France: A Social and Political Study of the Curés in a Diocese of Dauphiné, 1750–1791.* Princeton: Princeton University Press, 1977.

———. *Religion, Revolution, and Regional Culture in Eighteenth-Century France: The Ecclesiastical Oath of 1791.* Princeton: Princeton University Press, 1986.

Taillefer, Michel. *Une académie interprète des Lumières: L'Académie des sciences, inscriptions et belles lettres de Toulouse au XVIIIe siècle.* Paris, 1984.

Takats, Sean. *The Expert Cook in Enlightenment France.* Baltimore: Johns Hopkins University Press, 2011.

Todd, Christopher. *A Century of French Best-Sellers (1890–1990)*. Lewiston, NY: E. Mellen Press, 1994.

——. "French Advertising in the Eighteenth Century." *Studies on Voltaire and the Eighteenth Century* 266 (1989): 513–47.

Tonelli, Giorgio. "The 'Weakness' of Reason in the Age of Enlightenment." In *Scepticism in the Enlightenment*, edited by Richard H. Popkin, Ezequiel de Olaso, and Giorgio Tonelli, 217–44. Dordrecht, Netherlands: Kluwer Academic, 1997.

Tortarolo, Edoardo. *The Invention of Free Press: Writers and Censorship in Eighteenth Century Europe*. Dordrecht, Netherlands: Springer, 2016.

Tulchin, Allan A. "Weekly Enlightenment: The *Affiches de Bordeaux*, 1758–1765." *French Historical Studies* 42, no. 2 (April 2019): 175–202.

Turnovsky, Geoffrey. *The Literary Market: Authorship and Modernity in the Old Regime*. Philadelphia: University of Pennsylvania Press, 2010.

Van Cleve, John V. *Deaf History Unveiled: Interpretations from the New Scholarship*. Washington, DC: Gallaudet University Press, 1993.

Vardi, Liana. "Imagining the Harvest in Early Modern Europe." *American Historical Review* 101, no. 5 (December 1996): 1357–97.

——. *The Physiocrats and the World of the Enlightenment*. Cambridge: Cambridge University Press, 2012.

Vareschi, Mark. *Everywhere and Nowhere: Anonymity and Mediation in Eighteenth-Century England*. Minneapolis: University of Minnesota Press, 2018.

Venturi, Franco. *Utopia and Reform in the Enlightenment*. Cambridge: Cambridge University Press, 1971.

Vovelle, Michel. *Les mots de la Révolution*. Toulouse-Le Mirail: Presses universitaires du Mirail, 2004.

——. *Piété baroque et déchristianisation en Provence au XVIIIe siècle; Les attitudes devant la mort d'après les clauses des testaments*. Paris: Plon, 1973.

Wade, Ira O. *The Intellectual Development of Voltaire*. 2nd ed. Princeton: Princeton University Press, 2016.

Wahl-Jorgensen, Karin. *Journalists and the Public: Newsroom Culture, Letters to the Editor, and Democracy*. Cresskill, NJ: Hampton Press, 2007.

Walker, Lesley H. *A Mother's Love: Crafting Feminine Virtue in Enlightenment France*. Lewisburg: Bucknell University Press, 2008.

Walshaw, Jill Maciak. *A Show of Hands for the Republic: Opinion, Information, and Repression in Eighteenth-Century Rural France*. Rochester: University of Rochester Press, 2014.

Walter, Gérard. *Marat*. Paris: A. Michel, 1933.

——. *Hébert et le "Père Duchesne."* Paris: J. B. Janin, 1946.

Walton, G. Charles. "Between Trust and Terror: Patriotic Giving in Revolutionary France." In *Experiencing the French Revolution*, edited by David Andress, 47–67. Oxford: Voltaire Foundation, 2013.

——. *Policing Public Opinion in the French Revolution: The Culture of Calumny and the Problem of Free Speech*. Oxford: Oxford University Press, 2009.

Warner, Michael. *The Letters of the Republic: Publication and the Public Sphere in Eighteenth-Century America*. Cambridge, MA: Harvard University Press, 1990.

——. *Publics and Counterpublics*. Brooklyn, NY: Zone Books, 2005.

Warren, Christopher N., Daniel Shore, Jessica Otis, Lawrence Wang, Mike Finegold, and Cosma Shalizi. "Six Degrees of Francis Bacon: A Statistical Method for Reconstructing Large Historical Social Networks." *Digital Humanities Quarterly* 10, no. 3 (2016), http://www.digitalhumanities.org/dhq/vol/10/3/000244/000244.html.

Watts, Duncan J., and Peter Sheridan Dodds. "Influentials, Networks, and Public Opinion Formation." *Journal of Consumer Research* 34 (December 2007): 441–58.

Watts, Duncan J., and Steven H. Strogatz. "Collective Dynamics of 'Small-World' Networks." *Nature* 393, no. 4 (June 1998): 440–42.

Wawro, Geoffrey. *The Franco-Prussian War: The German Conquest of France in 1870–1871.* Cambridge: Cambridge University Press, 2003.

Weiner, Dora B. "A Provincial Doctor Faces the Paris Establishment, Philippe Pinel, 1778–1793." In *Enlightenment, Passion, Modernity: Historical Essays in European Thought and Culture*, edited by Mark Micale and Robert L. Dietle, 66–87. Palo Alto: Stanford University Press, 2000.

Wetherell, Charles. "Historical Social Network Analysis." *International Review of Social History* 43, no. 6 (1998): 125–44.

Weulersse, Georges. *Le mouvement physiocratique en France (de 1756 à 1770).* 2 vols. Paris: F. Alcan, 1910.

Weygand, Zina. *The Blind in French Society from the Middle Ages to the Century of Louis Braille.* Stanford: Stanford University Press, 2009.

White, D. R., and H. Gilman McCann. "Cites and Fights: Material Entailment Analysis of the Eigtheenth-Century Chemical Revolution." In *Social Structures: A Network Approach*, edited by Barry Wellman and Stephen D. Berkowitz, 380–400. Cambridge: Cambridge University Press, 1988.

Williams, Abigail. *The Social Life of Books: Reading Together in the Eighteenth-Century Home.* New Haven: Yale University Press, 2017.

Winterer, Caroline. *American Enlightenments: Pursuing Happiness in the Age of Reason.* New Haven: Yale University Press, 2016.

Withers, Charles W. J. *Placing the Enlightenment: Thinking Geographically about the Age of Reason.* Chicago: University of Chicago Press, 2007.

Wittman, Reinhard. "Was There a Reading Revolution at the End of the Eighteenth Century?" In *A History of Reading in the West*, edited by Guglielmo Cavallo and Roger Chartier, translated by Lydia G. Cochrane, 284–312. Amherst: University of Massachusetts Press, 1999.

Woloch, Isser. "From Charity to Welfare in Revolutionary History." *Journal of Modern History* 58 (1986): 779–812.

Yang, Tze-I, Andrew J. Torget, and Rada Mihalcea. "Topic Modeling on Historical Newspapers." In *Proceedings of the 5th ACL-HLT Workshop on Language Technology for Cultural Heritage, Social Sciences, and Humanities*, edited by Kalliopi Zervanou and Piroska Lendvai, 96–104. Portland, OR: Association for Computational Linguistics, 2011.

Yeo, Richard. "A Solution to the Multitude of Books: Ephraim Chambers's *Cyclopaedia* (1728) as 'the Best Book in the Universe.'" *Journal of the History of Ideas* 64, no. 1 (January 2003): 61–72.

INDEX

academies/*académisme*, 94–95
advertisements, 2, 23
affective spaces, 7
affiches, scholarship on, 2–3. *See also*
    information press; newspapers
Affiches d'Aix-en-Provence, 35
Affiches d'Angers, 28fig, 74, 92–93, 96, 131,
    146, 149, 177
Affiches d'Artois (Arras), 105
Affiches de Bordeaux, 30
Affiches de Dijon, 50, 55, 82, 93, 104, 146,
    160, 174
Affiches de Franche-Comté, 106
Affiches de la Basse-Normandie (Caen), 26,
    31
Affiches de l'Orléanois, 27–28, 31, 116, 117,
    129, 131, 139, 174, 177
Affiches de Lyon, 19
Affiches de Montpellier, 22, 28fig, 98, 152, 171,
    177
Affiches de Nantes, 30
Affiches de Normandie, 30, 50, 83, 170–71
Affiches de Paris, 20
Affiches de Picardie et Soissonnais (Amiens),
    22, 125, 159, 169, 174
Affiches de Provence, 36
Affiches de Province, 18–19, 30
Affiches de Reims, 35, 36
Affiches de Rennes, 22, 26, 78
Affiches des Trois-Évêchés et Lorraine, 30,
    83–84, 96, 98, 142, 147
Affiches de Toulouse, 28–29, 30, 86, 87, 97,
    102, 116, 176
Affiches de Troyes, 48, 102–3, 115, 117,
    130–31, 155–56
Affiches du Beauvaisis (Compiègne), 1, 81
Affiches du Dauphiné (Grenoble), 28fig,
    55–56, 90–91, 95–96, 97, 124, 141, 150,
    152, 172
Affiches du Poitou, 28fig, 97–98, 112, 115, 117,
    128, 133

agriculture, 112–32
    food insecurity, 118–19, 123–24, 159–60
    letters on, 15, 112–13, 115–18, 120–30,
        159–60, 181; authority of writers, 48,
        128–32; on disease and pests, 124–26,
        160; influence of, 128
    physiocracy, 113–14, 116–17
    reform of, 114–15, 118–19, 121–24
Agulhon, Maurice, 10
Alembert, Jean le Rond d', 21, 62, 78
Altman, Janet Gurkin, 214n7
ambiguous signatures, 42–43
American Revolution, 219n5
Anderson, Benedict, 10
Annales de la bienfaisance, 149
anonymity and pseudonyms
    anonymity, 41–42, 43, 49, 54, 110, 143,
        147–49, 172
    "a subscriber", 41, 54, 149, 171, 182,
        217n61
    censorship and, 217n54, 217n59
    initials only, 41–43, 54, 56–57, 182
    proportion of letters signed, 41–43, 110,
        217n53, 217n61, 217n65, 226n65
    pseudonyms, 41–43, 52–54, 129–30, 172
    unsigned letters, 54, 55–56, 182
approbation, 29
aristocratic plot, 235n36
"Artisanal Enlightenment", 208n44
artisans, 47–48
arts, frequency of letters on, 65fig, 66, 86
Auger, Émond, 74
authors, 57–59

balloons, 14, 87–100, 109–11
Baour, Jean-Florent, 30
Bastille, storming of, 161–62
Beaugeard, Ferréol, 177, 238n95
Bernardin de Saint Pierre, Jacques-Henri,
    75–76
Bertholon de Saint-Lazare, Pierre, 108

Bertier de Sauvigny, Louis-Bénigne-
    François, 162
Bertucci, Paola, 208n44
bienfaisance, 133–54
    letters on, 133–34, 136–38, 153–54,
        160–61, 181; on education, 144–47; on
        model benefactors, 147–54, 160; by
        representatives of organizations, 138–44
    role of information press, 134–35, 136,
        147, 149–50, 154, 160–61
    understandings of, 135–36, 147, 153
Blair, Ann, 79
Blouet, Jean-François, 21
Bonafous, Louis Abel, 21
Bonneval, Abbé de, 169
books and reading, 60–61, 85–86
    author citations, 71–73
    book title references, 62–71, 180
    collective reading, 37, 74, 83–85, 214n95
    criticism, 78–80
    experiences of reading, 60, 61, 73–77, 79,
        180
    literature, 63fig, 64–66, 69, 80–82
    poetry, 69, 80–83
    proliferation of titles, 79
    referencing of previous content, 61–62
Bouche, Charles-François, 169
bourgeoisie, 8, 45, 215n14
Brondex, Albert, 21
Broussonet, Pierre Marie Auguste, 130
Buissart, Antoine-Joseph, 101, 105
bureaux d'adresse, 19, 209n3
Burson, Jeffrey, 12

cabinets de lecture, 36
Cadet de Vaux, Antoine-Alexis, 123
cahiers de doléances, 158
Caplan, Jay, 34
Caradonna, Jeremy, 9, 11
Carra, Jean-Louis, 107, 108, 225n60
Cassirer, Ernst, 207n42
Castilhon, Jean-Louis, 83
celebrity and celebrities, 50, 204n14
Censer, Jack, 23, 24
censorship
    anonymity and pseudonyms and, 217n54,
        217n59
    ending of, 15, 156, 157–59, 161, 168–69,
        170, 172
    nonattribution of titles and, 71
    system of, 29–33
chambres de lecture, 36–37
chancellerie, 30–31
charity. See bienfaisance

Charles, Jacques-Alexandre-César, 89, 93
Charlot, Élisabeth, 22
Chartier, Roger, 8–9
children, 85, 144–47
Chisick, Harvey, 9
church property, 170–71
circulation, 35–38
citizenship, 236n68
clandestine publication, 29
Clay, Lauren, 9
clergy
    letters about, 139–40
    letters from, 44–45, 116, 117, 138–39, 142,
        151, 170–71
closings and signatures. See anonymity and
    pseudonyms; signatures and closings
coin collectors, 220n16
collective reading, 36–38, 74, 83–85, 214n95
Collot, Pierre, 130–31
community, 9–11
Comsa, Maria Teodora, 207n42
Condorcet, Nicolas de, 43
conseils souverains, 224n42
Constituent Assembly, 168–69, 170, 171,
    173–74, 176
Corneille, Pierre, 71, 72tab, 81
correspondence
    cost of receiving, 213n77
    golden age of, 5, 39–40
counterfeit books, 62
Courayer, Pierre François le, 68, 220n18
Couret de Villeneuve, Louis, 21
Courier de l'Europe, 219n5
Courmont, Le Bas de, Louis Dominique,
    18–19, 22, 29

Darnton, Robert, 8
Daujon, François, 172
deaf children, 146
debtors, 143–44
Declaration of Rights of Man and of Citizen,
    175
Delandine, Antoine-François, 75–76
Delaroche, Aimé, 19
Desmoulins, Camille, 176
Dictionnaire lyrique portatif, 78, 85
Diderot, Denis, 21, 78, 135–36
distribution, 33–35
doctors and surgeons
    anonymity and, 55, 56
    letters from, 46, 47, 57, 105–6, 117, 137,
        148, 152, 167–68
domestic workers, 47, 79–80
Dorat, Claude Joseph, 77

Dubreuil, Jean, 78, 85
Ducarne de Blangy, Jacques Joseph, 127
Dupont de Nemours, Pierre-Samuel, 113–14

Edelstein, Dan, 207n42
editors
  backgrounds of, 20–23
  content control by, 24–26
  writers' appeals to, 4, 6, 51, 129–30, 131,
    152, 183
electricity, 87–88, 100–111, 224n41
"electric kiss", 107
emotional communities, 77
empiricism, 7, 88, 112
Encyclopédie, 11, 78, 113
Encyclopedists, 6, 71–72
Enlightenment, the, 11–12, 72, 115, 181–82,
    207n42
epilepsy, 106, 107–8
essay competitions, 9, 94–95, 123
Estates General, 157–58
Estourmel, Louis Marie, marquis d', 169

families, collective reading among, 85
farmers and farm laborers, 48. See also
    agriculture
Faujas Saint-Fond, Barthélemy, 91
Félix-Nogaret, François, 81
Feuille du Bureau d'Adresse, 18–19, 209n3
Feyel, Gilles, 24
fires, 141–43
Flesselles, Jacques de, 94, 224n21
Flour War, 119
fodder crops, 121, 122
Fond, Jacques Dumoustier de la, 226n12
food insecurity, 118–19, 123–24, 159–60,
    164–65
Foreign Affairs, Department of, 18, 29, 30, 62
Foullon de Doué, Joseph, 162
foundlings and orphans, 140–41, 149, 152
Franklin, Benjamin, 100, 101, 103, 105
freedom of speech, 175–76
freedom of the press, 175–76, 177

Gaucher, Charles-Étienne, 39
Gay, Peter, 207n42
Gazette de France, 18–19, 29, 209n3, 229n3
Gazette de Leyde, 38
Gazette de Paris, 176
Gelbart, Nina, 235n51
Genty, Abbé, 125–26
Giroud, Justine Souverant, 22, 26
Giroud de Villette, André, 92, 95–96
Goodman, Dena, 6

Goudar, Sarah, 17
Gough, Hugh, 158
government administrators, 46–47
Greek, 81–82
Grosley, P.-J., 218n73
Grub Street writers, 8–9
guilds, 29
Guyton, Louis-Bernard, baron de Morveau,
    225n51

Habermas, Jürgen, 7–8
Hardy, Siméon-Prosper, 39, 56
Haüy, Valentin, 145
healthcare. See medicine and healthcare
Hébert, Jacques, 172
Hesse, Carla, 6, 51
history, letters on, 63fig, 65fig, 67
Homer, 80–81
hot-air balloons, 14, 87–100, 109–11
Hunt, Lynn, 10, 76

Iliad, 80–81
information press
  as critical sphere of public exchange, 12–13
  definition, 1–2, 203n2
  goal of, 179
  role of during Revolution, 157–59, 179
  See also newspapers
initials only, as signature, 41–43, 56, 182
Israel, Jonathan, 207n42

Jacob, Margaret, 207n44
Jaucourt, Louis de, 11
Joly, M., 102–4
Journal de Lyon, 139
Journal de Paris, 162
  censorship of, 30
  founders of, 20–21
  frequency of, 23
  Goudar's reading of, 17
  letters to: on agriculture, 121, 123; by
    amateur writers, 59; on ballooning,
    95–96, 99; on bienfaisance, 135, 136,
    137, 141, 145, 148, 150, 152, 160–61;
    on chimneys, 74; on experience of
    reading, 60, 74, 76, 84, 85; on novels,
    76; on reference works, 78; during
    Revolution, 158, 160–61, 162, 171, 174,
    175, 176; types of people writing, 47,
    48, 49–50; using connections to get
    published, 39; by women, 50–51
  price of, 35
  readers of, 47
  as source for provincial media, 28fig

Journal de Provence, 36, 142
Journal des dames, 58
Journal des sçavans, 18, 23, 212n59
Journal général de France
    editors of, 21, 26
    letters to: on agriculture, 122, 126,
        127–28; on experience of reading, 79;
        on literary reviews, 81; on poetry, 82;
        on reference works, 78
    as source for provincial media, 28fig
journalistes, use of term, 21
Journal patriote de Romans, 51
Jouyneau-Desloges, René, 21
Jullien, Rosalie, 50–51

king and royal family, 160, 166

laboureurs, 48
Latin, 53, 81–82
Laureau de Saint-André, Pierre, 82
Laurendeau, Jean-Charles, 169
Lavoisier, Antoine, 119
law, letters on, 63fig, 65fig, 68, 86
lawyers, 46, 170
Lefebvre, Georges, 234n36
Lefebvre Marchand, Barbe-Thérèse,
    22
Legislative Assembly, 176
Le Saulnier du Vauhello, Jeanne, 22
letters
    manuscripts of, 57–58
    motives of writers of, 6
    overview of, 24–25, 40–41
    profiles of writers, 44–49, 51, 57, 59
    public sphere and, 7–9
    research on, 2–4, 24
    as self-fashioning, 5–7, 59
    as terrain of contestation, 11
    as virtual sociability, 4, 85, 111, 180,
        183
    writers' arguments for publishing, 4, 6,
        51, 129–30, 131, 152, 183
    See also specific topic
Levasseur, Thérèse, 50, 62–63
libraries and reading rooms, 36–37,
    83–84
licensing, 15, 18–19, 29, 31
lightning rods, 102–5
literacy, 79–80, 220n60
literature, letters on, 63fig, 64–66, 69, 80–82.
    See also novels
Little Ice Age, 118–19
livestock, 124–25, 160

local *affiches*
    censorship of, 29–30, 31–32
    distribution of, 33–34
    information flows to, 26–29
    rise of, 17–20
    See also specific title

Malesherbes, Guillaume-Chrétien de
    Lamoignon, 31–32
Marat, Jean-Paul, 66, 95, 176
Maupin, 70, 112–13, 128–29
medicine and healthcare
    by doctors, 46, 47, 57, 105–6, 137, 167–68
    frequency of, 65fig
    by patients, 74, 137–38
Medlin, Dorothy, 54–55
mental health, 167–68
Mercure de France, 18, 101, 212n59, 213n77,
    225n46
Mesmer, Franz, 101–2
methodology of study, 12–14
Milcent, Jean, 21, 234n24
military, numbers of, 45
Mirabeau, Victor de Riqueti, marquis de,
    114, 115
monopolies, 18
Montansier, Madame (Marguerite Brunet),
    50
Montgolfier brothers, 88–89, 93
Morellet, André, 54–55
Morveau, Louis-Bernard Guyton de, 104
Mustel, François-George, 228n53

National Assembly, 155, 156
natural philosophy. *See* science
Necker, Jacques, 119
nécrologie, 140
network analysis, 13
newspapers
    collective reading of, 36–38, 74, 83–85
    community creation by, 9–11
    distribution of, 33–35
    experiences of reading, 73
    format and content, 23–26
    information flows between, 26–29
    readership of, 35–38
    Revolution, proliferation of during, 158,
        172, 177
    as site for conversations, 2–4, 25, 38, 86
    See also information press
nobility, 45, 147–48
Nollet, Jean-Antoine, 105
notes du rédacteur, 26

Nouvelles ordinaires, 209n3
novels, 75–77. *See also* literature, letters on

Observateur hollandaise, 212n59
Öffentlichkeit (public sphere), 7–8
orphans and foundlings, 140–41, 149, 152

Pagès-Marinier, Marguerite, 22
Panckoucke, Charles-Joseph, 21
Paris media, 20, 27–29. *See also Affiches de
    Paris; Gazette de Paris; Journal de Paris*
Parmentier, Antoine-Augustin, 123
patriotism, 165–66
peasants, 103, 147–48
pen names, 53
petites postes, 34
philanthropy. *See* bienfaisance
philosophy and philosophers, 6, 65fig, 66,
    71–72, 139–40
physiciens
    ballooning and, 90, 91–92, 96–97, 100, 110
    electricity and, 100–101, 103, 104, 108–9,
        110
    use of term, 223n8
physiocracy, 113–14, 116–17
Pichichero, Christy, 45
Pîlatre de Rozier, Jean-François, 91–92, 93,
    223n10
Pinel, Philippe, 167–68
Pocock, J.G.A., 12
poetry, 69, 80–83
Popkin, Jeremy, 38, 236n94
postal distribution, 33–34
potatoes, 122–23, 159
"presse d'information", 203n2
Price, Leah, 73
prices
    of licenses, 19
    of newspapers, 213n79
    for receiving correspondence, 213n77
    of subscriptions, 34–35
priests. *See* clergy
professionals, 45–46
prospectuses, 23, 31, 179
provincial media. *See* local affiches; *specific title*
pseudonyms, 41–43, 52–54, 129–30, 172
public, the, concept of, 8
public opinion, formation of, 7–9

Quesnay, François, 113–14, 115

Rabiot de Meslé, Denis, 18–19
Racine, Jean, 71, 72tab, 81

Raimond, Louis Filiol de, 225n58
Rambouillet Farm, 121–22, 159–60
Rancière, Jacques, 220n23
reading. *See* books and reading
reading rooms and libraries, 36–37, 83–84
Reddy, William, 77
reference books cited in letters, 65fig, 69,
    78–79, 85
regional media. *See* local affiches; *specific title*
Reigny, Beffroy de, 220n20
religion and theology, 63fig, 65fig, 67–68,
    71, 86
Renaudot family, 18, 229n3
Revolution, 155–78
    information press's role, 155–56, 176–78
    letters during, 155–68, 170–72, 176–78; to
        correct the record, 172–75, 177; decline
        in, 175; from deputies, 168–70; on
        public's role, 155–56, 165–66
    revolutionary crowd, 161–62
    social egalitarianism during, 163–64, 166
Richardson, Samuel, 39–40, 65, 69, 72tab, 76
Robespierre, Maximilien, 101, 168
Roche, Daniel, 118
root vegetables, 122–23
Rosenberg, Daniel, 221n48
Rosenfeld, Sophia, 204n7
rosières, 151
Rothschild, Emma, 13
Rouelle, Guillaume-François, 49, 216n38
Rousseau, Jean-Jacques, 50, 71, 76–77,
    94–95, 136, 213n77
Rozier, Pîlatre de, 223n10

Saint-Lambert, Jean-François, 82–83
salonnières, 84
science, 87–111, 181
    authors and target audiences, 109–11
    chemistry, 88–89
    electricity, 87–88, 100–111, 224n41
    frequency of letters on, 63fig, 65fig, 66,
        67, 86, 88
    hot-air balloons, 14, 87–100, 109–11
scissors editors, 26
Shalev, Eran, 217n54, 217n59
signatures and closings
    proportion of letters signed, 41–43, 110,
        217n53, 217n61, 217n65, 226n65
    range of, 24, 41–43
    as reflecting social value, 51–52
    See also anonymity and pseudonyms
sociability, 10–11, 206n33. *See also* collective
    reading; virtual sociability

social reading, 36–38, 74, 83–85, 214n95
sociétés de lecture, 36
Spang, Rebecca, 235n65
Suard, Amélie, 21
subscriptions
    costs of, 34–35
    numbers of, 35–36, 38

Tessier, Henri-Alexandre, 121–22, 125
"textual communities", 206n31
Thélis, Claude Antoine, comte de, 145
Thouret, Jacques-Guillaume, 169
trade reforms, 118–19
Turgot, Anne-Robert-Jacques, 119

United States, pen names in, 53
unsigned letters, 54, 55–56, 182. *See also*
    anonymity and pseudonyms

Villot, André, 234n25
virtual sociability, 4, 85, 111, 180, 183
Vissery de Bois-Valé, Charles Dominique
    de, 101
Voltaire, 62, 71, 72tab, 82–83

Walton, Charles, 236n80
widows, 49–50
women
    as benefactors, 148, 150
    collective reading and, 83–84
    as editors and printers, 22
    letter writing by, 43, 49–51, 130
    morality competitions for, 151
    newspapers for, 58
    during Revolution, 162–63
    self-fashioning by, 6
    working classes, 47–48, 79–80, 149

Lightning Source UK Ltd.
Milton Keynes UK
UKHW011056270122
397802UK00004B/195